Practical Algorithms for Programmers

Andrew Binstock and John Rex

Addison-Wesley Publishing Company

Reading, Massachusetts • Menlo Park, California • New York
Don Mills, Ontario • Wokingham, England • Amsterdam
Bonn • Sydney • Singapore • Tokyo • Madrid • San Juan
Paris • Seoul • Milan • Mexico City • Taipei

Library of Congress Cataloging-in-Publication Data

Binstock, Andrew.
    Practical algorithms for programmers / Andrew Binstock and John Rex.
        p.   cm.
    Includes index.
    ISBN 0-201-63208-X
    1. C (Computer program language)   2. Computer algorithms.
I. Rex, John.   II. Title
QA76.73.C15B5   1995
005.13'3—dc20   95.6582
                                                        CIP

Sponsoring Editor: Keith Wollman
Project Editor: Sarah Weaver
Production Coordinator: Erin Sweeney
Cover design: Imageset Design
Set in 11-point Times Roman by ST Associates

1 2 3 4 5 6 7 8 9 -MA- 9998979695
First printing, May 1995

Addison-Wesley books are available for bulk purchases by corporations, institutions, and other organizations. For more information please contact the Corporate, Government, and Special Sales Department at (800) 238-9682.

To my parents, Elisabetta and Julian Binstock,
in loving thanks for innumerable blessings—ALB

To my parents and wife,
whose love and support make all things possible—JR

Acknowledgments

The idea for this book was first put forth during the summer of 1991 by Phil Pistone, to whom we are indebted for setting us a task that took three years to accomplish. The many excellent folks at Addison-Wesley are the primary victims of this delay and we deeply thank them for their extraordinary patience and kindness. Not least of these is Keith Wollman, who heads up the computer trade books division and has made it one of Addison-Wesley's crown jewels. Claire Horne has also been with the project since its inception; she incarnates all the kindness and grace we associate with the company. Sarah Weaver has steered us ably through the production schedule, excelling where many others before her failed. Thanks also go to Steve Vinoski for a superb technical edit and to Barbara Milligan for a thorough copy edit. Any errors that survived despite their efforts are wholly ours.We sadly thank Phil Sutherland and Julie Stillman, who worked on the book's delivery but found new careers while waiting for the final manuscript. Who can deny them their share of our gratitude?

The ability to write this book came from many people who contributed in significant ways to the enlightenment of the authors as well as to many other programmers: in particular, Dennis Ritchie with the C language, Donald Knuth with the fundamental books on algorithms, and Jon Bentley with frequent eloquent reminders of how to apply simple principles to complex problems.

On a more personal level, we wish to thank Bill Hunt for one of the first really good books of C programming for PCs (notable, especially, for the clarity of the code); Allen Holub for teaching us (and a whole generation of programmers) how to use C to solve very difficult programming tasks; Mark DeSmet and the Farleys for a stunning compiler that was our entry into C programming; and not least, the many readers and contributors to the *C Gazette*, who made it all worthwhile.

Andrew Binstock and John Rex
April 1995

Contents

Contents

Preface

The purpose of this book is to provide a practical compendium of algorithms for use in applications. Unlike most works on algorithms, this book is not a text-book: you will not find implementation details left as an exercise for the reader, nor will you find highly theoretical discussions of algorithms with small snippets of code to show how the implementation might be undertaken. Rather, in keeping with our belief that the best explanation is a functioning program, you will find a wide selection of algorithms fully implemented in C with substantial practical discussion of their best use in a variety of applications. Theoretical material is presented only to enable programmers to change the implementation to suit specific needs or to more wisely select an algorithm for a particular use. When it arises in these contexts, the theory is presented in an approachable manner. References to more abstract material are provided at the end of each chapter.

A Word on the Code

While C++ continues to gain in popularity, we have used C in this book for several reasons. First, C still remains the programming *lingua franca* and is widely used and understood. Second, C can be compiled by C++ compilers with near-identical results to compilation by a C compiler. Finally, porting to C++ from C is not difficult, while a port in the other direction can be tedious. Thus, use of C makes the code available to the widest possible audience.

The code in this book was developed with two goals in mind: readability and portability. Portability has been assured by testing all the code in this book under Borland, Microsoft, and Watcom compilers for MS-DOS. The Watcom compilation was tested under extended DOS using DOS extenders from Phar-Lap or Rational Systems. In addition, other than a single exception in Chapter 1, all the code has been ported and recompiled under UNIX. Specifically, the port was to the UnixWare implementation of SVR4. Ports to other UNIX platforms and other operating systems are currently underway. All the latest ported versions, along with the appropriate makefiles and test data, can be obtained on the latest source code diskette. A coupon for obtaining this diskette is printed at the back of this volume.

ANSI *Externs*

In our porting efforts, a rarely discussed porting concern arose. The ANSI C standard offers several different ways in which items declared as `extern` in several modules are linked together. Many leading compilers today do not *require* any local definition of the variable declared as `extern`: the linker will simply define one in the linked program and point all declarations to it. However, this behavior is not guaranteed to work by the ANSI standard.

The only way to guarantee behavior under ANSI is for all variables declared as `extern` to have at least one source module where the variable is actually defined (that is, without the `extern` specifier). This affect can be achieved while still maintaining the declaration of all `extern` variables in a common header file. The technique is to declare the variables as follows in a header file that is included by all modules:

```
Extern int GlobalVariable1;
Extern int GlobalVariable2;
```

Then in some module, such as the one containing `main()` for example, you add the following line:

```
#define Extern
```

This has the effect of undefining `Extern` and transforming the declaration into a definition. In all other modules, you have the line

```
#define Extern extern
```

This will mean that in all other modules the header declares `extern` variables.

This approach has certain limitations. Mostly, it requires the user to make sure that `Extern` is properly `#defined` in all modules. An easier approach is to have the one local module identify itself with a manifest constant. Using our example, the `main()` module might announce itself with the following manifest constant:

```
#define IN_MAIN_MODULE
```

Then, the header file with all the `Extern` declarations need only contain the following code:

```
#ifdef IN_MAIN_MODULE
#define Extern
#else
#define Extern extern
#endif
```

If you use this approach, one module will contain all the local definitions for the `extern` variables. This may not be desirable. For example, you might want the definitions for linked lists to appear in a different module than those for stacks. Hence in this book, rather than using `Extern` in all cases, we use `StkExtern` for the stack variables we want, `ListExtern` for linked lists, and then we define the meaning of `StkExtern` in the modules we want. Examples of this appear in the code for Chapters 2 and 3. In this way, we are guaranteed that ANSI will link our `extern` variables and match them to definitions in exactly the manner we choose.

Code Style

Finally, we have done all we can to make the code readable. To attain this end we have used the convention of `MixedCase` variable names when defining functions and global variables, and we have used the `k_and_r_style` when declaring local variables. In addition, we have used more white space (both horizontally and vertically) to make code more readable. The sole exception is Chapter 6 (binary trees and B-trees), where the code is so abundant that it was incumbent upon us to lessen the number of pages that are pure code. In this chapter, we used conventions that diminish the amount of space occupied by code, which slightly diminishes readability as well.

We hope that you find the book readable and useful. It is intended to provide immediately usable hands-on information and solutions. If it does not succeed in this goal, the fault is wholly ours and we hope you will tell us in the comment area marked on the coupon at the back of the book.

—Andrew Binstock and John Rex

Chapter 1

Introduction

Assessing Algorithms

Algorithms are the heart and soul of all programs other than the most straight-forward applications. Algorithms are generally designed to solve a specific problem efficiently and with a minimum of effort. The value of an algorithm is generally determined by two factors: how well it solves the problem it addresses and how efficiently it implements the solution. These are the qualitative and quantitative aspects of algorithmic analysis.

For many algorithms, quality is not an issue. For example, a sort algorithm must sort all items correctly every time. If it errs once, it must be discarded and cannot properly be considered an algorithm. In other areas, quality cannot be measured on such a simple pass/fail basis. For example, the Soundex algorithm presented in Chapter 4 allows the retrieval of words or names that sound the same. Unlike the sorting algorithm, Soundex can be adjusted to find close matches or fairly wide matches; it depends on the way the algorithm is implemented and on the needs of the developer. In this case, quality is a measurable and important aspect of the algorithm and may dictate the careful selection of a different solution.

The quantitative aspect of algorithm design tries to establish the resources required by the algorithm. Generally speaking, the most important measure is time: how fast does the algorithm work? Occasionally, computer resources such as available memory are an important factor as well.

Measuring Performance

The performance of algorithms, unlike that of benchmarks, is rarely stated in terms of time. You will almost never read a treatment of a sort routine that states it took 8.62 seconds to complete. There is a good reason for this: such timings are difficult to duplicate and often depend on specific characteristics of the data being processed. Rather than rely on timings, algorithms rely on a straightforward equation to show the relationship between size of input and performance. The traditional method for showing this relationship uses the symbol O and is known as **big-oh notation**. It works like this: suppose you have an algorithm that simply reads through a text file looking for the word `flea`. A reasonable approach is to look for every instance of the letter `f` (see Chapter 4). When an `f` is found, the algorithm tests the four-letter sequence for the word `flea`. In this example, it is clear that execution time is directly proportional to the size of the text file. If a given file has N characters, then we say that the execution time of the algorithm is bounded by $O(N)$. You will note that this formulation does not take into account other factors that might influence performance—for example, how often the letter `f` appears in the text. When searching for a string (such as `fleas rarely wear collars`), the length of the string and the frequency in which similar strings (such as `fleas rarely wear colors`) occur also affect performance. These factors, however, are a function of the data being processed and not a function of the algorithm proper. Hence, in O notation they do not appear in the formula. The notation states simply the relation between data size (generally represented by N, and occasionally by n) and the algorithm's typical performance.

Another example should suffice: in the famous bubble sort (see Chapter 5), a list of items is sorted by traversing the list once for each item in the list. On each traversal, one less item is examined. As the list of items is traversed, neighboring items are compared and swapped if they are out of sort order. In such a sort, the action that most affects the performance is the number of comparisons. On a list of three items, three traversals will generate six comparisons. A list of ten items requires 55 comparisons. It is clear, therefore, that the number of comparisons is always $N\,(N-1)/2$. In this notation, the relationship between data size and execution (this relationship is termed **performance**) would be designated as $O((N^2-N)/2)$. Performance such as this is unacceptably slow except for small values of N.

The science of algorithmics is concerned with analyzing and improving algorithms so that the performance equation is steadily enhanced. When designing and implementing algorithms, it is important that you have a feel for this performance equation. The reasons for this are compelling. Algorithms whose performance is worse than N^2 are generally considered unusable. If run on a computer whose operations take 1 nanosecond (a billionth of a second), an algorithm whose performance is $3N^3$ will require 95 *years* to handle an input of 1,000,000 items, while an algorithm on the order of 19,500,000N will require only 5.4 hours to handle the same number of items. What is clear from these enormous disparities is that it is the order of N that is critical and not the constant that precedes it. In the previous example, had the algorithm used N^3 rather than $3N^3$, it would still be useless. As a result, O notation does not use constants; it uses only the order of N. The O notation for the bubble sort, therefore, is $O\ (N^2–N)$.

In this book we present performance equations somewhat differently. We use performance equations as explained previously; however, we retain constants where we feel their presence is important. So as not to confuse casual students of computer science, we do not use O notation, as the presence of constants will look very strange to the trained eye.

The Average Case versus the Worst Case

It is not enough to discuss performance simply in terms of a single equation or measurement. Some algorithms perform quite acceptably in most cases but unacceptably in a worst-case scenario. Since it is rarely possible to limit the data to which a generic algorithm will be applied, it is important to be mindful of the worst case. The worst-case performance may at times be so bad that a generally slower algorithm that can handle worst-case scenarios with aplomb may be a better choice. Let us look at the famous quicksort algorithm (see Chapter 5), which is implemented in the standard C library as `qsort()`. It performs very well under most scenarios. Its average-case performance equation is $N \lg N$. (The abbreviation *lg* means the base 2 logarithm. A logarithm is the exponent to which the base (here, 2) must be raised to attain *n*. For example, lg 8 is 3 because 2^3 is 8.) What this means is that quicksort will require 8 * 3 time units to sort 8 items, or 32 * 5 time units to sort 32 items. The result is that quadrupling the input from 8 to 32 items increases the sort time from 24 to 160 time units. Likewise, 1,024 items require 10,240 time units. Performance such as this is considered efficient.

However, when quicksort is applied against an input file that is already sorted, it exhibits worst-case performance. The performance equation suddenly becomes N^2. As shown in Table 1-1, if this single worst-case scenario is at all likely, quicksort cannot be used. (Fortunately for most C programmers, compiler vendors watch out for this case in their implementations of `qsort()`, and so the problem doesn't arise often.)

Table 1-1.   Average-case and worst-case performances for quicksort, in time units for *N* items

N	Average case: $N \lg N$	Worst case: N^2
8	24	64
32	160	1024
1,024	10,240	1,048,576

The Worst-Case Performance

When analyzing algorithms for worst-case behavior, it is not enough that you try simply to estimate the likelihood of the worst case occurring. You must also consider the consequences of the worst case, should it occur. In the example of quicksort, it is clear that the primary cost is the performance penalty; that is, the worst that will happen is that the sort will proceed slowly. With some algorithms, however, the worst-case performance penalty may be so great that, for practical purposes, the algorithm hangs the system. (Suppose, for example, a worst-case sort were to take fifteen days.)

Certain classes of problems have such severe worst-case consequences that the algorithm must be written to make certain that the worst case is detected and handled appropriately. One area in which such problems frequently occur is scheduling. Scheduling algorithms are not presented in this volume; however, since they are so illustrative of this point, we'll look briefly at one of the classics of the genre: the "dining philosophers" problem.

This problem, first devised by E. W. Dijkstra in 1965, now has many variations. It essentially goes like this. Five philosophers are seated at a round dinner table to enjoy a meal of noodles (see Figure 1-1). Between any two plates is a single chopstick. To eat, a philosopher must use two chopsticks: one from either side of her plate. As a result, if either neighbor is eating, the philosopher cannot eat, and must wait. She can attempt to eat at any time, by first picking up one chopstick and then looking to see whether the other one is available. If it is not, she must put down the one chopstick. Under most scenarios (the average case, in our parlance), all the philosophers will get to eat although some will have to wait their turn. In the worst case, however, the philosophers will all die of starvation. (If you are unfamiliar with this problem, stop here and try to work out what the worst case would be.) Suppose the philosophers all decide to eat at the same time. They all pick up the right chopstick. They then turn to look for the left one, which is, of course, unavailable. They put down their chopsticks and immediately attempt to eat again. The scenario is repeated. As long as they all want to eat at the same time (the worst case), they will, in unison, pick up and put down the right chopstick until they die of starvation. In algorithmic terms, the program will begin an endless loop. The worst case has killed the philosophers and the algorithm.

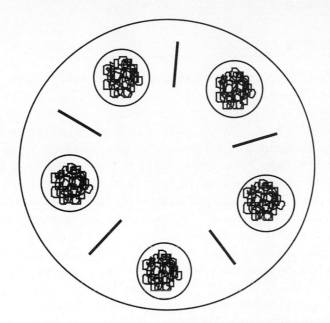

Figure 1-1.   Table with noodles for philosophers who could manage to starve.

The point of this problem is that when considering an algorithm, the worst case should be examined from the perspective of both its likelihood and its consequences. If the consequences are disastrous and you cannot change algorithms, then the worst case *must* be provided for.

The Best-Case Performance

An algorithm's best-case performance is rarely analyzed. This is because the best case has no effects that will bring an application to a complete standstill, and hence it represents no danger. In addition, as in the worst-case scenario, its occurrence tends to be rare and intensely dependent on the data being manipulated. However, this is not to say that best-case analysis should not be performed. Many algorithms show extraordinary performance increases when run against best-case data. A classic example is the bubble sort discussed earlier. Its typical performance is $O(N^2-N)$, while its best-case performance is $O(N)$. This means that for most applications the bubble sort is far too slow, while in the best case it runs as fast as a sort routine can go. This has implications for the applications developer because there are scenarios for which the quality of the data being processed is known in advance. A typical situation occurs when the output of one algorithm serves as the input for another. As we'll see later, in such circumstances best-case performance (even with the bubble sort) can be used effectively.

Modifying an Algorithm

One ongoing effort in the field of computer science is the refinement of algorithms to obtain optimal performance. This effort often takes one of two tacks: the optimization of an existing algorithm or the development of a new algorithm. These tacks have distinctly different goals and should be viewed differently. When optimizing an algorithm, you are generally not trying to reduce its performance equation. For example, we know that the bubble sort averages $O(N^2-N)$ performance. If you are forced to use the bubble sort, you will want to make sure that the activities performed in the bubble sort are of extremely short duration. Namely, you will want its two primary operations (comparing two elements in a list and swapping them) to be extremely quick. In the context of your application, you will therefore expend considerable effort making sure that the implementation of the algorithm is completely optimized. For example, you will make sure that the elements are swapped in memory, not on disk. By tackling the time required to process each data item, you can save substantially at run time. You have effectively optimized the algorithm by tailoring it to your application. However, you will not be able to get around the fact that bubblesort's performance grows geometrically with input size. To get around this issue, you will need to use or design a new algorithm.

It is at this point that the developer's work goes from the intensely practical (the optimization) to the abstract. You must now find a new method that performs better than $O(N^2-N)$. Should you succeed in lowering the performance equation, you will have developed a new algorithm. The distinction is important because it will condition your approach. In almost all cases, you will analyze a range of possible solutions, choose one, and then optimize it for your specific case. In the process, you will need to understand how the algorithm performs its work, so that you can identify where your optimization efforts are best directed.

Standard techniques should be applied first: you minimize I/O, you reduce the number of function calls, you limit computationally intensive operations such as floating-point calculations and the frequent use of division. Then you must identify the elements of the algorithm that are performed the most frequently. In the bubble sort, the comparison and swap should be the subject of intense scrutiny. Finally, you examine implementation details that may inadvertently generate especially slow performance. This last item tends to be akin to the search for the worst-case scenario. You are looking for any unusual situations that might bring performance to its knees. Typically, these situations will arise deep within the details of the implementation and will be the result of a fundamental assumption that is generally valid but occasionally expensive. A telling case in point is the previous discussion of quicksort.

Major Optimizations: I/O

The reduction of I/O and of function-call overhead is so important that a discussion of portable techniques to reduce their cost is warranted. I/O typically occurs in the millisecond time range, while CPU activities occur generally in the submicrosecond range. Hence, any I/O is devastatingly expensive to the performance of an algorithm. If I/O cannot be eliminated, its effects can be reduced by the use of intelligent buffering. Many programmers see this as an invitation to create and control their own buffers and thereby spend considerable effort and code in order to manage I/O buffers. ANSI C provides an elegant alternative with the `setvbuf()` function. This portable function allows the programmer to set the buffer size for the input streams. The question arises as to how big to make the buffers. Most compiler libraries tend to set the buffer size at a conservative but workable size. Expanding the buffer can significantly reduce I/O times. *bufsize.c*, the program in Listing 1-1, allows you to test the optimal buffer size on your own system. It accepts four arguments: a test file to copy, the name of the destination file, and two buffer sizes (one for the input buffer and one for the output buffer). The program then copies the input file four times and gives the minimum, maximum, and average duration of the copy process for the buffer sizes specified on the command line. As written, the program calls MS-DOS's clock and reports the timing in clock ticks. This should be changed for system-equivalent functions under UNIX. As an alternative, the beginning and ending times could be used and the time in seconds reported. Using seconds, however, gives a coarser measurement.

Listing 1-1. A program that tests optimal buffer sizes under MS-DOS.

```
/*--- BUFSIZE.C ----------------------- Listing 1-1 --------
 * Purpose:  Demonstrate use of setvbuf
 * Usage:    bufsize infile outfile [insize [outsize]]
 * Method:   Copies infile to outfile one character at a time,
 *           reporting elapsed time. Infile is set to use a
 *           buffer of insize bytes, while outfile uses an
 *           outsize bytes buffer. Default size is 512 bytes.
 * >> Should be changed per text for UNIX systems <<
 *-----------------------------------------------------------*/
```

```c
#include <bios.h>    /* for timer function */
#include <stdio.h>
#include <stdlib.h>
#include <limits.h>

#define DEF_BUF 512

#ifdef __TURBOC__                    /* Borland    */
#define get_clock_ticks(x) x=biostime(0,0L)
#else                               /* Microsoft and Watcom */
#define get_clock_ticks(x) \
        _bios_timeofday(_TIME_GETCLOCK, &x)
#endif

long CopyFile ( char *infilename, char *outfilename,
            size_t insize, size_t outsize )
{
    int  c;
    long starttime, donetime;
    FILE *infile, *outfile;

    /* open input file and setup its buffer */
    if (( infile = fopen ( infilename, "rb" )) == NULL)
    {
        printf ( "Can't open %s\n", infilename );
        exit ( 1 );
    }

    if ( setvbuf ( infile, NULL, _IOFBF, insize ))
    {
        printf ( "Couldn't set infile buffer to %u bytes.\n",
                insize );
        exit ( 1 );
    }


    /* open output file and setup its buffer */

    if (( outfile = fopen ( outfilename, "wb" )) == NULL )
    {
        printf ( "Can't open %s\n", outfilename );
        exit ( 1 );
    }

    if ( setvbuf ( outfile, NULL, _IOFBF, outsize ))
    {
        printf ( "Couldn't set outfile buffer to %u bytes.\n",
                outsize );
        exit ( 1 );
```

```
    }

    /* do it */

    get_clock_ticks ( starttime );     /* get timer value */
    while (( c = fgetc ( infile )) != EOF )
        fputc ( c, outfile );
    get_clock_ticks ( donetime );
    fclose ( infile );
    fclose ( outfile );

    return ( donetime - starttime );
}


int main ( int argc, char *argv[] )
{
    size_t insize, outsize;
    int    i;
    long   total, average, lo, hi, elapsed;

    insize = outsize = DEF_BUF;

    if ( argc < 3 || argc > 5 )
    {
        fprintf ( stderr,
         "Usage: BUFSIZE infile outfile [insize [outsize]]\n" );
        return ( EXIT_FAILURE );
    }

    /* get buffer sizes */
    if ( argc > 3 )
        insize = (unsigned) atoi ( argv[3] );

    if ( argc > 4 )
        outsize = (unsigned) atoi ( argv[4] );

    /* now, copy the file five times */
    total = hi = 0;
    lo = LONG_MAX;
    for ( i = 1; ; i++ )
    {
        elapsed = CopyFile ( argv[1], argv[2], insize, outsize );
        if ( elapsed > hi )
            hi = elapsed;
        if ( elapsed < lo )
            lo = elapsed;
        total += elapsed;
```

```
    if ( total > 500 ||    /* Change this value depending   */
                           /*   on how long you can wait    */
            i > 4 )        /* Do 4 passes, if time limit OK */
        break;
}

average = total / i;

printf ( "Average of %4ld ticks (%4ld - %4ld). "
         "Insize = %5u. Outsize = %5u.\n",
         average, lo, hi, insize, outsize );

return ( EXIT_SUCCESS );
}
```

The results from running this program on a variety of buffer sizes are shown in Figure 1-2. The vertical axis is in time units for copying a 64K file; the horizontal axis shows the input and output buffer sizes in bytes. This graph was generated on an MS-DOS system running in real mode. It is representative of performance improvements on other systems. Optimal performance is attained at buffer sizes of 4,096 bytes. Larger buffer sizes show no appreciable improvement in performance. In fact, for most applications where flat-out speed is not the most controlling need, buffer sizes of 1,024 bytes are entirely sufficient.

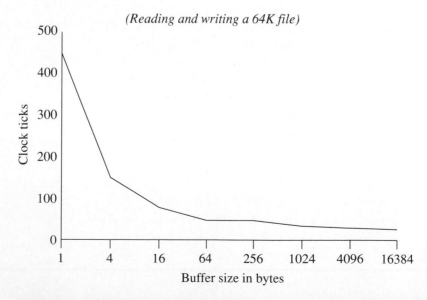

Figure 1-2. Performance of I/O as a function of buffer size, with time shown in clock ticks.

Major Optimization: Function Calls

Another significant optimization is the reduction of function calls. While many of today's compilers have performed substantial optimization of the function call, there is little doubt that functions carry significant overhead. To verify this, write a small program that makes 10,000 calls to a function that simply returns, and you will begin to appreciate the cost of function calls. Times are even longer if arguments are passed or returned by the function. A common practice is to use in-line code or macros to bury the function directly in your algorithm. Study your compiler's library (you should always get the source code if it is available), and you will find that a number of functions are already implemented as macros. Use these when possible, watching attentively for side effects. If you still must call functions and cannot obtain the performance you need, consider copying the vendor's source code directly into your algorithm. This is a risky business and should be considered only as a last resort when all other optimizations have been performed. The question of copyright notwithstanding, library source code is rarely portable and may address variables hidden within the library proper. However, many functions can be brought in easily or converted to macros. Either approach will increase code size, so beware not to overuse this technique.

Another common algorithmic technique is to eliminate recursion. Recursion is the practice of having a function call itself. In C, all functions can be recursive: they can all call themselves—at least, theoretically. In practice, functions such as `main()` and `exit()` can cause problems when called recursively. However, almost all other functions that do not terminate the program can call themselves. The technique of recursion is used frequently in algorithms because it can lead to short and elegant solutions. However, it is costly—in terms of both time and system resources, notably stack space. Chapter 5 shows some examples of how to remove recursion. Eliminate it where you can.

Under MS-DOS there are additional techniques for slashing the overhead of function calls. The first is to enable the optimization offered by many advanced compilers that allows arguments to be passed to a function in registers rather than on the stack. (Borland uses the *–pr* switch, Microsoft the */Gr* switch and the *_fastcall* keyword, while Watcom performs this optimization by default.) Care should be used when using these functions with third-party libraries; for further information consult your compiler documentation.

A second option for users of MS-DOS is the `pascal` keyword. This option affects how the called function manipulates the stack. When the keyword is used, both time and space savings can be realized. Like the previous option, the `pascal` keyword must be used with care. It cannot be used with functions that have a variable number of arguments, and it generally cannot be used in conjunction with the previous option. Again, read your compiler documentation carefully. If you must choose between the two approaches, you will have to inspect your program. If you frequently pass a small number of arguments (but not zero arguments), use the first option; if you have many kinds of functions that take either no arguments or many more than two or three, then the `pascal` option will be more efficient.

Finally, study the algorithm carefully and work at the pieces that are used the most frequently. A good profiler is of immeasurable benefit in this process. Buy one and use it; your code will accelerate with its regular application. In the chapters that follow, we emphasize clarity of code as an illustration of the algorithm. We forgo optimization if its presence will obscure the code. Whenever possible, we give tips and information regarding places where the algorithm can be optimized.

Resources and References

Rex, John. "The pascal Keyword." *C Gazette*, Vol. 3, No. 4. This is a good analysis of the benefits and dangers of using the `pascal` option.

Tanenbaum, Andrew. *Operating Systems: Design and Implementation.* Englewood Cliffs, NJ: Prentice Hall, 1987. The dining philosophers problem has been presented many times, but nowhere better than in this classic book.

Chapter 2

Basic Data Structures

Algorithms are the means by which we manipulate data to achieve a certain end. Algorithms are often applied to problems that handle simple data in complex ways. A compiler, for example, translates simple strings and characters into a binary product that is executable on a specific machine. The compiler's internal workings are the interplay of numerous algorithms that sequentially transform the source-code characters into intermediate representations. These representations are themselves translated by other algorithms into an object code that bears little resemblance to the original characters and strings. Programs that are less ambitious than compilers also rely heavily on algorithms to handle data in a predictable way. Consequently, it is impossible to talk much about algorithms without understanding the basic routines for manipulating data. Developers who want to be proficient in using algorithms must first learn how to manipulate data. Subsequently, they can apply algorithmic techniques to render the data according to their needs.

The algorithmic manipulation of data is concerned most with the techniques of representing data in memory. How can data be stored, accessed, and transformed to most efficiently solve a given problem? Most problems require the developer to be fluent in the use of certain basic **data structures**. These data structures are forms of storing or processing data. The simplest data structures are the **array**, the **linked list**, the **stack**, and the **queue**.

For the purposes of this book, it is assumed that you are already familiar with arrays in C. Whether these are arrays of characters (such as strings), of integers, or of `struct`s, the principles of operation are the same. If you are not comfortable with these operations, you should consult an introductory text on C before proceeding. This chapter explores linked lists, stacks, and queues in detail. Linked lists are examined again in Chapter 3, which discusses hash tables in considerable depth; and in Chapter 6 while exploring the labyrinth of binary trees.

Linked Lists

Arrays in C (and in many languages) must be defined when the program is written. That is, to define an array in C, you must also define its size. Even arrays that are declared or defined at a global level (that is, outside any function), such as

```
#include <stdio.h>

char BigArray[];

int main ( int argc, char *argv[] )
{
    ...
```

must be allocated at some point to a specific size, generally by the use of the `malloc` function or some similar mechanism.

Whether or not `malloc()` is used, the size must be specified before the array can be used. This leaves the problem of how to allocate space when you cannot know beforehand how many elements will need to be created.

Suppose, for example, that you need to write a program that reads a file containing cities and their temperatures from an input file. You will ultimately need to sort the cities by temperature and determine the median temperature (that is, the middle temperature that has an equal number of colder and hotter temperatures on either side). A simple array would be a poor choice for this problem. How large would you make the array? You could declare an array far larger than you would ever expect to need, and then hope that the input file never exceeds this size. However, not only does this approach waste space, but it is likely to fail if the input is suddenly larger than expected.

One solution might be to read through the file twice: once to determine the size of the array and to allocate it, the second time to actually process the data. However, this solution is inefficient. Disk I/O, even on a RAM disk, is extremely slow—in fact, it is almost always the slowest part of any program, generally by an order of magnitude—so reading data twice is something you want to avoid doing if at all possible.

A more elegant solution is the linked list, which is a way of storing data as it is received. The linked list is as accurate as the second method but far more efficient. A linked list consists of a chain of elements called **nodes**. Each node contains the data item to be stored and a pointer pointing to the next node in the list. As each data item is read, a new node is created (using `malloc`) and tacked on to the end of the list. At the end of the input, the computer memory holds a list of nodes, each containing the data (such as the city's name and the temperature) and a pointer to the next node. The last node has a pointer whose value is NULL, the value defined in ANSI C as a pointer to nowhere. When stepping through the list to find the median temperature, the NULL pointer tells us that we have reached the end of the linked list. The pointer in each node is termed the **link**, hence the term *linked list*. Each linked list starts with a simple pointer that points to the first item in the list. This pointer is called the **head**. A short linked list is shown in Figure 2-1.

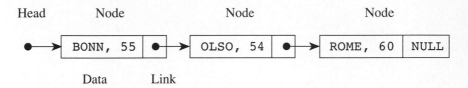

Figure 2-1. A linked list with three nodes.

The linked list shown in Figure 2-1 could be represented in C as follows:

```
struct Node {
     char *City;
     int   Temp;
     struct Node *Next;
};

typedef struct Node * Link;

Link Head;
```

The `typedef` is created to make the code more readable. Predictably, a `Link` is a pointer to a `Node`. The first `Link` we define is `Head`, which is `NULL` when the linked list is empty. Otherwise it points to the first node.

Initializing a new linked list of this kind requires simply initializing the appropriate variables:

```
Head = NULL;
NodeCount = 0;
```

The integer `NodeCount` will be useful in processing the linked list later on. As soon as the first node is added, `Head` points to it. Adding nodes can be easy or tedious. If you are adding nodes without being concerned about what place they occupy in the list (an unordered list), you simply add the node at the head. As each node is allocated, its link points to the current `Head`, and then `Head` is updated to point to the new `Node`, as shown in Figure 2-2.

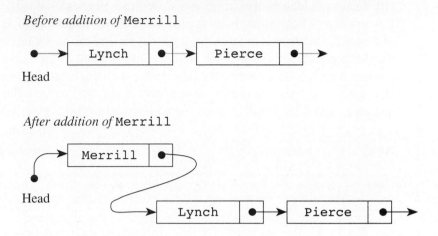

Figure 2-2. An unordered addition of a node to a linked list.

Adding nodes to a list whose elements are in some kind of order (an ordered list) requires more effort. First, you provide a way to compare the data of two nodes and determine which node is higher or lower on the list. You must also determine what should be done when a new node duplicates an existing node: should the new node be added, should the new node be discarded, or should the existing node's data be modified? In Listing 2-1 these tasks are performed by two functions: `NodeCmp()` and `DuplicateNode()`, respectively. With these functions defined, the actual addition of the node can then be undertaken.

As you traverse the linked list, you will know that you have found the insertion point only when you have passed it or when you have reached the end of the list. As a result, you will need to save the address of the previously examined node (`prev` in `AddNodeAscend()` in Listing 2-1). The insertion takes place between the currently examined node (`curr`) and the previous node. If `pn` points to the node you are trying to add, then the process is as follows:

```
prev->Next = pn; /* prev must now point to pn */
pn->Next = curr; /* and pn must now point to curr */
```

Several special cases must be considered: adding a node to an empty list, adding a node ahead of the first node, and adding a node at the end of the list. One method for succinctly handling all these cases is shown in `AddNodeAscend()`. Rather than test for all the special cases, we create a dummy node and hang the current list from this node. Thus, we know that our list is never empty, and our logic can be substantially simplified. Listing 2-1, *citytemp.c*, reads a data file of cities and temperatures, inserts the records into a linked list (in ascending order by temperature and city name), discarding any duplicates, and then prints the ordered list, indicating which entry is the median. The data records are simple lines of a text file, with the first 3 characters representing the temperature, followed by up to 124 characters for the city name.

   Notice that without some dynamic structure like a linked list, it would be impossible to determine the median temperature without reading the data twice. The final loop that prints the records in the list shows how simple it is to traverse a linked list.

Listing 2-1.   Printing an ordered linked list of cities and temperatures.

```
/*--- citytemp.c-------------------------- Listing 2-1 ---------
 *  Reads a text file of cities and temperatures in the
 *  following format:    TempCity
 *      where Temp is a number of three digits or
 *      a sign and two digits; City is a string of length < 124
 *  Examples:       -10Duluth
 *                  096Phoenix
 *  The records are read into a singly linked list by order
 *  of temperature and city; duplicates are discarded. At EOF,
 *  the whole list is printed with an indication of the median
 *  temperature. And then, the list is progressively shortened
 *  and reprinted showing the median.
 *              Usage: citytemp filename.ext
 *-----------------------------------------------------------*/

#include <stdio.h>
#include <stdlib.h>
#include <string.h>

/*--- data definitions ---*/

struct Node {           /* a node in our linked list */
    char *City;
    int   Temp;
    struct Node *Next;
};

typedef struct Node * Link; /* Links are pointers to nodes */
```

```
Link Head;                /* head of our linked list */
int  NodeCount;           /* how many nodes in the list */

/*--- functions declarations for linked lists ---*/

int  AddNodeAscend ( Link );        /* add a node           */
void CreateList ( void );           /* initialize list      */
int  DeleteNode ( Link );           /* delete a node        */
int  DuplicateNode ( Link, Link );  /* handle duplicate inserts */
void FreeNode ( Link );             /* free a node's memory */
void ShowNodes ( void );            /* show list of nodes   */
int  NodeCmp ( Link, Link );        /* compare two nodes    */

/*--- function definitions ---*/

int AddNodeAscend ( Link to_add )
{
    Link   pn,    /* local copy of node to be added */
           prev, /* points to previous node */
           curr; /* points to node being examined */
    struct Node dummy;
    int    i;

    /* Make a copy of the input node */
    pn = ( Link ) malloc ( sizeof ( struct Node ));
    if ( pn == NULL )
        return 0;
    memcpy ( pn, to_add, sizeof ( struct Node ));

    /* set up a dummy node to simplify logic */
    dummy.Next = Head;
    prev = &dummy;
    curr = Head;

    /* insert node pn */
    for ( ;; prev = curr, curr = curr->Next )
    {
        if ( curr == NULL )
            break; /* reached the end */

        i = NodeCmp ( pn, curr );
        if ( i <= 0 )
            break; /* pn precedes curr */
    }

    if ( curr && i == 0 ) /* we have a duplicate */
        if ( DuplicateNode ( curr, pn ) == 0 )
            return ( 1 ); /* bail out if DuplicateNode says to */
```

```
        prev->Next = pn;
        pn->Next = curr;

        Head = dummy.Next;
        return ( 1 );
}


/*-------------------------------------------------------------
 * Handle the duplicate node. In this program,
 * we just delete the duplicate.
 *-----------------------------------------------------------*/
int DuplicateNode ( Link inlist, Link duplicate )
{
    FreeNode ( duplicate );
    return ( 0 );
}

int DeleteNode ( Link to_delete )
{
    Link curr,  /* the current node */
         prev;  /* the previous node */
    int  i;

    /*--- Is there anything in the list? ---*/
    if ( Head == NULL )
        return ( 0 );

    /*--- If so, step through the list looking for the node ---*/
    for ( prev = NULL, curr = Head;
        curr != NULL && ( i = NodeCmp ( to_delete, curr )) > 0;
        prev = curr, curr = curr->Next )
        /* loop around */ ;

    /*--- Found a match, so delete it ---*/
    if ( curr != NULL && i == 0 )
    {
        if ( prev )
            prev->Next = curr->Next;
        else                /* deleting Head */
            Head = curr->Next;

        FreeNode ( curr );
        NodeCount -= 1;
        return ( 1 );
    }

    return ( 0 );
}
```

```
int NodeCmp ( Link a, Link b )
{
    /* returns 1, 0, -1, depending on whether the data in
     * a is greater than, equal, or less than b.
     */

    /* if temps are unequal, return based on temp */
    if ( a->Temp != b->Temp )
        return ( a->Temp - b->Temp );

    /* else, return based on city's name */
    return strcmp ( a->City, b->City );
}

void CreateList ( void )
{
    Head = NULL;
    NodeCount = 0;
}

void FreeNode ( Link n )
{
    free ( n->City );
    free ( n );
}

void ShowNodes( void )
{
    Link pn;
    int count, median;

    /* count the nodes */
    for ( count = 0, pn = Head; pn; pn = pn->Next )
        count += 1;

    /* compute the median node */
    median = count / 2 + 1;

    /* step through the list printing cities and
     * temperatures. Announce the median temperature.
     */
    if ( count ) /* only print if there's a node */
    {
        /* initialize the needed variables */
        count = 0;       /* count of nodes we've printed */
        for ( pn = Head; pn; pn = pn->Next )
        {
            printf ( "%-20s: %3d", pn->City, pn->Temp );
            count += 1;
```

```
            if ( count == median )
                printf ( " --Median--" );
            printf ( "\n" );
        }
    }
    else
        printf ( "Empty list\n" );
}

/*--- main line ---*/
int main ( int argc, char *argv[] )
{
    FILE *fin;        /* file we'll be reading from */
    char buffer[128]; /* where we'll read the file into */

    struct Node n;    /* the node we add each time */

    if ( argc != 2 )
    {
        fprintf ( stderr, "Usage: citytemp filename.ext\n" );
        exit ( EXIT_FAILURE );
    }

    fin = fopen ( argv[1], "rt" );
    if ( fin == NULL )
    {
        fprintf ( stderr, "Cannot open/find %s\n", argv[2] );
        exit ( EXIT_FAILURE );
    }

    /* Create and initialize the linked list to empty */
    CreateList();

    /*--- main loop ---*/
    while ( ! feof ( fin ))
    {
        /* read a record consisting of a line of text */
        if ( fgets ( buffer, 127, fin ) == NULL )
            break;

        /* get rid of the trailing carriage return */
        buffer [ strlen ( buffer ) - 1 ] = '\0';

        /* copy the city name to the node to be added */
        n.City = strdup ( buffer + 3 );

        /* mark off the temperature and convert to int */
        buffer[3] = '\0';
        n.Temp = atoi ( buffer );
```

```
        /* add the node to the list */
        if ( AddNodeAscend ( &n ) == 0 )
        {
            fprintf ( stderr, "Error adding node. Aborting\n" );
            exit ( EXIT_FAILURE );
        }
    }

    ShowNodes();

    /* Now, delete something */
    printf( "\n" );
    DeleteNode ( Head );
    ShowNodes();

    while (Head && Head->Next)
    {
        printf ( "\n" );
        DeleteNode ( Head->Next );
        ShowNodes();
    }

    printf ( "\n" );
    DeleteNode ( Head );
    ShowNodes();

    fclose ( fin );
    return ( EXIT_SUCCESS );
}
```

A sample data file for this program might look like this:

```
-10Boise, ID
-05Missoula, MT
-05Missoula, MT
040Hartford, CT
060Chicago, IL
080Los Angeles, CA
080Albuquerque, NM
100Phoenix, AZ
100Yuma, AZ
030Detroit, MI
000Franchot, MN
10 Kankakee, IL
098Hilo, HI
```

The output from this file will look like this:

```
Boise, ID           : -10
Missoula, MT        :  -5
Franchot, MN        :   0
Kankakee, IL        :  10
Detroit, MI         :  30
Hartford, CT        :  40
Chicago, IL         :  60 --Median--
Albuquerque, NM     :  80
Los Angeles, CA     :  80
Hilo, HI            :  98
Phoenix, AZ         : 100
Yuma, AZ            : 100
```

Listing 2-1 shows how to create and traverse a list, add nodes in order, and compare two nodes. It also contains a function, `DeleteNode()`, that shows how to delete a node even though it is unused in the main program. Deleting a node requires a traversal of the list until the correct node is found. Once the node is located, the pointer from the previous node is made to point to the next node in the list, such that the list now completely bypasses the current node. The current node is then returned to available memory by means of the standard `free()` function.

Note that to have the previous node ready to point to the next node, a separate pointer, called `prev`, must be maintained as the linked list is traversed, so as to keep track of which node precedes the node that should be deleted. This requirement suggests one of the major shortcomings of the linked lists examined so far: without special accommodations, you do not know which node points to the current node. The node itself tells you only what the next node is, not what the previous node is.

While there is no way to avoid the requirement for this piece of information, it is possible to maintain both the current pointer and the previous pointer as one pointer, namely `prev`. We do this by realizing that `curr = prev->Next`, so everywhere we have used `curr`, we simply used `prev->Next`.

An even more subtle technique is to maintain `prev` not as a pointer to a node of the list, but as a pointer to the `Next` element of the previous node. To do so, we define `prev` as `Link *prev`. An example of this technique is shown in Chapter 5 (Listing 5-16, *linsert.c*). This technique is especially valuable when you want to process a subset of a linked list without excising the subset from the main list. We make extensive use of this technique in our implementation of Quicksort for linked lists in Chapter 5 (Listing 5-17, *lquick1.c*, and Listing 5-18, *lquick2.c*). The advantage of having a pointer to the `Next` element of the previous node is that you can readily make any desired modification to the subset list without disturbing the larger, containing list.

Whichever technique you use, you are trying to get around the major shortcoming of linked lists that have just one link: you cannot tell where you came from. The solution is to use linked lists with two links in each node: one pointing to the previous link, and the other pointing to the following link. Such lists are called **doubly linked lists**.

Note that in Listing 2-1 the functions that manipulate the linked list directly are generic. They are coded so that they can be used regardless of what data the nodes contain. The only requirement is that the link to the next node be called `Next`. Actually, two functions are necessarily data dependent: `NodeCmp()`, which compares the data in two nodes to determine the insertion order, and `DuplicateNode()`, which handles the processing when inserting a node that has the same data as an existing node. All generic implementations of generic linked lists require that at least these two functions be tailored to the specific data being processed. In Listing 2-1, `DuplicateNode()` does not actually touch the data, but in other programs (such as those presented in Chapter 3), the same function may have to manipulate data.

To use the routines in Listing 2-1 for your own needs, define `Node` as required, carefully keeping the link named `Next`. Then recode `DuplicateNode()` and `NodeCmp()`, and you will be ready to go.

The functions presented in Listing 2-1 illustrate the basic operations of a linked list. They are suitable for quick and dirty applications, but they do not address needs that could arise in complex programs. For example, suppose you need to maintain multiple linked lists with differing data types. These functions will be insufficient. The following section describes in detail how to solve such a problem and how to address other subtleties that prevent quick-and-dirty linked lists from being truly robust.

Doubly Linked Lists

Doubly linked lists use nodes that contain data as well as links to the previous *and* succeeding nodes. Having links to both neighboring nodes confers certain advantages—notably, the ability to traverse the list backward and forward. Also, when traversing the list there is no need to maintain a pointer to the previous node. As a result, doubly linked lists offer greater facility. Because traversal in both directions is often performed on linked lists, the implementation suggests the definition of an additional pointer that keeps track of the last node in the list. This pointer, called the **tail**, serves the same function as the head pointer—but at the back end of the list. A standard doubly linked list looks like the one shown in Figure 2-3.

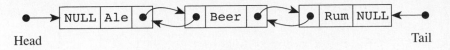

Head   Tail

Figure 2-3.   A short, doubly linked list of important liquids.

Notice the great similarity to a list with singly linked nodes. The code for implementing the doubly linked list is somewhat more complex, because each insertion and deletion requires the manipulation of an additional pointer. In addition, the tail pointer, generally called `Tail`, must be updated when actions occur at the end of the list. Anybody who has worked with doubly linked lists knows the tedium of coding them carefully so that all pointers point where they should. As a result, good programmers have a set of generic routines that they always use to implement the list. A comprehensive set of functions for handling doubly linked lists appears in Listing 2-2 through 2-4b. These functions, known as **primitives** (so named because they do all the low-level work), are presented in two parts: those that are data independent and those that access the data. A sample of the latter kind appears in Listings 2-4a and 2-4b.

Listing 2-2. Header file for generic doubly linked lists.

```
/*--- llgen.h -------------------------- Listing 2-2 ---------
 *  Declarations for generic doubly linked lists.
 *  Used in conjucntion with llgen.c (Listing 2-3).
 *------------------------------------------------------------*/
#ifndef LLGEN_H        /* make sure it's included only once */
#define LLGEN_H      1


struct Node {
    struct Node     *prev;  /* link to previous node */
    struct Node     *next;  /* link to next node */
    void            *pdata; /* generic pointer to data */
};

typedef struct Node *Link;

/* a linked list data structure */
struct List {
    Link            LHead;
    Link            LTail;
    unsigned int    LCount;
    void * ( * LCreateData )     ( void * );
    int    ( * LDeleteData )     ( void * );
```

```
    int      ( * LDuplicatedNode ) ( Link, Link );
    int      ( * LNodeDataCmp )     ( void *, void * );
};
```

```
/* The four functions specific to an individual linked list are:
```

LCreateData: is passed a pointer to an application-defined
               object and is expected to return a pointer to
               whatever is to be stored in the linked list.

LDeleteData: is passed a pointer to the object an application
               has stored in a linked list. LDeleteData must
               destroy the object.

LDuplicatedNode: is passed two pointers. The first pointer is
               to a node that you would like to add to a
               linked list and the second is to a node that
               is already in the list but is a duplicate of
               the first pointer.
               LDuplicatedNode returns:
                       0 -> do nothing to list
                       1 -> destroy duplicate
                       2 -> add duplicate to list

LNodeDataCmp: is passed pointers to two application data
               objects and must compare them, returning a
               number that is < 0, zero, or > 0, depending on
               the relationship between the first and second
               objects.
```
*/
```

```
/*--- generic linked-list primitives ---*/
int  AddNodeAscend ( struct List *, void * );
int  AddNodeAtHead ( struct List *, void * );
struct List * CreateLList (
               void * ( * ) ( void * ),         /* create data */
               int    ( * ) ( void * ),         /* delete data */
               int    ( * ) ( Link, Link ),   /* duplicate   */
               int    ( * )  ( void *, void * )); /* compare */
Link CreateNode       ( struct List * , void * );
int  DeleteNode       ( struct List *, Link );
Link FindNode         ( struct List *, void * );
Link FindNodeAscend ( struct List *, void * );
Link GotoNext         ( struct List *, Link );
Link GotoPrev         ( struct List *, Link );
#endif
```

This file warrants some careful attention. The initial test for `LLGEN_H` makes sure that the header file is only included once. This seemingly minor provision is a good habit to acquire on all header files. Not only does it give you direct control over what the compiler is doing, but it also leads to quicker compilations. One of the slowest aspects of a compiler's work is reading the source files. A case in point is the recent tendency of compiler vendors to provide the option of precompiled headers (for example, the Borland and Microsoft compilers, among others on the MS-DOS and Windows environments). Therefore, making sure that the compiler reads the relevant files only once boosts compilation speed.

Note the definition of `Node`. It contains the two links, `prev` and `next`, and then defines `NodeData`, a pointer to `void`. Pointers to `void` are C's generic pointers. They can be cast to any data type without error. To make our implementation of doubly linked lists truly generic, we do not want to specify in the generic functions what our data looks like. The generic functions are designed to manipulate only the links in a node. Therefore, they have no need to know what our data looks like. In this manner, the generic functions can be used on any number of dissimilar linked lists without having to be changed. When we define the application-specific functions, we will be required to cast our `void` pointers to reflect the type of data we are manipulating. Two sample data definitions appear as `NodeData1` and `NodeData2` in Listing 2-4a (*llapp.h*).

Having defined our nodes, we now define our lists. The structure `List` contains all the data items and functions that are specific to a given linked list. The first two pointers point to the head and the tail. The `LCount` field contains the number of nodes in the list. Finally, four pointers to functions that are specific to a given list appear in the structure. These four functions are the only ones that actually manipulate the data in our list's nodes. They are application-specific and must be defined for each list we implement. Examples of these functions appear in Listing 2-4b, *llapp.c*.

Defining a list as a structure containing all list-specific matters means that new lists can be easily added to a program, even when these lists store widely different types of data. Listing 2-5 (*lldriver.c*) is a program that exercises most of the linked-list primitives. It creates two linked lists, traverses the lists in both directions simultaneously, adds and deletes nodes, and prints the lists. Its input consists of a text file with one word per line. This driver program shows how to use the generic and application-specific functions. To create the executable file, you need to compile *llgen.c*, *llapp.c*, and *lldriver.c*. These programs should then be linked to form the executable file. A program illustrated in Chapter 3 (Listing 3-4, *wordlist.c*) shows how to use these functions to initialize and manipulate two lists with separate data types. One of the lists has hundreds of instances that appear in a table.

Listing 2-3 contains the generic primitives for linked lists. These functions manipulate only the links in a node; hence they are completely generic and should not be altered for use.

Listing 2-3.   Primitives for a doubly linked list.

```
/*--- llgen.c ---------------------------- Listing 2-3 --------
 * Generic primitive functions for doubly linked lists.
 * Contains no application-specific functions.
 * Functions are in alphabetical order.
 *----------------------------------------------------------*/

#include <stdlib.h>
#include <string.h>

#define IN_LL_LIB   1    /* in the library of primitives */

#include "llgen.h"

/*--- Aliases to make the code more readable ---*/

#define LLHead (L->LHead)        /* The head of the current list */
#define LLTail (L->LTail)        /* The tail of the current list */
#define NodeCount (L->LCount)    /* Nodes in the current list */

#define CreateData      (*(L->LCreateData))
#define DeleteData      (*(L->LDeleteData))
#define DuplicatedNode  (*(L->LDuplicatedNode))
#define NodeDataCmp     (*(L->LNodeDataCmp))

/*----------------------------------------------------
 * Add a node at head: first allocate the space for
 * the data, then allocate a node with a pointer to
 * the data, then add the node to the list.
 *----------------------------------------------------*/
int AddNodeAtHead ( struct List *L, void *nd )
{
    Link pn;

    pn = CreateNode ( L, nd );
    if ( pn == NULL )
        return ( 0 );

    /*--- Add the node ---*/
    if ( LLHead == NULL )    /* is it the first node? */
    {
        LLHead = LLTail = pn; /*--- yes ---*/
```

```
    }
    else                         /*--- no  ---*/
    {
        LLHead->prev = pn; /* first goes node before Head */
        pn->next = LLHead; /* put Head next */
        LLHead = pn;       /* then point Head to us */
    }

    NodeCount += 1;
    return ( 1 );
}


/*---------------------------------------------------
 * Add ascending. Adds a node to an ordered list.
 *--------------------------------------------------*/
int AddNodeAscend ( struct List *L, void *nd )
{
    Link        pn;          /* to node we're creating */
    Link        prev, curr; /* our current search */
    struct Node dummy;       /* a dummy node */
    int         compare;

    pn = CreateNode ( L, nd );
    if ( pn == NULL )
        return ( 0 );

    /* attach dummy node to head of list */
    dummy.next = LLHead;
    dummy.prev = NULL;
    if ( dummy.next != NULL )
        dummy.next->prev = &dummy;

    prev = &dummy;
    curr = dummy.next;
    for ( ; curr != NULL; prev = curr, curr = curr->next )
    {
        compare = NodeDataCmp ( pn->pdata, curr->pdata );
        if ( compare <= 0 )
            break; /* new node equals or precedes curr */
    }

    if ( curr != NULL && compare == 0 )
    {
        compare = DuplicatedNode ( pn, curr );
        if ( compare == 2 )
            /* do nothing -- will get inserted */;
        else
        {
```

```
                    /* first, repair the linked list */
                    LLHead = dummy.next;
                    LLHead->prev = NULL;

                    /* delete the duplicated node, if appropriate */
                    if ( compare == 1 )
                    {
                        DeleteData( pn->pdata );
                        free ( pn );
                    }
                    return ( 1 );
                }
            }

        prev->next = pn;
        pn->prev = prev;
        pn->next = curr;
        if ( curr != NULL )
            curr->prev = pn;
        else
            LLTail = pn; /* this node is the new tail */

        NodeCount += 1;

        /* now, unhook the dummy head node */
        LLHead = dummy.next;
        LLHead->prev = NULL;
        return ( 1 );
    }


/*-------------------------------------------------------------
 * Creates a linked-list structure and returns a pointer to it.
 * On error, returns NULL. This functions accepts pointers
 * to the four list-specific functions and initializes the
 * linked-list structure with them.
 *-----------------------------------------------------------*/
struct List * CreateLList (
                void * ( * fCreateData ) ( void * ),
                int    ( * fDeleteData ) ( void * ),
                int    ( * fDuplicatedNode ) ( Link, Link ),
                int    ( * fNodeDataCmp )  ( void *, void * ))
{
    struct List * pL;

    pL = (struct List *) malloc ( sizeof ( struct List ));
    if ( pL == NULL )
        return NULL;
```

```
    pL->LHead = NULL;
    pL->LTail = NULL;
    pL->LCount = 0;

    pL->LCreateData = fCreateData;
    pL->LDeleteData = fDeleteData;
    pL->LDuplicatedNode = fDuplicatedNode;
    pL->LNodeDataCmp = fNodeDataCmp;

    return ( pL );
}


/*-------------------------------------------------------------
 * Creates a node and then calls the application-specific
 * function CreateData() to create the node's data structure.
 * Returns NULL on error.
 *-----------------------------------------------------------*/
Link CreateNode ( struct List *L, void *data )
{
    Link new_node;

    new_node = (Link) malloc ( sizeof ( struct Node ));
    if ( new_node == NULL )
        return ( NULL );

    new_node->prev = NULL;
    new_node->next = NULL;

    /*--- now call the application-specific data allocation ---*/
    new_node->pdata = CreateData( data );
    if ( new_node->pdata == NULL )
    {
        free ( new_node );
        return ( NULL );
    }
    else
        return ( new_node );
}


/*-------------------------------------------------------------
 *  Deletes the node pointed to by to_delete.
 *  Function calls list-specific function to delete data.
 *-----------------------------------------------------------*/
int DeleteNode ( struct List *L, Link to_delete )
{
    Link pn;
```

```c
    if ( to_delete == NULL )        /* Double check before */
        return ( 0 );               /* deleting anything.  */

    if ( to_delete->prev == NULL )  /* we're at the head */
    {
        LLHead = to_delete->next;   /* update head */
        LLHead->prev = NULL;        /* update next node */
    }

    else if ( to_delete->next == NULL )
    {                               /* we're at the tail */
        pn = to_delete->prev;       /* get the previous node */
        pn->next = NULL;
        LLTail = pn;                /* update tail */
    }

    else                    /* we're in the list */
    {
        pn = to_delete->prev;       /* get the previous node */
        pn->next = to_delete->next; /* update previous node to */
                                    /* point to the next one. */
        pn = to_delete->next;       /* get the next node */
        pn->prev = to_delete->prev; /* update it to point to */
                                    /* the previous one. */
    }

    DeleteData ( to_delete->pdata ); /* delete the data */
    free ( to_delete );              /* free the node */

    NodeCount -= 1;

    return ( 1 );
}

/*-----------------------------------------------------------------
 * Finds node by starting at the head of the list, stepping
 * through each node, and comparing data items with the search
 * key. The Ascend version checks that the data in the node
 * being examined is not larger than the search key. If it is,
 * we know the key is not in the list. Returns pointer to node
 * on success or NULL on failure.
 *-----------------------------------------------------------*/
Link FindNode ( struct List *L, void *nd )
{
    Link pcurr;             /* the node we're examining */

    if ( LLHead == NULL )           /* empty list */
```

```
          return ( NULL );

     for ( pcurr = LLHead; pcurr != NULL; pcurr = pcurr->next)
     {
          if ( NodeDataCmp ( nd, pcurr->pdata ) == 0 )
               return ( pcurr );
     }
     return ( NULL );                 /* could not find node */
}

Link FindNodeAscend ( struct List *L, void *nd )
{
     Link      pcurr;           /* the node we're examining */
     int cmp_result;

     if ( LLHead == NULL )        /* empty list */
          return ( NULL );

     for ( pcurr = LLHead; pcurr != NULL; pcurr = pcurr->next)
     {
          cmp_result =  NodeDataCmp ( nd, pcurr->pdata );

          if ( cmp_result < 0 )
               return ( NULL );    /* too far */

          if ( cmp_result == 0 )   /* just right */
               return ( pcurr );
     }

     return ( NULL );              /* could not find node */
}
```

Each function takes as its first parameter the address of the structure containing the linked list's individual data items. For the sake of brevity, this pointer is called L. You will note that some functions need to be able to examine, but not modify, a node's data. For example, the function AddNodeAscend( ), which adds a node in ascending order, needs to be able to compare the data of the node to be added with the data of the node that it is currently examining (pointed to by LLCurr). To do so, it calls the list-specific comparison function pointed to by LNodeDataCmp in the List structure. The syntax for calling a function through a pointer to it is made simple by the macro that appears at the top of the listing:

```
#define NodeDataCmp (*(L->LNodeDataCmp))
```

LNodeDataCmp is the name in `List` of the pointer to the function. `L` is a pointer to the `List` structure we are accessing; therefore, `L->LNodeDataCmp` is the actual function pointer. Dereferencing it by using `*` calls the function. Hence, using the macro, `NodeDataCmp (a, b)`, has the effect of calling the function and passing it arguments `a` and `b`. All the application-specific functions follow this approach.

Note that if you simply want to add a node to a list without worrying about whether it is in ascending order, you use `AddNodeAtHead()`. All these functions, and the data-dependent functions, except for the comparison, return 0 if an error occurs. Success returns a 1. If `AddNodeAscend()`, which adds nodes in ascending order, encounters a node with a matching value, it first calls the application-specific function `DuplicatedNode()` to let you decide what to do. It then returns one of three possible values: 0 indicates an error, 1 means get rid of the duplicate node, and 2 means add the duplicate node to the list.

Because of an interesting subtlety, deleting a node requires an application-specific function. Suppose the node's data contains a pointer to a string. If you simply delete the node—using `free()`, for example—the pointer to the string disappears, as it should, but the string itself remains allocated in memory, occupying space. It has become an orphan; it is still live data, but no pointer knows of its existence. As a result, to dispose of a node properly, you must first delete the data (using the application-specific `LDeleteData()`), and then you can free the node.

The same is true for creating a node. You cannot simply copy a pointer to data. Suppose the pointer points to a buffer that will be reused as soon as the node is added to the list. The generic function has no way of knowing the permanence of the data it is handed. As a result, to create a node, you must write another application-specific function, `LCreateNode`. This function copies the string to a new area (using `strdup()`) and uses that address as the address of the string. In this way, the generic functions are always sure of the integrity of the data they handle. This set of issues, generally overlooked in most treatments of linked lists, is referred to as the problem of **data endurance**.

The header file shown in Listing 2-4a declares the application-specific data and functions. In this case, data for two linked lists are defined. The first is a structure containing `word`, a pointer to a string, and `u`, an unsigned integer; the second is a structure containing only a string.

Listing 2-4a.   Header file of the application-specific aspects of the linked list.

```
/*--- llapp.h --------------------------- Listing 2-4a -------
 *  Application-specific data for linked list in lldriver.c (2-5)
 *  Used in conjunction with llapp.c (Listing 2-4b).
 *------------------------------------------------------------*/
#ifndef LLAPP_H
#define LLAPP_H 1

/*
 *  Our first list's nodes consist of a pointer to
 *  a word and a count of occurrences.
 */

struct NodeData1 {
    char *word;
    unsigned int u;
};

typedef struct NodeData1 * pND1;

extern void * CreateData1 ( void * );
extern int    DeleteData1 ( void * );
extern int    DuplicatedNode1 ( Link, Link );
extern int    NodeDataCmp1 ( void *, void * );


/*
 *  Our second list's nodes consist of a
 *  pointer to a word.
 */

struct NodeData2 {
    char *word;
};

typedef struct NodeData2 * pND2;

extern void * CreateData2 ( void * );
extern int    DeleteData2 ( void * );
extern int    DuplicatedNode2 ( Link, Link );
extern int    NodeDataCmp2 ( void *, void * );

#endif
```

In Chapter 3, these structures are used in a program for scanning text. The first list contains unique words and a count of their occurrences, and the second contains words that are suspect. The four application-specific functions that touch the data are also declared for each list. These functions are defined in Listing 2-4b.

Listing 2-4b.   Code for the application-specific aspects of the linked list in Listing 2-5.

```
/*--- llapp.c --------------------------- Listing 2-4b --------
 *  Application-specific functions for linked-list examples.
 *  Replace these routines with your own.
 *-----------------------------------------------------------*/

#include <stdlib.h>          /* for free() */
#include <string.h>          /* for strcmp() and strdup() */

#include "llgen.h"
#include "llapp.h"

/* data is a pointer to a string */
void * CreateData1 ( void * data )
{
    struct NodeData1 * new_data;

    /*--- allocate our data structure ---*/
    if ((new_data = malloc ( sizeof ( struct NodeData1 ))) == NULL)
        return ( NULL );

    /*--- move the values into the data structure ---*/
    new_data->u    = 1;
    new_data->word =  strdup ( (char *) data );

    if ( new_data->word == NULL )    /* error copying string */
    {
        free ( new_data );
        return ( NULL );
    }
    else
        return ( new_data ); /* return a complete structure */
}

int DeleteData1 ( void * data )
{
    /*
     * In this case, NodeData1 consists of: a pointer and an int.
     * The integer will be returned to memory when the node
     * is freed. However, the string must be freed manually.
```

```
         */
         free ( ((pND1) data)->word );
         return ( 1 );
}
/*-------------------------------------------------------------
 * This function determines what to do when inserting a node
 * into a list if an existing node with the same data is found
 * in the list. In this case, since we are counting words, if a
 * duplicate word is found, we simply increment the counter.
 *
 * Note this function should return one of the following values:
 *      0         an error occurred
 *      1         delete the duplicate node
 *      2         insert the duplicate node
 * Any other processing on the duplicate should be done in this
 * function.
 *-----------------------------------------------------------*/

int DuplicatedNode1 ( Link new_node, Link list_node )
{              /* adding an occurrence to an existing word */

    pND1 pnd = list_node->pdata;
    pnd->u += 1;
    return ( 1 );
}

int NodeDataCmp1 ( void *first, void *second )
{
    return ( strcmp ( ((pND1) first)->word,
                      ((pND1) second)->word ));
}

/*=== Now the functions for the second linked list ===*/

void * CreateData2 ( void * data )
{
    struct NodeData2 * new_data;

    /*--- allocate the data structure ---*/
    if ((new_data = malloc ( sizeof ( struct NodeData2 ))) == NULL)
        return ( NULL );

    /*--- move the values into the data structure ---*/
    new_data->word =  strdup ( (char *) data );

    if ( new_data->word == NULL )    /* error copying string */
    {
        free ( new_data );
```

```
        return ( NULL );
    }
    else
        return ( new_data );
}

int DeleteData2 ( void * data )
{
    /*
     * In this case, NodeData2 consists of a pointer.
     * The string must be freed manually.
     */

    free ( ((pND2) data)->word );
    return ( 1 );
}

/* this list inserts duplicated nodes */
int DuplicatedNode2 ( Link new_node, Link list_node )
{
    return ( 2 );
}

int NodeDataCmp2 ( void *first, void *second )
{
    return ( strcmp ( ((pND2) first)->word,
                      ((pND2) second)->word ));
}
```

Now comes a driver program for these functions in Listing 2-5.

Listing 2-5.   A driver program to exercise the linked-list primitives.

```
/*--- lldriver.c ----------------------- Listing 2-5 -------
 *  Reads in text words from the file specified on the command
 *  line and places them into two linked lists. Then exercises
 *  a variety of linked-list activities, printing the results
 *  at every step.
 *  Must be linked to linked-list primitives in Listings 2-2
 *  through 2-4b.
 *-----------------------------------------------------------*/

#include <stdio.h>
#include <stdlib.h>
#include <string.h>

#include "llgen.h"              /* Header for generic linked lists */
```

```c
#include "llapp.h"          /* Header for appl.'s linked lists */

int main ( int argc, char *argv[] )
{
    char    word[64];        /* the raw word from the file */
    int     count;

    struct  List *L1, *L2;   /* two different linked lists */
    Link    w1, w2, w3;      /* cursors used to walk lists */

    FILE    *fin;            /* the input file              */

    if ( argc != 2 )
    {
        fprintf ( stderr, "Error! Usage: lldriver filename\n" );
        exit ( EXIT_FAILURE );
    }

    fin = fopen ( argv[1], "rt" );
    if ( fin == NULL )
    {
        fprintf ( stderr, "Could not find/open %s\n", argv[1] );
        exit ( EXIT_FAILURE );
    }

    /*--- set up linked-list data structures ---*/
    L1 = CreateLList ( CreateData1,      /* in llapp.c */
                       DeleteData1,      /*    "       */
                       DuplicatedNode1,  /*    "       */
                       NodeDataCmp1 );   /*    "       */

    L2 = CreateLList ( CreateData2,      /* in llapp.c */
                       DeleteData2,      /*    "       */
                       DuplicatedNode2,  /*    "       */
                       NodeDataCmp2 );   /*    "       */

    if ( L1 == NULL || L2 == NULL )
    {
        fprintf ( stderr, "Error creating linked list\n" );
        exit ( EXIT_FAILURE );
    }

    /*--- begin processing file ---*/

    while ( fgets ( word, 64, fin ) != NULL )
    {
        if ( strlen ( word ) > 0 )
            word[strlen ( word ) - 1] = 0; /* strip tail \n */
```

```
        /* now, add the word to both lists */
        if ( ! AddNodeAscend ( L1, word ))
            fprintf ( stderr,
                    "Warning! Error while adding node to L1.\n" );
        if ( ! AddNodeAtHead ( L2, word ))
            fprintf ( stderr,
                    "Warning! Error while adding node to L2.\n" );
    }
    fclose ( fin );

    /* now, walk the lists */

    printf( "L1 contains %u items:\n", L1->LCount );
    for ( w1 = L1->LHead; w1 != NULL; w1 = w1->next )
        printf("  %s occured %d times.\n",
                ((pND1) (w1->pdata))->word,
                ((pND1) (w1->pdata))->u );

    printf( "L2 contains %u items:\n", L2->LCount );
    for ( w1 = L2->LHead; w1 != NULL; w1 = w1->next )
        printf ( "  %s\n", ((pND2) (w1->pdata))->word );

    /* both ways at once */

    printf ( "L2 contains %u items:\n", L2->LCount );
    w1 = L2->LHead;
    w2 = L2->LTail;
    for ( ; w1 != NULL && w2 != NULL;
                        w1 = w1->next, w2 = w2->prev )
        printf( "  %30s  %30s\n",
                ((pND2) (w1->pdata))->word,
                ((pND2) (w2->pdata))->word );

    /* "Find" each node and delete every other one */

    count = 0;
    w1 = L2->LHead;
    while ( w1 != NULL )
    {
        w3 = FindNode ( L2, w1->pdata );
        if ( w3 != 0 )
        {
            printf ( "Found node %s",
                        ((pND2) (w3->pdata))->word );
            count += 1;
            w1 = w3->next;
            if ( count & 1 )
            {
```

```
            DeleteNode ( L2, w3 );
            printf ( " and deleted it." );
        }
        printf( "\n" );
    }
    else
        w1 = NULL;
}

printf ( "L2 contains %u items:\n", L2->LCount );
w1 = L2->LHead;
w2 = L2->LTail;
for ( ; w1 != NULL && w2 != NULL;
                    w1 = w1->next, w2 = w2->prev )
    printf ( "  %30s  %30s\n",
                ((pND2) (w1->pdata))->word,
                ((pND2) (w2->pdata))->word );

return ( EXIT_SUCCESS );
}
```

Further Characteristics of Linked Lists

Linked lists are called dynamic data structures because you can expand them and contract them. This characteristic distinguishes them from arrays and other static structures whose maximum size is specified once and is not easily changed later. Anytime you need to store an indeterminate amount of data items in memory, dynamic data structures are likely the best approach. The largest handicap imposed by linked lists is their potential length. Searching through long linked lists can be time-consuming, and this cost can become intolerable if a long list has to be searched repeatedly. Several techniques can help decrease the overhead. One technique is to put the nodes in some order in the list so that the entire list does not need to be examined when you want to determine whether it contains a given node. Another approach is to place the most recently accessed nodes at the head of the list. This will save considerable time if the data being examined tends to be bunched. That is, if a node is manipulated once, it is likely to be examined again soon. This approach can be used in building a cache or in building a compiler for a language like C where local variables, for example, are defined within the function that will use them. Hence, once a local variable appears in a function, it is likely that it will appear soon again in several places. Thereafter, its use will fall off and the node containing it will fall further back in the list as other more recently accessed nodes are moved to the head.

These approaches are beneficial only if the list is not very long. If you anticipate storing hundreds of pieces of data in memory, the linked list will be too inefficient, and you should use other dynamic data structures. The hash table, presented in Chapter 3, maintains a table of linked lists and determines which list should be used for storing a node based on the value of the data. A data structure that guarantees near-optimal performance regardless of how many data items it stores is the binary tree, whose many variations are examined in Chapter 6.

The functions in Listings 2-3, 2-4a, and 2-4b have been carefully segregated so that you can use them easily. But you may wonder which type of list should be used on a generic basis—singly or doubly linked. If your application does not require the use of doubly linked lists, you have a comfortable choice. If performance and space considerations are critically important, use singly linked lists; for all other situations (the vast majority of cases), use doubly linked lists. The extra overhead of setting up the second pointer imposes an almost imperceptible burden on performance. You can easily verify this by using a profiler. The advantage of the doubly linked list is that if your application should ever change and you need to have greater access to the list, the doubly linked list would provide this. The singly linked list, however, would have to be converted to a list with double links.

Stacks and Queues

We will now examine two other simple data structures: the **stack** and the **queue**. These useful structures often find roles in applications. They can be implemented equally well with arrays or linked lists. Once again, the linked-list implementations permit endless resizing, while the array requires that you determine a maximum size at an early point in the development process. With stacks and queues, it is recommended that maximum sizes be established at compilation time rather than at run time; hence, arrays are a reasonable way of implementing these structures. Implementing stacks and queues with linked lists is not a difficult task. All the needed primitives are presented in Listings 2-3, 2-4a, and 2-4b.

Characteristics of Stacks

The stack is a simple data structure that is most easily represented as an array in which items are added and removed from the *same* end. It is called a stack because it is reminiscent of a stack of plates. Plates are placed on the top of the stack and are removed from the top. The bottom plate can be touched only when all other plates have been removed. As with the plates, the important feature of the stack is that the last item placed on the stack is the first one removed. This method of storing data is generally termed **LIFO**—last in, first out.

Stacks have many applications. In most cases, stacks are used when the programmer needs to know what actions or data preceded an action currently in progress. For example, most compilers today implement high-level languages by using stacks. When a function or subroutine is called, the address of the next instruction of the main line is placed on the stack. Then when the function returns, the program retrieves the address from the stack and continues executing from that point. In the case of functions calling other functions, each return address is placed on the stack. In this manner, as the functions finish, they find the address that they placed on the stack.

Many other applications need to keep track of where they have been or how they came to a certain point, and almost invariably, the stack is the data structure of choice for this purpose. The act of placing an item, such as an address or a data item, on the stack is known as **pushing** the item onto the stack (Figure 2-4). Removing an item is called **popping** an item from the stack. The topmost entry of a stack is referred to as the **top**, and other items are considered to be further **down** the stack. At times, this terminology can be confusing; be sure to use it correctly.

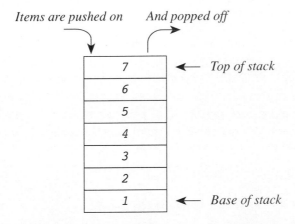

Figure 2-4. A typical stack. Note that item 7 was the last item pushed onto the stack. It will also be the first item popped off.

The primitive functions for manipulating a stack are as follows: creating the stack, clearing the stack (getting rid of everything that is on it), pushing an item, popping an item, and viewing an arbitrary item without disturbing the stack. The stack primitives are presented in Listings 2-6 (*stacks.h*) and 2-7 *(stacks.c)*. The code makes use of the doubly linked list primitives from Listings 2-3 through 2-4b. The application-specific material in Listing 2-5 declares each element in the stack as a structure containing an integer and a character. This structure will be used in Listing 2-8.

Listing 2-6.   The header file for stack primitives implemented as an array.

```
/*--- stacks.h -------------------------- Listing 2-6 ---------
 *  Header file for stack operations
 *-----------------------------------------------------------*/

#ifndef STACKS_H
#define STACKS_H     1

#ifdef IN_STACK_LIB
#define StkExtern
#else
#define StkExtern    extern
#endif

struct stack_struct {
    struct StkElement *base;       /* point to base of stack */
    int               stack_size;  /* number of elements */
    int               min_stack;   /* bottom-most element */
    int               max_stack;   /* last possible element */
    int               top;         /* current top */
};

typedef struct stack_struct Stack;

StkExtern void    ClearStack    ( Stack * );
StkExtern Stack*  CreateStack   ( int );
StkExtern int     PopElement    ( Stack *, struct StkElement * );
StkExtern int     PushElement   ( Stack *, struct StkElement * );
StkExtern struct StkElement *
                  ViewElement   ( Stack *, int );

/*--- Application-specific material goes below ---*/

StkExtern struct StkElement  {
            int    line_no;
            char   opener;
};

#endif
```

Listing 2-7 implements the stack as a simple array of elements that are defined in Listing 2-6. The function `CreateStack` allocates the memory for an array of `how_many` elements. It then initializes the variables that hold the maximum and minimum range of the stack: `MaxStack` and `MinStack`, respectively. These variables are important, because the functions must make sure that items are not pushed beyond the maximum size of the stack (this would overwrite other data items in memory) and that they are not popped past the bottom (this would return incorrect data items that are not actually on the stack). Finally, the function initializes `StackTop`—the variable that keeps track of which stack element is the top—to an illegal value (−1) indicating that the stack is empty.

Listing 2-7. Stack primitives.

```
/*--- stacks.c -------------------------- Listing 2-7 ---------
 * Primitives for array-based stacks
 *------------------------------------------------------------*/

#define IN_STACK_LIB 1

#include <stdlib.h>
#include <string.h>
#include <assert.h>
#include "stacks.h"

/*-------------------------------------------------------------
 *   clear the stack by pointing the top of the stack
 *   at an invalid item; that is, the stack is empty.
 *-----------------------------------------------------------*/
void ClearStack ( Stack *this_stack )
{
    this_stack->top = -1;
}

/*-------------------------------------------------------------
 *   allocate the stack, set the maximum and minimum bounds
 *   on the stack, and show that the stack is empty.
 *-----------------------------------------------------------*/
Stack *CreateStack ( int how_many )
{
    Stack *pstk;

    assert ( how_many > 0 );    /* make sure the size is legal */

    pstk = (Stack *) malloc ( sizeof ( Stack ));
    if ( pstk == NULL )
```

```
        return ( NULL );

    pstk->stack_size = how_many;

    pstk->base = ( struct StkElement * )
        malloc ( how_many * sizeof ( struct StkElement ));

    if ( pstk->base == NULL ) /* error in allocating stack */
        return ( NULL );

    pstk->min_stack = 0;
    pstk->max_stack = how_many - 1;

    ClearStack ( pstk );

    return ( pstk );
}

/*-----------------------------------------------------------------
 *  pop an element from the stack. If stack is not already empty,
 *  copy the element, and decrement stack top.
 *-------------------------------------------------------------*/
int PopElement ( Stack *this_stack,
                 struct StkElement * destination )
{
    if ( this_stack->top == -1 ) /* stack empty, return error */
        return ( 0 );

    memmove ( destination,
              &(( this_stack->base )[this_stack->top] ),
              sizeof ( struct StkElement ));

    this_stack->top -= 1;

    return ( 1 );
}

/*-----------------------------------------------------------------
 *  push an element onto the stack. If stack is not already full,
 *  point StackTop to the next slot, and copy the new element.
 *-------------------------------------------------------------*/
int PushElement ( Stack *this_stack, struct StkElement * to_push )
{
    /* is stack full? */
    if ( this_stack->top == this_stack->max_stack )
        return ( 0 );

    this_stack->top += 1;
```

```
    memmove ( &(( this_stack->base )[this_stack->top] ), to_push,
                        sizeof ( struct StkElement ));


    return ( 1 );
}


/*----------------------------------------------------------------
 *  view an element on the stack. Function is passed a value that
 *  specifies the element's position in terms of its distance
 *  from the top. 0 is the top, 1 is the element below the top,
 *  2 is the element below that. If an invalid value is passed,
 *  the function returns NULL; otherwise, it returns a pointer
 *  to the requested element.
 *----------------------------------------------------------*/
struct StkElement * ViewElement ( Stack *this_stack,
                                  int which_element )
{
    if ( this_stack->top == -1 )
        return ( NULL );

    if ( this_stack->top - which_element < 0 )
        return ( NULL );

    return ( &(( this_stack->base )
                    [this_stack->top - which_element] ));
}
```

As items are pushed onto the stack by `PushElement()`, `StackTop` is incremented to refer to the next available element, and the element to be pushed is then copied there. Popping an element merely copies the topmost element to a specified destination and then decrements `StackTop` to point to the next item on the stack. If the popped item is the last one on the stack (so that it was at `Stack[0]`), then `StackTop` is still decremented and its –1 value indicates that the stack is empty once again.

Listing 2-8 (*braces.c*) exercises the stack primitives by reading through a C program to find out whether there are any unbalanced parentheses, brackets, or braces. It reads through a program, one line at a time; as an opening brace or related item is found, that item is pushed onto the stack along with its line number. Then, as a closing item is found, the topmost stack item is popped. If the popped item is the correct one for the current closing character, processing continues. If the items do not complement each other, an error message is generated, stating the character and line numbers of the opening and closing items.

Listing 2-8.   An informative C program checker for braces, brackets, and parentheses.

```
/*--- braces.c -------------------------- Listing 2-8 ---------
 * Checks that braces, brackets, and parentheses are properly
 * paired in a C program. If they're not, an error message
 * is printed to stderr saying at what line the unmatched
 * opening item is found. Uses a stack.
 *
 * Usage: braces filename.ext
 *------------------------------------------------------------*/

#include <stdio.h>
#include <stdlib.h>
#include <string.h>
#include "stacks.h"

int main ( int argc, char *argv[] )
{
    FILE *fin;                  /* file we'll be reading from */
    char buffer[128];           /* read file into this buffer */

    int line_count;            /* current line count */
    struct StkElement *stk_el;  /* scratch stack element */
    Stack *stk;                 /* the stack we will use */
    char ch;                    /* character we're examining */
    int i;                      /* for loop count */

    if ( argc != 2 )
    {
        fprintf ( stderr, "Usage: braces filename.ext\n" );
        exit ( EXIT_FAILURE );
    }

    fin = fopen ( argv[1], "rt" );
    if ( fin == NULL )
    {
        fprintf ( stderr, "Cannot open/find %s\n", argv[1] );
        exit ( EXIT_FAILURE );
    }

    /* Create and initialize the stack */

    stk = CreateStack ( 40 );   /* create a stack of 40 items */
    if ( stk == NULL )
    {
        fprintf ( stderr, "Insufficient Memory\n" );
        exit ( EXIT_FAILURE );
    }
```

```c
/* Create the scratch stack element */

stk_el = (struct StkElement *)
            malloc ( sizeof ( struct StkElement ));
if ( stk_el == NULL )
{
    fprintf ( stderr, "Insufficient memory\n" );
    exit ( EXIT_FAILURE );
}

line_count = 0;

while ( ! feof ( fin ))
{
    /* read a line of a C program */
    if ( fgets ( buffer, 127, fin ) == NULL )
        break;

    line_count += 1;

    /* scan and process braces, brackets, and parentheses */
    for ( i = 0; buffer[i] != '\0'; i++ )
    {
        switch ( ch = buffer[i] )
        {
        case '(':
        case '[':
        case '{':
            stk_el->opener  = ch;
            stk_el->line_no = line_count;
            if ( ! PushElement ( stk, stk_el ))
            {
                fprintf ( stderr, "Out of stack space\n" );
                exit ( EXIT_FAILURE );
            }
            break;
        case ')':
        case ']':
        case '}':
            if ( ! PopElement ( stk, stk_el ))
                fprintf ( stderr, "Stray %c at line %d\n",
                            ch,  line_count );
            else
            if (( ch == ')'&& stk_el->opener != '(' ) ||
                ( ch == ']'&& stk_el->opener != '[' ) ||
                ( ch == '}'&& stk_el->opener != '{' ))
                fprintf ( stderr,
                  "%c at line %d not matched by %c at line %d\n",
```

```
                        ch, line_count,
                        stk_el->opener, stk_el->line_no );
                break;
            default:
                continue;
            }
        }
    }

    /*  We are at the end of file. Are there unmatched items? */

    if ( ViewElement ( stk, 0 ) != NULL )
        while ( PopElement ( stk, stk_el ) != 0 )
            fprintf ( stderr, "%c from line %d unmatched\n",
                        stk_el->opener, stk_el->line_no );

    fprintf ( stderr, "Error checking complete\n" );

    fclose ( fin );
    return ( EXIT_SUCCESS );
}
```

Once the entire C source file has been read, the program checks to see whether any items remain on the stack. These are opening items for which no closing items were found. They are then printed out, along with error messages. Note that the use of a stack was suggested in this program by the need to know where we had come from when a closing item was discovered.

This program is only an illustration. It can be fooled by comments and by characters appearing in literals. You should keep in mind also that this program always pops an element when a closing item is found. This works in some cases; in other cases you may want to retain the unmatched opening item. These improvements, simple as they appear, are too involved to implement within the scope of this discussion. However, if you do not use parentheses and the like in literals and comments (or if you do and you keep them matched), this program will intelligently inform you of any errors. For purposes of simplicity, the program assumes that no line is longer than 127 characters and that every line ends with a '\n'.

Characteristics of Queues

Queues are similar to stacks. However, rather than requiring you to add and remove data items from the same end of the stack, queues allow you to add at one end and remove from the other. In this manner, the first item placed in a queue is the first to be removed (Figure 2-5). The queue approximates the common activity of waiting in line.

To place an item at the end of the queue (the tail), you must **enqueue** it; to remove an item from the head, you must **dequeue** it. These are the two fundamental actions of the queue.

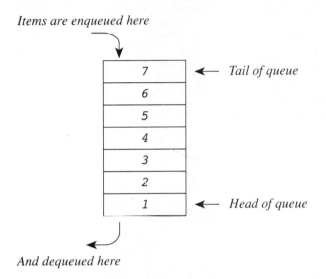

Items are enqueued here

7 ← *Tail of queue*
6
5
4
3
2
1 ← *Head of queue*

And dequeued here

Figure 2-5.   A typical queue. Note that item 1 was the first item enqueued and will be the first item dequeued.

In its simplest form, the queue is an easy data structure to implement. However, it soon becomes clear that the apparent simplicity hides a number of subtleties. The first is the question of memory representation. You would generally represent a queue by using either an array or a linked list. In both cases a singular problem arises: if you keep adding elements to the tail and deleting them from the head, the queue's data structure will migrate slowly through memory. When you use arrays to implement queues, you can circumvent this issue by making the array circular, such that once you have accessed the last element in the array, you continue to the first element in the array. These arrays are commonly called **circular buffers**.

The linked-list implementation suffers the same handicap in a slightly different form: if you keep adding and deleting nodes to a queue, you will fragment available memory as the nodes are allocated and freed. In the case of the linked-list queue—which is implemented in the Listings 2-9, 2-10, and 2-11—you have two options. One option is to use your own function to allocate and return memory. This function would allocate a pool of nodes that are then used and returned. The second option, implemented in Listing 2-9, is to create a linked list of unused nodes. As items are placed in the queue, nodes are moved from the free list to the queue; as items are dequeued, the nodes are returned to the free list. We use the linked-list function introduced earlier in the chapter. (Listings 2-3 through 2-4b.)

Listing 2-9.   Header file for linked-list implementation of queues.

```
/*--- qapp.h ----------------------------- Listing 2-9 --------
 *  Application-specific data items for linked-list queues.
 *-----------------------------------------------------------*/
#ifndef QAPP_H
#define QAPP_H 1

/*
 *  Our first list's nodes consist of a pointer to
 *  text and a priority level.
 */

#define TEXT_SIZE 60    /* the maximum size of our text string */

extern int DataCopy ( void *, void * );

/*
 * The data and functions for the queue
 */

struct NodeData1 {
    char *text;
    unsigned int priority;
};

typedef struct NodeData1 * pND1;

extern void * CreateData1 ( void * );
extern int    DeleteData1 ( void * );
extern int    DuplicatedNode1 ( Link, Link );
extern int    NodeDataCmp1 ( void *, void * );


/*
 *  The free list has identical nodes
 */

struct NodeData2 {
    char *text;
    unsigned int priority;
};
```

```
typedef struct NodeData2 * pND2;

extern void * CreateData2 ( void * );
extern int    DeleteData2 ( void * );
extern int    DuplicatedNode2 ( Link, Link );
extern int    NodeDataCmp2 ( void *, void * );

#endif
```

The file shown in Listing 2-9 should look very familiar to you. Listing 2-10 shows the implementation of the application-specific functions for the two linked lists.

Listing 2-10.   The application-specific functions for linked-list queues.

```
/*--- qapp.c --------------------------- Listing 2-10 --------
 *  Application-specific functions for queue examples.
 *  Replace these routines with your own.
 *-----------------------------------------------------------*/

#include <stdio.h>
#include <stdlib.h>            /* for free() */
#include <string.h>            /* for strcmp() and strdup() */

#include "llgen.h"
#include "qapp.h"

/*=== linked-list functions for queue ===*/

/*
 * our nodes come from the free list,
 * so this function is never called.
 */
void * CreateData1 ( void * data )
{
    return ( NULL );
}

int DeleteData1 ( void * data )
{
    /*
     * In this case, NodeData1 consists of a pointer and an int.
     * The integer will be returned to memory when the node
     * is freed. However, the string must be freed manually.
     */
    free ( ((pND1) data)->text );
```

```
        return ( 1 );
}
/*-----------------------------------------------------------------
 * This function determines what to do when inserting a node
 * into a list if an existing node with the same data is found
 * in the list. In this case, since we are counting words, if a
 * duplicate word is found, we simply increment the counter.
 *
 * Note this function should return one of the following values:
 *       0           an error occurred
 *       1           delete the duplicate node
 *       2           insert the duplicate node
 * Any other processing on the duplicate should be done in this
 * function.
 *-----------------------------------------------------------------*/

int DuplicatedNode1 ( Link new_node, Link list_node )
{
        return 2;
}

/* compare only the priority of the queue data */
int NodeDataCmp1 ( void *first, void *second )
{
        return (   ( ((pND2) first)->priority -
                     ((pND2) second)->priority ));
}

/*=== Now the functions for the list of free nodes ===*/

/* data is a priority level (int) and text (string) */
void * CreateData2 ( void * data )
{
        struct NodeData1 * new_data;

        /*--- allocate our data structure ---*/

        new_data = malloc ( sizeof ( struct NodeData1 ));
        if ( new_data == NULL )
            return ( NULL );

        /*--- move the values into the data structure ---*/

        /*
         * we assign a priority of 0
         * and allocate a string of TEXT_SIZE + 1
         */
```

```
    new_data->priority =  0;
    new_data->text      = (char *) malloc ( TEXT_SIZE + 1);

    if ( new_data->text == NULL )    /* error copying string */
    {
        free ( new_data );
        return ( NULL );
    }
    else
        return ( new_data ); /* return a complete structure */
}

int DeleteData2 ( void * data )
{
    /*
     * In this case, NodeData2 consists of a pointer.
     * The string must be freed manually.
     */

    free ( ((pND2) data)->text );
    return ( 1 );
}

/* this list inserts duplicated nodes */
int DuplicatedNode2 ( Link new_node, Link list_node )
{
    return 2;
}

/* this function is never called */
int NodeDataCmp2 ( void *first, void *second )
{
    return ( 0 );
}

/* function to copy our data */

int DataCopy ( void * dest, void * src )
{
    pND2 s, d;
    s = src;
    d = dest;

    if ( dest == NULL || src == NULL )
        return ( 0 );


    printf ( "About to copy %d - %s \n",
```

```
                        s->priority, s->text );

    d->priority = s->priority;
    strncpy ( d->text, s->text, TEXT_SIZE );

    return ( 1 );
}
```

Listing 2-11, the final listing, is the main driver, which shows how queues are implemented with these functions. Notice that the items in the queue can be assigned priorities.

Listing 2-11.   An implementation of a priority queue.

```
/*--- qdriver.c -------------------------- Listing 2-11 --------
 * Reads in a data file consisting of lines of text of the form
 *                       X9Message
 * where X = A for add to queue, D = delete, P = print the queue
 *        9 = priority of the queued item
 *        Message = string to enqueue
 * Note: actions D and P have no priority or message.
 * As each action is performed, a status message is printed.
 *
 * Must be linked with object files from qapp.c and llgen.c
 *--------------------------------------------------------------*/

#include <stdio.h>
#include <stdlib.h>
#include <string.h>

#include "llgen.h"
#include "qapp.h"

int dequeue ( struct List *, struct List *, void * );
int enqueue ( struct List *, struct List *, void * );

#define QMAX 100     /* maximum number of elements in a queue */

main ( int argc, char *argv [] )
{
    char      record[64];       /* the raw word from the file */
    int       count;
    void *    temp;             /* temporary data area */

    struct  List *queue,
                 *free_list; /* our two queues */
```

```
FILE      *fin;                /* the input file */

if ( argc != 2 )
{
    fprintf ( stderr, "Error! Usage: qdriver filename\n" );
    exit ( EXIT_FAILURE );
}

fin = fopen ( argv[1], "rt" );
if ( fin == NULL )
{
    fprintf ( stderr, "Could not find/open %s\n", argv[1] );
    exit ( EXIT_FAILURE );
}

/*--- set up linked-list data structures for queues ---*/

queue
    = CreateLList ( CreateData1,      /* in qapp.c */
                    DeleteData1,      /*     "     */
                    DuplicatedNode1,  /*     "     */
                    NodeDataCmp1 );   /*     "     */
free_list
    = CreateLList ( CreateData2,      /* in qapp.c */
                    DeleteData2,      /*     "     */
                    DuplicatedNode2,  /*     "     */
                    NodeDataCmp2 );   /*     "     */

if ( queue == NULL || free_list == NULL )
{
    fprintf ( stderr, "Error creating queue\n" );
    exit ( EXIT_FAILURE );
}

/*--- allocate the free list ---*/

for ( count = 0; count < QMAX; count++ )
{
    if ( ! AddNodeAtHead ( free_list, record ))
    {
        fprintf
            ( stderr, "Could not create queue of %d\n",
              QMAX );
        exit ( EXIT_FAILURE );
    }
}

/*--- begin processing file ---*/
```

```c
temp = CreateData2 ( NULL );
if ( temp == NULL )
{
    fprintf ( stderr, "Error creating temporary data area\n" );
    exit ( EXIT_FAILURE );
}

while ( fgets ( record, 64, fin ) != NULL )
{
    if ( strlen ( record ) > 0 )
        record[strlen ( record ) - 1] = 0; /* strip CR/LF */

    if ( *record == 'A' )   /* add */
    {
        ((pND2)temp)->priority = *( record + 1 ) - '0';
        ((pND2)temp)->text = record + 2;

        if ( enqueue ( queue, free_list, temp ) == 0 )
        {
            printf ( "Error enqueueing %d %s\n",
                        ((pND2)temp)->priority,
                        ((pND2)temp)->text );
            exit ( EXIT_FAILURE );
        }
        else
        {
            printf ( "Enqueued %d %s\n",
                        ((pND2)temp)->priority,
                        ((pND2)temp)->text );

            if ( queue->LCount == 0 )
                printf ( "Empty queue\n" );
            else
            {
                Link curr;
                printf ( "-------- List so far-------\n" );
                for ( curr = queue->LHead;
                        curr != NULL;
                        curr = curr->next )
                    printf ( "%d %s\n",
                        ((pND2)(curr->pdata))->priority,
                        ((pND2)(curr->pdata))->text );
            }
        }
    }
    else
    if ( *record == 'D' )   /* delete */
    {
```

```
            if ( dequeue ( queue, free_list, temp ) == 0 )
            {
                printf ( "Error dequeueing %d %s\n",
                         ((pND2)temp)->priority,
                         ((pND2)temp)->text );
                return ( EXIT_FAILURE );
            }
            else
                printf ( "Dequeued %d %s\n",
                         ((pND2)temp)->priority,
                         ((pND2)temp)->text );
        }
        else
        if ( *record == 'P' )    /* print */
        {
            if ( queue->LCount == 0 )
                printf ( "Empty queue\n" );
            else
            {
                Link curr;
                printf ( "\n-------- List so far-------\n" );
                for ( curr = queue->LHead;
                        curr != NULL;
                        curr = curr->next )
                    printf ( "%d %s\n",
                             ((pND2)(curr->pdata))->priority,
                             ((pND2)(curr->pdata))->text );
            }
        }
        else
            fprintf ( stderr, "Data error: %s\n", record );
    }

    fclose ( fin );
    return ( EXIT_SUCCESS );
}
/*----------------------------------------------------------------
 * enqueue loads the data items in entry into the head node of
 * the free list, then adds that node to the queue based on
 * priority.
 *----------------------------------------------------------------*/

int enqueue ( struct List *lqueue, struct List *lfree,
              void *new_entry )
{
    Link curr, new_node;

    /* Are there any free nodes left? */
```

```
if ( lfree->LCount == 0 )
{
    fprintf ( stderr, "Exceeded maximum queue size\n" );
    return ( 0 );
}

/* load the data into the head of the free list */

new_node = lfree->LHead;

if ( DataCopy ( new_node->pdata, new_entry ) == 0 )
    return ( 0 );

/* adding to an empty list? */

if ( lqueue->LCount == 0 )
{
    lfree->LHead = lfree->LHead->next;

    new_node->prev = NULL;
    new_node->next = NULL;

    lqueue->LTail = new_node;
    lqueue->LHead = new_node;

    lqueue->LCount = 1;
    lfree->LCount -= 1;

    return ( 1 );
}
else
/* Traverse the list to find the insertion position */

for ( curr = lqueue->LHead; ; curr = curr->next )
{
    if ( curr == NULL           /* at end of queue */
            ||                   /* or at insertion point */
            NodeDataCmp1 ( new_entry, curr->pdata ) < 0 )
    {
        new_node = lfree->LHead;
        lfree->LHead = lfree->LHead->next;

        if ( curr == NULL )   /* if end of list */
        {
            new_node->prev = lqueue->LTail;
            new_node->next = NULL;
            new_node->prev->next = new_node;
            lqueue->LTail = new_node;
```

```
            }
            else
            {
                if ( curr->prev == NULL )   /* adding at head? */
                    lqueue->LHead = new_node;

                new_node->prev = curr->prev;
                new_node->next = curr;

                if ( curr->prev != NULL )
                    curr->prev->next = new_node;
                curr->prev = new_node;
            }

            lqueue->LCount += 1;

            /* update the free list */

            lfree->LCount -= 1;

            return ( 1 );
        }
        else
        {
            pND2 p1, p2;
            p1 = curr->pdata;
            p2 = new_entry;
            printf ( "searched at %d %s to insert %d %s\n",
                        p1->priority, p1->text,
                        p2->priority, p2->text );
        }
    }
}


/*---------------------------------------------------------------
 * dequeue takes a pointer that will be set to the data in the
 * node at the head of the queue. It then moves the node being
 * dequeued from the queue to the free list. Note that if you do
 * not use the dequeued data before next queue operation, the
 * data is lost, so copy it if you need to. Returns 0 on error.
 *---------------------------------------------------------*/

int dequeue ( struct List *lqueue, struct List *lfree,
             void * our_data )
{
    Link dequeued_link;

    /* is there anything to dequeue? */
```

```
    if ( lqueue->LCount == 0 )
    {
        fprintf ( stderr, "Error dequeue from empty queue\n" );
        return ( 0 );
    }

    /* make a copy of the data being dequeued */

    if ( DataCopy ( our_data, lqueue->LHead->pdata ) == 0 )
        return ( 0 );

    /* remove the node from the queue */

    dequeued_link = lqueue->LHead;
    lqueue->LHead = lqueue->LHead->next;
    lqueue->LCount -= 1;

    /* add the node to the free list */

    dequeued_link->prev = NULL;
    dequeued_link->next = lfree->LHead;
    lfree->LHead = dequeued_link;
    lfree->LCount += 1;

    return ( 1 );
}
```

Chapter 3

Hashing

Linked lists provide a means of storing data in memory when the number of data items is not known beforehand. The drawback of linked lists is that their construction requires that nodes be accessed sequentially. That is, to get to any node, you must access every node that precedes it in the list. Various techniques, such as ordering the nodes or placing the most recently accessed nodes near the head of the list, reduce the time required by sequential searches; but these approaches do not do away with the requirement that the search itself be sequential.

To provide quick, random access to data items stored in memory, an elegant solution is the **hash table**. Regular tables in C, such as arrays of `structs`, require you to specify in advance the number of elements in the table. Hash tables, however, can hold an indeterminate number of items in a table without giving up quick, near-random access.

Hashing Concepts

The secret of a hash table is the way it figures out where in the table to store a particular piece of data. This determination is performed by a **hash function**, which accepts a piece of data to be placed in the table and generates a number that specifies the slot in the table where the data will be placed. This number is called a **hash key**. For example, if you had a table with 26 possible slots, it wouldn't be difficult to devise a hash function that would allow you to place English words in the table. You could use the first letter of each word as a hash key as shown here:

```
char *word_to_hash;
hash_key = tolower (*word_to_hash) - 'a';
```

The slot in the table would then be `table [hash_key]`. While this hash function is simple, the table it uses is too small to hold many words. In the real world, a larger table would have to be used.

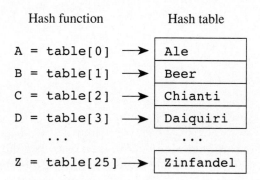

Hash function   Hash table

```
A = table[0]  ──▶  │ Ale       │
B = table[1]  ──▶  │ Beer      │
C = table[2]  ──▶  │ Chianti   │
D = table[3]  ──▶  │ Daiquiri  │
    ...               ...
Z = table[25] ──▶  │ Zinfandel │
```

Figure 3-1.   An elementary hash table based on the first letter of words.

One immediate consideration is how to resolve the problem of two entries hashing to the same slot in the table. Such an occurrence is called a **collision**. If we used the simple hash table of Figure 3-1, the words *scotch* and *soda* would hash to the same slot in the table (`table[18]`). How should the collision be resolved? A number of approaches exist. All collision-resolution approaches fall into two categories: **rehashing**, in which a new hash value is computed, and **chaining**, in which colliding elements are added to a table by means of a linked list. Chaining and rehashing are discussed later in this chapter.

Listing 3-1, `birthday.c`, shows the construction of a simple hash table. The program reads a text file in which each line consists of a birthday and the name of the person whose birthday it is. As the file is read, the names are stored in a hash table. When a collision occurs, the program prints the name of the two people born on the same day.

Listing 3-1.   A simple hash table to identify duplicate birthdays.

```
/*--- birthday.c ---------------------------- Listing 3-1 --------
 * Reads input file of birthdays and lists any duplicates.
 * Uses a simple hash table to identify the duplicates.
 *
 * Input records consists of lines of text of the form
 * MMDDName where MM = month, DD = day, Name. For example:
```

```
*                   0212Abraham Lincoln
* Note: for simplicity, no error checking is done on records.
*------------------------------------------------------------*/

#include <stdio.h>
#include <stdlib.h>
#include <string.h>

#define TABLE_SIZE 366   /* Maximum days in a year */

FILE *fin;              /* Birthday file */
int  NameCount,         /* Number of names read */
     DupeCount;         /* Number of dupes found */

int hash_birthday ( char * );    /* Our hash function */

#ifdef __STDC__         /* in ANSI C, there's no strdup() */
/* the source code for this function is discussed in Ch. 2 */
char *strdup ( const char * );  /* string duplication */
#endif

int main ( int argc, char *argv[] )
{
    char buffer[128];   /* where the records will be read */
    int  hash_value;    /* the hash value we will compute */
    char *name;         /* pointer to birthday name        */

    char *Table[TABLE_SIZE];   /* table of birthday folks */
    int i;              /* subscript to init the table     */

    if ( argc < 2 )
    {
        fprintf ( stderr, "Error! Expecting birthday file\n" );
        exit ( EXIT_FAILURE );
    }

    if (( fin = fopen ( argv[1], "rt" )) == NULL )
    {
        fprintf ( stderr, "Error! Cannot open %s\n", argv[1] );
        exit ( EXIT_FAILURE );
    }

    for ( i = 0; i < TABLE_SIZE; i++ )
        Table[i] = NULL;

    while ( ! feof ( fin ))
    {
        if ( fgets ( buffer, 128, fin ) == NULL )
```

```
            break;

        /* get rid of the '\n' at end of record */
        buffer [strlen ( buffer ) - 1] = '\0';

        NameCount += 1;

        hash_value = hash_birthday ( buffer );
        name = strdup ( buffer + 4 );

        if ( Table[hash_value] == NULL )  /* No duplicate, */
        {                                 /* so add name.  */
            Table[hash_value] = name;
            continue;
        }
        else
        {                                    /* Is duplicate, */
            DupeCount += 1;                  /* so tell 'em.  */
            printf ( "%s and %s have the same birthday.\n",
                    name, Table[hash_value] );
            continue;
        }
    }

    if ( DupeCount == 0 )
    {
        printf ( "No duplicate matches found among %d people.\n",
                NameCount );
        if ( NameCount > 50 )
            printf ( "How rare!\n" );
    }
    else
        printf ( "Among %d people, %d matches were found\n",
                NameCount, DupeCount );

    return ( EXIT_SUCCESS );
}

/*------------------------------------------------------------
 * A simple hash algorithm. It converts the month and day
 * to the number of the day in the year. Adds the day in the
 * month to the number of days elapsed before that month began.
 *------------------------------------------------------------*/

int hash_birthday ( char *data )
{
    const int days_elapsed[12] =
        { 0, 31, 60, 91, 121, 152, 182, 213, 244, 274, 305, 335 };
```

```
int mm, dd;
char record [128];   /* where we store our copy of the data */

strcpy ( record, data );   /* make our own copy */

record [4] = '\0';   /* Mark the spot where the name begins */
dd = atoi ( record + 2 );   /* Convert the day to an int */
record [2] = '\0';   /* Mark off the spot where day begins */
mm = atoi ( record );        /* Convert the month to an int */

/* since mm is going to be an index into days_elapsed,
 * it must be checked for the correct range.
 */

if ( mm < 1 || mm > 12 )
{
    fprintf ( stderr, "Error in record for %s: %02d/%02d\n",
            (char *) data + 4, mm, dd );
    exit ( EXIT_FAILURE );
}

return ( days_elapsed[mm - 1] + dd );
}
```

In `main( )`, a hash table named `Table` is defined, consisting of `TABLE_SIZE` elements: one for each possible day of the year. The table elements consist of pointers to characters. Eventually, these pointers will point to the name of some birthday person. The hash function, `hash_birthday`, converts the incoming month and day digits into a unique number smaller than `TABLE_SIZE`. It does this by simply converting the date into the Julian date and subtracting 1, to fit C's zero-based array. This hash algorithm converts January 1 to 0, February 1 to 31, and December 31 to 365. The program then looks at the pointer at `Table[hash_value]`. If it is `NULL`, no one yet has this birthday; so the current person's name is stored, and a pointer to the name is inserted in `Table[hash_value]`. If the pointer at `Table[hash_value]` is not `NULL`, a collision has occurred: two records have hashed to the same element in the table. In this case, we know this means that two people have the same birthday. We print their names, discard the duplicate, and go on to read the next record. At the end, we summarize the number of duplicates we have found.

Note that this problem is well suited to a hash table but would fare poorly if implemented with a linked list. A linked list of all birthdates could be as long as 366 entries. At that length, the average lookup would take 183 queries. With the hash table, even if all 366 birthdays are loaded into the table, a birthday never requires more than one query to determine whether it is a duplicate.

This implementation, while better than a linked list, seems like little more than the management of an array of pointers. This is certainly true, but only because the hash table selected here is a simple one. As we shall see, hash tables quickly become more complicated.

Hash Functions

The hash function that converted birthdays into unique numbers between 0 and 365 is a special case. It is called a **perfect hash function**. It is perfect because for every piece of data it is handed it generates a unique hash value. No two dates in a year have the same hash value. To generate perfect hash values, you must know all possible inputs to the hash function and you must be able to write a function that can generate a unique value for every input. In the case of birthdays, we know the range of dates and how to construct a unique number for each date. We could have written a nonperfect hash function such as

```
hash_value = dd * mm - 1;
```

This would have generated keys in the range of 0 to 371 (about the size of our range). It is nonperfect because it does not generate unique values for every unique input: March 10 and October 3 both generate hash values of 29. Worse yet, the duplicates tend to congregate at the low end of the table, while the high end mostly contains empty slots (all primes greater than 31 are unused, as are all hash values that are the product of primes greater than 12). The choice of a nonperfect algorithm means that access to a table element in no more than one lookup cannot be assured. Where they can be devised, perfect hash algorithms are highly efficient.

In real-life situations, however, perfect hash algorithms are almost impossible to construct, and effort you spend looking for them is often effort wasted. They are impossible to write because most often the complete set of data to be hashed is rarely known in advance. For example, in a program we shall look at shortly, a hash table is used to count duplicate words in a text. Since we do not know beforehand what words appear in the text, we cannot write a perfect algorithm. As a result, we attempt to write a good general-case algorithm.

A good hash function has two desirable traits: it is quick and it disperses hash keys evenly throughout the table. It must also compensate for clustering that might occur in the incoming data (clustering is the tendency of data to have elements that are close in value), and it must always generate the same hash key for the same data item.

    Instead of searching for perfect hash functions, you need to devise hash functions that simply minimize the frequency of collisions for a data set. For example, let's take a hash table that stores words taken from English texts. Our initial attempt at a hash function for such a table (see Figure 3-1) was to use the first letter of each word as a hash key. While this function is undoubtedly fast, it suffers from two problems: it does not avoid clustering and it generates too few unique hash keys. To generate a maximum number of keys, hash functions often generate fairly large results that are then divided by the size of the table.

    Typically, a hash function has this form:

$$hash\text{-}key = calculated\text{-}key \% tablesize$$

where % is the modulo operator. To heighten dispersal of the key values, *tablesize* should be a prime number. The process of generating *calculated-key* has been the subject of many computer-science papers. As it turns out, however, applications spend very little time computing hash keys; and slow performance is rarely the product of poor hashing algorithms. Hash functions will generally work quickly if the following conditions are met:

- They contain, at most, one division (generally, the final modulo operation).
- They generate a wide range of keys.
- They do not rely on attributes of data that will encourage clustering.

    A quick, generic algorithm for generating hash keys was developed by Peter J. Weinberger of AT&T Bell Labs (who is the W in AWK, the UNIX pattern-matching language), and is published in the famous "dragon book" [Aho et al. 1986]. A version based on an adaptation by Allen Holub [Holub 1990] appears in Listing 3-2.

Listing 3-2.   A generic hash function, adapted from Peter Weinberger's algorithm.

```
/*--- HashPJW ----------------------------- Listing 3-2 ---------
 *     An adaptation of Peter Weinberger's (PJW) generic hashing
 *  algorithm based on Allen Holub's version.
 *
 *  Accepts a pointer to a datum to be hashed and returns an
 *  unsigned integer. This integer is called "calculated-key"
 *  in the text.
 *------------------------------------------------------------*/

#include <limits.h>

#define BITS_IN_int     ((UINT_MAX + 1) / (UCHAR_MAX + 1)) / CHAR_BIT
#define THREE_QUARTERS      ((int) ((BITS_IN_int * 3) / 4))
```

```
#define ONE_EIGHTH           ((int) (BITS_IN_int / 8))
#define HIGH_BITS            ( ~((unsigned int)(~0) >> ONE_EIGHTH ))

unsigned int HashPJW ( const char * datum )
{
    unsigned int hash_value, i;

    for ( hash_value = 0; *datum; ++datum )
    {
        hash_value = ( hash_value << ONE_EIGHTH ) + *datum;
        if (( i = hash_value & HIGH_BITS ) != 0 )
            hash_value =
                ( hash_value ^ ( i >> THREE_QUARTERS )) &
                    ~HIGH_BITS;
    }

    return ( hash_value );
}
```

The algorithm works quickly because all the work is done as bit operations. The division that appears in the `#define` statements is performed at compilation time and the results are inserted into the code as constants. The `#define` statements merely test for the numbers of bits in an integer (it is curious that this constant is not defined by the ANSI standard, since it would be a helpful value) and then use the result to know how much to shift the emerging hash value. The code is implemented this way to assure portability. On 16-bit implementations, `THREE_QUARTERS` and `ONE_EIGHTH` have the values 12 and 2 respectively, while `HIGH_BITS` is a mask with the value `0x3FFF`.

The modulo operator should be applied to the return value from `HashPJW( )`, and the result (the remainder after dividing the return value by *tablesize*) is the hash value. As with all implementations, it is possible that a generic algorithm such as `HashPJW( )` will not be as effective as one expressly tailored to the expected data set. Pure empirical work is the only answer. As a result, whenever you are implementing hash tables, you should write a function that will check the hash table to see how well the hash function works. These statistics will allow fine tuning of the algorithm.

A different version of Weinberger's hash function is used by UNIX to perform hashing when constructing object files in the ELF format. (ELF is the Executable and Linking Format introduced in UNIX SVR4 in 1990. It supersedes COFF, the Common Object File Format.) The function, as published by UNIX Systems Laboratories (now part of Novell) in its official UNIX documentation, appears in Listing 3-3. Note that this version expects long integers of at least 32 bits. Since this assumption is true on all MS-DOS and most (if not all) versions of UNIX, it probably does not subvert portability. Unlike the hash function in Listing 3-2, however, this function returns an unsigned long. Its performance results are discussed at the end of this chapter.

Listing 3-3.   The hash function used in ELF object files.

```
/*--- ElfHash ----------------------------- Listing 3-3 ---------
 *  The published hash algorithm used in the UNIX ELF format
 *  for object files.
 *
 *  Accepts a pointer to a string to be hashed and returns an
 *  unsigned long. Algorithm is similar to that implemented
 *  in HashPJW (see Listing 3-2).
 *-------------------------------------------------------------*/

unsigned long ElfHash ( const unsigned char *name )
{
    unsigned long   h = 0, g;

    while ( *name )
    {
        h = ( h << 4 ) + *name++;
        if ( g = h & 0xF0000000 )
            h ^= g >> 24;

        h &= ~g;
    }
    return h;
}
```

The implementation in Listing 3-3 is taken from the *System V Application Binary Interface* [UNIX Press 1990]. The last line of this function is sometimes printed incorrectly as h &= g (see the *Programming in Standard C* manual for UnixWare, 1992). The missing tilde means that the incorrect function will always return zero—hardly a desirable hash function!

Unless you have special needs for which the generic hash functions in Listings 3-2 and 3-3 are insufficient, these functions should be used. They're quick and they do a reasonably good job of scattering keys through a table. In addition, they're fairly portable. Despite the fondness of academics for perfecting hash functions, the time spent optimizing hash functions is almost always better spent enhancing performance on some other part of the program. Profiler timings for the programs presented in this chapter consistently show that performance is slowed mostly by I/O operations (including the abysmally slow `printf` function) and then by the constant `malloc` and `free` of memory. Only then do the hash functions appear, consuming typically less than 2 percent of the programs' time. So, work first on the I/O and memory-management functions.

Collision Resolution

With the exception of situations in which perfect hash functions can be devised, hash tables must be equipped to handle collisions gracefully. A collision occurs when two different data items are given the same hash value by the hash function. When two different elements have the same hash value, how is the second one added to the table? There are three widely used approaches to this problem: (1) **linear rehashing** simply steps sequentially through the table, looking for the next available slot; (2) **nonlinear rehashing** computes a new hash value; and (3) **external chaining** views each slot in the hash table as the head of a linked list of data items with the same hash value. The table adds the colliding entry to the linked list.

Linear Rehashing

Linear rehashing is the simplest form of collision resolution. Upon discovering a collision, the algorithm simply steps through the table until it finds the next empty slot in the table, and places the element in that slot. Thereafter, any search for the element starts at the table slot pointed to by the hash value. If there is no match, the table is stepped through until (1) the element is found, (2) an empty slot is found (indicating that the searched-for element is absent), or (3) the entire table has been examined (indicating that the element is absent and that the table is full).

When stepping through a table, there is no need to step one slot at a time. For example, a search could examine every third slot. As long as the search wraps around to the start of the table and the total number of slots in the table is not a multiple of three, every slot will be examined. In fact, as long as the size of the table and the number of slots stepped over are relatively prime (they have no common divisors), every slot in the table will be examined. A step size of one is not desirable because it fosters clustering. If a few collisions occur in the same general area of the table, a step size of one means that that portion of the table will quickly become filled with duplicates to the point that any activity in that area of the table will involve extensive stepping. A step of five or more quickly moves the search away from congestion and decreases the opportunity for heavy clustering.

While simple to implement, linear rehashing suffers from two drawbacks: elements cannot be deleted from the table, and performance drops significantly as the table gets full. Deletions represent a vexatious problem. If the search stops at the first empty slot, then deletions cannot be made from the table at all. For example, suppose we have the table of 26 elements that we first used to hold words, hashed on the basis of their first letter. We read the word `elephant`, and we want to insert it into the table (see Figure 3-2). We go to the slot for `E` only to find that it is occupied by `Eel`. We examine the next slot and find that it is occupied by `Elk`. We examine the next slot and find it empty. At this point, we insert `Elephant`. If our next operation is to delete `Elk`, a search for `Elephant` will never be successful because before finding it we will encounter the slot vacated by `Elk`. As a result, deletions can be done only by marking a used slot as invalid. If in the search for `Elephant` we come across an invalid slot, we simply keep searching.

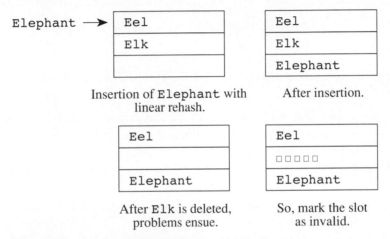

Insertion of `Elephant` with linear rehash.

After insertion.

After `Elk` is deleted, problems ensue.

So, mark the slot as invalid.

Figure 3-2.   Linear rehashing and its dangers.

Nonlinear Rehashing

The approach we have just examined is called linear because it starts at the point of collision and steps through the table in a sequential fashion searching for an available slot. Nonlinear rehashing avoids stepping through the table. Rather, it calculates a new hash key that jumps to a completely different part of the table. The idea is that by jumping to a different part of the table, clustering of similar values (see Figure 3-2) will be avoided. If the slot to which the rehash function jumps is already occupied, another rehash and jump are performed. If the hash table is nearly full, nonlinear rehashes may have to be performed numerous times on the same element before an available slot is found. To avoid this problem, rehashing algorithms should be used only when it is unlikely the hash table will ever be more than 50 percent full.

In our earlier discussion of hash functions, it was shown that a practical approach for computing hash values is to compute a number that is then divided by the number of slots in the table. The remainder from this division (the modulo) is the hash value. One approach to rehashing is to make use of the quotient generated by the division, rather than the remainder. This quotient can be multiplied by the length of the input string and the numeric value of the second character (provided it is not null). Other kinds of multiplications or bit shifts can be investigated. Ultimately, a new number is generated, which like the original value is divided by the number of slots.

Another approach that can be a little slower but very effective is to use C's random number generator. The `rand()` function generates a pseudorandom number when started with a seed. Use the some portion of the colliding entry other than the hash value as the seed and then call `rand()`. Use the returned random number as your new hash value.

You need to understand the workings of the `rand()` function before you adopt this approach. The `rand` mechanism is first seeded with a value; then the `rand()` function is called repeatedly, generating the next value in a pseudorandom sequence with each call. For example, the following piece of code seeds the `rand` mechanism by calling `srand()` with a value of 100. It then prints the values generated by five successive calls to `rand()`. The result of this program when compiled with Microsoft's C compiler is 365, 1,216, 5,415, 16,704, and 24,504.

```c
#include <stdio.h>
#include <stdlib.h>

int main ( void )
{
    int i;

    srand ( 100u );

    for ( i = 0; i < 5; i++ )
    {
        printf ( "%6d\n", rand() );
    }

    return ( i );
}
```

Note that whenever this compiler's `rand` mechanism is seeded with 100, this same set of random numbers is always generated. This is important because it means that the `rand` mechanism can be used for rehashing, since when you go to look up an element the hash function will give you the same random hash value used to place that element in the hash table. This trait, however, is the reason the colliding hash value should not be used as the seed to `rand()`. Instead of the colliding hash value, use some other aspect of the data being hashed.

A concept that greatly affects the performance of hash tables is termed **load factor**. The load factor (α) is the number of elements (n) inserted into the table, divided by the total number of available slots. Hence,

$$\alpha = n / tablesize$$

A load factor of 1.00 means there are as many elements inserted into the table as there are slots. As the load factor increases, the performance of the hash table drops correspondingly. An important consideration in the design of any hash table is how it handles high load factors.

Whether you use linear or nonlinear rehashing, you can use rehashing only in situations in which the hash table will not be close to full. As the load factor for the table increases, the time you spend rehashing increases dramatically. A theoretical analysis of probes necessary to find an element in a hash table is provided in the text by Kruse et al. [Kruse 1991]. Table 3-1, which is derived from that analysis, shows clearly that for a load factor greater than 0.50, rehashing is not a viable solution. This is especially true where lookups in the table are likely to be unsuccessful. The best scenario of random rehashing, 5.0 probes for a load factor of 0.80, is unacceptably slow. If the previously described use of `rand()` to perform rehashing is implemented, every search must seed the `rand` function and then call the function an average of five times. You would spend more time computing random rehash values than performing any other aspect of hash table operations.

Table 3-1. The theoretical number of probes required by rehashing

Load Factor>	0.10	0.50	0.80	0.90	0.99
Successful Linear	1.06	1.5	3.0	5.5	50.5
Successful Nonlinear	1.05	1.4	2.0	2.6	4.6
Unsuccessful Linear	1.12	2.5	13.0	50.0	5000
Unsuccessful Nonlinear	1.10	2.0	5.0	10.0	100

The rehashing approach should be used only in quick-and-dirty situations or in rapid prototyping contexts. Its chief advantage is that it is easy to code on the fly and that it is sufficiently quick in situations in which low table loads are assured and deletions are unlikely. For all other needs, use external chaining.

External Chaining

The technique of external chaining sees the hash table as an array of linked lists. Each slot in the table is either empty or is pointing to a linked list of entries that have hashed to that slot. You perform collision resolution by adding the element to the linked list. Likewise, you perform deletions by removing elements from the linked list. Collision resolution is, therefore, no more expensive than adding a node to a list; no rehashing is necessary. Unlike rehashing, in which the maximum number of entries is determined by the original number of slots in the table, external chaining accommodates as many elements as will fit in memory.

Using the first hash table we examined, where words were hashed based on the first letter of the word, a table using external chaining would appear as in Figure 3-3. Suppose an input file contains `Eel`, `Elephant`, `Dog`, `Cat`, `Giraffe`, `Elk`, `Zebra`, `Goat`, and `Donkey`.

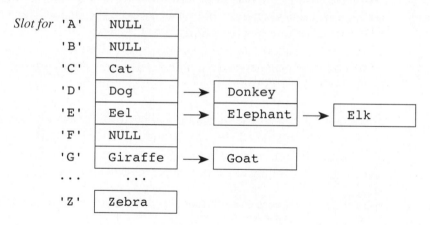

Figure 3-3.   A hash table using external chaining.

You will notice that the elements in the linked lists have been placed in alphabetical order. This accelerates searches, since the entire list does not need to be traversed in order to identify whether an element is present in the list. The average search time is therefore half the length of the list, plus one for the original examination of the table slot. Likewise, the average number of probes, whether the search is successful or unsuccessful, is proportional to half the length of the average linked list, where empty lists are considered to have a length of one. This calculation shows that tables that use external chaining with ordered linked lists must have a load factor of more than 1.0 before the average number of probes exceeds 2.0. Equally interesting is the fact that unsuccessful searches tend to be shorter than successful searches. The down sides of external chaining are that it requires somewhat more space to implement, since the addition of any element requires the addition of a pointer to a mode, and that each probe takes slightly more time since it requires the dereferencing of pointers rather than direct access to the elements. Given the low cost of memory these days and the availability of very fast CPUs, these drawbacks are considered minor. As a result, most professional developers use external chaining to resolve hash-table collisions.

Listing 3-4, *wordlist.c*, accepts an input text file and counts the number of duplicate words. The table elements consist of a pointer to a word and an integer that keeps track of how often the word appears in the text file. Depending on the switches set at the beginning of the text, the words can be printed to the screen with their respective counts. As you should do with all programs that rely heavily on hash tables, you need the ability to print out on command all statistics relating to the performance of the hash algorithm and the hash table. This is the best way of monitoring whether any unusual aspect of the data has undermined the efficiency of the hashing algorithm. Listing 3-4 relies heavily on the linked-list functions presented in Chapter 2.

Listing 3-4.   A program that counts word occurrences in a text file with the use of a hash table and external chaining to resolve collisions.

```
/*--- wordlist.c ------------------------ Listing 3-4 -------
 *  Lists all words in a text file by storing them in a hash
 *  table. Must be linked to the linked-list primitives of
 *  Chapter 2 and to ElfHash() of Listing 3-3.
 *-----------------------------------------------------------*/

   /* uncomment the following line to print all words
    * with their associated hash value.
    */

/* #define LIST_HASH  1 */

   /* uncomment the following line to print the unique words
    * and a count of their frequency.
    */

/* #define LIST_WORDS 1 */

   /* comment out the following line if you do not want
    * an analysis of the hash function and hash table load.
    */

#define LIST_TABLE_STATS 1
```

```
      /* uncomment the following line if you want a listing
       * of all words > 10 letters. Such words are often typing
       * or scanning errors in the text or odd constructs.
       */

#define LIST_LONG_WORDS 1

#include <stdio.h>
#include <stdlib.h>
#include <string.h>
#include <ctype.h>

#include "llgen.h"          /* Header for generic linked lists */
#include "llapp.h"          /* Header for appl.'s linked lists */

extern unsigned long ElfHash ( char *);

/*--- the hash table portion ---*/

#define TABLE_SIZE  1999     /* Number of slots; a prime number */

Link    *Table;              /* Our table is an array of Links */

#if 0
int CreateTable ( Link **t )
{
    *t = calloc ( TABLE_SIZE, sizeof ( Link ));
    return ( *t == NULL ? 0 : 1 );
}
#endif

/*-------------------------------------------------------------
 * We use calloc() to allocate the table. However, on some
 * compilers the bit pattern used by calloc() for initialization
 * is not the same as NULL (which is what we want). So we check
 * for this condition and, if it occurs, intialize the table by
 * hand to NULLs. If this is not an issue, use the routine above.
 *-----------------------------------------------------------*/
int CreateTable ( Link **t )
{
    int i;

    *t = (Link *) calloc ( TABLE_SIZE, sizeof ( Link ));
    if ( *t == NULL )
        return ( 0 );

    if ( **t != NULL )        /* is the calloc'd memory == NULL? */
    {
```

```
        for ( i = 0; i < TABLE_SIZE; i++, t++ )
            **t = NULL;
    }

    return ( 1 );
}


/*-----------------------------------------------------------
 * Function to convert a string to upper case. Exists in most
 * PC C libraries but missing from many UNIX C libraries.
 *---------------------------------------------------------*/
char *strupr ( char *str )
{
    char *s = str;

    while ( *s )
    {
        *s = toupper ( *s );
        s += 1;
    }

    return ( str );
}

/* === main line === */

int main ( int argc, char *argv[] )
{
    char    word[64];        /* the raw word from the file */
    char    *pw;             /* pointer to the word */
    int     c, i, j;
    int     chains,          /* counts how many chains    */
            chain_table[33]; /* table of chain lengths    */
                             /*    for our report.        */
    int     add_status;      /* return value from table add*/

    unsigned hash_key;

    struct List *L1,         /* list for hash table entries*/
                *long_wd;    /* list of long words        */

    struct NodeData1 nd;     /* the node we add each time  */
    struct Node      n;      /* used for scratch purposes  */

    FILE    *fin;            /* the input file            */

    if ( argc < 2 )
```

```
{
    fprintf ( stderr, "Error! Usage: wordlist filename\n" );
    exit ( EXIT_FAILURE );
}

if ( argc > 2 )
    fprintf
        ( stderr, "Warning: Usage: wordlist filename\n" );

fin = fopen ( argv[1], "rt" );
if ( fin == NULL )
{
    fprintf ( stderr, "Could not find/open %s\n", argv[1] );
    exit ( EXIT_FAILURE );
}

/*--- create the table ---*/

if ( ! CreateTable ( &Table ))
{
    fprintf ( stderr, "Error! Could not create table\n" );
    exit ( EXIT_FAILURE );
}

/*--- set up linked-list data structures ---*/

L1 = CreateLList ( CreateData1,      /* in llapp.c */
                   DeleteData1,      /*     "      */
                   DuplicatedNode1,  /*     "      */
                   NodeDataCmp1 );   /*     "      */

long_wd = CreateLList ( CreateData2, /* in llapp.c */
                   DeleteData2,      /*     "      */
                   DuplicatedNode2,  /*     "      */
                   NodeDataCmp2 );   /*     "      */

if ( L1 == NULL || long_wd == NULL )
{
    fprintf ( stderr, "Error creating linked list\n" );
    exit ( EXIT_FAILURE );
}

/*--- begin processing file ---*/

c = ' ';

while ( ! feof ( fin ))
{
```

```
      /*--- skip white space ---*/

      while ( c != EOF && isspace ( c ))
          c = fgetc ( fin );

      /*--- pick up the word ---*/
      i = 0;
      while ( c!= EOF && !isspace ( c ))
      {
          word[i++] = c;
          c = fgetc ( fin );
      }

      if  ( c == EOF )
          break;

      word[i] = '\0';

      /*--- strip off trailing punctuation ---*/

      while ( i >= 0 && ispunct ( word[--i] ))
          word[i] = '\0';

      pw = strupr ( word );

      /*--- get the hash value ---*/

      hash_key = (unsigned int) ElfHash ( pw );
      hash_key %= TABLE_SIZE;

#ifdef LIST_HASH
      printf ( "%15s  %3d\n", pw, hash_key );
#endif

      /*--- insert into table ---*/

      L1->LHead = Table[hash_key];

      nd.word =  pw;              /* the string we're adding */
      nd.u    =  1;              /* adding one occurrence   */

      add_status =  AddNodeAscend ( L1, &nd );
      if ( add_status == 0 )     /* an error occurred */
          printf ( "Warning! Error while allocating node.\n" );

      Table[hash_key] = L1->LHead;

      /*--- handle long words ---*/
```

```
                /* if a word is longer than ten chars, put it in the
                 * long word list for subsequent display.
                 */

            if ( strlen ( pw ) > 10 )
                AddNodeAscend ( long_wd, &nd );

                /* if a word is longer than 20 chars, it's likely to
                 * be a typo or other error; so delete it. This pro-
                 * cessing is included primarily to exercise these
                 * functions. It should be removed for real text
                 * processing.
                 */

            if ( strlen ( pw ) > 20 )
            {
                Link pl;

                pl =  FindNodeAscend ( Ll, &nd );
                if ( pl == NULL )
                    printf ( "processing error!\n" );
                else
                    DeleteNode ( Ll, pl );
            }
        }

    /*--- now dump the table ---*/

    for ( j = 0; j < 33; j++ )
        chain_table[j] = 0;

    for ( i = 0; i < TABLE_SIZE; i++ )
    {
        Link pcurr;      /* Node we're examining */

        pcurr = Table[i];            /* set to start of list */
        if ( pcurr == NULL )         /* skip empty slots */
            continue;
        else
        {
            int chain_len;

            for ( chain_len = 0; ; pcurr = pcurr->next )
            {
                memcpy ( &n, pcurr, sizeof ( struct Node ));

#ifdef LIST_WORDS
```

```
                    /* Print each word and the count of occurrences */
                      printf ( "%-20s  %3u\n",
                                  ( (pND1) n.pdata)->word,
                                  ( (pND1) n.pdata)->u );
#endif

                 chain_len += 1;

                 if ( pcurr->next == NULL )
                     break;
             }

             if ( chain_len > 32 )
                 chain_len = 32;

             chain_table[chain_len] += 1;
         }
     }

#ifdef LIST_LONG_WORDS
    if ( long_wd->LCount < 1 )
        printf ( "No long words!\n" );
    else
    {                          /* step thru the list and print it*/
        Link pcurr;

        for ( pcurr =  long_wd->LHead;
              pcurr != NULL;
              pcurr =  GotoNext ( long_wd, pcurr))
              printf ( "%-20s\n",
                          ((pND2)( pcurr->pdata ))->word );
    }
#endif

#ifdef LIST_TABLE_STATS

    chains = 0;
    for ( i = 32; i > 0; i-- )
    {
        if ( chain_table[i] == 0 )
            continue;
        else
        {
            printf ( "%3d chains of length %2d\n",
                        chain_table[i], i );
            chains += chain_table[i];
        }
    }
```

```
    if ( chains != 0 )
    {
        printf ( "\n%d Nodes in %u chains\n\n",
                 L1->LCount, chains );

        printf ( "Size of hash table   = %u\n",
                   (unsigned) TABLE_SIZE );

        printf ( "Average chain length = %f\n",
                 L1->LCount / (double)chains );

        printf ( "Slot Occupancy       = %f \n",
                 ( (double)chains ) / TABLE_SIZE );

        printf ( "Load Factor          = %f \n",
                 ( (double)L1->LCount ) / TABLE_SIZE );
    }
    else
        printf ( "Error! No chains found.\n" );
#endif

    return ( EXIT_SUCCESS );
}
```

When *wordlist.c* is run against a text file consisting of Arthur Conan Doyle's 1904 classic "The Adventure of the Abbey Grange," the program reads through 9,286 words, of which 1,956 are identified as unique. Of these unique words, 1,335 are placed in chains of 2 or fewer entries. The statistics printed by the LIST_TABLE_STATS option are shown in Figure 3-4. These statistics tell us quite a bit about the quality of the hashing process. The first thing to point out is the **slot occupancy** presented in the figure. Previously, the load factor was defined as the number of entries in a table, divided by the number of available slots. In the case of a table that uses external hashing, this statistic is only marginally useful, since load factors greater than 1.0 are common and not of significant concern. The slot occupancy (a term coined by us) indicates the number of slots in the hash table that were actually used to head linked lists. It is a measure of the quality of the hashing algorithm. In this case, 59 percent of the slots pointed to linked lists. What is interesting is the average length of the individual chains. At 1.65 nodes in each chain, the average successful search requires 1.62 probes (see the explanation in the next paragraph). Had we used rehashing, the table would have a load factor of 0.98, meaning that the best searches would require either 5.2 or 126 probes, depending on whether the search was successful or not. The benefits of external chaining are clear.

Figure 3-4. The results of wordlist.c for "The Adventure of the Abbey Grange."

```
  1 chains of length 10
  1 chains of length  9
  1 chains of length  7
  4 chains of length  6
 16 chains of length  5
 35 chains of length  4
117 chains of length  3
330 chains of length  2
675 chains of length  1

1956 Nodes in 1180 chains

Size of hash table   = 1999
Average chain length = 1.657627
Slot occupancy       = 0.590295
Load Factor          = 0.978489
```

How do we know the average successful search requires 1.62 probes? Suppose we were to search once for every element in the table. The chain of 10 items would require 1 probe for the first item, 2 probes for the second, 3 for the third, and so on until it performed 10 probes for the last item on the list. The 10-node chain would require 10+9+8 . . . +1=55 probes to find all its elements successfully. Numbers that have the form $n + n–1 + n–2 . . . + n–n$ are informally called triangular numbers. The equation for finding a triangular number is $x = (n^2 + n) / 2$. In the previous example, $n = 10$, and x (the total number of probes) = 55. Table 3-2 gives the total number of probes needed to find all elements in the table.

Table 3-2. How to calculate probe count

Count	Chain Length	Triangle	Product
1	10	55	55
1	9	45	45
1	7	28	28
4	6	21	84
16	5	15	240
35	4	10	350
117	3	6	702
330	2	3	990
675	1	1	675
		Total Probes	3169
		Total Elements	1956
		Average Number of Probes	1.620143

You will note that these counts show the number of probes required to access every element in the table. If the linked lists are in order, the average search will traverse only half the list before finding the element or determining that it's not there. Hence, on successful searches, the averages shown in Table 3-2 will be substantially improved.

Returning to the program, it simply reads in the file, finds a word based on separation by white space, strips off any trailing punctuation, and converts the word to uppercase letters. It then computes a hash value, hash_key, and attempts to add the word and a count of 1 to the hash table by using the AddNodeAscend function provided in Chapter 2. This function adds a node to a linked list in ascending order. If a duplicate entry occurs (meaning that the word is already in the table), the count associated with the word already in the table is incremented by 1.

Listing 3-4 uses the generic linked-list functions of Chapter 2. As discussed in that chapter, all uses of generic linked-list functions require application-specific code. This code is kept in the file, *llapp.c*. For this program, Listing 3-5 shows that the changes when compared to *llapp.c* in Chapter 2 are fairly minor.

Listing 3-5.   The application-specific portions of the linked-list operations for Listing 3-4.

```
/*--- llapp.c --------------------------- Listing 3-5 ---------
 *  Application-specific functions for linked-lists.
 *  Here used for hash table of words and word counts.
 *------------------------------------------------------------*/

#include <stdlib.h>          /* for free() */
#include <string.h>          /* for strcmp() and strdup() */

#include "llgen.h"
#include "llapp.h"


void * CreateData1 ( void * data )
{
    struct NodeData1 * new_data;

    /*--- allocate the data structure ---*/

    new_data = (pND1) malloc ( sizeof ( struct NodeData1 ));

    if ( new_data == NULL )
        return ( NULL );

    /*--- move the values into the data structure ---*/
```

```
      new_data->u    =  1;
      new_data->word =  strdup ( (char *) ((pND1) data)->word );

      if ( new_data->word == NULL )   /* error copying string */
      {
          free ( new_data );
          return ( NULL );
      }
      else
          return ( new_data );
}

int DeleteData1 ( void * data )
{
    /*
     * In this case, NodeData1 consists of: a pointer and an int.
     * The integer will be returned to memory when the node
     * is freed. However, the string must be freed manually.
     */

    free ( ((pND1) data)->word );
    return ( 1 );
}
/*----------------------------------------------------------------
 * This function determines what to do when inserting a node
 * into a list if an existing node with the same data is found
 * in the list. In this case, since we are counting words, if a
 * duplicate word is found, we simply increment the counter.
 *
 * Note this function should return one of the following values:
 *       0           an error occurred
 *       1           delete the duplicate node
 *       2           insert the duplicate node
 * Any other processing on the duplicate should be done in this
 * function.
 *----------------------------------------------------------------*/

int DuplicatedNode1 ( Link new_node, Link list_node )
{              /* adding an occurrence to an existing word */

    pND1 pnd = list_node->pdata;
    pnd->u += 1;
    return ( 1 );
}

int NodeDataCmp1 ( void *first, void *second )
{
    return ( strcmp ( ((pND1) first)->word,
                      ((pND1) second)->word ));
```

```
}

/*=== Now the functions for the second linked list ===*/

void * CreateData2 ( void * data )
{
    struct NodeData2 * new_data;

    /*--- allocate the data structure ---*/

    new_data = (pND2) malloc ( sizeof ( struct NodeData2 ));

    if ( new_data == NULL )
        return ( NULL );

    /*--- move the values into the data structure ---*/
    new_data->word =  strdup ( (char *) ((pND1) data)->word );

    if ( new_data->word == NULL )   /* error copying string */
    {
        free ( new_data );
        return ( NULL );
    }
    else
        return ( new_data );
}

int DeleteData2 ( void * data )
{
    /*
     * In this case, NodeData2 consists of a pointer.
     * The string must be freed manually.
     */

    free ( ((pND2) data)->word );
    return ( 1 );
}

/* do nothing on a duplicated nodes */
int DuplicatedNode2 ( Link new_node, Link list_node )
{
    return ( 1 );
}

int NodeDataCmp2 ( void *first, void *second )
{
    return ( strcmp ( ((pND2) first)->word,
                      ((pND2) second)->word ));
}
```

The changes include a different way of handling duplicates in `DuplicatedNode2()`. All other linked-list functions are provided by the generic functions.

Once the input text file has been read and processed, the program creates and initializes a small table, `chain_table`, that will be loaded with a count of how many chains attained a given length. If a linked list has 6 nodes, then `chain_table[6]` is increased by 1. The program then reads through the hash table, ascertaining the length of all linked lists by stepping through each list, and updating `chain_table` after reaching the end of the list. Once this has been done, the statistics for the hash table are printed and the program exits.

Earlier, we proposed that you order the linked lists so as to make searches quicker. However, ordering nodes in ascending or descending order is not always the best solution. In some instances, it is better to insert new nodes at the head of the list. This creates a last-in, first-out order similar to that of the stack discussed in Chapter 2. An instance in which such an approach is useful is in analyzing a C program. Compilers always use hash tables to store the identifiers in a program. As identifiers are defined they are stored in the table. As they go out of scope they are removed from the table. Suppose we are examining the following program fragment that defines the variable `i` in several places:

```
#include <stdio.h>
int i;                  /* global i */
main ( void )
{
    int i;              /* main i */
    ...
    if ( a > 2 )
    {
            int i;      /* block-level i */
            ...
    }
}
```

Once we are in the `if` block, no other `i` but the one declared at the block level is accessible. Hence, all references to `i` must refer to it and cannot be confused for references to the `i` in `main()` or the global-level `i`. Since all the instances of `i` would hash to the same slot in the table, we have to be careful how we add them to the table. In fact, they are three different variables with the same name. If we were simply to use an ordered list, we would be obliged to do a fair amount of work to determine which `i` in the table was being accessed. A more elegant solution is to add the `i`'s to the *head* of the list as they are defined. This creates a table list as shown in Figure 3-5.

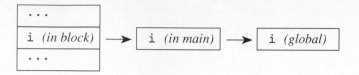

Figure 3-5.   Storing multiple definitions of `i` in a hash table.

Now any access to the variable `i` will first find the local block definition and thereby access the correct instance of `i`. When the block goes out of scope, the first `i`, the one from the local block, is deleted, leaving all further references to `i` pointing to the version declared at the top of `main()`. This is an elegant solution and one provided for in the generic linked-list routines by `AddNodeAtHead()`.

Another approach moves a node to the head of a list when the node is accessed. This approach capitalizes on the tendency of some kinds of data to cluster around certain values. A good example is taken from programming in which local variables are defined just prior to use. As a program is scanned and identifiers are looked up in a hash table, it is likely that a recently accessed variable will be referred to repeatedly in this section; hence moving it to the top of the list shortens any subsequent searches. When you use this model, the least recently used data items migrate to the end of the list.

Performance Issues

You can obtain good performance in hash tables by following broad guidelines and by monitoring results. Every hash table has unique aspects, and every hash table is called on to handle unique data. If you learn as much as you can about how your hashing operations work, you will know how to obtain excellent results quickly. Examine the following suggestions in the context of your own needs and your own results:

- Create hash tables that are reasonably large. However, tables with load factors under 0.20 will not offer better performance if they are expanded.
- Be sure that the number of slots in each hash table is a prime number.
- Test your hash algorithm on representative data, and measure the results. If no representative data is available, be sure to test extreme data ranges. Limit your hash function to one division operation—preferably a modulo with the table size.
- Anticipate collisions and use external chaining where possible.

Table 3-3. Primes for hash tables

Desired Size	Closest Prime
100	97
250	241
400	397
500	499
750	743
1000	997
1500	1499
2000	1999
4000	3989
5000	4999
7500	7499
10,000	9973

Let's examine all but the first point in detail.

Be sure that the number of slots in each hash table is a prime number. Common sense tells us that the maximum dispersal of remainders occurs when we divide by a prime number. Practice bears out this assumption. The worst possible division is to divide by a multiple of 2, since this serves only to mask off bits in the number being divided. Because our hash number (the result of the hash function) is put through the modulo operation using the table size, we can obtain the best results if the table has a prime number of slots. Table 3-3 lists prime numbers in the range likely to be required for typical tables. The number on the right is the basic size of the hash table you might want; the figure on the left is the largest prime number smaller than the desired table size.

Test your hash algorithms. The *wordlist.c* program presented earlier in Listing 3-4 shows how to measure the performance of hash algorithms. It shows how long the average chains are and how full the table is. It also prints a list of all chain sizes. Very long chains indicate a problem. If there are many long chains, the table is too small; if there are just a few very long chains, an aspect of the data is affecting the results of the hash function. Listings 3-2 and 3-3 present two general-purpose hash functions. Table 3-4 shows the results when the *wordlist.c* program uses these hash functions on the text of Arthur Conan Doyle's *The Hound of the Baskervilles*. The novel contains 60,250 words, of which 6,027 are unique.

Table 3-4.   The performance of two hash algorithms when reading *The Hound of the Baskervilles*

	HashPJW()	ElfHash()
Average chain length	6.83	3.30
Slot occupancy	0.44	0.91
Number of chains of length <= 4	439	1402
Execution time	30.62 secs	30.08 secs

Based on these results, `ElfHash()` does a far better job of hashing words. You can experiment to see if `HashPJW()` might work better on other data. The results offer interesting insights. It is clear that the ELF function does a much better job of distributing the keys throughout the table. The slot occupancy shows a better than 2-to-1 effectiveness in dispersing the keys. As a result, the average chain is about half the size of the chains generated by PJW. Even without the ELF figures for comparison, it is clear that the PJW does not work very well with strings. Consider that, despite loading over 6,000 unique words into a table with fewer than 2,000 slots, it could fill up only 44 percent of the slots. If you print out the words and the hash values that `HashPJW()` generated, you will see that the function is very sensitive to the length of the input strings. Strings of equal length tend to get hash values that are close in range. If you dump the table, you will find most of the occupied slots clustered at the low end of the table. We know that this is not the case with the ELF algorithm, because it used 91 percent of the available slots. Finally, it is interesting to note that the relative quality of the hash algorithms had little impact on the performance of the program. Optimization of hash algorithms, while necessary, should occur after the other optimizations have been performed. For hardware fanatics, the run times were obtained on a PC, using an Intel 386 chip running at 33Mhz. The program was compiled with no optimizations. Most of the execution time was spent reading the input file.

Anticipate collisions. If you are using a hash table that resolves collisions through rehashing, do not assume that if your table is large enough you can avoid collisions. Such a perspective is bound to be wrong in nearly all instances. Consider the famous puzzle about birthdays. It can be demonstrated that if 24 people are chosen at random, odds are better than 50 percent that two of them will have the same birthday. If you take 50 people at random, the odds are near certainty. Likewise, in a table of 365 elements, a standard hash function will generate a collision more than half the time after hashing only 24 values. If you don't believe this, try it out at your next large party. The program in Listing 3-1, *birthday.c*, will make this process especially convenient.

Resources and References

Aho, Alfred, Setli Ravi, and Jeffrey Ullman. *Compilers: Principles, Techniques, and Tools*. Reading, MA: Addison-Wesley, 1986.

Holub, Allen. *Compiler Design in C*. Englewood Cliffs, NJ: Prentice Hall, 1990. The best book available on compiler implementations. The discussion of hashing begins on p. 482.

Kruse, Robert, Bruce Leung, and Clovis Tondo. *Data Structures and Program Design in C*. Englewood Cliffs, NJ: Prentice Hall, 1991. A moderately good textbook introducing data structures.

UNIX Press. *System V Application Binary Interface—UNIX System*. Englewood Cliffs, NJ: UNIX Press, Prentice Hall, 1990.

Chapter 4

Searching

Comparing two strings and searching one string for another are closely related fundamental programming operations. String comparison operators answer the question "Are two given strings similar, or are they the same?" The ANSI C `strcmp()` family of functions provides this operation. String search operators, in contrast, look through a large body of text for any substring that matches a target string. To solve this problem, ANSI C has provided `strstr()`. These ANSI functions are related in that any search operation, at its heart, must repeatedly compare various substrings of the search text. However, these ANSI C functions provide only the most rudimentary type of search-and-compare operations.

This chapter presents a variety of alternatives to the ANSI C string search-and-compare functions (see Table 4-1). The algorithms differ from the ANSI C string functions in two ways. One group of algorithms reduces search time by taking advantage of string properties (the Boyer-Moore algorithm) or by searching simultaneously for more than one target string (the Aho-Corasick algorithm as well as regular expression searching). The second group of algorithms looks for *approximate* matches. The type of approximate match may be specified with a template (grep), by a distance metric, or even by how two words would sound when spoken (Soundex and Metaphone).

Table 4-1.   A comparison of different search techniques and their corresponding algorithms

String Searches and Comparisons	Approaches
Search for an exact copy* of one string	Brute-force algorithms; the Boyer-Moore algorithm
Search simultaneously for an exact copy* of two or more strings	The Aho-Corasick algorithm; regular expression searching
Search for an approximate match to a given string	Regular expression searching; string difference metrics
Phonetic comparisons	Soundex; Metaphone

*Easily modified to ignore case differences

Characteristics of Searches

All search techniques have a common goal, but the means used by a technique affects its suitability for a given situation. While the type of search may limit your choices, there are three main features to consider when choosing a technique (see also Table 4-2).

Setup Time

Some comparison techniques require you to do a substantial amount of computation before they can begin searching. If this takes a lot of time and if the amount of text to be searched is small, the setup time may outweigh any savings you achieve by using an algorithm with a higher theoretical speed.

Running Time

All string-search algorithms perform on the order of $a + bn$, where n is the number of characters in the text being searched, b is a constant indicating the number of comparisons performed for each character n, and a is setup time to begin the search. The effectiveness of the algorithms discussed in this chapter is determined by how much they manage to lower the value of b. Good searches perform less than one comparison per character searched; in other words, $b < 1$ (such searches are termed **sublinear**), while inefficient searches could have $b > 1.5$. Add to these any setup time (generally necessary only when you are searching for multiple strings) and you have the elements of search performance. For readers accustomed to standard algorithmic notation, searching

Table 4-2.   A comparison of searching methods for exact strings. A is the number of characters in the alphabet used by the text, `TLen` is the length of the text to be searched, and `PatLen` is the length of the search pattern.

	Brute Force	**Aho-Corasick**	**Boyer-Moore**
Setup time	None	O(sum of length of *all* target patterns)	O(`PatLen+A`)
Worst case	O(`PatLen * TLen`)	O(`TLen`)	O(`TLen`)
Typical case	O(`TLen`)	O(`TLen`)	O(`TLen/PatLen`)
Backtrack?	Yes	No	Yes

algorithms are all of order $O(N)$, where N is the number of characters in the text being searched.

The Need for Backtracking

Some algorithms proceed linearly through the search text, while others move back and forth through it. If the search text exists as a block of data in memory, moving back and forth is not difficult, but if the search text is a stream of data being sent to the program, the use of a back-and-forth algorithm may entail some form of buffering.

Brute-Force Searches

Brute-force searches simply plod through a piece of text looking for a specified string. They are about the simplest of algorithms and involve no particular magic. They are the sort of algorithms you are likely to write when you need to solve a simple problem quickly and without much imagination. Listing 4-1, *brute1.c*, shows a simple but slow brute-force search.

Listing 4-1.   A simple brute-force search that is slow.

```
/*--- brute1.c -------------------------- Listing 4-1 ---------
 *   Simple brute search with no optimization.
 *   Easy to write but slow to execute.
 *
 *   #define DRIVER to have a command-line version compiled.
 *-----------------------------------------------------------*/

#include <stdio.h>
#include <stdlib.h>
#include <string.h>
```

```
#define DRIVER  1    /* if #defined, runs test routine */

/*---------------------------------------------------------
 * Search for string in text. Return pointer to first
 * instance of string, or NULL at end of text.
 *-------------------------------------------------------*/

char * BruteSearch ( const char *text, const char *string )
{
    int len = strlen ( string );

    for ( ; *text; text++ )
        if ( strncmp ( text, string, len ) == 0 )
            return ( (char *) text );

    return ( NULL );
}

/*---------------------------------------------------------
 * The main driver: accepts a string to search for and
 * a filename from the command line. It then searches
 * through the first 10,000 chars of the file and prints
 * the first 30 characters of the first match, if any,
 * and then quits.
 *-------------------------------------------------------*/
#ifdef DRIVER

int main ( int argc, char *argv[] )
{
    char *search_for, *filename,
         *site;                     /* Site of match */
    FILE *fin;                      /* File to search */
    char *buffer;                   /* buffer from file */

    if ( argc < 3 )
    {
        fprintf ( stderr,
                    "Error! Usage: BRUTE1 string filename\n" );
        return ( EXIT_FAILURE );
    }
    else
    {
        search_for = argv[1];
        filename   = argv[2];
    }

    if (( fin = fopen ( filename, "rt" )) == NULL )
    {
```

```
            fprintf ( stderr, "Error: Cannot open %s\n", filename );
            return ( EXIT_FAILURE );
        }

    buffer = (char *) calloc ( 1, 10001 );
    if ( buffer == NULL )
    {
        fprintf ( stderr,
                    "Error! Cannot allocate buffer space.\n" );
        return ( EXIT_FAILURE );
    }

    fread ( buffer, 10000, 1, fin );

    site = BruteSearch ( buffer, search_for );

    if ( site == NULL )
        printf ( "%s NOT found\n", argv[1] );
    else
    {
        char solution[31];
        strncpy ( solution, site, 30 );
        solution [30] = '\0';

        printf ( "\nFound:\n%s\n", solution );
    }

    fclose ( fin );
    return ( EXIT_SUCCESS );
}
#endif
```

The principal searching function, `BruteSearch`, reads through a piece of text and calls `strncmp()` at every character to test for a match of `String`.

Many optimizations can be made on this process. First, `strncmp()` needs to be called only when a match occurs on the first character of `string`, rather than being called for every character. However, even if we test for this match before calling `strncmp()`, we will be performing two tests on every character: one for the match and one for the end-of-text marker. As we indicated previously, good search performance expects fewer than one comparison per character. Right now, the proposed optimized version is performing at least two comparisons.

One solution is to use a `switch` statement. Many compilers implement a `switch` not as a series of `if`/`else` conditions but as a jump table. (A **jump table** is an array of known size whose elements consist of pointers to executable code.) This is especially true when the `switch` statement controls to a large number of cases. In other words, when a jump table is used, the variable in the `switch` is tested just once and a jump is made to the code for the corresponding `case` statement. It would be ideal to use the following code in the `BruteSearch` function, particularly if the compiler implements the `switch` statement as a jump table.

```
switch ( *text )

{
   case '\0':              /* test for end of text */
          return NULL;
   case *string:           /* test for match with string */
          // call to strncmp()
   default:
          text += 1;       /* look at next character */
}
```

Unfortunately, C does not permit `case` statements to be evaluated at run time; hence code such as `case *string` is illegal. The value of each `case` must be known at compilation time. Further, such a small `switch` statement would almost certainly be implemented as a series of `if`/`else` statements, meaning that each character of the search text will still be examined several times. We overcome these problems in *brute2.c* (see Listing 4-2). The code is the same as *brute1.c*, except for the `BruteSearch` function.

Listing 4-2.   Brute-force search using a look-up table.

```
/*------------------------------------------------------
 *   Search for string in text using lookup table.
 *   Returns a pointer to the first instance of
 *   string, or NULL at end of text.
 *------------------------------------------------------*/

char * BruteSearch ( const char *text, const char *string )
{
    int len  = strlen ( string );

    /* the table. "static" assures its initialized to '\0's */
    static char lookup[UCHAR_MAX + 1];
    lookup[0]                            = 1;      /* EOT process */
    lookup[(unsigned char) (*string)] = 2;      /* a match */

    for ( ;; text++ )
    {
```

```
        switch ( lookup [(unsigned char) (*text)] )
        {
            case 0:
                break;            /* it's not EOT or a match */
            case 1:
                return ( NULL );          /* EOT */
            case 2:
                if ( strncmp
                        ( string + 1, text + 1, len - 1 ) == 0 )
                    return ( (char *) text );      /* a match */
                break;
            default:     /* good coding to include default */
                break;
        }
    }
}
```

This second routine implements a lookup table. The table, `lookup`, contains 256 values, one for each possible character in an 8-bit byte. (We assume that all text we will be scanning uses 8-bit bytes.) The values in `lookup` are all initialized to 0 by use of the `static` keyword. We then go into the table and assign special values to the characters we are interested in: the initial character in `string` is assigned a value of 2 in the table (`lookup[*string]`), and the end-of-text character (whose value is 0) is assigned a value of 1. We then ascertain the lookup value of each input character by using a `switch` statement: 0's are characters we are not interested in, 1 indicates end-of-text and we return, and 2 triggers a call to the string-comparison function.

This version of the brute-force search is fast for three reasons: (1) it retains only one comparison per character examined; (2) the table lookups are fast (a single pointer dereference); and (3) the setup time for the lookup is short, since most of the initialization is performed at startup (due to the `static` keyword). Initializing the table in this fashion means that we cannot search for a string that contains a zero byte. Should we want to look for strings with that value, the table would have to be initialized explicitly to a value other than 0.

This optimized brute-force approach has another advantage. Additional search strings can be searched for without generating more comparisons. For example, to perform a case-insensitive search, the lookup table could be set so that both upper- and lowercase versions of `*string` would return a 2. Then, `case 2` would invoke a call to a case-insensitive version of `strncmp()`. If multiple strings were being searched for, and they differed in their first character, they could be added to the lookup process—again, without generating any extra comparisons. This is an expandable, easy-to-implement, and reasonably efficient brute-search algorithm.

Notice one aspect of this algorithm's behavior. When a match is found between `*string` and `*text`, the search for additional occurrences should resume at the next character in `text`. We may be tempted to jump the length of `*string`, but this is imprudent in a number of cases. For example, suppose we are searching for the string `ff` and we find it in the text `fffff`. There are actually four occurrences of `ff` in the text, but if we skip ahead the full length of the string after every match, we would find only two of them: those beginning on the first and third `f`s. In the brute-search approach, it is advisable to skip the length of the whole string only when the string has no repeating characters. An algorithm that capitalizes on the possibility of skipping more than one character is presented in this chapter as the **Boyer-Moore** algorithm.

The optimized brute-force approach has essentially no setup time and is at its worst when searching a text of all `a`s for the pattern `aa...aab`. In that case, it will try all `PatLen` characters (the length of the search string) at every possible position, which gives this approach an execution time proportional to `PatLen * TextLen`. However, with any luck, it may need to look only once at each character of the search text, such as when searching for `a b` in a text of all `a`s. The typical case lies somewhere between these extremes.

The optimized brute-force search is easily understood and works acceptably well. It can be used in most situations where a simple string search is needed and where every bit of speed does not have to be extracted from the code.

The Boyer-Moore Search

In 1977 R. S. Boyer and J. S. Moore published their classic paper "A Fast String Searching Algorithm." The Boyer-Moore technique showed a new solution to the problem of string searches: by taking advantage of two approaches, it became possible to search a text without examining all the characters in the text. These two approaches, known as **heuristics** (techniques that use previous information to find a solution), involve the use of precomputed tables—a concept presented in the preceding discussion of brute-force searches, and one that appears frequently throughout the rest of this chapter.

Heuristic #1: Skipping Characters

The first heuristic is surprisingly simple. Boyer-Moore lays out the text to search, the pattern to search for, and a marker that points at the location where the search process is currently looking:

Target pattern	→ `corn`
Current marker of search	→ `*`
Search text	→ `Oaks from acorns grow`

Notice that the search pointer starts at the *right* end of the search pattern. Since the s in the text does not match any character of the search pattern, the search can be shifted to the right by 4 characters—that is, the length of the search string:

```
(Original pattern location)   → corn
Location after 1 shift        →     corn
Current marker                →        *
Search text                   → Oaks from acorns grow
```

Now the n of the search pattern is lined up with an o. Since o appears in the search pattern, we again shift right, but this time by only 2 characters, the number necessary to test for a match:

```
(Original location)           → corn
Location after 1 shift        →     corn
Location after 2 shifts       →       corn
Current marker                →          *
Text to search                → Oaks from acorns grow
```

This time, the n is lined up with a space. Since there is no space in the search pattern, we shift by 4:

```
(Original location)           → corn
Location after 1 shift        →     corn
Location after 2 shifts       →       corn
Location after 3 shifts       →           corn
Current marker                →              *
Search text                   → Oaks from acorns grow
```

Now the n is lined up with an r. Because an r exists in the target pattern, a shift of just 1 is made:

```
(Original location)           → corn
Location after 1 shift        →     corn
Location after 2 shifts       →       corn
Location after 3 shifts       →           corn
Location after 4 shifts       →            corn
Current marker                →              *
Text to search                → Oaks from acorns grow
```

Finally, a match. This trick allows rapid skipping through the text: only four characters were examined in order to eliminate the first *eleven* characters from consideration.

Implementing this concept requires the use of a table (`CharJump` in the code) that contains one unsigned integer for every possible character used by the text and pattern strings. Each entry in this table tells us how far to move the search string to the right to perform the next comparison. Clearly, if we are examining a character that does not appear in the search string at all, we can move ahead by the length of the entire string. If the letter does appear in the search string, we can move ahead only by the distance between that character and the right end of the string. For example, in the preceding text, when the n in `corn` had lined up with the r in `acorn`, we moved to the right by 1 character, the distance between the r and the right end of the string. The calculation is summarized as follows and is coded in Listing 4-3: If `t[ ]` is the search text and `p[ ]` the target pattern, and if `PatLen` is the length of `p`, then, for each possible alphabetic character c, find the rightmost occurrence of c in p. If c is not found, then `CharJump[c]` = `PatLen`. Otherwise, if c is found at position i, then `CharJump[c]` = `PatLen - i`.

Thus, for the preceding example, `CharJump` would be computed as follows:

```
CharJump['c'] = 3
CharJump['o'] = 2
CharJump['r'] = 1
CharJump['n'] = 0
CharJump [all others] = 4
```

The values in this table represent the distance that the search pointer is to be moved to the right from its current position when two strings fail to compare. Consider the following:

Target pattern	→	corn
Current marker	→	*
Search text	→	planting new crops

Match the ns and move the pointer:

Target pattern	→	corn
Current marker	→	*
Search text	→	planting new crops

We have a mismatch. Consulting `CharJump['a']` indicates that the pointer is to be moved 4 spaces to the right. When the pointer passes the end of the search pattern, it "hooks" the search pattern and pulls it along:

Target pattern	→	corn
Current marker	→	*
Search text	→	planting new crops

It is important to see that shifting the pointer by 4 moved the search pattern by only 3 positions.

Heuristic #2: Repeating Patterns

Boyer-Moore's second heuristic comes into play when the search string contains a repeating pattern. It is somewhat more involved. Assume the following search:

Target pattern　　　　　　　→ `door to door`
Marker　　　　　　　　　　→ 　　　　　　`*`
Search text　　　　　　　　→ `He went door to door`

The marker would match successfully until

Target pattern　　　　　　　→ `door to door`
Marker　　　　　　　　　　→ 　　　`*`
Search text　　　　　　　　→ `He went door to door`

Using only the `CharJump` table, we may be tempted to move the marker forward by `CharJump['t'] = Patlen-5-1`, or 6 spaces. (Remember that when the marker passes the end of the search pattern it hooks the search pattern and pulls it along.)

Target pattern　　　　　　　→ 　`door to door`
Marker　　　　　　　　　　→ 　　　　　　　`*`
Search text　　　　　　　　→ `He went door to door`

This would align the `ts` (but not much more), and after a few more moves, the match ultimately would be found. However, it is possible to do even better. Since the last 5 characters of the search pattern have already been matched, there is automatically a partial match for (in this case) the first 4 characters of the search pattern. In other words, to take advantage of the fact that the search pattern repeats itself, move the marker forward 13 spaces rather than 6:

Target pattern　　　　　　　→ 　　　　　　`door to door`
Marker　　　　　　　　　　→ 　　　　　　　　　　`*`
Search text　　　　　　　　→ `He went door to door`

The trick here is to know how far to move. The distance is computed by the use of a second auxiliary table, called `MatchJump` in the code. Using the same notation we used previously, we want to calculate `MatchJump[k]` as follows: First, look for the rightmost substring of p that matches `p[k+1]` ... `p[Patlen-1]`. Let s be the largest value of s such that `strncmp (p+s, p+k+1, PatLen-k-1) == 0` and `p[s-1] != p[k]`. Then,

MatchJump[k] = PatLen - s. If there is no such matching substring, look for a matching prefix. If q is the largest value of q such that strncmp(p, p+Patlen-1-q, q) == 0, then MatchJump[k] = 2*Patlen-q-k-1.

While it is easy to see in principle how to compute MatchJump[], an efficient algorithm to handle all cases is tricky to devise, and even harder to explain. If you're interested, check Smit in the references [Smit 1982] for details on the computation of MatchJump[].

Because Boyer-Moore works best when given large blocks of text to search and it does not stop at '\0' characters, the implementation in Listing 4-3 has to be told the length of the text block it is to search. The code also includes a test driver that searches a file for every occurrence of a specified string.

Listing 4-3.   An implementation of the Boyer-Moore string search.

```
/*-- boyermor.c -------------------------- Listing 4-3 --------
 * Boyer-Moore string search routine
 *
 *    Preprocessor switches: if #defined:
 *
 *        DEBUG will cause the search routine to dump its tables
 *              at various times--this is useful when trying to
 *              understand how MatchJump is generated
 *
 *        DRIVER will cause a test driver to be compiled
 *
 *-----------------------------------------------------------*/

#define DRIVER  1
/* #define DEBUG    1 */

#if defined(DEBUG)
#define SHOWCHAR for (uT=1; uT<= PatLen; uT++)  \
                    printf(" %c ", String[uT-1])
#define SHOWJUMP for (uT=1;uT<= PatLen;uT++)      \
                    printf("%2d ", MatchJump[uT])
#define SHOWA     printf("  uA = %u  ", uA)
#define SHOWB     printf("  uB = %u", uB)
#define SHOWBACK for (uT=1;uT<= PatLen;uT++)      \
                    printf("%2d ", BackUp[uT])
#define NL        printf("\n")

unsigned uT;
#else
#define SHOWCHAR
#define SHOWJUMP
#define SHOWA
```

```
#define SHOWB
#define SHOWBACK
#define NL
#endif

#include <stdio.h>
#include <limits.h>
#include <stdlib.h>
#include <string.h>

#define AlphabetSize (UCHAR_MAX + 1)    /* For portability */

#ifndef max
#define max(a,b) ((a) > (b) ? (a) : (b))
#endif

char *BoyerMoore ( const char * String, /* search for this */
                   const char * Text,   /* ...in this text */
                   size_t TextLen )     /* ...up to here.  */
{
            /* array of character mismatch offsets */
    unsigned CharJump[AlphabetSize];

            /* array of offsets for partial matches */
    unsigned *MatchJump;

            /* temporary array for MatchJump calculation */
    unsigned *BackUp;
    size_t   PatLen;
    unsigned u, uText, uPat, uA, uB;


    /* Set up and initialize arrays */
    PatLen = strlen ( String );
    MatchJump = (unsigned *)
        malloc ( 2 * sizeof ( unsigned ) * ( PatLen + 1 ));
    BackUp = MatchJump + PatLen + 1;

    /* Heuristic #1 -- simple char mismatch jumps ... */

    memset ( CharJump, 0, AlphabetSize * sizeof(unsigned) );
    for ( u = 0 ; u < PatLen; u++ )
        CharJump[((unsigned char) String[u])]
                  = PatLen - u - 1;

    /* Heuristic #2 -- offsets from partial matches ... */
    for ( u = 1; u <= PatLen; u++ )
```

```
        MatchJump[u] = 2 * PatLen - u;
                               /* largest possible jump */
    SHOWCHAR; NL;
    SHOWJUMP; NL;

    u  = PatLen;
    uA = PatLen + 1;
    while ( u > 0 )
    {
        BackUp[u] = uA;
        while ( uA <= PatLen &&
                String[u - 1] != String[uA - 1] )
        {
            if ( MatchJump[uA] > PatLen - u )
                MatchJump[uA] = PatLen - u;
            uA = BackUp[uA];
        }
        u--;
        uA--;
    }

    SHOWJUMP; SHOWA; SHOWBACK; NL;

    for ( u = 1; u <= uA; u++ )
        if ( MatchJump[u] > PatLen + uA - u )
            MatchJump[u] = PatLen + uA - u;

    uB = BackUp[uA];
    SHOWJUMP; SHOWB; NL;

    while ( uA <= PatLen )
    {
        while ( uA <= uB )
        {
            if ( MatchJump[uA] > uB - uA + PatLen )
                MatchJump[uA] = uB - uA + PatLen;
            uA++;
        }
        uB = BackUp[uB];
    }
    SHOWJUMP; NL;

    /* now search */
    uPat =  PatLen;          /* tracks position in Pattern */
    uText = PatLen - 1;      /* tracks position in Text */
    while ( uText < TextLen && uPat != 0 )
    {
        if ( Text[uText] == String[uPat - 1])  /* match? */
```

```
        {
            uText--;     /* back up to next */
            uPat--;
        }
        else  /* a mismatch - slide pattern forward */
        {
            uA = CharJump[((unsigned char) Text[uText])];
            uB = MatchJump[uPat];
            uText += max(uA, uB);  /* select larger jump */
            uPat = PatLen;
        }
    }

    /* return our findings */
    if ( uPat == 0 )
        return ( (char *) ( Text + ( uText + 1 ))); /* a match */
    else
        return ( NULL );                    /* no match */
}

/*------------------------------------------------------------
 * The main driver, activated by #defining DRIVER.
 * Will print all occurrences of a match in the first
 * 10,000 characters of the target file.
 *----------------------------------------------------------*/

#ifdef DRIVER

#define MAX_TEXT_SIZE 10000u

int main ( int argc, char *argv[] )
{
    char *SearchFor, *Filename;

    FILE *Fin;                    /* File to search */
    char *Buffer;                 /* Buffer from file */

    char *start, *p;
    int i;
    size_t   TextSize;
    unsigned count;

    if ( argc != 3 )
    {
        puts ( "Usage is: boyermor search-string filename\n" );
        return ( EXIT_FAILURE );
    }
    else
```

```
{
    SearchFor = argv[1];
    Filename  = argv[2];
}

if (( Fin = fopen ( Filename, "r" )) == NULL )
{
    fprintf ( stderr, "Can't open %s\n", Filename );
    return ( EXIT_FAILURE );
}

/* allocate search buffer and fill it with target file */
Buffer = (char*) malloc ( MAX_TEXT_SIZE + 1 );
if ( Buffer == NULL )
{
    puts ( "Error! Could not allocate buffer space\n" );
    return ( EXIT_FAILURE );
}

TextSize = fread ( Buffer, 1, MAX_TEXT_SIZE, Fin );
fclose ( Fin );

p = Buffer;
count = 0;
while ( count < TextSize )
{
    if ( *p == '\n' )
        *p = '\0';
    p++;
    count++;
}

/* now search repeatedly */

start = BoyerMoore ( SearchFor, Buffer, TextSize );
if ( start == NULL )                 /* no match found */
    printf ( "\n%s Not Found.\n", SearchFor );
else                                 /* match found */
    while ( start != NULL )
    {
        for ( p = start; ; p-- )  /* find start of line */
        {
            if ( *p == '\0' )
            {
                p++;
                break;
            }
            else
```

```
            if ( p == Buffer )
                break;
        }                           /* print the match */
        printf( "Found:\n%s\n", p );
        for ( i = start - p; i > 0; i-- )
            fputc ( ' ', stdout );
        printf ( "%s\n\n", SearchFor );
        start =                     /* continue the search */
            BoyerMoore ( SearchFor, start + 1,
                    TextSize - ( start - Buffer ) - 1 );
    }
    return ( EXIT_SUCCESS );
}
#endif
```

The code first calculates the `MatchJump` and `CharJump` arrays. It then steps through the search text; when it finds a character mismatch, it picks the larger of the appropriate `MatchJump` and `CharJump` entries.

Note that you can simplify the Boyer-Moore code by eliminating the `MatchJump` table. Under the right circumstances this still allows Boyer-Moore to retain most of its speed while reducing its setup time and space requirements. To do so, you need to replace the calculation of uB in the search loop with uB = `Patlen - uPat + 1`. This calculation is identical to the lowest legal result obtained when calculating `MatchJump`. Without this value the search loop could actually slip backward.

The calculation of the running times for Boyer-Moore is somewhat more complex. It is easy to derive that its setup time is proportional to `Patlen+AlphabetSize`, but the worst-case running time is very difficult to establish. It has been shown that if the text does not contain a match for the pattern, the algorithm does at most 6*`TextLen` character comparisons. Other authors have conjectured that this boundary may be as low as 2*`TextLen` characters. It is in the average case that Boyer-Moore shows its importance. In general, it requires only the time proportional to `TextLen/PatLen`. In other words, Boyer-Moore usually examines only a fraction of the text. As an example, remember that the first sample search performed only four comparisons to skip eleven characters. This sublinearity is what makes the Boyer-Moore algorithm so attractive.

Multiple-String Searches

Suppose we need to search a large database for several strings at the same time. This problem is a common one; we might, for example, want to search a medical database for any and all references to chest pain, angina pectoris, or heart attack. Of course, we could simply search the database once for each of these phrases, but there is a more elegant solution that will search for any number of phrases in a single pass.

The approach presented here was first described by Alfred Aho and M. J. Corasick [Aho 1975]. The technique they developed revolves around the construction of a finite-state machine that can locate the keywords. (**Keywords** here refer to the strings being searched for.) This approach identifies all the substrings of a given text that belong to a list of keywords. The substrings may overlap.

We can best describe the algorithm by first considering an example. Suppose we want to search a text for the keywords tale, tool, and ale. An appropriate state machine for these three keywords is described in the three tables shown in Figure 4-1.

a) a Goto Function

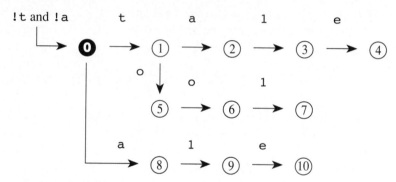

All undefined transitions are to a state known as FAIL_STATE. Note that all transitions from state 0 *are* defined; if only as a transition back to state 0.

b) a Failure Function

state	(1)	(2)	(3)	(4)	(5)	(6)	(7)	(8)	(9)	(10)
Fail[state]	0	8	9	10	0	0	0	0	0	0

c) an Output Function

state	Output[state]
(4)	**tale, ale**
(7)	**tool**
(10)	**ale**

Figure 4-1.   A finite-state machine for multiple string searches.

The key to the state machine is the `Goto` function in Figure 4-1a. It defines a network of states that keep track of what we have seen. We start in state 0, and then examine each character of the input stream. For example, if an `a` is seen in state 0, we then move to state 8. A `1` would then take us to state 9. If, however, the next character is not an `e`, we consult `fail[9]` and change to state 0. Note carefully that from state 9, `Goto[9, 'e'] == 10`, but `Goto[9, anything else] == FAIL_STATE`. If we arrive at a state with a nonempty `Output` function, we have found a matching string. Here is the pseudocode:

```
state = 0;
while ((c = getchar()) != EOF)   /* read text */
{
     while (Goto[state, c] == FAIL_STATE)
          state = Fail[state];

     state = Goto[state, c];
     if (Output[state] != NULL)
          report(Output[state]);
}
```

As you can see, once the various tables of Figure 4-1 are available, the searching process is straightforward. Constructing these tables is the difficult aspect of this algorithm. We approach the problem in two steps. First, we construct the `Goto` function and partially construct the `Output` function. We start with an empty `Goto` function and step by step we add each character from the search words. Where possible, we "overlay" words that begin with the same characters. For example, to build the `Goto` function in Figure 4-1, we start with an empty `Goto` function (as in Figure 4-2a), insert the word `tale` (Figure 4-2b), the word `tool` (Figure 4-2c), and finally the word `ale` (Figure 4-1a).

We also define the beginning of the `Output` function at the same time. The rough pseudocode for these computations is as follows:

```
HighState = 0;
for(word=list_of_words; word!=NULL; word=next_word)
{
     state = 0;
     j = 1;
     /* try to overlay on existing word(s) */
     while (Goto[state, word[j]] != FAIL_STATE)
     {
          state = Goto[state, word[j]);
          j += 1;
     }
```

a) an empty Goto Function

all characters ⟶ ⓿

b) after adding `Tale`

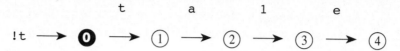

c) after adding `Tool`

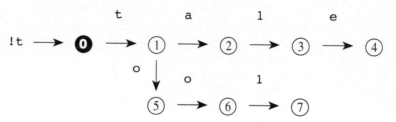

Figure 4-2. Loading the finite-state table.

```
/* now create new states as needed */
while (word[j] != '\0')  /* scan to end of string */
{
      HighState += 1;      /* a new state */
      Goto[state, word[j]] = HighState;
      state = HighState;
}

      /* we are at the end of word[].  Add to Output */
      Output[state] += word;  /* append word */
}

/* eliminate all FAIL_STATE transitions from state 0 */
for(i=0; i<MAXCHARS; i++)
      if (Goto[0, i] == FAIL_STATE)
            Goto[0, i] = 0;
```

Computing the `Fail` function is the second and final step in constructing the tables. Here we must account for (1) overlapping search words and (2) the possibility that a given state might find multiple search words. We proceed with a step-by-step examination of all the states of `Goto`. If we define *depth* to be the distance of state *x* from state 0, then states 1 and 8 are at depth 1 while states 2, 5, and 9 are at depth 2. Intuitively, `Fail[depth 1 states]` must take us to state 0. The `Fail` function for depth 2 states now depends on the `Fail` and `Goto` functions of the depth 0 and 1 states. To generalize, the `Fail` function for the depth *n* states depends on the `Fail` and `Goto` functions of all states of lesser depth.

Consider, for example, the computation of `Fail[2]` shown previously in Figure 4-1. The character that brought us from state 1 to state 2 was a. We now search all the transitions from state 0 to state 1 to find another transition that also makes use of a. We find just such a one: a takes us from state 0 to state 8. Thus, `Fail[2]` is set to 8. Note how the calculation of `Fail` has turned up the overlap of the keywords `tale` and `ale`.

`Output` is updated at the same time. When an overlap is discovered, we need only concatenate the `Output` functions of the two overlapping states. In this pseudocode, a `queue` is a first-in-first-out list. The code `queue = queue + x` adds x to the end of the queue, while `queue = queue - x` removes x from the head of the queue:

```
queue = empty;

/* examine state 0 first */
for (i=0; i<MAXCHARS; i++)
    if (Goto[0, i] != 0)  /* find all depth 1 states */
    {
        s = Goto[0, i];
        Fail[s] = 0;
        queue = queue + s;
    }

/* now examine states of depth 2 and greater */
while (queue != empty)
{
    r = next state from queue;
    queue = queue - r;
    for (i=0; i<MAXCHARS; i++)
    {
        if (Goto[r, i] != FAIL_STATE)
        {
            s = Goto[r, i];  /* i takes us from r to s */
            queue = queue + s;
            state = Fail[r]; /* look back one to n levels */

            /*  find a valid transition that uses i. Note
             *  that we can always find such a transition
             *  because at the very least,
             *   Goto[0, i] = 0 or some other valid state.
             */
            while (Goto[state, i] == FAIL_STATE)
```

```
                              state = Fail[state];
                      Fail[s] = Goto[state, i];
                      Output[s] = Output[s] + Output[Fail[s]];
               }
           }
     }
```

   The actual code for implementing this pseudocode is presented in Listing 4-4. We must deal with a number of implementation issues that affect the speed and memory requirements of the algorithm. First, we must decide how many possible states our machine might have. A reasonable choice is to store the states as integers. The next critical issue is how to store the `Goto` function. The simplest algorithm would involve a jump table for each state. The table would contain a next state for each possible character. Unfortunately, this would require 512 bytes (256 chars at a minimum of 2 bytes per integer) so that each state could deal with ASCII text. A 100-state machine would then consume 50 KB for the `Goto` function. Since many applications of this algorithm might need only 20 to 40 states (that is, the total length of all search phrases is 20 to 40 characters), such an approach would be tolerable. Indeed, if the number of states were limited to 256, then a single 8-bit byte could be used to store each state, thus halving the memory required for the jump table.

Listing 4-4.   Search for multiple strings.

```
/*--- msrch.c ---------------------------- Listing 4-4 --------
 * Purpose: search text for multiple keywords simultaneously
 * Switches: DRIVER  - will cause a test driver to be compiled
 *           MAXCHAR - maximum number of symbols recognized
 *
 * Usage: The sample driver illustrates all the key points.
 *        There are three routines:
 *
 *        (1) MsrchInit ( struct kword *) is passed list of
 *            words to search for
 *
 *        (2) MsrchGo ( int (*MsrchData) (),
 *                      void (*MsrchSignal) (char *) );
 *            does the work. It uses two pointers to functions:
 *            the first retrieves a character, the second is
 *            called when a match is found.
 *
 *        (3) MsrchEnd ( void ) cleans up the work areas
 *
 *------------------------------------------------------------*/

#define DRIVER 1              /* compile a test driver */
```

```c
#include <stdio.h>
#include <stdlib.h>
#include <string.h>

struct kword {              /* linked list of keywords */
    unsigned char *word;    /*    to search for.       */
    struct  kword *next;
};


#define MAXCHAR  256        /* max number of different chars
                                            we search for */
static int MaxState;        /* max number of states
                                            we have room for */


static int *MatchArray;     /*  First level of matching.
                             *  Possible values:
                             *      (1) EMPTY_SLOT  -2
                             *      (2) a character
                             *      (3) MULTI_WAY   -1
                             */

#dcfine MULTI_WAY   -1      /* flags for match_array */
#define EMPTY_SLOT  -2

union GotoTable {        /* values in MatchArray take us here:  */
    int GotoState;       /* go here if MatchArray is a character*/
    int *BranchTable;  /* or to this MULTI_WAY branching table*/
} static *GotoArray;

#define FAIL_STATE  -1      /* in GotoState or BranchTable,
                                this means failure */

/* OutArray[] is the Output function */
                        /* list of keywords 'found' by states */
static struct kword **OutArray;

/* FailArray[] is the Fail function */
static int *FailArray;      /* failure transition array */


/* variable to track next free state */
static int HighState;

/* functions we use */
static void AddStateTrans ( int, int, int );
static void ComputeFail ( void );
static void Enter ( unsigned char * );
```

```
static void FindFail ( int state, int s, int a );
static void QueueAdd ( int *queue, int qbeg, int new );

/* set up tables needed by MsrchGo() */
void MsrchInit ( struct kword *klist )
{
    int i;
    struct kword *ktemp;

    /* compute maximum number of possible states */
    MaxState = 1;
    for ( ktemp = klist; ktemp != NULL; ktemp = ktemp->next )
        MaxState += strlen ( ktemp->word );

    /* allocate space for arrays */

    MatchArray = (int *) malloc ( sizeof(int) * MaxState );
    GotoArray  = (union GotoTable *) malloc (
                        sizeof(union GotoTable) * MaxState );
    OutArray   = (struct kword **) malloc (
                        sizeof(struct kword *) * MaxState );
    FailArray  = (int *) malloc ( sizeof(int) * MaxState );

    /* initialize state arrays */
    for ( i = 0; i < MaxState; i++ )
    {
        MatchArray[i] = EMPTY_SLOT;
        OutArray[i]   = NULL;
    }

    /* initialize state_array[0] */
    HighState = 0;
    AddStateTrans ( 0, 'a', FAIL_STATE );
        /* force a multiway table */
    AddStateTrans ( 0, 'b', FAIL_STATE );

    /* step through keywords */
    for ( ; klist != NULL; klist = klist->next )
        Enter ( klist->word );

    /* setup return to zero transitions for state[0] */
    for ( i = 0; i < MAXCHAR; i++ )
        if ( GotoArray[0].BranchTable[i] == FAIL_STATE )
            GotoArray[0].BranchTable[i] = 0;

    /* and compute failure array */
    ComputeFail();
}
```

```
/* add transition from OldState -> NewState for MatchChar */
static void AddStateTrans ( int OldState,
                            int MatchChar,
                            int NewState )

{
    int i, *temp;

    /* is this slot empty? */
    if ( MatchArray[OldState] == EMPTY_SLOT )   /* this is easy */
    {
        MatchArray[OldState] = MatchChar;
        GotoArray[OldState].GotoState = NewState;
    }
        /* is there already a multi-way table? */
    else
    if ( MatchArray[OldState] == MULTI_WAY ) /* easy, too */
        GotoArray[OldState].BranchTable[MatchChar] = NewState;

        /* need to convert to multi-way table */
    else
    {
        temp = (int *) malloc ( sizeof(int) * MAXCHAR );
        for ( i = 0; i < MAXCHAR; i++ )
            temp[i] = FAIL_STATE;

        /* copy data from single way branch */
        temp[MatchArray[OldState]] =
            GotoArray[OldState].GotoState;

        /* and new data */
        temp[MatchChar] = NewState;

        /* and load it all into state_array */
        MatchArray[OldState] = MULTI_WAY;
        GotoArray[OldState].BranchTable = temp;
    }
}

/* add kword to list of words our machine recognizes */
static void Enter ( unsigned char *kword )
{
    int state, k;
    char *save;
    struct kword *ktemp;

    state = 0;
    save = kword;    /* keep a copy */
```

```
    /*  first, see whether we can place this word
     *  on top of an existing one
     */

    for ( ; *kword != '\0'; kword++ )
    {
        /* is this a single char slot? */

        if ( MatchArray[state] == *kword )
            state = GotoArray[state].GotoState;

        else        /* multi-way? */
        if ( MatchArray[state] == MULTI_WAY )
        {
            if (( k = GotoArray[state].BranchTable[*kword] )
                    == FAIL_STATE )
                break;
            else    /* we have a transition for this char */
                state = k;
        }
        else        /* no match for this char */
            break;
    }

    /* now add new states as needed */
    for ( ; *kword != '\0'; kword++ )
    {
        HighState += 1;
        if ( HighState >= MaxState )  /* uh-oh ... */
        {
            fputs( "INTERNAL ERROR: too many states\n", stderr );
            exit ( EXIT_FAILURE );
        }
        AddStateTrans ( state, *kword, HighState );
        state = HighState;
    }

    /* now add this keyword to output list for final state */
    ktemp = (struct kword *) malloc ( sizeof ( struct kword ));
    ktemp->word = save;
    ktemp->next = OutArray[state];
    OutArray[state] = ktemp;
}

/* build FailArray and update GotoArray */
static void ComputeFail()
{
    int *queue, qbeg, r, s;
```

```
int i;

/* allocate a queue */
queue = (int *) malloc ( sizeof ( int ) * MaxState );
qbeg = 0;
queue[0] = 0;

/* scan first level and setup initial values for FailArray */
for ( i = 0; i < MAXCHAR; i++ )
    if (( s = GotoArray[0].BranchTable[i] ) != 0 )
    {
        FailArray[s] = 0;
        QueueAdd ( queue, qbeg, s );
    }

/* now scan lower levels */
while ( queue[qbeg] != 0 )
{
    /* pull off state from front of queue and advance qbeg*/

    r = queue[qbeg];
    qbeg = r;

    /* now investigate this state */
    if ( MatchArray[r] == EMPTY_SLOT )
        continue;         /* no more to do */
    else
    if ( MatchArray[r] == MULTI_WAY )
    {
        /* scan its subsidiary states */
        for ( i = 0; i < MAXCHAR; i++ )
                            /* scan BranchTable */
            if (( s = GotoArray[r].BranchTable[i] )
                    != FAIL_STATE )
            {                   /* add new state to queue */
                QueueAdd ( queue, qbeg, s );
                FindFail ( FailArray[r], s, i );
            }
    }
    else  /* single char */
    {
        QueueAdd ( queue, qbeg, GotoArray[r].GotoState );
        FindFail ( FailArray[r], GotoArray[r].GotoState,
                    MatchArray[r] );
    }
}

/* tidy up */
```

```
        free ( queue );
}

/*-------------------------------------------------------------------
 * Actually compute failure transition.  We know that 'a'
 * would normally cause us to go from state s1 to s2.
 * To compute the failure value, we backtrack in search
 * of other places 'a' might go.
 *-------------------------------------------------------------------*/
static void FindFail ( int s1, int s2, int a )
{
    int on_fail;
    struct kword *ktemp, kdummy, *out_copy, *kscan;

    for ( ; ; s1 = FailArray[s1] )
        if ( MatchArray[s1] == a )
        {
            if (( on_fail = GotoArray[s1].GotoState )
                        != FAIL_STATE )
                break;
        }
        else
        if ( MatchArray[s1] != EMPTY_SLOT )
            if (( on_fail = GotoArray[s1].BranchTable[a] )
                        != FAIL_STATE )
                break;

    FailArray[s2] = on_fail;

    /* merge output lists */

    /* first, make a copy of OutArray[on_fail] */
    if ( OutArray[on_fail] == NULL )
        out_copy = NULL;
    else
    {
        kscan = OutArray[on_fail];
        out_copy = malloc ( sizeof ( struct kword ));
        out_copy->word = kscan->word;
        out_copy->next = NULL;
        for ( kscan = kscan->next;
              kscan != NULL;
              kscan = kscan->next )
        {
            ktemp = malloc ( sizeof ( struct kword ));
            ktemp->word = kscan->word;
            ktemp->next = out_copy->next;
            out_copy->next = ktemp;
        }
```

```
    }

    /* now merge them */
    if (( kdummy.next = OutArray[s2] ) != NULL )
    {
        ktemp = &kdummy;
        for ( ; ktemp->next->next != NULL; ktemp = ktemp->next )
                ;
        ktemp->next->next = out_copy;
    }
    else
        OutArray[s2] = out_copy;
}

/* add new to end of queue */
static void QueueAdd ( int *queue, int qbeg, int new )
{
    int q;

    q = queue[qbeg];
    if ( q == 0 )               /* is list empty? */
        queue[qbeg] = new;   /* yes */
    else                        /* no: scan to next-to-last link */
    {
        for ( ; queue[q] != 0; q = queue[q] )
                ;
        queue[q] = new; /* put this state at end of queue */
    }

    /* and terminate list */
    queue[new] = 0;
}

/* do the actual search */
void MsrchGo ( int  (*MsrchData) (),
               void (*MsrchSignal) (char *) )
{
    int state, c, g, m;
    struct kword *kscan;

    state = 0;
    while (( c = MsrchData() ) != EOF )
    {
        /* what is goto ( state, c ) ? */
        for ( ;; )
        {
            /*-------------------------------------------------
             *  We cheat slightly in the interest of
             *  speed/simplicity. The machine will spend most
```

```
             *   of its time in state==0, and this state is
             *   always a MULTI_WAY table. Since this is a
             *   simple test, we make it first and try to save
             *   the calculation of an array index
             *-----------------------------------------------*/

             if ( state == 0 ||
                  ( m = MatchArray[state] ) == MULTI_WAY )
                  g = GotoArray[state].BranchTable[c];
             else
             if ( m == c )
                  g = GotoArray[state].GotoState;
             else
                  g = FAIL_STATE;

             if ( g != FAIL_STATE )
                  break;

             state = FailArray[state];
         }
         state = g;

         /* anything to output? */
         if (( kscan = OutArray[state] ) != NULL )
             for ( ; kscan != NULL; kscan = kscan->next )
                  MsrchSignal ( kscan->word );
     }
}

/* free all the arrays we created */
void MsrchEnd ( void )
{
    int i;
    struct kword *kscan;

    for ( i = 0; i < MaxState; i++ )
         if ( MatchArray[i] == MULTI_WAY )
              free ( GotoArray[i].BranchTable );

    free ( MatchArray );
    free ( GotoArray );
    free ( FailArray );

    for ( i = 0; i < MaxState; i++ )
        if ( OutArray[i] != NULL )
            for ( kscan = OutArray[i];
                  kscan!=NULL;
                  kscan = kscan->next )
```

```
                    free ( kscan );
        free ( OutArray );
}


/*------------------------------------------------------------
 * This test driver expects a command line of the form
 *    msrch file word-1 word-2 word-3 .... word-n
 *
 * It will then search file for all words on the command line.
 * The results are written to stdout. This illustrates all the
 * features of using the multisearch routines.
 *
 * This is an admittedly simple design--the search routine would
 * certainly be faster if the character fetch routine was put
 * directly into the MsrchGo() module.  However, to avoid using
 * application-specific code in the demonstration version of
 * these routines, it is coded as a separate subroutine.
 *------------------------------------------------------------*/

#ifdef DRIVER

#define BUFSIZE 200

FILE *infile;
char inbuf[BUFSIZE];
char *inbufptr;
int  linecount;

/* declare the routines that MsrchGo() will use */
int RetrieveChar ( void );
void FoundWord();

int main ( int argc, char **argv )
{
    char infile_name[80];
    struct kword *khead, *ktemp;
    int i;

    if ( argc < 3 )
    {
        fprintf ( stderr,
            "Usage: msrch infile word-1 word-2 ... word-n\n" );
        exit ( EXIT_FAILURE );
    }

    strcpy ( infile_name, argv[1] );

    if (( infile = fopen ( infile_name, "r" )) == NULL )
```

```
    {
        fprintf ( stderr, "Cannot open %s\n", infile_name );
        exit ( EXIT_FAILURE );
    }
    linecount = 0;
    inbufptr = NULL;

    /* turn command-line parameters into a list of words */
    khead = NULL;
    for ( i = 3; i <= argc; i++ )
    {
        ktemp = (struct kword *) malloc ( sizeof ( struct kword ));
        ktemp->word = argv[i-1];
        ktemp->next = khead;
        khead = ktemp;
    }

    MsrchInit ( khead ); /* setup system; pass list of words */

    /* Now search. Note call to functions by use of pointers */
    MsrchGo ( RetrieveChar, FoundWord );

    MsrchEnd();                 /* clean up */
    return ( EXIT_SUCCESS );
}


/* get next character from input stream.  Routine returns either
 *    (a) a character (as an int without its sign extended), or
 *    (b) EOF
 */
int RetrieveChar ( void )
{
    int c;

    if ( inbufptr == NULL || *(++inbufptr) == '\0' )
    {   /* read a new line of data */
        if ( fgets ( inbuf, BUFSIZE, infile ) == NULL )
        {
            fclose ( infile );
            return ( EOF );
        }
        inbufptr = inbuf;
        linecount += 1;
    }

    c = *inbufptr;
    c &= 0x00FF;    /* make sure it is not sign extended */
```

```
        return ( c );
}

/* FoundWord: called by MsrchGo() when it finds a match */
void FoundWord(char *word)
{
    int i;

    fprintf ( stdout, "Line %d\n%s", linecount, inbuf );

    i = ( inbufptr - inbuf ) - strlen ( word ) + 1;
    for ( ; i > 0; i-- )
        fputc ( ' ', stdout );

    fprintf ( stdout, "%s\n\n", word );
}
#endif
```

The objective of the code in Listing 4-4 is to conserve memory. Since most
states have only one valid transition leading from them (in Figure 4-1, 8 of 10
qualify), we implement each state by using two arrays. These two arrays are,
in effect, the Goto function:

```
int MatchArray[];
union GotoTable {
    unsigned GotoState;
    unsigned *BranchTable;
} GotoArray[];
```

To determine Goto[state, c], we proceed as follows:

1. If MatchArray[state] == c, then the next state is
    GotoArray[state]. GotoState.
2. If MatchArray[state] == the special value MULTI_WAY, then the
    next state is GotoArray[state].BranchTable[c].
3. Otherwise, the next state is FAIL_STATE.

Using this structure, we need to implement a full jump table only for those
states that have multiple possible characters leading from them. It would be
easy, however, to modify the code to eliminate this feature and use a
BranchTable for every state. The other functions (Output and Fail) have
been implemented as simple lookup tables, as their memory requirements are
not excessive under any circumstance.

The code is written so that the input and reporting functions are separate from the actual search code. The search code is passed pointers to the functions it should use. This approach was chosen to keep the search engine as a separate piece of code, insulated from the concerns of I/O. This is relatively inefficient however; the I/O operations would be best performed in-line in production versions of the code.

An analysis of the time complexity of this algorithm is straightforward. It requires a single pass through each keyword to set up its tables, thus using the time proportional to the total length of the keywords. The search phase then requires only the time proportional to the size of the text being searched.

String Searches for Regular Expressions: grep

Users of most operating systems are familiar with the concept of **wildcards**. Wildcards are special characters that refer to a series of characters. For example, a familiar command-line argument for MS-DOS involves the characters `*.*` when referring to all files. In this example, the asterisk means any set of zero or more characters—specifically, any characters followed by a period (which retains its normal meaning), followed by any other set of characters. The result of `*.*` then refers to all files with a name and an extension, such as *command.com*.

Characters such as the asterisk in the preceding example are referred to as **metacharacters** (the Latin *meta* means "change"). Metacharacters have special meanings or they change the meanings of otherwise regular characters. The metacharacter in C, for example, is the backward slash: \. In context, the backward slash changes the meaning of the next character. For example, \n is not a two-character combination, rather it is the symbol for the new-line character (ASCII 0x0D). Likewise, \a is the representation of the single character for alarm (ASCII 0x07). Notice that in C, as in all situations that rely upon metacharacters, there is an escape mechanism that signals when a metacharacter should be treated as a regular character with no special meaning. In C, a regular slash is written as \\.

As we'll see shortly, an entire alphabet of metacharacters has grown up over the years, mainly evolving within the UNIX arena, where metacharacters have been very popular. Expressions that use metacharacters are called **regular** expressions, for reasons one could only speculate on. String searches involving metacharacters are commonly performed by a utility called **grep**, an acronym for **g**eneral **r**egular-**e**xpression **p**arser. (Because UNIX has a case-sensitive command line and UNIX users avoid capital letters, even acronyms such as grep are always in lowercase letters.) grep reads through an input file and then prints all lines containing strings that match a regular expression typed at the command line.

We will now examine a grep engine: how it accepts and understands regular expressions (this is the parser we just referred to) and how it searches through text to find matches for the regular expression. Before we begin, however, we should examine the metacharacters that will be allowed in the regular expressions. Table 4-3 lists a set of common metacharacters and their standard meanings.

Table 4-3.   Some common metacharacters and their meaning

Metacharacter	Meaning
^	Anchors the expression at the beginning of a line. For example, `^From` will search for `From` starting at the beginning of a line only.
$	Anchors the expression at the end of a line. For example, `tops$` will find `tops` at the end of a line. Note that the `$` specifies location only; the new-line character is not a part of the string. See comments for `^`.
.	Matches any character except a new-line character.
?	Indicates an optional element. That is, the preceding regular-expression element can occur zero times or one time. For example, `tom?e` will find both `toe` and `tome`. Quite a difference!
*	Indicates that the previous element can be repeated zero or more times. It is similar to the `?` except that the `?` is limited to a maximum of one occurrence, while the `*` can appear many times in succession.
+	Works the same as a `*` except that it matches an element if the element occurs one or more times. It is similar to `?`, except that the `?` is limited to a maximum of one occurrence of the element.
[ ]	A class of characters. For example, `to[klmn]e` will find the words `toke`, `tole`, `tome`, and `tone`. Hyphens may be used as shorthand. In the preceding example, `to[k-n]e` would have indicated the same search string. Several ranges can be specified within a set of brackets by simply juxtaposing the ranges. For example, if you were looking through a C program, `0x[0-9a-fA-F]` would find hexadecimal constants. A `^` at the beginning of a range means all characters *except* those specified in the range: `[^0-9]` matches everything that is *not* a digit.
\	An escape character that removes any special significance from the characters previously listed. However, it also leads certain escape sequences such as those in C.

Note also the escape sequences listed in Table 4-4. These can be used freely in regular expressions.

Table 4-4.   Escape sequences for some regular expressions

Escape Sequence	Description
\b	Backspace
\e	ASCII escape character
\f	Form feed
\n	New line
\r	Carriage return
\s	Space
\t	Tab
\DDD	Number (D is a digit) formed by 1–3 octal digits
\xDDD	Number (D is a digit) formed by 2–3 hex digits
\x^C	A control code (C is a character), i.e., ctrl-c.

The strategy in this implementation of grep is to use a brute-force search to detect all instances of a string specified by a regular expression. Rather than slowing down to interpret the regular expression from scratch inside the comparison function, the regular expression is predigested into a **pattern string** that is interpreted by the comparison function. The pattern string is a mixture of regular ASCII characters (whose ASCII values are less than 0x7F) and special characters, or **tokens**, that represent an action of some sort. The tokens, which are listed in Table 4-5, all have values greater than 0x80 and all have symbolic names. (The MT_ prefix in each token refers to *metacharacter token*.) A pattern string without tokens is handled by the comparison function just like a regular comparison: each character in the pattern has to match the character at the equivalent position in the input string.

Table 4-5.   Metacharacters and their corresponding tokens

Metacharacter	Meaning	Token	Token Value
^	Beginning of line	MT_BOL	0x80 | '^'
$	End of line	MT_EOL	0x80 | '$'
[	Start of character class	MT_CCL	0x80 | '['
]	End of character class		
^ (inside a class)	Negates character class, if first character		
*	Kleene closure (matches 0 or more)	MT_CLOSE	0x80 | '*'
+	Positive closure (matches 1 or more)	MT_PCLOSE	0x80 | '+'
?	Optional (matches 0 or 1 occurrences)	MT_OPT	0x80 | '?'

The tokens are handled differently, however. For example, if a MT_ANY token is found in the pattern string, the comparison function will successfully match any character in the input string. When the comparison function finds an MT_PCLOSE token, it advances the pattern pointer to the following token and then looks for one or more repetitions of the following token in the input string.

A regular expression like a.*[0-9]x+$ is represented by the following pattern: 'a' MT_CLOSE MT_ANY MT_CCL <bit_map> MT_PCLOSE 'x' MT_EOL. Note that MT_CLOSE, MT_PCLOSE, and MT_OPT tokens *precede* their operands in the pattern string, while they follow their operands in the input regular expression.

The only token that is not perfectly straightforward is the MT_CCL. This token flags a group of 17 bytes that represent a character class in the pattern string. The first byte is the MT_CCL token, and the following 16 bytes are a bitmap, with each bit in the map corresponding to one ASCII character. Bit 97 represents the presence of an a (which in ASCII has the decimal value of 97), 98 represents a b, and so forth.

The code that translates regular expressions to pattern templates is in Listing 4-5 (*minigrep.c*).

Listing 4-5.   A grep engine that matches regular expressions.

```
/*--- minigrep.c ------------------------- Listing 4-5 --------
 *   Find substrings represented by regular expressions
 *   in some other string or text
 *
 *   #define DRIVER to have a command-line version compiled.
 *------------------------------------------------------------*/

#define DRIVER 1    /* Compile the main driver */

#include <stdio.h>
#include <ctype.h>
#include <stdlib.h>
#include <string.h>

#ifndef max
#define max(a,b) ((a) > (b) ? (a) : (b))
#endif

/*------------------------------------------------------
 * If DEBUG is defined, D(printf("hello");) expands
 * to printf("hello"). If DEBUG isn't defined, D(...)
 * is expanded to an empty string, effectively
 * removing the printf() statement from input
 *----------------------------------------------------*/
```

```
#ifdef DEBUG
#define D(x) x
#else
#define D(x)
#endif

/*--- Metacharacters in the input:  ---*/
#define BOL      '^'      /* start-of-line anchor              */
#define EOL      '$'      /* end-of-line anchor                */
#define ANY      '.'      /* matches any character             */
#define CCL      '['      /* start a character class           */
#define CCLEND   ']'      /* end a character class             */
#define NCCL     '^'      /* negates character class if 1st char */
#define CLOSURE  '*'      /* Kleene closure (matches 0 or more) */
#define PCLOSE   '+'      /* Positive closure (1 or more)      */
#define OPT      '?'      /* Optional closure (0 or 1)         */


/*--- These are the tokens representing metacharacters -------*/

#define    MT_BOL      ( 0x80 | '^' )
#define    MT_EOL      ( 0x80 | '$' )
#define    MT_ANY      ( 0x80 | '.' )
#define    MT_CCL      ( 0x80 | '[' )
#define    MT_OPT      ( 0x80 | '?' )
#define    MT_CLOSE    ( 0x80 | '*' )
#define    MT_PCLOSE   ( 0x80 | '+' )

/*--- pattern strings are unsigned char ---*/
typedef unsigned char pattern;

/* maximum number of pattern elements. Remember that
 * character classes require 17 pattern elements.
 */
#define MAXPAT  128

/*--- need this many bytes for character-class bitmap ---*/
#define MAPSIZE 16

/*  Advance a pointer into the pattern template
 *  to the next pattern element, this is a +1 for
 *  all pattern elements but MT_CCL, where you
 *  to skip past both the MT_CCL character and the
 *  bitmap that follows that character
 */

#define ADVANCE(pat) (pat += (*pat == MT_CCL) ? (MAPSIZE+1) : 1)

/* Bitmap functions. Set bit b in the map and */
/* test bit b to see if it was set previously */
```

```
#define SETBIT(b,map) ( \
         (map)[((b) & 0x7f) >>3] |= (1<< ((b) & 0x07)) )
#define TSTBIT(b,map) ( \
         (map)[((b) & 0x7f) >>3] &  (1<< ((b) & 0x07)) )

#define ISHEXDIGIT(x) isxdigit(x)

#define ISOCTDIGIT(x) ('0'<=(x) && (x)<='7')


/*--- Return values from PatternError() and MakePattern() -----*/
#define E_NONE        0
#define E_ILLEGAL     1
#define E_NOMEM       2
#define E_PAT         3

static int Error = E_NONE;      /*--- error flag, like errno ---*/

/*--- Declare the functions we wiil create and use ------------*/
static  pattern * DoCCL      ( pattern *, unsigned char *);
static  int       DoEscapeSeq( char ** );
static  int       HexToBinary( int );
static  int       MatchOne   ( char **, pattern *, char * );
static  pattern * MakePattern( char * );
extern  char    * MatchString( char *,  pattern *, int );
static  int       OctToBinary( int );
static  char    * PatternCmp ( char *,  pattern *, char * );
extern  int       PatternErr ( void );


/*--- returns current error status ---*/
int PatternErr ( void )
{
    return ( Error );
}


/*------------------------------------------------------------
 *  Make a pattern template from the regular-expression
 *  string pointed to by exp.
 *  Stop when '\0' or '\n' is found in exp.
 *  Return:  a pointer to the pattern template on success, NULL
 *           on failure (in which case, PatternErr()
 *           will return one of the following values:
 *
 *                  E_ILLEGAL       Illegal input pattern.
 *                  E_NOMEM         out of memory
 *                  E_PAT           pattern too long.
 *------------------------------------------------------------*/
static pattern *MakePattern ( char *exp )
```

```
{
    pattern *pat;  /* pattern template being assembled   */
    pattern *cur;  /* pointer to current pattern element */
    pattern *prev; /* pointer to previous pattern element */

    pat   = NULL;
    Error = E_ILLEGAL;
    if( ! *exp || *exp == '\n' )
        return ( pat );

    if( *exp == CLOSURE || *exp == PCLOSE || *exp == OPT )
        return ( pat );

    /* get pattern buffer  */
    Error = E_NOMEM;
    if (( pat = (pattern *) malloc ( MAXPAT )) == NULL )
        return ( pat );

    /* zero the buffer if debugging */
    D( memset ( pat, 0, MAXPAT); )

    prev  = cur = pat;
    Error = E_PAT;

    while ( *exp  &&  *exp != '\n' )
    {
        if ( cur >= &pat[MAXPAT-1] )
        {
            free ( pat );
            return ( NULL );
        }

        switch ( *exp )
        {
            case ANY:
                *cur = MT_ANY;
                prev = cur++;
                ++exp;
                break;

            case BOL:
                *cur = ( cur == pat ) ? MT_BOL : *exp;
                prev = cur++;
                ++exp;
                break;

            case EOL:
```

```
                    *cur = ( !exp[1] || exp[1]=='\n' ) ?
                            MT_EOL : *exp;
                    prev = cur++;
                    ++exp;
                    break;

            case CCL:
                    if ((( cur - pat ) + MAPSIZE ) >= MAXPAT )
                    {
                        /* need more room for bitmap */

                        free ( pat );
                        return ( NULL );
                    }

                    prev   = cur;
                    *cur++ = MT_CCL;
                    exp    = DoCCL ( cur, exp );
                    cur   += MAPSIZE ;
                    break;

        case OPT:
        case CLOSURE:
        case PCLOSE:
                switch ( *prev )
                {
                    case MT_BOL:
                    case MT_EOL:
                    case MT_OPT:
                    case MT_PCLOSE:
                    case MT_CLOSE:
                        free ( pat );
                        return ( NULL );
                }

                memmove ( prev+1, prev, cur-prev );
                *prev = ( *exp == OPT ) ? MT_OPT :
                        ( *exp == PCLOSE ) ? MT_PCLOSE :
                        MT_CLOSE;
                ++cur;
                ++exp;
                break;

        default:
                prev   = cur;
                *cur++ = DoEscapeSeq ( &exp );
                break;
        }
}
```

```
    *cur  = '\0';
    Error = E_NONE;

    return ( pat );
}

/*-------------------------------------------------------------------
 *  Set bits in the map corresponding to characters
 *  specified in the src character class.
 *-----------------------------------------------------------------*/

static pattern *DoCCL ( pattern *map, pattern *src )
{
    int first, last, negative;
    pattern *start = src;

    ++src;                                  /* skip past the [       */
    if( negative = ( *src == NCCL )) /* check for negative CCl*/
        ++src;
    start = src;                 /* start of characters in class */
    memset ( map, 0, MAPSIZE );      /* bitmap initially empty */

    while ( *src && *src != CCLEND )
    {
        if ( *src != '-' )
        {
            /* Use temp variable to avoid macro side effects */

            first = DoEscapeSeq ( &src );
            SETBIT( first, map );
        }
        else
        if ( src == start  )
        {
            SETBIT( '-', map );       /* literal dash at      */
            ++src;                    /* start or end.        */
        }
        else
        {
            ++src;             /* skip to end-of-sequence char */
            if ( *src < src[-2] )
            {
                first = *src;
                last  = src[-2];
            }
            else
            {
                first = src[-2];
```

```
                last  = *src;
            }

            while ( ++first <= last )
                SETBIT( first, map );
            src++;
        }
    }

    if ( *src == CCLEND )
        ++src;                      /* Skip CCLEND */

    if ( negative )
        for ( first = MAPSIZE; --first >= 0 ; )
            *map++ ^= ~0;       /* invert all bits */

    return ( src );
}

/*-----------------------------------------------------------------
 * Uses PatternCmp() to look for a match of pat anywhere in
 * str using a brute-force search. str is a character string
 * while pat is a pattern template made by MakePattern().
 * Returns:
 *     o  NULL if no match was found.
 *     o  A pointer the last character satisfying the match
 *          if ret_endp is true.
 *     o  A pointer to the beginning of the matched string
 *          if ret_endp is false.
 *-----------------------------------------------------------------*/

char *MatchString ( char *str, pattern *pat, int ret_endp )
{
    char  *start;
    char  *end = NULL;

    /*-----------------------------------------------------------------
     * This test lets you do MatchString(str, MakePattern(...),?);
     * without grave consequences if MakePattern() fails.
     *-----------------------------------------------------------------*/

    if ( !pat )
        return NULL;

    if ( !*str )
    {
        if (( *pat == MT_EOL ) ||
            ( *pat == MT_BOL &&
                ( !pat[1] || pat[1] == MT_EOL )))
```

```
                    end = str;
    }
    else
    {
        /*--------------------------------------------------
         * Do a brute-force search for substring, comparing
         * a pattern against the input string.
         *-----------------------------------------------*/
        start = str;
        while ( *str )
        {
            if( !( end = PatternCmp ( str, pat, start )))
                str++;
            else                    /* successful match */
            {
                if ( !ret_endp )
                    end = str ;
                break;
            }
        }
    }
    return ( end );
}


/*------------------------------------------------------------------
 * Like strcmp, but compares str against pat. Each element of
 * str is compared with the template until either a mismatch is
 * found or the end of the template is reached. In the former
 * case, a 0 is returned; in the latter, a pointer into str
 * (pointing to the last character in the matched pattern)
 * is returned. strstart points at the first character in the
 * string, which might not be the same thing as line if the
 * search started in the middle of the string.
 -----------------------------------------------------------*/
static char *PatternCmp ( char *str, pattern *pat, char *start )
{
    char *bocl,     /* beginning of closure string.        */
         *end;      /* return value: end-of-string pointer. */

    if ( !pat )              /* make sure pattern is valid    */
        return ( NULL );

    while ( *pat )
    {
        if ( *pat == MT_OPT )
        {
            /*-------------------------------------------------
             *  Zero or one matches. It doesn't matter if MatchOne
             *  fails---it will advance str past the character on
```

```
    *  success. Always advance the pattern past both
    *  the MT_OPT and the operand.
    *-------------------------------------------------*/

    MatchOne ( &str, ++pat, start );
    ADVANCE ( pat );
}
else
if ( !( *pat == MT_CLOSE || *pat == MT_PCLOSE ))
{
   /*------------------------------------------------
    *  Do a simple match. Note that MatchOne() fails
    *  if there's still something in pat when we are
    *  at end of string.
    *-------------------------------------------------*/

    if ( !MatchOne ( &str, pat, start ))
        return NULL;

    ADVANCE ( pat );
}
else            /* process a Kleene or positive closure */
{
    if ( *pat++ == MT_PCLOSE )   /* one match req'd */
        if ( !MatchOne ( &str, pat, start ))
                return NULL;

    /* Match as many as possible, zero is OK */

    bocl = str;
    while ( *str  && MatchOne ( &str, pat, start ))
        ;

   /*------------------------------------------------
    *  str now points to the character that made
    *  made us fail. Try to process the rest of the
    *  string. If the character following the closure
    *  could have been in the closure (as in the pattern
    *  "[a-z]*t") the final 't' will be sucked up in the
    *  while loop. So, if the match fails, back up a
    *  notch and try to match the rest of the string
    *  again, repeating this process recursively until
    *  we get back to the beginning of the closure. The
    *  recursion goes, at most, one level deep.
    *-------------------------------------------------*/

    if ( *ADVANCE ( pat ))
    {
```

```
                for ( ; bocl <= str; --str )
                    if ( end = PatternCmp( str, pat, start ))
                            break;
                return ( end );
            }
            break;
        }
    }

    /*-------------------------------------------------------------
     *  MatchOne() advances str to point at the next
     *  character to be matched. So str points at the
     *  character following the last character matched
     *  when you reach the end of the template. The
     *  exceptions are templates containing only a
     *  BOLN or EOLN token. In these cases, MatchOne doesn't
     *  advance. Since we must return a pointer to the last
     *  matched character, decrement str to make it point at
     *  the end of the matched string, making sure that the
     *  decrement hasn't gone past the beginning of the string.
     *
     *  Note that $ is a position, not a character, but in the
     *  case of a pattern ^$, a pointer to the end of line
     *  character is returned. In ^xyz$, a pointer to the z
     *  is returned.
     *
     *  The --str is done outside the return statement because
     *  max() is often a macro that has side effects.
     *-------------------------------------------------------------*/

    --str;
    return ( max ( start, str ));
}


/*-------------------------------------------------------------
 *  Match one pattern element, pointed at by pat, against the
 *  character at **strp. Return 0 on a failure, 1 on success.
 *  *strp is advanced to skip over the matched character on a
 *  successful match. Closure is handled one level up by
 *  PatternCmp().
 *
 *  "start" points at the character at the left edge of the
 *  line. This might not be the same thing as *strp if the
 *  search is starting in the middle of the string. Note,
 *  an end-of-line anchor matches '\n' or '\0'.
 *-------------------------------------------------------------*/
static int MatchOne ( char **strp, pattern *pat, char *start )
{
```

```
        /* amount to advance *strp, -1 == error  */
        int advance = -1;

        switch ( *pat )
        {
          case MT_BOL:                    /* First char in string? */
            if ( *strp == start )         /* Only one star here.    */
                advance = 0;
            break;

          case MT_ANY:                    /* . = anything but newline */
            if ( **strp != '\n' )
                advance = 1;
            break;

          case MT_EOL:
            if ( **strp == '\n'  ||  **strp == '\0' )
                advance = 0;
            break;

          case MT_CCL:
            if ( TSTBIT ( **strp, pat + 1 ))
                advance = 1;
            break;

          default:                        /* literal match */
            if ( **strp == *pat )
                advance = 1;
            break;
        }

        if ( advance > 0 )
            *strp += advance;

        return ( advance + 1 );
}

/*------------------------------------------------------------*/
static int HexToBinary ( int c )
{
        /* Convert the hex digit represented by 'c' to an int. 'c'
         * must be one of: 0123456789abcdefABCDEF
         */
        return (isdigit(c) ? (c)-'0': ((toupper(c))-'A')+10)  & 0xf;
}

static int OctToBinary ( int c )
{
```

```
        /* Convert the hex digit represented by 'c' to an int. 'c'
         * must be a digit in the range '0'-'7'.
         */
        return ((( c ) - '0' )  &   0x7 );
}


/*-------------------------------------------------------------
 *  Map escape sequences into their equivalent symbols.
 *  Return the equivalent ASCII character. *s is advanced
 *  past the escape sequence. If no escape sequence is
 *  present, the current character is returned and
 *  the string is advanced by one.
 *
 *  The following escape sequences are recognized:
 *
 *    \b        backspace
 *    \f        formfeed
 *    \n        newline
 *    \r        carriage return
 *    \s        space
 *    \t        tab
 *    \e        ASCII ESC character ('\033')
 *    \DDD      number formed of 1-3 octal digits
 *    \xDDD     number formed of 1-3 hex digits
 *    \^C       C = any letter. Control code
 *-------------------------------------------------------------*/
static int DoEscapeSeq ( char **s )
{
    int rval;

    if ( **s != '\\' )
        rval = * (( *s )++ );
    else
    {
        ++( *s );                      /* Skip the \ */
        switch ( toupper ( **s ))
        {
          case '\0':  rval = '\\';           break;
          case 'B':   rval = '\b' ;          break;
          case 'F':   rval = '\f' ;          break;
          case 'N':   rval = '\n' ;          break;
          case 'R':   rval = '\r' ;          break;
          case 'S':   rval = ' '  ;          break;
          case 'T':   rval = '\t' ;          break;
          case 'E':   rval = '\033';         break;

          case '^':
            rval = *++( *s ) ;
```

```
              rval = toupper ( rval ) - '@' ;
              break;

          case 'X':
            rval = 0;
            ++( *s );
            if ( ISHEXDIGIT ( **s ))
            {
                  rval  = HexToBinary ( *(*s)++ );
            }
            if ( ISHEXDIGIT(**s) )
            {
                  rval <<= 4;
                  rval  |= HexToBinary ( *(*s)++ );
            }
            if ( ISHEXDIGIT(**s) )
            {
                  rval <<= 4;
                  rval  |= HexToBinary ( *(*s)++ );
            }
            --( *s );
            break;

          default:
            if( !ISOCTDIGIT ( **s ))
                  rval = **s;
            else
            {
                  ++ ( *s );
                  rval = OctToBinary ( *(*s)++ );
                  if ( ISOCTDIGIT ( **s ))
                  {
                        rval <<= 3;
                        rval  |= OctToBinary ( *(*s)++ );
                  }
                  if ( ISOCTDIGIT ( **s ))
                  {
                        rval <<= 3;
                        rval  |= OctToBinary ( *(*s)++ );
                  }
                  --( *s );
            }
            break;
        }
        ++ ( *s );
    }
    return rval;
}
```

```
/*-----------------------------------------------------------
 * Driver is compiled so as to make this program a command-line
 * utility. In its absence, you have a grep engine that can be
 * called by other applications using the format below.
 *---------------------------------------------------------*/

#ifdef DRIVER

#include <limits.h>        /* to access CHAR_BIT */

int main ( int argc, char **argv )
{
    static pattern *pat;
    static FILE    *inp;
    static char    inp_buf[ 1024 ];

    /*-----------------------------------------------------
     * This implementation is so dependent on 8-bit bytes
     * that they must be checked for. Since 8-bit bytes are
     * almost universal, this should not hinder portability.
     *-------------------------------------------------*/

    if ( CHAR_BIT != 8 )  /* ANSI-defined as bits in a char */
    {
        fprintf ( stderr, "Error: Requires 8-bit bytes\n" );
        exit ( EXIT_FAILURE );
    }

    if ( argc < 2 || argv[1][0] == '-' )
    {
        fprintf ( stderr,
                     "Usage: minigrep reg_exp filename\n" );
        fprintf ( stderr,
                     "Usage: minigrep reg_exp < filename\n" );
        exit ( EXIT_FAILURE );
    }

    if( !( pat = MakePattern ( argv[1] )))
    {
        fprintf ( stderr, "Can't make expression template\n" );
        exit ( EXIT_FAILURE );
    }

    if ( argc == 2 )
        inp = stdin;
    else
    if( !( inp = fopen ( argv[2], "r" )))
    {
```

```
            perror ( argv[2] );
            exit ( EXIT_FAILURE );
    }

    while ( fgets ( inp_buf, sizeof(inp_buf), inp ))
            if ( MatchString ( inp_buf, pat, 0 ))
                fputs ( inp_buf, stdout );

    return ( EXIT_SUCCESS );
}
#endif
```

The macros at the beginning of the listing define the metacharacters as they appear in the input regular expression. In this manner, they are easy to change if you don't like the UNIX-style regular-expression syntax. Immediately following the macros are the definitions of the tokens used to represent metacharacters in the pattern string. Note that the pattern strings are `typedef`'d to unsigned `char`s. This is required for compilers that default to signed `char`s, since the tokens will have their high bit set. Without this step, sign extension would get in the way every time you looked at the token. The `MAXPAT` macro limits the size of the pattern. (Patterns are `MAXPAT`-element arrays of unsigned `char`.) Patterns are made a fixed length in order to simplify the memory-allocation process. The current default of 128 characters per pattern is a good compromise. Patterns this size are big enough to be useful but do not waste too much memory with unused pattern elements.

The `ADVANCE (p)` macro advances `p` past the current pattern element. This is an increment for everything except character classes, where you have to advance the pointer by the size of the bit map (`MAPSIZE`) plus one more for the `MT_CCL` token. Note that `ADVANCE()` has significant side effects. It also evaluates to the incremented value of `p`, so you can say `*ADVANCE (p)` if you like. Think of it as the equivalent of `*++p`. The bitmaps are manipulated by the `SETBIT()` and `TSTBIT()` macros, defined immediately after `ADVANCE`. The two macros differ only by one operator (`|=`) in `SETBIT()`. The first half of the macro isolates the array element that holds the bit we are interested in. When simplified a little, it looks like this:

```
map[ (b & 0x7F) >>3 ]
```

The `& 0x7F` makes sure that the requested bit number (b) is in range, and the `>>3` is equivalent to an integer divided by eight; there are eight bits per array element. (Our implementation requires an 8-bit byte. Note the test for this in the `main()` driver). The shift is more efficient than division on most compilers, although most optimizers today substitute shifts for divisions where possible. The second half of the macro creates a mask. All bits in the mask will be zero except that a 1-bit will be positioned at the place corresponding to the bit we are looking for. This positioning is accomplished with the following code:

```
1 << (b & 0x07)
```

The b & 0x07 (a more efficient equivalent to b % 8) evaluates to the offset from the beginning of the current array element to bit b. The mask is created by shifting the number 1 to the left by that many bits. A bit is set to 1 by OR'ing the mask into the proper array element. A bit is tested for true (1) with a bitwise AND of the mask and the array element.

With all the preliminaries out of the way, we finally come to the actual code. Patterns are manufactured by the MakePattern function. It returns either the pattern template (which is in malloc()ed memory) or NULL if there was a problem. In the latter case, you can call PatternErr() to find out what went wrong. Possible errors are defined just prior to the code for MakePattern().

The call to memmove() in the case for OPT, CLOSURE, and PCLOSE is the only tricky bit of code in this function. The problem is that in the regular expression the *, ?, and + tokens follow their corresponding expression, while they need to precede their expression in the encoded form. Thus, the previous pattern needs to be shifted one notch to the right so that a MT_CLOSE, MT_PCLOSE, and MT_OPT token can precede their operands. (This makes the comparison function's life a lot easier.) The trick here is to use memmove() rather than memcpy(). Both copy strings, but only memmove() can handle overlapping source and destination strings. The bitmap for a character class is set up by DoCCL(). The next and last case in the big switch statement that makes up MakePattern() handles nonmetacharacters. You do this by calling DoEscapeSeq(). This routine handles both ordinary characters and escape sequences. Note that it is passed a pointer to the string pointer. This allows it to return the ASCII value of the character or escape sequence pointed to by the string pointer as well as to advance the string pointer past that character or escape sequence. Returning to the code that does the actual pattern matching, the highest-level function is this:

```
char *MatchString( char *str, pattern *pat, int ret_endp );
```

It is passed a pointer to a pattern (pat) generated by MakePattern(), a string to search through (str), and a flag (ret_endp for "return endpoint") that tells whether the returned pointer should point to the beginning or to the end of the matched string, if one is found. For example,

```
MatchString ( "1234567890", MakePattern ( "4[0-9]*7" ), 0 );
```

returns a pointer to the 4, and

```
MatchString ( "1234567890", MakePattern ( "4[0-9]*7" ), 1 );
```

returns a pointer to the 7. Note that success status is returned when the pattern string is made up only of BOL or EOL tokens and the input string is either empty or comprised of a single newline. In this case, a pointer to the terminating '\n' or '\0', whichever is leftmost in the string, is returned. This behavior lets you process the expression ^$ correctly. MatchString() returns NULL if it cannot find a match. Note that the function uses a simple brute-force approach.

A final function of interest is char *PatternCmp (char *str, pattern *pat, char *start). It is the actual comparison function. It returns a pointer to the end of the matching substring if there is one. (The beginning of the substring must be pointed to by str, so you do not need to return this value.) The start argument is used only for processing the beginning-of-line anchor (^). Note that at the actual start of the string, str can point anywhere in the string, so it cannot be used for this purpose.

The one curiosity in PatternCmp() is the recursive PatternCmp() call. This call is needed for closure (* and +) processing in order to use a greedy algorithm, which finds the longest string that matches the regular expression. (There is also a nongreedy algorithm that finds the first string that matches the expression, but this algorithm tends not to be as useful in practice.) The problem is exemplified by a search for a substring that matches the expression [a-z]*ed (all words that end in ed) in a string like educated turnips. A nongreedy algorithm would stop at the first ed; a greedy algorithm gets the whole first word. The problem here is that the trailing e and d are legitimate members of the character class [a-z]. Consequently, the closure processing will suck up the ed as it processes the character class. The situation is corrected with the loop that calls PatternCmp(). When the closure-processing is finished (when a character that does not match the operand to the closure operator is found), PatternCmp() tries to match the rest of the input string against the rest of the regular expression with a single recursive call. If this attempt fails, PatternCmp() backs up the end-of-input-string pointer one notch and tries again, continuing in this way until it backs up all the way to the start of the substring that matched the closure. In the current example, the initial closure processing terminates with str pointing at the second d in educated and the pattern pointer (pat) pointing at the e in the pattern. The recursive PatternCmp() call fails, so str is backed up a notch to point at the rightmost e in educated. Since this fails too, the algorithm backs up another notch, and finally succeeds. In this example, bocl points at the first e in educated, and it makes sure that you do not back up past the left edge of the substring.

There is a small driver at the very end of the listing that implements a small grep-like filter. It is used as follows:

```
minigrep  regular-expression [optional-file]
```

Standard input is used if [`optional_file`] is missing; otherwise, input is taken from the file. Only the lines that contain a match of the regular expression passed as the second argument are printed to the output. You can use this program in much the same way that you use the UNIX grep utility or the MS-DOS `find` utility.

Don't be fooled by the simplicity or the theoretical inefficiency of these functions. Their behavior is entirely satisfactory in most situations in which regular expressions are used.

Approximate String-Matching Techniques

All the search techniques presented so far in this chapter are geared to finding exact string matches. Even the grep function specifies a set of permissible strings that have to be matched exactly. Sometimes, however, an application needs to perform searches that are only approximately right. The need arises most often when the exact string to be searched for is unknown, and this problem is the subject of the remaining three algorithms in this chapter. We will first consider a string-searching algorithm where the match needs to be only approximate and the degree of acceptable variation can be specified.

Applications in which close but inexact string matches are needed include comparisons of sequences of amino acids or DNA bases for homology with other sequences. While the following implementation uses text phrases, you will see that the algorithm can be adapted to any type of data.

Consider a pattern, P, and a text to be searched, T. A k-approximate match of P in T will be a substring of T that differs in, at most, k places from P. The differences may be any one of these three types:

1. The corresponding characters in P and T are different.
2. P is missing a character that appears in T.
3. T is missing a character that appears in P.

As an example, take the case in which T is `compiler` and P is `cmpxleer`. P is a 3-approximate match for T:

```
P =  c   m p x l e e r
         |     |     |
T =  c o m p i l e   r
```

The mismatches illustrate the three possible types of differences.

You can locate the k-approximate matches by computing an array of minimum differences between P and T. The formal notation is as follows:

Let P be the string $p[1]\ p[2]\ ...\ p[n]$.
Let T be the string $t[1]\ t[2]\ ...\ t[n]$.

You compute the difference array, $D[i,j]$, as the minimum number of differences between $p[1]\ ...\ p[n]$ and a substring of T ending at $t[j]$. You calculate D by following three rules step by step. These rules consider each of the three possible types of mismatches noted earlier.

$D[i,j]$ is the minimum of the following three values:
1. $D[i-1,j-1] + diff(p[i], t[j])$
       where $diff(p[i], t[j]) = 0$ if $p[i] == t[j]$,
                           $= 1$ otherwise.
2. $D[i-1,j] + 1$
3. $D[i,j-1] + 1$

A k-approximate match will be found at $t[j]$ for any j, such that $D[n,j] <= k$. (Remember that n is the last element of P).

As an example, consider the calculation of D for $P =$ add and $T =$ andadd, as shown in Figure 4-3. The outside row and column are initialized as shown. The top row is all zeros because a zero-length P differs by, at most, zero positions from any T. Steadily larger integers are assigned to the left column because a P of length n must differ in n places from a zero-length T. Now array D is filled in.

```
        a n d a d d
    0 | 0 0 0 0 0 0
-----+--------------
a   1 |
d   2 |
d   3 |
```

Figure 4-3. The initial difference array.

The first value to calculate is $D[1,1]$, for $p[1] =$ a, and $t[1] =$ a. (In this discussion, string indexes, unlike arrays in C, start with 1, not 0.) We consider the three rules and the values of the elements of D that are above, to the left of, and above and to the left of $D[1,1]$:

Rule 1: Since $p[1] == t[1]$, Rule 1's value is $D[0,0] + 0$ or 0.
Rule 2: $D[0,1] + 1 == 0 + 1 == 1$
Rule 3: $D[1,0] + 1 == 1 + 1 == 2$

Taking the minimum of these three values gives $D[i,j]$, as shown in Figure 4-4.

```
        a n d a d d
    0 | 0 0 0 0 0 0
-----+--------------
a   1 | 0
d   2 |
d   3 |
```

Figure 4-4.   The computation of first $D[i,j]$.

It helps to consider this calculation as being based on the three values marked with an x as shown in Figure 4-5.

```
        a n d a d d
    x | x 0 0 0 0 0
-----+--------------
a   x | 0
d   2 |
d   3 |
```

Figure 4-5.   The values used in Figure 4-4.

The calculation then proceeds column by column until the array is filled in, as shown in Figure 4-6.

```
        a n d a d d
    0 | 0 0 0 0 0 0
-----+--------------
a   1 | 0 1 1 0 1 1   <-- Row 1
d   2 | 1 1 1 1 0 1
d   3 | 2 2 1 2 1 0   <-- Row 3
```

Figure 4-6.   The completed difference array.

Row 3 of this array is now examined for k-approximate matches. There are two 1-approximate matches. The first is easy: the substring and differs by one letter from add. The 1 in Row 3 shows the end of the matching substring, while the 0 that is above and to the left in Row 1 shows the beginning of the substring. The second 1-approximate match is more interesting. Once again, the 1 on the bottom row shows the endpoint, while the 0 above and to the left reveals the beginning of the string ad. This substring differs from add by the deletion of a d.

Note also the 0-approximate match. This is the exact match of `add` in `andadd`.

While determining the endpoint of a k-approximate match is easy (you just examine the last row of D), determining the beginning of the matching substring can be tricky. Consider the values for P and T in Figure 4-7. A single 1-approximate match can be seen in Row 4. But scanning up and to the left in Row 1 shows two zeros. Indeed, the strings `ffod` and `fod` are both 1-approximate matches for `food`.

```
          f  f  o  d
      0 | 0  0  0  0
  -----+---------
  f   1 | 0  0  1  1    <-- Row 1
  o   2 | 1  1  0  1
  o   3 | 2  2  1  1
  d   4 | 3  3  2  1    <-- Row 4
```

Figure 4-7. Finding the start of match.

The shortest and least costly method of locating the start of a mismatched substring is to search for the path from the bottom row to the top row. You can best understand the algorithm by thinking of the difference array as a topographic map. The higher the number, the higher the elevation. Imagine a marble at the lower right-hand corner; then gently lift that corner of the array. The marble first rolls from a to b, as shown in Figure 4-8.

```
          f  f  o  d
      0 | 0  0  0  0
  -----+---------
  f   1 | 0  0  1  1    <-- Row 1
  o   2 | 1  1  0  1
  o   3 | 2  2  b  1
  d   4 | 3  3  2  a    <-- Row 4
```

Figure 4-8.   Working backward to find a match.

The marble can now see an even lower level, and so it rolls to c and then to d, as shown in Figure 4-9. Now that the marble has reached the top row, it stops, thus marking the beginning of the matching substring.

```
          f f o d
    0  |  0 0 0 0
  -----+----------
  f  1 |  0 d 1 1   <-- Row 1
  o  2 |  1 1 c 1
  o  3 |  2 2 b 1
  d  4 |  3 3 2 a   <-- Row 4
```

Figure 4-9.   Finding the start of a match.

One simple way to compute the path of the marble is to maintain a separate array of offsets. These offsets are added to the current column location to calculate the beginning of the substring. In technical terms, the offset is calculated for the array $O[i,j]$ for $D[i,j]$ by following these rules:

1. if $D[i-1,j-1] < D[i,j]$ look up and to left
   then $O[i,j] = O[i-1,j-1] - 1$
2. else if $D[i,j-1] < D[i,j]$ look up
   then $O[i,j] = O[i,j-1]$
3. else if $D[i-1,j] < D[i,j]$ look to left
   then $O[i,j] = O[i-1,j] - 1$
4. else, $D[i-1,j-1]$ must equal $D[i,j]$, so
   set $O[i,j] = O[i-1,j-1] - 1$

The beginning of the k-approximate match $D[i,j]$ can then be calculated as follows:

$$\text{Starting column} = j + O[i,j]$$

The preceding calculation can be expanded by putting the offsets in parentheses. We'll start with the array shown in Figure 4-10. The top row of offsets is set to 0 because the marble will always stop when it gets to this row. The left column is set to $+1$ because intuitively any match that ends in this column must begin in the column to the right (although this actually cannot happen). Now start filling in the offsets. Examining the offset marked with an a, we see that the marble at $[2,2]$ would roll straight up. Thus, $O[2,2] = O[1,2]$, or zero.

```
                   f         f         o         d
      0       |  0         0         0         0
  ------------+----------------------------------------
  f  1 (+1)  |  0  (0)    0  (0)    1  (0)    1  (0)
  o  2 (+1)  |  1  (a)    1  (?)    0  (?)    1  (?)
  o  3 (+1)  |  2  (?)    2  (?)    1  (?)    1  (?)
  d  4 (+1)  |  3  (?)    3  (?)    2  (?)    1  (?)
```

Figure 4-10.   Expanding the offsets.

Continuing this calculation, fill in the array as shown in Figure 4-11. It is important to note that each column of offsets can be computed based solely on the column of offsets to the left and the two related columns of the difference array.

```
              f         f         o         d
    0      |  0         0         0         0
-----------+------------------------------------
f   1 (+1) |  0 (0)    0  (0)    1  (0)    1  (0)
o   2 (+1) |  1 (0)    1 (-1)    0 (-1)    1 (-2)
o   3 (+1) |  2 (0)    2 (-1)    1 (-1)    1 (-2)
d   4 (+1) |  3 (0)    3 (-1)    2 (-1)    1 (-2)
```

Figure 4-11. Completed offsets.

The code in *approx.c* (Listing 4-6) shows you how this algorithm is implemented. To conserve memory, the code does not compute and save the entire array *D*. Instead, since the values in any given column depend only on the column immediately to the left, only these two columns are kept in memory. This same technique is also used to maintain the data in the offset array.

You invoke the code by first initializing its data areas with a call to `AppInit()` and then repeatedly calling `AppNext()`. The test driver and comments demonstrate the syntax of these functions.

Listing 4-6. Approximate string matching.

```c
/*--- approx.c --------------------------- Listing 4-6 -------
 *
 * Approximate string search
 *
 * Usage:
 *   approx pattern text-to-search degree-of-approximation
 *
 *   if DRIVER is #defined, a test driver is compiled
 *-----------------------------------------------------------*/

#define DRIVER 1

#include <stdio.h>
#include <stdlib.h>
#include <string.h>

/* local, static data */

static char *Text, *Pattern;/* pointers to search strings      */
```

```
static int Textloc;         /* current search position in Text */
static int Plen;            /* length of Pattern               */
static int Degree;          /* max degree of allowed mismatch  */
static int *Ldiff, *Rdiff;  /* dynamic difference arrays        */
static int *Loff,  *Roff;   /* used to calculate start of match*/

void AppInit ( char *pattern, char *text, int degree )
{
    int i;

    /* save parameters */
    Text    = text;
    Pattern = pattern;
    Degree  = degree;

    /* initialize */

    Plen    = strlen ( pattern );
    Ldiff   = (int *) malloc ( sizeof(int) * ( Plen + 1 ) * 4 );
    Rdiff   = Ldiff + Plen + 1;
    Loff    = Rdiff + Plen + 1;
    Roff    = Loff +  Plen + 1;
    for ( i = 0; i <= Plen; i++ )
    {
        Rdiff[i] = i;   /* initial values for right column */
        Roff[i]  = 1;
    }

    Textloc = -1; /* current offset into Text */
}

void AppNext ( char **start, char **end, int *howclose )
{
    int *temp, a, b, c, i;

    *start = NULL;
    while ( *start == NULL )  /* start computing columns    */
    {
        if ( Text[++Textloc] == '\0' ) /* no more text      */
            break;

        temp    = Rdiff;  /* move right column to left    */
        Rdiff   = Ldiff;  /*  so that we can compute new  */
        Ldiff   = temp;   /*  right-hand column.          */
        Rdiff[0] = 0;      /* top (boundary) row           */

        temp    = Roff;    /* and swap offset arrays, too */
        Roff    = Loff;
        Loff    = temp;
```

```
Roff[1]  = 0;

for ( i = 0; i < Plen; i++ )  /* run thru pattern  */
{
    /* compute a, b, & c as the 3 adjacent cells...*/
    if ( Pattern[i] == Text[Textloc] )
        a = Ldiff[i];
    else
        a = Ldiff[i] + 1;
    b = Ldiff[i+1] + 1;
    c = Rdiff[i] + 1;

    /* ... now pick minimum ... */
    if ( b < a )
        a = b;
    if ( c < a )
        a = c;

    /* ... and store */
    Rdiff[i+1] = a;
}
/*-------------------------------------------------------
 *  Now update offset array:
 *  the values in the offset arrays are added to the
 *  current location to determine the beginning of the
 *  mismatched substring. See text for details.
 *-----------------------------------------------------*/

if ( Plen > 1 )
    for ( i = 2; i <= Plen; i++ )
    {
        if ( Ldiff[i-1] < Rdiff[i] )
            Roff[i] = Loff[i-1] - 1;
        else
        if ( Rdiff[i-1] < Rdiff[i] )
            Roff[i] = Roff[i-1];
        else
        if ( Ldiff[i] < Rdiff[i] )
            Roff[i] = Loff[i] - 1;
        else    /* Ldiff[i-1] == Rdiff[i] */
            Roff[i] = Loff[i-1] - 1;
    }

  /* now, do we have an approximate match? */

if ( Rdiff[Plen] <= Degree )  /* indeed so! */
{
    *end     = Text + Textloc;
    *start   = *end + Roff[Plen];
```

```
                *howclose = Rdiff[Plen];
            }
        }

    if ( start == NULL ) /* all done: free dynamic arrays */
        free ( Ldiff );
}

#ifdef DRIVER

int main ( int argc, char *argv[] )
{
    char *begin, *end;
    int howclose;

    if ( argc != 4 )
    {
        fprintf ( stderr,
                    "Usage is: approx pattern text degree\n" );
        return ( EXIT_FAILURE );
    }

    AppInit ( argv[1], argv[2], atoi ( argv[3] ));
    AppNext ( &begin, &end, &howclose );

    while ( begin != NULL )
    {
        printf ( "Degree %d: %.*s\n",
                    howclose, end-begin + 1, begin );
        AppNext ( &begin, &end, &howclose );
    }

    return ( EXIT_SUCCESS );
}
#endif
```

The basic algorithm can be modified in several ways. One useful change allows it to recognize the special case of transposition of adjacent characters. You can do this by adding a fourth case to the list of values from which to choose a minimum:

$$D[i-2, j-2] + diff(p[i-1], t[j]) + diff(p[i], t[j-1]) + 1$$

Another possible modification gives different weights to different errors. For example, the weight attached to the difference between a and p can be large, while the weight for the difference between m and n can be made small. This favors finding mismatches that represent simple keyboard mishaps.

Phonetic Comparisons: Soundex

Searching through databases for a person's name by using surnames works only if you know exactly how the name is spelled. Suppose, however, that you are running an airline reservation system and you need to look up names when the exact spelling is unknown. What you would need is a method of encoding names based on their pronunciation—in other words, a phonetic key to search on. A search would then deliver entries bearing similar-sounding names; Dickson and Dixon, for example, would be found on the same search, you would hope.

M. K. Odell and R. C. Russell applied for two patents (one in 1918, the other in 1922) for a system to encode surnames so that names that sound alike would have the same code. The system, called **Soundex**, became widely used. It is based on a concept familiar to linguists and speed writers: that English words and names can be distinguished based on the consonants alone. Note, for example, the last few words of this sentence when represented by consonants alone: *th lst fw wrds f ths sntnc whn rprsntd b cnsnnts alne*. The meaning is clear, even though the spelling looks a little strange.

Soundex reads a name and assigns one of seven values to the incoming letters, as shown in Table 4-6. Letters that will be dropped are assigned a value of 0. These include all vowels and all silent consonants.

Table 4-6. Soundex codes assigned to various letters

Incoming Letters	Value
A E I O U H W Y	0
BFPV	1
CGJKQSXZ	2
DT	3
L	4
MN	5
R	6

After all letters are assigned their respective digits, the zeros are removed and runs of the same digit are reduced to one digit (effectively removing double consonants and repetitions of the same consonant group). The first three remaining digits are used in the code. If fewer than three digits remain, the code is padded with spaces (although a few implementations pad with zeros). The Soundex code consists of the first letter of the word or name being coded, followed by the three digits of code. In this manner, `Lincoln` is converted to `L524`.

When we use Soundex, the names `Dickson` and `Dixon` have the same code: `D25`. `Smith`, `Smyth`, and `Smythe` would also share a common Soundex code. The Soundex method is effective for the database retrieval of names. It will often pick up excess names that are vaguely similar to the search name, but it tends not to skip names that it should find. It also has the advantage of being fast and of creating compact codes. It suffers from the drawback that the first letter of the search name must be known exactly. As a hashing algorithm, Soundex produces, at most, 8918 codes that tend to group around pronunciations.

The attached program, *soundex.c* (Listing 4-7) implements the algorithm as described. The main routine, `Soundex()`, accepts a pointer to a string, which it then traverses, performing the encoding as it goes down the string. A second pointer, `SoundexOut`, shows where the Soundex code should be copied. Notice that `Soundex()` returns an integer: an error code if an invalid input string was encountered, or a 1 if the encoding was performed correctly.

Listing 4-7.   An implementation of the Soundex phonetic search.

```
/*--- soundex.c --------------------------- Listing 4-7 -------
*    Will generate the soundex code for a name or word.
*
*    Usage: int Soundex ( char *name, char *soundex_code )
*
*    if DRIVER is #defined a driver routine is compiled.
*-----------------------------------------------------------*/

#include <ctype.h>
#include <string.h>

#define DRIVER 1

int Soundex ( const char *str, char *soundex_out )
{

#define SOUNDEX_ERR 0
#define SOUNDEX_OK   1

    static const char table[] =

      /* ABCDEFGHIJKLMNOPQRSTUVWXYZ */
        "01230120022455012623010202";

    int count = 0;               /* Valid code letters done */
    char this_char, prev_char;   /* Current and previous    */
    char code [5];               /* will hold Soundex code  */
```

```c
    strcpy ( code, "    " );        /* Initialize string       */

    this_char = toupper ( *str );   /* The first character is  */
    if ( isalpha ( this_char ))     /* preserved albeit as     */
    {                               /* uppercase.              */
        code[0] = this_char;
        count = 1;
        str += 1;
    }
    else
        return ( SOUNDEX_ERR );

    prev_char = ' ';                /* previous char empty now */

    while ( count < 4 && isalpha ( *str ))
    {
        char c;

        this_char = toupper ( *str );
        c = table[this_char - 'A'];

        /*-------------------------------------------------------
         *  Remove 0's and repeated sequences from output
         *  and then insert the next character into the string.
         *------------------------------------------------------*/

        if ( c != prev_char && c != '0' )
        {
            code[count++] = c;
            prev_char = c;
        }
        str += 1;
    }

    /* Next, if it's neither '/0' or a letter, it's an error */

    if ( *str != '\0' && ! ( isalpha( *str )))
        return ( SOUNDEX_ERR );
    else
    {
        strcpy ( soundex_out, code );
        return ( SOUNDEX_OK );
    }
}

#ifdef DRIVER          /* Driver to demo soundex results */

#include <stdio.h>
```

```
#include <stdlib.h>

int main ( int argc, char *argv[] )
{
    char code[5];

    if ( argc != 2 )
    {
        fprintf ( stderr,
                    "Error! Usage: soundex word-to-code\n" );
        return ( EXIT_FAILURE );
    }

    if ( Soundex ( argv[1], code) == 0 )
        printf ("%s is not a valid name or word\n", argv[1] );
    else
        printf ( "Soundex for %s is %s\n", argv[1], code );

    return ( EXIT_SUCCESS );
}
#endif
```

Soundex is used in many databases and in many cataloguing systems. This fact should discourage the reader from changing the algorithm. It is undoubtedly imperfect, but to maintain compatibility with systems that use the Soundex codes, you need to use the presented method without changes. Occasions may arise, however, in which it is not necessary to maintain compatibility with other systems. You can use one of two approaches: The first is to tinker with Soundex, in the hope of improving it, by either narrowing or widening the field of possible matches. A presentation of this approach appears in [Celko89]. A more systematic approach is to come up with a wholly new, and more comprehensive, method of generating Soundex-like codes. Such a system can be found in Metaphone.

Metaphone: A Modern Soundex

Rather than simply coding letters based on their approximate sound, Metaphone uses a series of rules to transform one sound into another. Unlike Soundex, it does not restrict itself to consonants, but rather examines groups of letters known as **diphthongs**.

Metaphone removes nonalphabetic characters from the search key and converts the remaining letters to uppercase as shown in Table 4-7. It then discards all vowels, unless the word begins with a vowel, in which case the vowel is retained. The remaining consonants are mapped to their Metaphone code, with two additions: the letter X represents the "sh" sound, and the digit 0 represents the "th" sound. If any of the consonants except C are doubled, the second consonant is removed. Table 4-7 shows the transformations.

Table 4-7. Transformations performed by Metaphone

From	To
GN- KN- PN-	N
AE-	E
WH-	H
WR-	R
X-	S
B	B (unless in -MB)
C	X if in -CIA-, -CH-
	else S if in -CI-, -CE-, -CY-
	else dropped if in -SCI-, SCE-, -SCY-
	else K
D	J if in -DGE-, -DGI-, or -DGY-
	else T
G	F if in -GH and not B--GH, D--GH, -H--GH, -H---GH
	else dropped if -GNED, -GN, -DGE-, -DGI-, or -DGY-
	else J if in -GE-, -GI, -GY, and not GG
	else K
H	H if before a vowel and not after C, G, P, S, T
K	dropped if after C, else K
P	F if before H, else P
Q	K
S	X in -SIO- or -SIA-, else S
T	X in -TIA- or -TIO-
	else O before H
	else T
V	F
W	W after a vowel, else dropped
X	KS
Y	Y unless followed by a vowel
Z	S
F, J, L, M, N, R	never transformed

As you can readily see, Metaphone performs much more specific transformations on words than does Soundex. You will notice that the transformations very closely fit the way English is spoken. For example, B is left alone unless it appears as part of the -MB combination at the end of a word (such as *bomb* or *comb*), where it is silent. The sequence PH is compressed into an F (meaning that *haphazard* will not be correctly found—but how specific can you make the rules without creating a dictionary of all words?). Q is converted into K in all cases (recall that the U that invariably succeeds Q has already been removed), which rightly results in a match for *cake* and *quake* or *kick* and *quick,* and so forth. Soundex, unlike Metaphone, cannot handle the possibility of special cases at all. It converts PH into a P sound, which is then lumped with all B and V sounds. The result of Metaphone's greater specificity is that Metaphone tends to be more accurate than Soundex in its searches, since the words are better encoded. Listing 4-8 (*metaphon.c*) shows how the rules from Table 4-7 are implemented.

Listing 4-8.   Metaphone, a more accurate phonetic search.

```
/*--- metaphon.c ----------------------- Listing 4-8 ---------
*
* Usage: the calling function must pass three arguments:
*
*     char *word      - the word to be converted to a 'metaph'
*     char *result    - a MAXMETAPH+1 byte field for the result
*     int  flag       - a flag
*
* If flag is 1, then a code will be computed for word and
* stored in result. If flag is 0, then the function will compute
* a code for word and compare it with the code passed in
* result. It will return 0 for a match, else -1. The function
* will also return -1 if word is 0 bytes long.
*-----------------------------------------------------------*/

#define DRIVER 1

#include <ctype.h>

#define MAXMETAPH  4

int Metaphone ( const char *, char *, int );

/* Character coding array */
static char codes[26] =  {
   1,16,4,16,9,2,4,16,9,2,0,2,2,2,1,4,0,2,4,4,1,0,0,0,8,0
/* A  B C  D E F G  H I J K L M N O P Q R S T U V W X Y Z*/
   };

/*--- Macros to access character coding array ------------*/
```

```c
#define ISVOWEL(x)  (codes[(x) - 'A'] & 1)      /* AEIOU */

    /* Following letters are not changed */
#define NOCHANGE(x) (codes[(x) - 'A'] & 2)       /* FJLMNR */

    /* These form diphthongs when preceding H */
#define AFFECTH(x) (codes[(x) - 'A'] & 4)       /* CGPST */

    /* These make C and G soft */
#define MAKESOFT(x) (codes[(x) - 'A'] & 8)       /* EIY */

    /* These prevent GH from becoming F */
#define NOGHTOF(x)  (codes[(x) - 'A'] & 16)      /* BDH */

int Metaphone ( const char *word, char *result, int flag )
{
    char *n, *n_start, *n_end; /* pointers to string */
    char *metaph, *metaph_end; /* pointers to metaph */
    char ntrans[32];           /* word with uppercase letters */
    char newm[8];              /* new metaph for comparison */
    int  KSflag;               /* state flag for X to KS */

    /*---------------------------------------------------------
     *  Copy word to internal buffer, dropping non-alphabetic
     *  characters and converting to uppercase.
     *---------------------------------------------------------*/

    for ( n = ntrans + 1, n_end = ntrans + 30;
          *word && n < n_end; word++ )
            if ( isalpha ( *word ))
                *n++ = toupper ( *word );

    if ( n == ntrans + 1 )   /* return if 0 bytes */
        return -1;
    n_end = n;               /* set n_end to end of string */

    /* ntrans[0] will always be == 0 */
    *n++ = 0; *n = 0;        /* pad with nulls */
    n = ntrans + 1;          /* assign pointer to start */

    /* if doing a comparison, redirect pointers */
    if ( !flag )
    {
        metaph = result;
        result = newm;
    }
```

```
/*-----------------------------------------------------------
 *  check for all prefixes:
 *          PN KN GN AE WR WH and X at start.
 *-------------------------------------------------------*/

switch ( *n )
{
    case 'P':
    case 'K':
    case 'G':
        if ( *( n + 1 ) == 'N')
            *n++ = 0;
        break;

    case 'A':
        if ( *( n + 1 ) == 'E')
            *n++ = 0;
        break;
    case 'W':
        if ( *( n + 1 ) == 'R' )
            *n++ = 0;
        else
        if ( *(n + 1) == 'H')
        {
            *( n + 1 ) = *n;
            *n++ = 0;
        }
        break;
    case 'X':
        *n = 'S';
        break;
}

/*-----------------------------------------------------------
 *  Now, loop step through string, stopping at end of string
 *  or when the computed metaph is MAXMETAPH characters long
 *-------------------------------------------------------*/

KSflag = 0; /* state flag for KS translation */

for ( metaph_end = result + MAXMETAPH, n_start = n;
      n <= n_end && result < metaph_end; n++ )
{

    if ( KSflag )
    {
        KSflag = 0;
        *result++ = *n;
    }
```

```
else
{
    /* drop duplicates except for CC */
    if ( *( n - 1 ) == *n && *n != 'C' )
        continue;

    /* check for F J L M N R or first letter vowel */
    if ( NOCHANGE ( *n ) ||
            ( n == n_start && ISVOWEL ( *n )))
        *result++ = *n;
    else
    switch ( *n )
    {
    case 'B':          /* check for -MB */
        if ( n < n_end || *( n - 1 ) != 'M' )
            *result++ = *n;
        break;

    case 'C':    /* C = X ("sh" sound) in CH and CIA */
                 /*   = S in CE CI and CY            */
                 /*      dropped in SCI SCE SCY      */
                 /* else K                           */
        if ( *( n - 1 ) != 'S' ||
            !MAKESOFT ( *( n + 1 )))
        {
            if ( *( n + 1 ) == 'I' && *( n + 2 ) == 'A' )
                *result++ = 'X';
            else
            if ( MAKESOFT ( *( n + 1 )))
                *result++ = 'S';
            else
            if ( *( n + 1 ) == 'H' )
                *result++ = (( n == n_start &&
                            !ISVOWEL ( *( n + 2 ))) ||
                                *( n - 1 ) == 'S' ) ?
                                (char)'K' : (char)'X';
            else
                *result++ = 'K';
        }
        break;

    case 'D':  /* J before DGE, DGI, DGY, else T */
        *result++ =
            ( *( n + 1 ) == 'G' &&
                MAKESOFT ( *( n + 2 ))) ?
                    (char)'J' : (char)'T';
        break;
```

```
case 'G':   /* complicated, see table in text */
    if (( *( n + 1 ) != 'H' || ISVOWEL ( *( n + 2 )))
        && (
            *( n + 1 ) != 'N' ||
            (
                (n + 1) < n_end  &&
                (
                    *( n + 2 ) != 'E' ||
                    *( n + 3 ) != 'D'
                )
            )
        )
        && (
            *( n - 1 ) != 'D' ||
            !MAKESOFT ( *( n + 1 ))
            )
        )
            *result++ =
                ( MAKESOFT ( *( n  + 1 )) &&
                *( n + 2 ) != 'G' ) ?
                        (char)'J' : (char)'K';
    else
    if( *( n + 1 ) == 'H'    &&
        !NOGHTOF( *( n - 3 )) &&
        *( n - 4 ) != 'H')
            *result++ = 'F';
    break;

case 'H':   /* H if before a vowel and not after */
            /* C, G, P, S, T */
    if ( !AFFECTH ( *( n - 1 )) &&
        ( !ISVOWEL ( *( n - 1 )) ||
        ISVOWEL ( *( n + 1 ))))
                *result++ = 'H';
    break;

case 'K':    /* K = K, except dropped after C */
    if ( *( n - 1 ) != 'C')
        *result++ = 'K';
    break;

case 'P':     /* PH = F, else P = P */
    *result++ = *( n +  1 ) == 'H'
            ? (char)'F' : (char)'P';
    break;
case 'Q':   /* Q = K (U after Q is already gone */
    *result++ = 'K';
    break;
```

```
case 'S':   /* SH, SIO, SIA = X ("sh" sound) */
    *result++ = ( *( n + 1 ) == 'H' ||
                  ( *(n  + 1) == 'I' &&
                    ( *( n + 2 ) == 'O' ||
                      *( n + 2 ) == 'A'))) ?
                        (char)'X' : (char)'S';
    break;

case 'T':  /* TIO, TIA = X ("sh" sound) */
           /* TH = 0, ("th" sound ) */
    if( *( n  + 1 ) == 'I' && ( *( n + 2 ) == 'O'
       || *( n + 2 ) == 'A') )
          *result++ = 'X';
    else
    if ( *( n + 1 ) == 'H' )
        *result++ = '0';
    else
    if ( *( n + 1) != 'C' || *( n + 2 ) != 'H')
        *result++ = 'T';
    break;

case 'V':     /* V = F */
    *result++ = 'F';
    break;

case 'W':     /* only exist if a vowel follows */
case 'Y':
        if ( ISVOWEL ( *( n + 1 )))
            *result++ = *n;
    break;

case 'X':     /* X = KS, except at start */
    if ( n == n_start )
        *result++ = 'S';
    else
    {
        *result++ = 'K'; /* insert K, then S */
        KSflag = 1; /* this flag will cause S to be
                inserted on next pass thru loop */
    }
    break;

case 'Z':
    *result++ = 'S';
    break;
}
}
```

```
                 /* compare new metaph with old */
                 if ( !flag && *( result - 1 ) !=
                         metaph[( result - newm ) - 1] )
                     return -1;
         }

         /* If comparing, check that metaphs were equal length */
         if ( !flag && metaph[result - newm] )
             return -1;

         *result = 0; /* null-terminate return value */
         return 0;
     }

#ifdef DRIVER    /* compile a driver to demo routine */

#include <stdio.h>
#include <stdlib.h>

main ( int argc, char *argv[] )
{
     char coded_word [MAXMETAPH+1];

     if ( argc != 2 )
     {
         fprintf ( stderr, "Usage: METAPHON word-to-be-coded\n" );
         return ( EXIT_FAILURE );
     }

     if ( Metaphone ( argv[1], coded_word, 1 ) == -1 )
     {
         fprintf ( stderr, "Invalid word/name to be coded\n" );
         return ( EXIT_FAILURE );
     }
     else
         printf ( "Metaphone for %s is %s\n",
                         argv[1], coded_word );

     return ( EXIT_SUCCESS );
}
#endif
```

As with Soundex, the goal in using Metaphone is to generate a short code that reflects the pronunciation of the word being searched for (the search key). This code is MAXMETAPH characters in length (default is 4). The length should balance two factors: how much space can be afforded and how narrow (precise) the match should be. The longer the code, the fewer candidate matches will be found. Depending on how wide you want the field of possibilities to be, this can be either a benefit or a drawback. If you begin a search with a name that you're very unsure how to spell, you'll want a wide search field, and therefore you'll find a long Metaphone code to be a hindrance. The reverse is true when spelling is likely to be correct. An optimal length for most purposes seems to be four or five characters. The algorithm works until it has reached the end of the search key or has generated a code MAXMETAPH characters long.

The list of consonant transformations is by no means comprehensive. It can easily be expanded and refined, at the cost of adding overhead to the Metaphone process. As improvements are made, small increments in accuracy will occur. It is important to think carefully before you make changes: you might provide for a small subset of exceptions while accidentally excluding a far larger group of words you failed to consider. Several extensions can be made safely. For example, names (and the few words) that start with X are generally pronounced with a leading Z sound. Metaphone translates all Zs to S, so a safe translation might be to check for a leading X and convert it to S in all instances. The changes and the tweaking can go on ad infinitum, each time adding slightly to processing time.

A word of caution should be sounded, however. If you use the Metaphone code as a database field, it is critical that you do not change the Metaphone algorithm once you have settled on a formulation you like. For example, if you have a list of customers that you frequently search by name, you might want to add a field for the Metaphone code. In this way a search needs to look for a match only on this field, rather than compute the Metaphone for each customer. If you then change the Metaphone algorithm even slightly, you will miss exact matches that you would have found previously. If you must change the Metaphone algorithm at that point, you need to recompute it everywhere it is saved.

Choosing a Technique

This chapter has surveyed a wide variety of techniques to search and compare strings. Many techniques are appropriate only for specific situations; others, such as brute-force and Boyer-Moore, can be used anytime a string search must be performed. An interesting aspect of the algorithms presented in this chapter is how many rely on the brute-force search. This fact testifies to the acceptable speed of an optimized brute search. However, where the exact search string is known, Boyer-Moore will almost always outperform brute-force approaches.

This does not mean that every string-search routine should be replaced with Boyer-Moore. Consider the following:

1. Boyer-Moore has a high setup time. If the text isn't long enough, you may not be able to recover the time you spent in the setup routine.

2. If the search pattern is short, Boyer-Moore's tricks lose their punch; the largest possible jump is limited by the length of the pattern. (Remember that, as shown in Table 4-1, if `PatLen == 1`, then the typical case running times for the three routines become similar.) Smit (1982) shows that for patterns of length 2 or 3, Boyer-Moore could easily be slower than either of the other techniques [Smit 1982].

3. Boyer-Moore's performance degrades when the alphabet is small, because a small alphabet means that most characters are likely to appear at least once in the search pattern; thus `CharJump` will not be able to take such large leaps. A typical example of a small alphabet is one that is used for searching DNA sequences. Here there are only four "letters," and any realistic search pattern would very likely include all four. One possible solution to this problem is to compound adjacent letters to produce a larger alphabet. For example, adjacent DNA "letters" can be compounded into sets of double "letters," thus producing a sixteen-letter alphabet.

4. Boyer-Moore needs to be able to back up through the text and scan some characters multiple times. While this may be acceptable for operations in which all the data is in memory, the added buffering complexities for testing a stream of data might outweigh the other advantages of the algorithm.

5. Finally, keep in mind that the actual performance of a specific implementation is the true test. Even the best algorithm can be implemented poorly or can run poorly due to external constraints. The analysis in Table 4-2 looks at "time proportional to n," but it does not (and cannot) give the proportionality constant.

Even with these caveats, if you are searching a large text for a lengthy pattern, and the text uses a large alphabet, then the Boyer-Moore technique is usually the best.

Resources and References

General Reference

Baase, Sara. *Computer Algorithms*. Reading, MA: Addison-Wesley, 1988. This is a general reference work on algorithms, with good explanations of searching—especially with Boyer-Moore and approximate string-matching techniques.

Boyer-Moore

Apostolico, A., and R. Giancarlo. "The Boyer-Moore-Galil String Searching Strategies Revisited." *Siam J Comput*, Vol. 15, pp. 98–105, 1986. This paper and Galil's paper address the issue of improving the worst-case performance of Boyer-Moore.

Boyer, R. S., and J. S. Moore. "A Fast String Searching Algorithm." *Communications of the ACM*, Vol. 20, pp. 762–772, 1977. This is the original. The development of the `MatchJump` table was subsequently improved by Knuth and Rytter.

Galil, Z. "On Improving the Worst Case Running Time of the Boyer-Moore String Matching Algorithm." *Communications of the ACM*, Vol. 22, pp. 505–508, 1979. See the comment on Apostolico.

Knuth, Donald E., J. H. Morris, and V. R. Pratt. "Fast Pattern Matching in Strings." *Siam J Comput*, Vol. 6, pp. 323–350, 1977. This is the original Knuth-Morris-Pratt paper. It includes a detailed discussion of Boyer-Moore and an improved `MatchJump` algorithm.

Rytter, W. "A Correct Preprocessing Algorithm for Boyer-Moore String Scarching." *Siam J Computing*, Vol. 9, pp. 509–512, 1980. This paper explains how to fix a bug in the `MatchJump` algorithm.

Smit, G. de V. "A Comparison of Three String Matching Algorithms." *Software-Practice and Experience*, Vol. 12, pp. 57–66, 1982. This paper presents an interesting comparison of KMP, Boyer-Moore, and the brute-force techniques. It fixes yet another subtle bug in the `MatchJump` algorithm. The code presented in Listing 4-3 in this chapter is based on the pseudocode presented in this paper.

Multiple-String Searching

Aho, Alfred V., and M. J. Corasick. "Efficient String Matching: An Aid to Bibliographic Search." *Communication of the ACM*, Vol. 18, pp. 333–340, 1975.

Purdum, Jack. "Pattern Matching Alternatives: Theory vs. Practice." *Computer Language*, Vol. 4, No. II, pp. 34–44, 1987.

Regular Expression Searching

Holub, Allen. "GREP: Searching for Regular Expressions." *C Gazette*, Vol. 5, No. 1 (Autumn) 1990. The code presented is a substantial rewrite of this excellent article. Several search patterns can be OR'd together by **egrep**, a utility in which grep has been extended. This utility allows you to search against one pattern of wildcards or against another in the same search. For information on how to process patterns in this form, consult Chapter 2 of Holub's excellent book *Compiler Design in C* (Englewood Cliffs, NJ: Prentice Hall, 1990). The chapter contains a definitive discussion of the state tables needed for such a search. The book, incidentally, is considered by many (including the authors of *this* book) to be the finest book written on the subject of compiler construction.

Approximate String-Matching

Hall, P., and G. Dowling. "Approximate String Matching." *ACM Computing Surveys*, Vol. 12, pp. 381–402, 1980. This paper, along with Baase's book, provides an excellent introduction to approximate string-matching.

Soundex and Metaphone

Celko, Joe. "Optimized Soundex." *C Gazette*, Vol. 4, No. 2, pp. 29–32, 1989.

Parker, Gary. "A Better Phonetic Search." *C Gazette*, Vol. 5, No. 4 (June/July), 1990. The code presented in this chapter is based on the public-domain C version presented in this article. That version was adapted and expanded from the original Metaphone algorithm by Lawrence Philips in *Computer Language* (Vol. 7, No. 12 [December], 1990). Philips's version was written in Pick BASIC.

Chapter 5

Sorting

Sorting is an important aspect of many applications. While ANSI C's qsort() is a basic workable sorting tool, it suffers from several potential problems. First, it sorts only an array of items. While the definition of qsort() is flexible enough to allow it to sort an array of structures or an array of pointers to structures, it cannot be used directly to sort linked lists. Second, as usually implemented, qsort() is not an inherently stable sort (see the next section if you are unfamiliar with the term *stable*). Finally, as usually implemented, qsort()'s performance may depend strongly on the data it is given to sort; a naive implementation can be seriously tripped by asking it to sort an already sorted list.

Despite these flaws, qsort() is generally an excellent choice because your compiler library's version will be well tested, easy to use, and usually very quick. Before considering any of the alternatives discussed in this chapter, you should give qsort() serious consideration. This chapter discusses the potential failings of the Quicksort algorithm that usually underlies qsort() in sufficient detail for you to decide how well behaved your local implementation is and whether it would be satisfactory for your particular problem. Before you can do that, however, you must consider some basic properties of all sorting algorithms.

The Basic Characteristics of Sorts

All sorts work by reordering records (or pointers to those records) based on a key contained within each record. The key is usually a single data item within the record, although you may also create the key by looking at several data

173

items within the record. As the key is the only part of the record used during a sort, the discussions in this chapter often refer to the key as if it were the record. Beyond the fact that all records have a key, however, sorts differ in almost every detail.

Stability

A **stable** sort is one that maintains preexisting order in the records being sorted. For example, if you have a list of transactions sorted by transaction date, a stable second sort by customer number would keep each customer's records sorted by transaction date. This is often an important property for a sort, but one that tends to be present only in simple sorts and tends to be lost by more sophisticated implementations. It is possible to make an unstable sort correctly sort a list of transactions by customer and by date—we could sort once, using a single key that is created by compounding the customer number and the transaction date—but such an approach is not always convenient. We will consider both stable and unstable sorts.

The Need for Sentinels

Some sorts are cumbersome to implement unless dummy records containing two special keys known as **sentinels** are provided. These two sentinel keys are sometimes represented as $-\infty$ and ∞ and are guaranteed to be respectively less than and greater than any keys in the records to be sorted. Providing such sentinel values is often inconvenient and may not even be possible. While it is usually feasible to replace a sentinel with some form of record counting, this imposes extra overhead on the sort. Other than in simple examples, we will not consider sorts that require sentinels.

The Ability to Sort a Linked List

While nearly all sorting algorithms are designed for use on an array of objects (or pointers to objects), some sorting algorithms are easily adapted to sorting linked lists; others are not. If your data is best handled as a linked list, converting it to an array solely to sort it is cumbersome. We will consider two sorts that work well for linked lists.

The Dependence of Order on Input

Sorting algorithms vary dramatically in their order or $O()$, with orders ranging from N to N^2. An additional problem with estimating the order of a sort is that the order may depend on the data being sorted. For example, some sorts have an order that varies from N on forward-sorted records (records that are already in ascending order) to N^2 on reverse-sorted records (records that are in descending order). Other sorts are fastest on random-ordered records and slowest on records that are already in order. The optimal situation is to have a sort with an order near N for all types of input. We will study examples of sorts with all these types of behaviors.

The Need for Additional Storage Space

Some sorts require additional temporary storage for one or more of the records being sorted. While requiring space equal in size to one record is common and is easily accommodated, requirements for more space may be difficult to meet, and we will not consider any sorts that require more than a trivial amount of extra storage space. A type of extra space that may not be immediately apparent is the requirement for stack space by sorts that are implemented recursively. While we will consider one such sort (Quicksort), our final implementations of this algorithm will make use of a technique that dramatically reduces stack requirements to levels that are met easily.

Internal versus External Sorting Techniques

An additional consideration is **internal** versus **external** sorting. In an internal sort, all records to be sorted can be loaded into main memory at one time. An external sort is the opposite situation: a portion of the records will always reside on a mass storage device during the sort. While the implementation details differ, the basic strategy of all external sorts is the same. The data to be sorted is divided into chunks that are small enough to fit into main memory, and these chunks are sorted one at a time with an internal technique. The chunks are then merged to produce the final sorted output. The major problem with external sorts has historically been not the technical details of merging the records but rather a more prosaic difficulty. The data were often stored on slow tape drives, and it was difficult to avoid spending more time rewinding the tapes than was spent reading and writing the data. With the increasing availability of large amounts of RAM and of operating systems that can provide additional memory by means of virtual-memory mechanisms, external sorts should not be needed often. When large amounts of data do need to be sorted, loading the data into a b-tree (see next chapter) is often an excellent solution. Therefore, we will not discuss external sorts in this book.

A Sorting Model

We will develop several kinds of sorts in this chapter, but all of them will share certain basic features. First, most of our sorting routines will sort an array of pointers to the following simple structure:

```
typedef struct sElement {
    char *text;
} Element;
```

The structure itself could be filled with any variety of items, but for our purposes we will use the single item `text`. Each structure will be a record to be sorted, and `text` will be both the record's data and its key.

We would define a 100-element array of these structures as

```
Element *array[100];
```

and, because we are programming in C, efficient programming requires that we use the C convention of numbering the *n* elements of such an array from 0 to *n*-1. If you study sorts described in other references, be aware that the elements of *n*-membered arrays are often numbered instead from 1 to *n*. Any conversion to C requires you to carefully adjust the algorithm to account for this change.

To further generalize our sort routines, we will always pass the sorting routine the address of a comparison routine that takes as its arguments pointers to two structures. The comparison routine must return a negative value if the first argument is "less" than the second, a zero if the two are equal, and a positive value if the first argument is "greater" than the second. This behavior is identical to that of the `strcmp()` function, and we will actually use `strcmp()` as the comparison function in our test routines.

Support routines that will allow us to test the behavior of the various array-oriented sorts in a consistent way are provided in *sortsub.c* (Listing 5-1), *sortsub.h* (Listing 5-2), and *sorthdr.h* (Listing 5-3). *sortsub.c* and *sortsub.h* collectively provide access to routines that can load and display an array of data items. The data are loaded from a simple text file, one data item to a line. The third file, *sorthdr.h*, provides a `typedef` for the structures that are to be sorted; it also provides a prototype for the comparison function that must be passed to each sort routine. The prototype, shown here, is a bit tricky:

```
typedef int (*CompFunc) ( void *, void * );
```

The code states that a `CompFunc` is a pointer to a function that takes two pointers to `void` for arguments and returns an `int`. Thus, the following is a valid comparison function:

```
int CFunc ( Element *L, Element *R )
{
    return ( strcmp ( L->text, R->text ));
}
```

Note that the real function takes pointers to two real structures as its arguments, not pointers to void. However, as the compiler will allow us to interchange pointers to void with pointers to real objects, the use of pointers to void in the typedef allows us to use the same typedef for all our comparison functions.

Listing 5-1. The code for *sortsub.c*.

```
/*--- sortsub.c ------------------------- Listing 5-1 ---------
 * I/O subroutines for sorting routines
 *
 * Note: Loads data into an array
 *-----------------------------------------------------------*/

#include <stdio.h>
#include <stdlib.h>
#include <string.h>
#include <ctype.h>
#include "sorthdr.h"
#include "sortsub.h"

#define MAX_ITEM_SIZE 500 /* maximum length of a text item */

/*-----------------------------------------------------------
 * Load up to MaxItems text strings from FileName into an array
 * of pointers to the text strings. Returns number of items
 * in array or -1 for failure.
 *-----------------------------------------------------------*/

int LoadArray ( char *FileName,
                int MaxItems,
                Element ***Array)
{
    FILE *infile;
    char buffer[MAX_ITEM_SIZE], *s;
    int i;

    if (( infile = fopen ( FileName, "r" )) == NULL )
    {
        fprintf ( stderr, "Can't open file %s\n", FileName );
        return ( -1 );
    }
```

```
*Array =
    (Element **) malloc ( sizeof(Element **) * MaxItems );

if ( *Array == NULL )
{
    fprintf ( stderr, "Can't allocate array of pointers\n" );
    return ( -1 );
}

i = 0;
while ( fgets ( buffer, MAX_ITEM_SIZE, infile ))
{
    if ( i >= MaxItems )   /* limit on # of items */
    {
        printf ( "Entire data file not loaded\n" );
        break;
    }

    /* trim trailing control characters */
    s = buffer + strlen ( buffer );
    while( iscntrl ( *s ))
        *s-- = 0;

    /* make space and store it */
    ( *Array )[i] = malloc ( sizeof ( Element ));
    if (( *Array )[i] == NULL )
    {
        fprintf ( stderr, "Can't get memory for data\n" );
        return ( -1 );
    }

    ( *Array )[i]->text = malloc ( strlen ( buffer ) + 1 );
    if (( *Array )[i]->text == NULL )
    {
        fprintf ( stderr, "Can't get memory for data\n" );
        return ( -1 );
    }
    strcpy (( *Array )[i++]->text, buffer );
}

/*
 * Special case: if the array contains only 1 item, and
 * the item is an empty string, return an empty array.
 */
if ( i == 1 && *(( *Array )[0]->text ) == 0 )
    i = 0;

fclose ( infile );
```

```
        return ( i );
}

/*--- Display array of items ---*/
void ShowArray ( Element **Array, int Items, CompFunc Compare )
{
    int i, sorted = 1, column = 1;

    for ( i = 0; i < Items; i++ )
    {
        if ( column > 61 )
        {
            printf ( "\n" );
            column = 1;
        }
        else  while (( column - 1 ) % 20 )
        {
            printf ( " " );
            column += 1;
        }
        printf ( "%3d: %s", i, Array[i]->text );
        column += 5 + strlen ( Array[i]->text );

        if ( i > 0 )
        {
            if ( Compare(Array[i-1], Array[i]) > 0 )
                sorted = 0;
        }
    }

    if ( sorted )
        printf ( "\n\nThe array is sorted.\n" );
    else
        printf ( "\n\nThe array is not sorted.\n" );
}
```

Listing 5-2. The code for _sortsub.h_.

```
/*--- sortsub.h -------------------------- Listing 5-2 ------
 * Prototypes of functions in sortsub.c
 *----------------------------------------------------------*/

int LoadArray ( char *FileName, int MaxItems, Element ***Array );
void ShowArray ( Element **Array, int Items, CompFunc Compare );
```

Listing 5-3.   The code for *sorthdr.h*.

```
/*--- sorthdr.h ------------------------- Listing 5-3 -------
 * General definitions for array-oriented sort routines
 *--------------------------------------------------------*/


/*----------------------------------------------------------
 * We sort an array of pointers to this structure. The
 * structure could contain anything you'd like: you only
 * need to define appropriate comparison functions.
 *--------------------------------------------------------*/

typedef struct sElement {
    char *text;
}
    Element;


/*----------------------------------------------------------
 * A type for the comparison function: a symbol with
 * type CompFunc is a pointer to a function that takes
 * two pointers to void and returns an int.
 *--------------------------------------------------------*/

typedef int (*CompFunc) ( void *, void * );
```

While many different sorts have been proposed, we will limit ourselves to the five sorts listed in Table 5-1. (Note that a sixth sort—one that is quite different—is not listed in this table. It is discussed at the end of the chapter). This group of sorts was chosen because it provides a broad range of techniques ranging from the simple to the sophisticated. While Quicksort is probably the most useful and popular of these five, each sort has points in its favor and is worthy of study. Finally, we will also modify two of the sorts (insertion sort and Quicksort) to sort linked lists. If none of these sorts is exactly what you're looking for, the tree algorithms described in Chapter 6 can also be viewed as sorting algorithms. To use them as a sort, simply load your data into the tree and then traverse it—sorted output will be produced.

Table 5-1. **Basic sort characteristics**

Name	Order	Stable?	Notes
Array Sorts			
Bubble sort	N^2	Yes	Worst on reverse-ordered records but linear on almost sorted records.
Insertion sort	N^2	Yes	Worst on reverse-ordered records, but linear on almost sorted records.
Shellsort	$N^{1.25}$	No	Order is largely insensitive to initial record order.
Quicksort	$N \lg N$	No	Worst case is N^2, but with careful programming this would be very rare.
Heapsort	$N \lg N$	No	Worst case is same as average case. Despite having the same order, Heapsort is slower than Quicksort.
Linked-List Sorts			
Insertion sort	N^2	Yes	Worst on almost sorted records and best on reverse-ordered records.
Quicksort	$N \lg N$	Varies	

Bubble Sort

The bubble sort is one of the first sorts many of us learn. Its great virtue is its simplicity. If for some reason `qsort()` is unavailable and you need a small sort that can be programmed quickly, bubble sort is an option. It is very fast on nearly sorted files, but its general performance is relatively poor. Thus we will study it mainly as a paradigm for the other sorts, not because it has performance characteristics that make it suitable for application programs.

The bubble sort algorithm is very simple: successive sweeps are made through the records to be sorted, and on each sweep the largest record is moved closer to the top, rising slowly like a bubble—hence the name. Because each sweep places one record into its final and correct position, the next sweep need not re-examine this record. The pseudocode for bubble sorting an array of *n* records is as follows:

```
for limit = n - 1 to 1 begin
    for i = 0 to limit begin
        if array[i] > array[i+1] then
            swap array[i] and array[i+1]
    end
end
```

An analysis of the order of this algorithm is straightforward: it makes *n* passes through the records, and on each pass it performs *n*-1 comparisons and possibly this number of swaps. Thus, the algorithm's running time will be proportional to $n(n-1)$, or more simply just n^2.

The bubble sort is implemented in *bubble.c* (Listing 5-4). The code takes advantage of the fact that if no swaps are made on any given pass, the records are sorted and the sort can terminate. This routine also shows the usage of the support routines discussed earlier. If the constant DRIVER is #defined, a test driver along with a simple comparison function are also compiled. This test driver uses LoadArray() from *sortsub.c* to read a file of items to be sorted and then uses ShowArray() to display the results. The prototype of the actual sort function is this:

```
void BubbleSort(Element **Array, int N, CompFunc Compare);
```

That is, the sort routine is passed a pointer to an array of pointers, a count, and a pointer to a comparison function. All of our array-oriented sort routines will make use of this interface.

Listing 5-4.   The code for a bubble sort.

```
/*--- bubble.c --------------------------- Listing 5-4 ---------
 * Bubble sort an array
 *
 * #define DRIVER to compile a test driver
 * Driver must be linked to sortsub.c (Listing 5-1).
 *-------------------------------------------------------------*/

#include "sorthdr.h"

#define DRIVER 1

void BubbleSort ( Element **Array, int N, CompFunc Compare )
{
    int limit;

    /* Make steadily shorter passes ... */
    for ( limit = N - 1; limit > 0; limit-- )
    {
        int j, swapped;

        /* On each pass, sweep largest element to end of array */
        swapped = 0;
        for ( j = 0; j < limit; j++ )
        {
```

```
                    if ( Compare ( Array[j], Array[j+1] ) > 0 )
                    {
                        Element *temp;

                        temp = Array[j];
                        Array[j] = Array[j+1];
                        Array[j+1] = temp;
                        swapped = 1;
                    }
                }

            if ( !swapped )
                break; /* if no swaps, we have finished */
        }
}


#ifdef DRIVER
#include <stdio.h>
#include <string.h>
#include <stdlib.h>
#include "sortsub.h"

/*
 * A comparison function
 */
int Cfunc ( Element *L, Element *R )
{
    return ( strncmp ( L->text, R->text, 5 ));
}

void main(int argc, char *argv[] )
{
    Element **Array;
    int Items = 2000;

    if ( argc != 2 && argc != 3 )
    {
        fprintf ( stderr, "Usage: bubble infile [maxitems]\n" );
        return;
    }

    if ( argc == 3 )
        Items = atoi ( argv[2] );

    if (( Items = LoadArray ( argv[1], Items, &Array )) == -1 )
        return; /* Couldn't load file */

    BubbleSort ( Array, Items, (CompFunc) Cfunc );
    ShowArray ( Array, Items, (CompFunc) Cfunc );
}
#endif
```

The comparison function used in the bubble sort is also used in the other sorts in this chapter. Note that it uses `strncmp()` to examine only the first five characters of each record's `text` field. This limited examination of the data allows you to test each sort for stability. For example, let's say you created an input file that contains these records:

```
00002 Am
00001 Unique key
00002 I
00002 stable?
00003 Another unique key
```

A stable sort would keep the records with the key `00002` in order, while an unstable sort might shuffle them. (Note that it only *might* shuffle them. Do not conclude on the basis of a single test that a sort is stable or unstable. It is really necessary to either analyze the algorithm carefully or test it thoroughly before concluding that a sort is stable. Alternatively, you can refer to Table 5-1, shown earlier.)

As Table 5-2 shows, this algorithm is sensitive to the data it is given to sort. If the records are already in order, the algorithm is very quick and has an

Table 5-2.   The behavior of sort routines

Sort Routine	Execution Time[1]	No. of Comparisons	No. of Swaps	Notes
Array Sorts				
bubble.c (Bubble sort)				
Forward[2]	14	999	0	Does $N(N-1)/2$
Reverse[3]	6,541	499,500	499,500	comparisons and swaps on
Random[4]	6,143	500,000	500,000	reverse-ordered records
insert.c (Insertion sort)				
Forward	18	99	500	Two moves counted as
Reverse	5,938	499,500	250,250	one swap, ignoring the
Random	2,766	250,000	125,000	move to `temp`
shell.c (Shellsort)				
Forward	95	4,821	4,821	Counted swaps as for
Reverse	159	9,894	5,406	*insert.c*
Random	204	14,000	7,300	
quick1.c (Basic Quicksort)				Stack Depth
Forward	5,988	501,497	999	1000
Reverse	6,044	501,498	999	1000
Random	163	12,500	2,400	23

Table 5-2. The behavior of sort routines *(continued)*

Sort Routine	Execution Time[1]	No. of Comparisons	No. of Swaps	Notes
quick2.c (Quicksort with median-of-three partitioning and insertion sort on small groups of records)				Stack Depth
Forward	108	8,133	754	26
Reverse	175	13,149	2,226	20
Random	141	11,000	3,100	17
quick3.c (*quick2.c* with removal of tail recursion)				Stack Depth
Forward	106	8,133	754	8
Reverse	172	13,149	2,226	8
Random	139	11,000	3,100	6
quick4.c (*quick3.c* with random pivot and pointers)				Stack Depth
Forward	133	10,900	840	6
Reverse	154	12,500	1,900	6
Random	127	11,000	3,100	6
heap.c				
Forward	178	10,379	8,925	
Reverse	189	10,769	9,791	
Random	171	10,308	8,929	
Linked-List Sorts				
linsert.c (Insertion sort for linked lists)				
Forward	5,686	499,500	1,000	
Reverse	15	999	1,000	
Random	2,700	250,000	1,000	
lquick1.c (Quicksort for linked lists using insertion sort on small groups of records, and tail-recursion removal)				Stack Depth
Forward	6,216	499,500	499,500	1
Reverse	6,340	499,500	499,500	2
Random	147	12,000	12,000	4
lquick2.c (Like *lquick1.c*, but uses random pivot selection)				Stack Depth
Forward	153	11,045	9,853	6
Reverse	134	9,531	9,853	6
Random	150	11,000	11,000	6

Note: For these tests, all programs were compiled by using the Borland C++ compiler with optimizations enabled. The timing data was collected on the sort routine alone; the time required to load the data and display the results is not included.

[1] Arbitrary time units.

[2] 1,000 forward-ordered records were sorted.

[3] 1,000 reverse-ordered records were sorted.

[4] Data are the average results from sorting five sets of 1,000 random-ordered records.

order proportional to n. With both reverse-ordered records and random-ordered records, however, the algorithm is miserably slow. As noted earlier, the bubble sort's only advantage is its simplicity.

The behavior of each routine presented in this chapter has been measured in several ways. First, the raw execution speed of the routine has been measured with the use of a profiler. While the absolute values of these timings will be reproduced only on an identical machine, a comparison of the relative values may be helpful. It is possible however, that the relative ranking by speed could vary slightly in other situations. These sample routines use a relatively simple comparison function, and they all sort an array of pointers to structures. If a more complex comparison function were required, the time cost to do the comparisons would rise. Alternatively, while swapping two pointers is very quick, other applications might well need to sort arrays of structures instead, and swapping multibyte structures will obviously take longer than swapping pointers. Thus, the comparison table also reports the numbers of comparisons and swaps that the routine performed while sorting test datasets of 1,000 records. While the faster algorithms always have lower numbers of both comparisons and swaps, you might want to consider the relative time costs of these two actions with respect to your particular situation.

Insertion Sort

An insertion sort works the way a bridge player might proceed in sorting a hand: as each successive card is picked up, it is inserted into the correct position relative to the cards that were previously picked up. To see this procedure in action, consider the problem of sorting the five letters shown in Table 5-3. The first is C, and inserting it into the sorted pile is easy. On subsequent passes the A is inserted in front of the C, the B between the A and the C, and so on.

Table 5-3. **An insertion sort**

Pass	Sorted Pile	Unsorted Pile
0		C A B E D
1	C	A B E D
2	A C	B E D
3	A B C	E D
4	A B C E	D
5	A B C D E	

Implementing an insertion sort is almost as simple as implementing a bubble sort. There is, however, one important design point to consider: as you pick up each new record and prepare to insert it into its place among the sorted records, do you look through the sorted records from first to last, or vice versa? This seemingly small decision has a large impact on the performance, and the correct answer really depends on the typical ordering of the unsorted records. First, suppose that the list of unsorted records would often be in reverse (or almost reverse) order, such as (E, D, C, B, A). As each successive record is examined, its value would usually be smaller than most of the records in the sorted pile. In this case, we could minimize our work by searching the sorted pile from first to last. However, if we expected the unsorted records to be typically in order (or almost in order), the value in each successive record from the unsorted pile would be expected to be *larger* than most of the other records. In this case our work will be minimized if we search the sorted pile from last to first. If there are no other constraints on our choice, the usual approach is to assume that if the records have any order at all, they would be (almost) in order. Thus, the algorithm should search the sorted pile from last to first as it tries to insert each successive record. Here is the pseudocode:

```
for step = 1 to N begin
    temp = array[step]
    for i = step - 1 to 0 begin
        if array[i] > temp then
            array[i+1] = array[i]
        else
            break
    end
    array[i+1] = temp
end
```

Note the way in which the pseudocode creates a "hole" in the sorted portion of the array by copying one element into a temporary storage element. This hole is then moved backward through the sorted records until the correct spot is found. At that point, the inner loop terminates and the new record is inserted into the hole.

The actual implementation of this algorithm is in *insert.c* (Listing 5-5). It is almost identical to the pseudocode. Estimating the order of this algorithm is relatively easy. Very loosely, an insertion sort makes one pass through the data for each record of input, but on each of these n passes we would expect to search backward through half of the sorted records in order to find the position for the new record. In the worst case, we would expect to search backward through all the records. In either case, the running time is proportional to $n^2/2$

or just n^2. This quadratic behavior is similar to the behavior predicted for bubble sort, and the data in Table 5-2 confirms these predictions where the two algorithms can be seen to have similar running times for reverse-ordered and random-ordered records. Insertion sort is generally faster, however. This is because it uses both fewer swaps and fewer comparisons than bubble sort uses. The use of fewer swaps is easier to see: bubble sort does a complete exchange at each step as it "bubbles" the largest record to the top, whereas insertion sort does what could be called "half exchanges" as it moves the hole through the sorted records. Insertion sort gets away with half as many comparisons because it typically looks through only half of the sorted records while inserting a new records. Bubble sort, in contrast, always bubbles the largest record all the way to the top on each pass. Thus, while neither is a speed demon in the average case, insertion sort does have the edge.

Listing 5-5.   The code for an insertion sort.

```
/*--- insert.c -------------------------- Listing 5-5 ---------
 * Insertion sort of an array
 *
 * #define DRIVER to compile a test driver
 * Driver must be linked to sortsub.c (Listing 5-1)
 *-------------------------------------------------------------*/

#include "sorthdr.h"

void InsertionSort ( Element **Array, int N, CompFunc Compare )
{
    int step;

    /* Look at 2nd thru Nth elements, putting each in place */
    for (step = 1; step < N; step++)
    {
        int i;
        Element *temp;

        /* Now, look to the left and find our spot */
        temp = Array[step];
        for ( i = step - 1; i >= 0; i-- )
        {
            if ( Compare(Array[i], temp ) > 0 )
            {
                /* Not there yet, so make room */
                Array[i+1] = Array[i];
            }
            else /* Found it! */
                break;
```

```
        }
        /* Now insert original value from Array[step] */
        Array[i+1] = temp;


    }
}

#ifdef DRIVER
#include <stdio.h>
#include <string.h>
#include <stdlib.h>
#include "sortsub.h"

/*
 * A comparison function
 */
int Cfunc ( Element *L, Element *R )
{
    return ( strncmp ( L->text, R->text, 5 ));
}

void main ( int argc, char *argv[] )
{
    Element **Array;
    int Items = 2000;

    if ( argc != 2 && argc != 3 )
    {
        fprintf ( stderr, "Usage: insert infile [maxitems]\n" );
        return;
    }

    if ( argc == 3 )
        Items = atoi ( argv[2] );

    if (( Items = LoadArray ( argv[1], Items, &Array )) == -1 )
        return; /* Couldn't load file */

    InsertionSort ( Array, Items, (CompFunc) Cfunc );
    ShowArray ( Array, Items, (CompFunc) Cfunc );
}
#endif
```

It's interesting that insertion sort, like bubble sort, runs in linear or near-linear time on records that are almost sorted. This important fact will be used to our advantage later when optimizing Quicksort.

The Shellsort

Shellsort is a clever variation of insertion sort. It starts with the observation that the reason insertion sort is slow is that it moves through the sorted pile one item at a time. Thus, records that are far from their final location will be correctly positioned only after many swaps. What is needed is a way to allow records to jump large distances during the early phases of sorting. Shellsort's solution to this problem is shown in Table 5-4.

Table 5-4. Shellsort in action

0: Items to be sorted E	F	B	G	H	D	C	A
1: Consider the items as			G				A
four pairs of two.		B				C	
	F				D		
E				H			
2: Sorting each pair gives E	D	B	A	H	F	C	G
this order.							
3: Now consider them as	D		A		F		G
two sets of four. E		B		H		C	
4: Sorting each set gives B	A	C	D	E	F	H	G
this order.							
5: Finally, sort as one set A	B	C	D	E	F	G	H
of eight items.							

The basic idea is simple: the records are subdivided into *interleaved* groups, and each group is sorted with the use of the now-familiar insertion sort. In this example, there are eight records to be sorted. First, they are subdivided into four interleaved pairs, and each pair is sorted. Then the records are subdivided into two interleaved sets of four records and again sorted. Finally, the entire set of records is sorted.

To see why this method is an improvement over plain insertion sort, consider the movement of record A. While it starts off completely out of place, it jumps half the distance to its ultimate position on each of the first two passes, arriving at its goal after only three swaps.

This repeated subdivision into interleaved sets of records by selecting every hth record is referred to as "h-sorting," and a Shellsort can be described in terms of the sequence of h's that it uses. For example, the records in Table 5-4 were h-sorted using values of 4, 2, and then 1 for h. The key to making Shellsort work is that any steadily decreasing sequence of h's can be used, as long as the last value of h is 1. Indeed, when h is 1, what we have is just a plain insertion sort. This last insertion sort pass gets everything into final order; all the previous passes have had the single goal of producing an "almost" sorted file that the last pass can sort in linear time.

The selection of an appropriate sequence of values of h has been the subject of a substantial amount of work. However, despite this work, the "best" sequence is not known. The implementation of Shellsort shown in Listing 5-6 (*shell.c*) uses the following scheme to determine a sequence of values of h:

> Let $h_1 = 1$ and n = number of records to sort
> Let $h_{s+1} = 3h_s + 1$, stopping when $h > n / 9$

This simple calculation produces a sequence of values of h that are well behaved. Both slightly better and much worse sequences can be generated by other methods. (See "Resources" at the end of this chapter for more details on methods of determining values of h.)

Listing 5-6. The code for a shellsort.

```
/*--- shell.c --------------------------- Listing 5-6 ---------
 * Shell's sort on an array
 *
 * #define DRIVER to compile a test driver
 * Driver must be linked to sortsub.c (Listing 5-1)
 *-----------------------------------------------------------*/

#include "sorthdr.h"

#define DRIVER 1

void ShellSort ( Element **Array, int N, CompFunc Compare )
{
    int step, h;

    /* Find starting h */
    for ( h = 1; h <= N / 9; h = 3*h + 1 )
                ;

    /* Now loop thru successively smaller h's */
    for ( ; h > 0; h /= 3 )
    {
        /* Look at hth thru Nth elements */
        for ( step = h; step < N; step++ )
        {
            int i;
            Element *temp;
```

```
                    /* Now, look to the left and find our spot */
                    temp = Array[step];
                    for ( i = step - h; i >= 0; i -= h )
                    {
                        if ( Compare ( temp, Array[i] ) < 0 )
                        {
                            /* Not there yet, so make room */
                            Array[i + h] = Array[i];
                        }
                        else /* Found it! */
                            break;
                    }
                    /* Now insert original value from Array[step] */
                    Array[i + h] = temp;
                }
            }
        }

#ifdef DRIVER
#include <stdio.h>
#include <string.h>
#include <stdlib.h>
#include "sortsub.h"
/*
 * A comparison function
 */
int Cfunc ( Element *L, Element *R )
{
    return ( strncmp ( L->text, R->text, 5 ));
}

void main ( int argc, char *argv[] )
{
    Element **Array;
    int Items = 2000;

    if ( argc != 2 && argc != 3 )
    {
        fprintf ( stderr, "Usage: shell infile [maxitems]\n" );
        return;
    }

    if ( argc == 3 )
        Items = atoi ( argv[2] );

    if (( Items = LoadArray ( argv[1], Items, &Array )) == -1 )
        return; /* Couldn't load file */
```

```
        ShellSort ( Array, Items, (CompFunc) Cfunc );
        ShowArray ( Array, Items, (CompFunc) Cfunc );
}
#endif
```

Analyzing the performance of this algorithm has proven tricky and is dependent on the sequences of h's that is chosen. Implementations that use the sequence of values of h that were discussed previously appear to have an order of roughly $N^{1.25}$. A demonstration that this algorithm is dramatically better than insertion sort is found in Table 5-2. While Shellsort does not have the blazing speed of insertion sort or bubble sort on already sorted records, it also does not suffer any significant speed degradation when presented with reverse-ordered or random-ordered records. Indeed, Shellsort's running time is comparatively insensitive to the input data. The only negative feature of Shellsort is that it is not a stable sort (see Table 5-1). Taken together, however, these features make it an excellent choice in almost any situation, and it should be one of the first sorts you consider.

Quicksort

Due to its favorable $N \lg N$ order, Quicksort is undoubtedly the most widely used advanced sorting algorithm. Even the ANSI C library sorting function, `qsort()`, has a name suggesting Quicksort. (Note that while `qsort()` is often based on Quicksort, nothing in the definition of ANSI C requires that it be implemented with Quicksort.) Quicksort, however, is somewhat tricky to implement correctly, and it is easy to create versions that behave badly under unusual circumstances. For these reasons we will study several variants of Quicksort. The discussion of these variants will give you enough information to test your compiler library's version of `qsort()` for implementation weaknesses that could seriously affect the performance of your applications.

Quicksort takes a "divide and conquer" approach to the records to be sorted. At each step of the sort, the records are divided into two partitions. This division is made on the basis of a record known as the **pivot**. All records that are less than the pivot go into one partition while all records that are greater than the pivot go into the other partition. Records that are equal to the pivot may go into either partition. By allowing records equal to the pivot to go into either partition, Quicksort minimizes degenerate behavior that is due to data sets containing many records with equal keys. Quicksort then recursively Quicksorts the two partitions. Here is some very loose pseudocode:

```
Quicksort (array A) begin
     If A has only one element, return.
     Choose an element, Array[i], as the pivot.
Create two subarrays, A1 and A2. Place elements <
     Array[i] into A1, elements > Array[i] into A2,
     and those equal to Array[i] into either A1 or
     A2. At the conclusion of this step, the array A
     contains the elements of A1, Array[i], and the
     elements of A2, in that order.
Quicksort (A1).
Quicksort (A2).
end
```

While this looks easy enough, the trick to implementing it in a useful fashion is to (1) select the pivot properly and (2) construct the subarrays `A1` and `A2` within the memory allocated to `A` itself, thus obviating the need for any extra storage. To see a basic example of how this can be done, examine *quick1.c* (Listing 5-7). Starting with the test driver, we see that it passes the array to be sorted along with a comparison function to the very short routine `Quicksort1()`. This interface routine is used to minimize stack-space requirements. Its only purpose is to store the addresses of the array and the comparison function into the `static` variables `StoredArray` and `StoredCompare` and then call `xQuickSort1()`, the actual sort routine. If this were not done, these addresses would have to be passed recursively during execution of the sort, thus slowing execution. The only down side to this approach is that these implementations are not reentrant. That is, if this code is used in a multitasking environment where only one copy of the executable code for this routine *and its static data* are loaded into main memory, simultaneous calls to this routine by different tasks will interfere with each other. If this is a concern, eliminate the `static` variables and pass the addresses of the array and the comparison function on each call to `xQuickSort1()`.

Listing 5-7.   The code for a basic Quicksort.

```
/*--- quick1.c -------------------------- Listing 5-7 ---------
 * A basic quicksort
 *
 * #define DRIVER to compile a test driver
 * Driver must be linked to sortsub.c (Listing 5-1)
 *-----------------------------------------------------------*/

#include "sorthdr.h"

#define DRIVER 1

static CompFunc StoredCompare;
```

```
static Element **StoredArray;

static void xQuickSort1 ( int L, int R )
{
    if ( R > L )
    {
        int i, j;
        Element *temp;

        /* First, partition the array using array[R] as pivot */
        i = L - 1; /* Scan up from here   */
        j = R;     /* Scan down from here */
        for ( ;; )
        {
            /*
             * Looking from left, find element >= Array[R].
             * No sentinel needed, as Array[R] will stop us.
             */
            while ( StoredCompare ( StoredArray[++i],
                                    StoredArray[R] ) < 0 )
                            ;

            /*
             * Looking from right, find element <= Array[R].
             * The loop provides boundary checking.
             */
            while ( j > 0 )
            {
                if ( StoredCompare ( StoredArray[--j],
                                     StoredArray[R]) <= 0 )
                    break;
            }

            if ( i >= j )
                break;

            /* swap ith and jth elements */
            temp = StoredArray[i];
            StoredArray[i] = StoredArray[j];
            StoredArray[j] = temp;
        }

        /* swap ith and Rth elements */
        temp = StoredArray[i];
        StoredArray[i] = StoredArray[R];
        StoredArray[R] = temp;
        xQuickSort1 ( L, i-1 );
```

```
            xQuickSort1 ( i+1, R );
        }
    }

    void QuickSort1 ( Element **Array, int Items, CompFunc Compare )
    {
        StoredCompare = Compare;
        StoredArray = Array;
        xQuickSort1 ( 0, Items - 1 );
    }

    #ifdef DRIVER
    #include <stdio.h>
    #include <string.h>
    #include <stdlib.h>
    #include "sortsub.h"

    /*
     * A comparison function
     */
    int Cfunc ( Element *L, Element *R )
    {
        return ( strncmp ( L->text, R->text, 5 ));
    }

    void main ( int argc, char *argv[] )
    {
        Element **Array;
        int Items = 2000;

        if ( argc != 2 && argc != 3 )
        {
            fprintf ( stderr, "Usage: quick1 infile [maxitems]\n" );
            return;
        }

        if ( argc == 3 )
            Items = atoi ( argv[2] );

        if (( Items = LoadArray ( argv[1], Items, &Array )) == -1 )
            return; /* Couldn't load file */

        QuickSort1 ( Array, Items, (CompFunc) Cfunc );
        ShowArray ( Array, Items, (CompFunc) Cfunc );
    }
    #endif
```

All the actual work is done in `xQuickSort1()`. It is passed two parameters, `L` and `R`, which are the first and last elements of the subarray of `StoredArray` to be sorted on this pass. Provided that `R` is greater than `L` (in other words, there is more than one element in the subarray to be sorted), `xQuickSort1()` partitions the subarray. It chooses `Array[R]` as its pivot, the last element of the subarray. It then partitions all the elements between `L` and `R-1` by steadily working inward from the two ends of this subarray. It does this by using the counters `i` and `j`, with `i` working from the left end of the subarray and `j` from the right end. Each counter is advanced until `i` finds an element that is greater than or equal to `Array[R]` and `j` finds one that is less than or equal to `Array[R]`. These two elements are out of order with respect to each other. (If the element is equal to `Array[R]`, it is not actually out of order, but, as discussed previously, there is a benefit in trying to place records equal to the pivot into both partitions.) Therefore, the elements are swapped and the counters are allowed to advance. When the counters cross, `Array[R]` is exchanged with `Array[i]`. The partitioning is now complete. All elements to the left of `Array[i]` are known to have keys that are less than or equal to the key of `Array[i]`, while all elements to its right are greater than or equal to it. Furthermore, the element in `Array[i]` is in its *final* position and never needs to be moved or examined again. The code then calls itself recursively on the subarrays `L` through `i-1` and `i+1` through `R`.

Take a few moments right now to prove to yourself that this method actually works. Make up an array of six or seven random-ordered items, and follow the algorithm step by step. Then do it again with an array of six or seven *already sorted* items. The behavior of the algorithm when given this type of input is striking and is very important to the upcoming discussion. Also, pay attention to the way the algorithm keeps itself from running out of bounds. Notice how the loop that increments `i` takes advantage of the fact that when `i` equals `R` the comparison function returns zero and terminates the loop. In contrast, the loop that decrements `j` must ensure that `j` is not decremented past zero. You could have avoided this test by creating a dummy record in `Array[0]` and ensuring that its key was less than any of the real keys. However, as noted in the introduction, this procedure is not always convenient.

If you try the pencil-and-paper exercise just suggested, you will discover that when Quicksort is given an array of already sorted items, its performance degenerates badly. Blindly choosing `Array[R]` as the pivot from an already sorted array means that *all* elements are put into only one partition on each pass, and this behavior occurs whether the array is sorted in forward or reverse order. The effect is shown clearly in Table 5-2, where *quick1.c* is speedy on random-ordered records but becomes as slow as insertion sort on both

forward- and reverse-ordered records. Another side effect is that stack requirements go up dramatically under these circumstances, with one recursive call
being made for each element to be sorted. Reducing the likelihood of this kind
of degenerate behavior is the object of our next version of Quicksort.

quick2.c (Listing 5-8) incorporates two modifications that improve the
behavior of the sort. The overall structure of this second version is the same as
the first, with most changes concentrated in the core routine `xQuickSort2()`.

The first change is that `xQuickSort2()` refuses to sort any subarray of
fewer than 10 elements. Why? Extensive analysis has shown that Quicksort
generally runs faster if you use an insertion sort on small subarrays rather than
invoke the recursive mechanisms needed to Quicksort a small subarray. The
definition of "small" is somewhat loose, but any value in the range of 5 to 25
works well. If you examine the sort driver, `QuickSort2()`, you will see that
after it calls `xQuickSort2()` it also calls `InsertionSort()` to complete
the work of sorting. As `xQuickSort2()` will have created an almost sorted
array by arranging the whole array into sorted groups of locally disordered
records, the insertion sort will run in roughly linear time.

The second change relates to the method of selecting the pivot. Rather than
blindly selecting the `R`'th element, the routine does a calculation known as
median-of-three. Three elements are examined: the `L`'th, the `R`'th, and one
(called `mid` in the code) roughly halfway between these two. These three
elements are sorted, and the `mid`'th and `R-1`'th elements are then exchanged.
Once this process is complete, we are assured that the following is true:

```
Array[L] <= Array[R-1] <= Arrray[R]
```

At this point, we take `Array[R-1]` as the pivot and partition the elements
between `L` and `R-2`. Our search loops can now use the elements `Array[L]`
and `Array[R]` as built-in sentinels, thus simplifying these loops. Note also
that the fact that `xQuickSort2()` does not sort subarrays smaller than 10
elements means that much special-case code can be left out of the routine; we
know that there are enough elements so that `L`, `mid`, `R-1`, and `R` will each be
separate and distinct.

Listing 5-8. The code for Quicksort with median-of-three partitioning.

```
/*--- quick2.c -------------------------- Listing 5-8 ---------
 * Quicksort with median-of-three partitioning
 *      and insertion sort on small subfiles.
 *
 * Uses InsertionSort() from insert.c (Listing 5-5)
 *
```

```
 * #define DRIVER to compile a test driver
 * Driver must be linked to sortsub.c (Listing 5-1)
 *------------------------------------------------------------*/

#include "sorthdr.h"

#define DRIVER 1

static CompFunc StoredCompare;
static Element **StoredArray;

static void xQuickSort2 ( int L, int R )
{
    if ( R - L >= 9 ) /* if if there are at least 10 elements */
    {
        int i, j, mid;
        Element *temp;

        /*
         * Sort Lth, Rth, and middle element. Then swap the
         * middle element with the R-1th element. This will
         * obviate the need for bound checking.
         */
        mid = ( L + R ) / 2; /* this is the middle element */
        if ( StoredCompare ( StoredArray[L],
                             StoredArray[mid] ) > 0 )
        {
            temp = StoredArray[L];
            StoredArray[L] = StoredArray[mid];
            StoredArray[mid] = temp;
        }
        if ( StoredCompare ( StoredArray[L],
                             StoredArray[R] ) > 0 )
        {
            temp = StoredArray[L];
            StoredArray[L] = StoredArray[R];
            StoredArray[R] = temp;
        }
        if ( StoredCompare ( StoredArray[mid],
                             StoredArray[R] ) > 0 )
        {
            temp = StoredArray[mid];
            StoredArray[mid] = StoredArray[R];
            StoredArray[R] = temp;
        }

        temp = StoredArray[mid];
        StoredArray[mid] = StoredArray[R-1];
```

```
            StoredArray[R-1] = temp;

        /*
         * Now, we know that Array[L] <= Array[R-1] <= Array[R].
         * We use Array[R-1] as the pivot, so this relationship
         * gives us known sentinels. Also, we need to
         * partition only between L+1 and R-2.
         */
        i = L;      /* Scan up from here    */
        j = R - 1; /* Scan down from here */
        for ( ;; )
        {
            /* Looking from left, find element >= Array[R-1] */
            while ( StoredCompare ( StoredArray[++i],
                               StoredArray[R - 1] ) < 0 )
                            ;

            /* Looking from right, find element <= Array[R-1] */
            while ( StoredCompare ( StoredArray[--j],
                               StoredArray[R - 1] ) > 0 )
                            ;

            if ( i >= j )
                break;

            /* swap ith and jth elements */
            temp = StoredArray[i];
            StoredArray[i] = StoredArray[j];
            StoredArray[j] = temp;
        }


        /* swap ith and R-1'th elements */
        temp = StoredArray[i];
        StoredArray[i] = StoredArray[R - 1];
        StoredArray[R - 1] = temp;

        /* and sort the two partitions */
        xQuickSort2 ( L, i-1 );
        xQuickSort2 ( i+1, R );
    }
}

void QuickSort2 ( Element **Array, int Items, CompFunc Compare )
{
    void InsertionSort ( Element **, int, CompFunc );

    /* Save some things */
```

```
        StoredCompare = Compare;
        StoredArray = Array;

        /* Quicksort to get nearly sorted file */
        xQuickSort2 ( 0, Items - 1 );

        /* Do an insertion sort on the now nearly sorted file */
        InsertionSort( Array, Items, Compare );
}

#ifdef DRIVER
#include <stdio.h>
#include <string.h>
#include <stdlib.h>
#include "sortsub.h"

/*
 * A comparison function
 */
int Cfunc ( Element *L, Element *R )
{
    return ( strncmp ( L->text, R->text, 5 ));
}

void main ( int argc, char *argv[] )
{
    Element **Array;
    int Items = 2000;

    if ( argc != 2 && argc != 3 )
    {
        fprintf( stderr, "Usage: quick2 infile [maxitems]\n" );
        return;
    }

    if ( argc == 3 )
        Items = atoi ( argv[2] );

    if (( Items = LoadArray ( argv[1], Items, &Array )) == -1 )
        return; /* Couldn't load file */

    QuickSort2 ( Array, Items, (CompFunc) Cfunc );
    ShowArray ( Array, Items, (CompFunc) Cfunc );
}
#endif
```

As Table 5-2 shows, the changes demonstrated in Listing 5-8 dramatically improve the behavior of Quicksort. It now runs equally well on random-, reverse-, and forward-ordered records. However, there are further improvements to be made in the areas of stack utilization and worst-case behavior. The first of these improvements is tackled by our third version, *quick3.c* (Listing 5-9).

Listing 5-9.   The code for an improved Quicksort that eliminates tail recursion.

```
/*--- quick3.c -------------------------- Listing 5-9 ---------
 * Quicksort with median-of-three partitioning,
 * insertion sort on small subfiles, and removal
 * of end recursion.
 *
 * Uses InsertionSort() from insert.c (Listing 5-5)
 *
 * #define DRIVER to compile a test driver
 * Driver must be linked to sortsub.c (Listing 5-1)
 *-----------------------------------------------------------*/

#include "sorthdr.h"

#define DRIVER 1

static CompFunc StoredCompare;
static Element **StoredArray;

static void xQuickSort3 ( int L, int R )
{
    while ( R - L >= 9 )   /* if there are at least 10 elements */
    {
        int i, j, mid;
        Element *temp;

        /*
         * Sort Lth, Rth, and middle element. Then swap the
         * middle element with the R-1'th element. This will
         * obviate the need for bound checking.
         */
        mid = ( L + R ) / 2; /* this is the middle element */

        if ( StoredCompare ( StoredArray[L],
                             StoredArray[mid] ) > 0 )
        {
            temp = StoredArray[L];
            StoredArray[L] = StoredArray[mid];
```

```
        StoredArray[mid] = temp;
}
if ( StoredCompare ( StoredArray[L],
                        StoredArray[R]) > 0 )
{
    temp = StoredArray[L];
    StoredArray[L] = StoredArray[R];
    StoredArray[R] = temp;
}
if ( StoredCompare ( StoredArray[mid],
                        StoredArray[R]) > 0 )
{
    temp = StoredArray[mid];
    StoredArray[mid] = StoredArray[R];
    StoredArray[R] = temp;
}

temp = StoredArray[mid];
StoredArray[mid] = StoredArray[R-1];
StoredArray[R-1] = temp;

/*
 * Now, we know that Array[L] <= Array[R-1] <= Array[R].
 * We use Array[R-1] as the pivot, so this relationship
 * gives us known sentinels. Also, we need to partition
 * only between L+1 and R-2.
 */
i = L;      /* Scan up from here    */
j = R - 1; /* Scan down from here */
for ( ;; )
{
    /* Looking from left, find element >= Array[R-1] */
    while ( StoredCompare ( StoredArray[++i],
                    StoredArray[R - 1] ) < 0 )
                ;

    /* Looking from right, find element <= Array[R-1] */
    while ( StoredCompare ( StoredArray[--j],
                    StoredArray[R - 1]) > 0 )
                ;

    if ( i >= j )
        break;

    /* swap ith and jth elements */
    temp = StoredArray[i];
    StoredArray[i] = StoredArray[j];
    StoredArray[j] = temp;
```

```
        }

        /* swap ith and R-1'th elements */
        temp = StoredArray[i];
        StoredArray[i] = StoredArray[R - 1];
        StoredArray[R - 1] = temp;

        /*
         * This, and the conversion of the main loop from
         * "if (R - L >= 9)" to "while (R - L >= 9)" are the
         * only places we differ from quick2.c. These small
         * changes have a big effect: by recursing only on the
         * small half and simply looping on the large half
         * of each partition, we eliminate the possiblity
         * that worst-case input could cause us to make N
         * recursive calls. Instead, the worst case becomes
         * log2 N calls.
         */
        if ( i - L > R - i )  /* left half is larger */
        {
            xQuickSort3 ( i + 1, R ); /* recurse on small half
*/
            R = i - 1;
        }
        else  /* right half is larger */
        {
            xQuickSort3 ( L, i - 1 );
            L = i + 1;
        }
    }
}

void QuickSort3 ( Element **Array, int Items, CompFunc Compare )
{
    void InsertionSort ( Element **, int, CompFunc );

    /* Save some things */
    StoredCompare = Compare;
    StoredArray = Array;

    /* Quicksort to get nearly sorted file */
    xQuickSort3 ( 0, Items - 1 );

    /* Do an insertion sort on the now nearly sorted file */
    InsertionSort ( Array, Items, Compare );
}
```

```
#ifdef DRIVER
#include <stdio.h>
#include <string.h>
#include <stdlib.h>
#include "sortsub.h"

/*
 * A comparison function
 */
int Cfunc ( Element *L, Element *R )
{
    return ( strncmp ( L->text, R->text, 5 ));
}

void main ( int argc, char *argv[] )
{
    Element **Array;
    int Items = 2000;

    if ( argc != 2 && argc != 3 )
    {
        fprintf( stderr, "Usage: quick3 infile [maxitems]\n" );
        return;
    }

    if ( argc == 3 )
        Items = atoi(argv[2]);

    if (( Items = LoadArray ( argv[1], Items, &Array )) == -1 )
        return; /* Couldn't load file */

    QuickSort3 ( Array, Items, (CompFunc) Cfunc );
    ShowArray ( Array, Items, (CompFunc) Cfunc );
}
#endif
```

---

    quick3.c removes **tail recursion**. To see how this works, observe that the last two things xQuickSort2() does are to make two recursive calls to itself. While there is little we can do about the first recursive call, routines that *end* with recursive calls to themselves are said to be tail recursive. This recursion can usually be removed by resetting the routine's parameters to match those that would have been passed recursively, and then simply looping back to the top of the routine. Because it doesn't matter in which order we Quicksort the two partitions, we may also choose which half we sort by recursion and which half we sort by looping. This choice is easy; it is to our advantage to use recursion on the smaller half and to loop on the larger half. That way, should worse come to worst and we hit a degenerate case, we will always recurse on a subarray that is, at most, half the size of the previous array and thus make, at most, lg *N* recursive calls instead of *N* such calls.

As you can see, the changes made to *quick2.c* to produce *quick3.c* are simple. By altering the test in xQuickSort2() from if (R-L >= 9) to while (R-L >= 9), we provide a looping mechanism. Then we remove tail recursion by modifying the calls at the end of the loop. We still make the call to sort the smaller half, but we just change the values of L and R to be those we have passed to sort the larger half, and then loop around to actually perform the sort.

The effect of these changes on the maximum stack depth can be seen in Table 5-2. In the worst case, a forward-sorted array of records, *quick2.c* reached a maximum stack depth of 26 while *quick3.c* made only 8 recursive calls.

It now looks as if we have done pretty well. We have a fast sort routine that uses a reasonable amount of stack space, that requires no additional storage space, and that handles forward-, reverse-, and random-ordered arrays of records with equal aplomb. Its only obvious failing is that it is not a stable sort.

There is however, one last problem relating to worst-case behavior. Consider what happens to the median-of-three pivot selection procedure if you give it an array of this form to sort:

A B C D E F G H G F E D C G A

That is, we first have a steadily increasing sequence and then the same sequence in reverse. On the first pass, the median-of-three procedure sorts the first, last, and middle entries (A, A, and H). After the middle element (one of the A's) is swapped with the next-to-last element (the G), we proceed to partition the elements by using the A as the pivot. Now we have a degenerate case, with all the elements being greater than the pivot. And, horror of horrors, this situation will tend to persist on each subsequent partitioning. We are clearly in trouble, but we should avoid the temptation to design an even more complex scheme (median-of-four? median-of-five?), because no matter what fixed scheme we select, we can always design an input pattern that will cause it to degenerate. The only true defense here is that of randomness. By simply modifying median-of-three to use the first and last elements and a *randomly* selected element for its partitioning, we can almost eliminate the chance of degenerate behavior.

The version of Quicksort shown in *quick4.c* (Listing 5-10) incorporates these refinements plus one other code enhancement. Instead of using the explicit array indices, this version directly uses the pointer equivalents. With these changes, not only do we have our most bulletproof version of Quicksort, but also the fastest (see Table 5-2).

Listing 5-10.   The code for a Quicksort with a randomly selected middle pivot element.

```
/*--- quick4.c ------------------------- Listing 5-10 --------
 * Quicksort with median-of-three partitioning
 * based on a randomly selected middle element,
 * insertion sort on small subfiles, removal of
 * end recursion, and use of pointer
 * incrementing rather than an index.
 *
 * Uses InsertionSort() from insert.c (Listing 5-5)
 *
 * #define DRIVER to compile a test driver
 * Driver must be linked to sortsub.c (Listing 5-1)
 *-----------------------------------------------------------*/

#include <stddef.h>      /* for typedef of ptrdiff_t */
#include <stdlib.h>      /* for rand() */
#include "sorthdr.h"

#define DRIVER 1

static CompFunc StoredCompare;

static void xQuickSort4 ( Element **pL, Element **pR )
{
    ptrdiff_t diff; /* ptrdiff_t is a signed type that can hold
                       the difference between two pointers */

    while (( diff = ( pR - pL )) >= 9 )   /* 10 elements a must */
    {
        int mid;
        Element *temp, **pmid, **pi, **pj, *ppivot;

        /* select a random mid element */
        mid = abs ( rand() ) % diff;
        if ( mid < 1 || mid > diff - 2 )
            mid = 1;
        pmid = pL + mid;

        /*
         * Sort Lth, Rth, and middle element. Then swap the
         * middle element with the R-1'th element. This will
         * obviate the need for bound checking.
         */
        if ( StoredCompare ( *pL, *pmid ) > 0 )
        {
            temp = *pL;
            *pL = *pmid;
```

```
        *pmid = temp;
    }
    if ( StoredCompare ( *pL, *pR ) > 0 )
    {
        temp = *pL;
        *pL = *pR;
        *pR = temp;
    }
    if ( StoredCompare ( *pmid, *pR ) > 0 )
    {
        temp = *pmid;
        *pmid = *pR;
        *pR = temp;
    }

    temp = *pmid;
    *pmid = *(pR-1);
    *(pR-1) = temp;

    /*
     * Now, we know that Array[L] <= Array[R-1] <= Array[R].
     * We use Array[R-1] as the pivot, so this relationship
     * gives us known sentinels. Also, we need to partition
     * only between L+1 and R-2.
     */
    pi = pL;        /* Scan up from here */
    pj = pR - 1;    /* Scan down from here */
    ppivot = *pj;
    for ( ;; )
    {
        /* Looking from left, find element >= Array[R-1] */
        while ( StoredCompare ( *++pi, ppivot ) < 0 )
                        ;

        /* Looking from right, find element <= Array[R-1] */
        while ( StoredCompare ( *--pj, ppivot ) > 0 )
                        ;

        if ( pi >= pj )
            break;

        /* swap ith and jth elements */
        temp = *pi;
        *pi = *pj;
        *pj = temp;
    }
```

```
        /* swap ith and the pivot */
        *(pR - 1) = *pi;
        *pi = ppivot;

        if ( pi - pL > pR - pi )   /* left half is larger */
        {
            xQuickSort4 ( pi+1, pR ); /* recurse on smaller half */
            pR = pi - 1;
        }
        else    /* right half is larger */
        {
            xQuickSort4 ( pL, pi-1 );
            pL = pi + 1;
        }
    }
}

void QuickSort4 ( Element **Array, int Items, CompFunc Compare )
{
    void InsertionSort ( Element **, int, CompFunc );

    /* Save some things */
    StoredCompare = Compare;

    /* Quicksort to get nearly sorted file */
    xQuickSort4 ( Array, Array + Items - 1 );

    /* Do an insertion sort on the now nearly sorted file */
    InsertionSort ( Array, Items, Compare );
}

#ifdef DRIVER
#include <stdio.h>
#include <string.h>
#include "sortsub.h"

/*
 * A comparison function
 */
int Cfunc ( Element *L, Element *R )
{
    return ( strncmp ( L->text, R->text, 5 ));
}

void main ( int argc, char *argv[] )
{
    Element **Array;
    int Items = 2000;
```

```
    if ( argc != 2 && argc != 3 )
    {
        fprintf ( stderr, "Usage: quick4 infile [maxitems]\n" );
        return;
    }

    if ( argc == 3 )
        Items = atoi ( argv[2] );

    if (( Items = LoadArray ( argv[1], Items, &Array )) == -1 )
        return; /* Couldn't load file */

    QuickSort4 ( Array, Items, (CompFunc) Cfunc );
    ShowArray ( Array, Items, (CompFunc) Cfunc );
}
#endif
```

To wrap this all up, one last version of Quicksort is presented as *quick5.c* (Listing 5-11). This version makes use of all the improvements discussed so far, but is also a "plug-compatible" replacement for your compiler's qsort(). Rather than assuming the array of items to be sorted is an array of pointers, this version sorts an array of elements of arbitrary size. It also avoids the use of static data items and is thus safe to use reentrantly. As discussed at the end of this chapter, you should test your compiler's version of qsort() to see whether it is well behaved; if it isn't, you may want to use the routine in *quick5.c* instead.

Listing 5-11.   The code for an optimized Quicksort that uses a `qsort()` syntax.

```
/*--- quick5.c -------------------------- Listing 5-11 --------
 * qsort() replacement derived from quick4.c
 * that may be used to replace your compiler's
 * version of qsort(). Just compile this routine
 * and then call xqsort() rather than qsort().
 *-----------------------------------------------------------*/

#include <stdio.h>
#include <stdlib.h> /* for rand() */
#include <string.h> /* for memcpy() */

typedef int ( *CF )();
#define A(x) (a + (x) * es)

static void InsertionSort ( char *a, int n, int es,
                            CF cf, char *b )
```

```
{
    int step, i;

    /* Look at 2nd thru Nth elements, putting each in place */
    for ( step = 1; step < n; step++ )
    {
        /* Now, look to the left and find our spot */
        memcpy ( b, A(step), es );
        for ( i = step - 1; i >= 0; i-- )
        {
            if ( cf ( A(i), b ) > 0 )
            {
                /* Not there yet, so make room */
                memcpy ( A(i+1), A(i), es );
            }
            else /* Found it! */
                break;
        }
        /* Now insert original value from Array[step] */
        memcpy ( A(i+1), b, es );

    }
}

static void xQuickSort5 ( char *a, int L, int R, int es,
                          CF cf, char *b )
{
    int diff;

    while (( diff = ( R - L )) >= 9 )  /* 10 elements a must */
    {
        int mid, i, j;
        char *ppivot;

        /* select a random mid element */
        mid = abs ( rand() ) % diff;
        if ( mid < 1 || mid > diff - 2 )
            mid = 1;
        mid += L;

        /*
         * Sort Lth, Rth, and middle element. Then swap the
         * middle element with the R-1'th element. This will
         * obviate the need for bound checking.
         */
        if ( cf ( A(L), A(mid) ) > 0 )
        {
```

```
        memcpy ( b, A(L), es );
        memcpy ( A(L), A(mid), es );
        memcpy ( A(mid), b, es );
    }
    if ( cf ( A(L), A(R) ) > 0 )
    {
        memcpy ( b, A(L), es );
        memcpy ( A(L), A(R), es );
        memcpy ( A(R), b, es );
    }
    if ( cf ( A(mid), A(R) ) > 0 )
    {
        memcpy ( b, A(mid), es );
        memcpy ( A(mid), A(R), es );
        memcpy ( A(R), b, es );
    }

    memcpy ( b, A(mid), es );
    memcpy ( A(mid), A(R-1), es );
    memcpy ( A(R-1), b, es );

    /*
     * Now, we know that Array[L] <= Array[R-1] <= Array[R].
     * We use Array[R-1] as the pivot, so this relationship
     * gives us known sentinels. Also, we need to partition
     * only between L+1 and R-2.
     */
    i = L;          /* Scan up from here */
    j = R - 1;      /* Scan down from here */
    ppivot = A ( j );
    for ( ;; )
    {

        /* Looking from left, find element >= Array[R-1] */
        while ( cf ( A(++i), ppivot ) < 0 )
                    ;

        /* Looking from right, find element <= Array[R-1] */
        while ( cf ( A(--j), ppivot ) > 0 )
                    ;

        if ( i >= j )
            break;

        /* swap ith and jth elements */
        memcpy ( b, A(i), es );
        memcpy ( A(i), A(j), es );
        memcpy ( A(j), b, es );
    }
```

```
            /* swap ith and the pivot */
            memcpy ( b, A(R-1), es );
            memcpy ( A(R-1), A(i), es );
            memcpy ( A(i), b, es );

            if ( i - L > R - i )    /* left half is larger */
            {
                xQuickSort5 ( a, i+1, R, es, cf, b );
                R = i - 1;
            }
            else  /* right half is larger */
            {
                xQuickSort5 ( a, L, i-1, es, cf, b );
                L = i + 1;
            }
        }
    }
}

void xqsort ( char *a, int n, int es, CF cf )
{
    #define DEFAULT_BUFFER 64
    char buf[DEFAULT_BUFFER], *b;

    printf ( "sorting %d elements of size %d\n", n, es );

    /* allocate space for making a copy of an item */
    b = buf;
    if ( es > DEFAULT_BUFFER )
    {
        b = (char *) malloc ( es );
        if ( b == NULL )
        {
            qsort (a, n, es, cf );
            return;
        }
    }

    /* Quicksort to get nearly sorted file */
    xQuickSort5 ( a, 0, n - 1, es, cf, b );

    /* Do an insertion sort on the now nearly sorted file */
    InsertionSort ( a, n, es, cf, b );

    /* Cleanup */
    if ( b != buf )
        free ( b );
}
```

Heapsort

A properly implemented Quicksort is, on average, hard to beat. However, Quicksort's worst-case performance is proportional to N^2, and there is always the possibility that your program will encounter a worst-case condition. Our final version of Quicksort takes many steps to defend itself against this, but there are times when what you need is certainty, not probability. We have already examined Shellsort, a good general-purpose sort with a guarantee of an order of approximately $N^{1.25}$. In this section we will study Heapsort, another sort with $N \lg N$ order that is usually slower than Quicksort but which lacks a worst case.

Heapsort works by viewing the array to be sorted as a binary tree. For example, if we have an array with 15 entries, each entry can be viewed as the corresponding node in the binary tree shown in Figure 5-1. We can define this tree by using three simple formulas:

Parent of `array[n]`:	`array[(n-1)/2]`
Children of `array[n]`:	`array[n * 2 + 1]`
	and `array[n * 2 + 2]`

That is, the children of `array[0]` would be `array[1]` and `array[2]`, while the parent of `array[5]` would be `array[2]`. Note that these formulas are for C-style zero-based arrays; if you read other works on Heapsort, they will usually use one-based arrays, in which the correct formulas are parent of `a[n]` is `a[n/2]` and `a[n]`'s children are `a[n*2]` and `a[n*2+1]`.

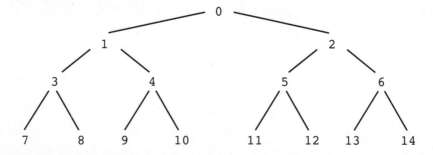

Figure 5-1.   A binary tree of 15 nodes.

Heapsort then ensures that the entries in this binary tree form a structure known as a **heap**. To create a heap, we need only ensure that the value at each node is greater than or equal to the values of that node's children. This does not mean that the entries are sorted so that a standard tree-walk algorithm (see the next chapter) would yield the data items in sorted order. The heap condition requires only that the data in node 3 be greater than or equal to the data in nodes 7 and 8; the data in nodes 4, 9, and 10 might be greater or less than the data in nodes 3, 7, and 8. But since the data in node 0 must be greater than or equal to the data in nodes 1 and 2—which must in turn be greater than or equal to the data in nodes 3, 4, 5, and 6, and so on—the data item in node 0 will be the largest data item in the heap. Thus, once the heap condition is enforced, finding the largest item is simple: it is in `array[0]`. If this data item is removed and the heap condition reenforced, the second largest item is now in `array[0]`. By repeating this process, the data items can be extracted in order.

The code to implement this sort is shown in *heap.c* (Listing 5-12). The key routine is `downheap()`. This routine is called with beginning and ending array indices (node numbers) and is responsible for enforcing the heap condition within this range. The routine is surprisingly simple because it assumes that the heap condition is already partially met; if disorder is present, it is limited to the first node and its children. This routine can thus be as simple as the following pseudocode:

```
downheap(first, last) {
    parent = first;
    child = parent * 2 + 1;
    while (child <= last)  {
        /* Find larger of two children */
        if (child + 1 <= last &&
            array[child+1] > array[child])
            child++;

        /* Exit if parent > largest child */
        if (array[parent] > array[child}
            break;

        /*
         * Child is larger than parent. Swap
         * that child with parent and keep
         * looking down heap to make sure
         * heap condition is satisified.
         */
        temp = array[child];
        array[child] = array[parent];
        array[parent] = array[child];
        parent = child;
        child = parent * 2 + 1;
    }
}
```

To actually perform the sort, the preceding routine is paired with code that first enforces the heap condition by starting at the deepest parent and working upward to node 0:

```
for (i = (N - 1) / 2; i >= 0; i--)
    downheap(i, N);
```

Because this routine starts with the smallest, deepest heap and works backward, the heap condition is gradually enforced on the entire heap. As noted previously, this approach allows downheap() to be fairly simple.

Listing 5-12.   The code for a Heapsort.

```
/*--- heap.c --------------------------- Listing 5-12 --------
 * Heapsort on an array. Uses basic heapsort
 * algorithm, with Floyd's modification to
 * reduce order from 2N lg N to N lg N.
 *
 * #define DRIVER to compile a test driver
 * Driver must be linked to sortsub.c (Listing 5-1)
 *------------------------------------------------------------*/

#include "sorthdr.h"

#define DRIVER 1

static CompFunc StoredCompare;
static Element **StoredArray;

/* Enforce heap condition between first and last */
static void downheap ( int first, int last )
{
    int child, parent, i;
    Element *temp;
    for ( i = first; ( child = i * 2 + 1 ) <= last; i = child )
    {
        if ( child + 1 <= last &&
            StoredCompare ( StoredArray[child + 1],
                            StoredArray[child] ) > 0 )
            child += 1;

        /* child is the larger child of i */
        temp = StoredArray[i];
        StoredArray[i] = StoredArray[child];
        StoredArray[child] = temp;
    }
```

```
    while ( 1 )
    {
        parent = ( i - 1 ) / 2;

        if ( parent < first || parent == i ||
             StoredCompare ( StoredArray[parent],
                             StoredArray[i] ) > 0 )
            break;
        temp = StoredArray[i];
        StoredArray[i] = StoredArray[parent];
        StoredArray[parent] = temp;

        i = parent;
    }
}

void HeapSort ( Element **Array, int N, CompFunc Compare )
{
    int i;
    Element *temp;

    /* Make array and compare function available to all */
    StoredCompare = Compare;
    StoredArray = Array;

    /* Make N equal to largest index */
    N -= 1;

    /* First, ensure heap property for array */
    for ( i = ( N - 1 ) / 2; i >= 0; i-- )
        downheap ( i, N );

    /*
     * Now sort by taking advantage of the fact that the
     * largest element is in Array[0]. If we remove this element
     * and move it to Array[N-1], that element is now in place.
     * We continue to sort by reenforcing the heap property on
     * Array[0 .. N-2] and then taking the next largest element
     * and moving it to Array[N-2]. By repeating this process,
     * we will ultimately sort the array.
     */
    for ( i = N; i > 0; )
    {
        temp = Array[i];
        Array[i] = Array[0];
        Array[0] = temp;
        downheap ( 0, --i );
    }
```

```
}

#ifdef DRIVER
#include <stdio.h>
#include <string.h>
#include <stdlib.h>
#include "sortsub.h"
/*
 * A comparison function
 */
int Cfunc ( Element *L, Element *R )
{
    return ( strncmp ( L->text, R->text, 5 ));
}

void main ( int argc, char *argv[] )
{
    Element **Array;
    int Items = 2000;

    if ( argc != 2 && argc != 3 )
    {
        fprintf ( stderr, "Usage: heap infile [maxitems]\n" );
        return;
    }

    if ( argc == 3 )
        Items = atoi ( argv[2] );

    if (( Items = LoadArray ( argv[1], Items, &Array )) == -1 )
        return; /* Couldn't load file */

    HeapSort ( Array, Items, (CompFunc) Cfunc );
    ShowArray ( Array, Items, (CompFunc) Cfunc );
}
#endif
```

The sort is then performed by repeatedly taking the element in `Array[0]` (which is now the largest element in the array), moving it to the end of the array, and reenforcing the heap condition on the remaining portion of the array.

```
for (i = N; i > 0; ) {
    temp = Array[i];
    Array[0] = temp;
    downheap(0, --i);
}
```

The actual code in *heap.c* follows this model closely but makes one change to `downheap()`. Empirical studies have found that `downheap()` is about twice as fast if it simply pushes the element in the initial parent node all the way to the bottom of the heap and then lets it float up to its final resting place. Thus, the production version of `downheap()` has two loops: the first repeatedly swaps the parent node with its largest child until the bottom of the tree is reached, and the second loop then walks the item in question back up the tree until that item is in place.

As you can see in Table 5-2, this implementation of Heapsort is a consistent but not fabulous performer. Even though it has the same $N \lg N$ order as Quicksort, its longer inner loop makes it slower than Quicksort. It is, however, a good all-around choice when you simply can't risk slowing a sort by a worst-case condition.

Insertion Sort on a Linked List

Insertion sort is the first of the two sorts we will modify to handle linked lists. Like array-based sorts, the list-based sorts make use of support routines and definitions given in *lsortsub.c* (Listing 5-13), *lsortsub.h* (Listing 5-14), and *lsorthdr.h* (Listing 5-15). The routines will sort singly linked lists built from structures of the form (from *lsorthdr.h*):

```
typedef struct sElement {
    char *text;
    struct sElement *next;
} Element;
```

Listing 5-13. Support routines for insertion sort of linked lists.

```
/*---lsortsub.c-----------------------Listing 5-13----------
 * I/O subroutines for sorting routines
 * Loads data into an array
 *-------------------------------------------------------*/

#include <stdio.h>
#include <stdlib.h>
#include <string.h>
#include <ctype.h>
#include "lsorthdr.h"
#include "lsortsub.h"

#define MAX_ITEM_SIZE 500 /* max length of a text item */
```

```
/*
 * Loads text strings from FileName into a linked list. Returns
 * the number of items in the list of -1 for failure.
 */
int LoadList ( char *FileName, Node **ListHead )
{
    FILE *infile;
    char buffer[MAX_ITEM_SIZE], *s;
    int i;
    Node **current;

    if (( infile = fopen ( FileName, "r" )) == NULL )
    {
        fprintf ( stderr, "Can't open file %s\n", FileName);
        return ( -1 );
    }

    i = 0;
    current = ListHead;
    while ( fgets ( buffer, MAX_ITEM_SIZE, infile ))
    {
        /* trim trailing control characters */
        s = buffer + strlen ( buffer );
        while ( iscntrl ( *s ))
            *s-- = 0;

        /* make space and store it */
        *current = malloc ( sizeof (Node) );
        if ( *current == NULL )
        {
            fprintf ( stderr, "Can't get memory for data\n" );
            return ( -1 );
        }

        (*current)->text = malloc ( strlen ( buffer ) + 1 );
        if ( (*current)->text == NULL )
        {
            fprintf ( stderr, "Can't get memory for data\n" );
            return ( -1 );
        }
        strcpy ( (*current)->text, buffer );

        current = &( (*current)->next ); /* advance */
        i++; /* keep count */
    }
    *current = NULL; /* terminate the list */

    /*
     * If the linked list contains only one element, and that
```

```
 * element is an empty string, return an empty list.
 */
if ( *ListHead != NULL &&
     (*ListHead)->next == NULL &&
     (*ListHead)->text[0] == 0 )
{

    *ListHead = NULL;
    i = 0;
}

fclose ( infile );
return ( i );
}


/* Display array of items */
void ShowArray ( Node *ListHead, CompFunc Compare )
{
    int i = 0, sorted = 1, column = 1;

    for ( ; ListHead != NULL; ListHead = ListHead->next )
    {
        if ( column > 61 )
        {
            printf ( "\n" );
            column = 1;
        }
        else  while (( column - 1 ) % 20 )
        {
            printf ( " " );
            column += 1;
        }
        printf ( "%3d: %s", i++, ListHead->text );
        column += 5 + strlen ( ListHead->text );
        if ( ListHead->next )
        {
            if ( Compare ( ListHead, ListHead->next ) > 0 )
                sorted = 0;
        }
    }

    if ( sorted )
        printf ( "\n\nThe linked list is sorted.\n" );
    else
        printf ( "\n\nThe linked list is not sorted.\n" );
}
```

Listing 5-14.   Prototypes for listing 5-13.

```
/*--- lsortsub.h ------------------------- Listing 5-14 -----
 * Prototypes of functions in lsortsub.c (Listing 5-13)
 *----------------------------------------------------------*/

int LoadList ( char *FileName, Node **ListHead );
void ShowArray ( Node *ListHead, CompFunc Compare );
```

Listing 5-15.   The code for *lsorthdr.h*.

```
/*--- lsorthdr.h ------------------------- Listing 5-15 -------
 * General definitions for linked-list oriented sort routines
 *----------------------------------------------------------*/

/*
 * We sort a linked list of these structures. The structure
 * could contain anything you'd like: you need only to define
 * appropriate comparison functions.
 */
typedef struct sNode {
    char *text;
    struct sNode *next;
} Node;

/*
 * A type for the comparison function: a symbol with type
 * CompFunc is a pointer to a function that takes two pointers
 * to void and returns int
 */
typedef int (*CompFunc) ( void *, void * );
```

Insertion sort is readily modified to sort a linked list, as shown in *linsert.c* (Listing 5-16). The linked-list version differs from the array version in two ways. First, the already sorted records must be searched from first to last as each new record is inserted. As discussed earlier, this causes the algorithm to be slowest on already sorted records and fastest on reverse-ordered records. Unfortunately, given that singly linked lists can be traversed only first to last, this is unavoidable.

The second modification is actually due to the first modification but is a bit more subtle. If you examine the comparison function used in the inner loop, you will see that the function continues to search as long as the test record (pointed to by walk) is greater than *or equal to* the record you are examining.

This small change makes the algorithm retain the important property of stability, and it is interesting to see how this works. Table 5-5 shows four records with keys A1, A2, B1, B2. The records have already been ordered based on the numeric portion: the sequence B1 A1 B2 A2. Our task is to sort them based on their alphabetic portion, using a forward-searching linked-list insertion sort. First, we do it the right way and use the >= test. On the first pass, we place A1 before B1. On the second pass, we must insert B2. Because we keep going as long as the new record is greater than or equal to (>=) the sorted record, we skip past A1 *and* B1, inserting B2 after B1. Finally, on the third pass, we insert A2 after A1, giving the final and correct sequence A1 A2 B1 B2. If we repeat this process by using just a test for >, we quickly get into trouble. The first pass is all right because A is less than B, but as we are inserting B2 during the second pass we stop our search when we see B1 (rather than after we see it), and we thus put B2 before B1. The same thing happens with A2, giving the final order A2 A1 B2 B1. While these records are correctly sorted with respect to their alphabetic portion, the sort has lost the numeric ordering present in the input sequence.

Table 5-5.   The choice of comparisons determines the stability of insertion sorts of linked lists. Already sorted records are shown in italics.

Pass	Test for >=	Test for >
0	*B1* A1 B2 A2	*B1* A1 B2 A2
1	*A1 B1* B2 A2	*A1 B1* B2 A2
2	*A1 B1* B2 A2	*A1 B2 B1* A2
3	*A1 A2 B2 B1*	A2 *A1 B2 B1*

Listing 5-16.   The code for insertion sort of linked lists.

```
/*--- linsert.c ------------------------ Listing 5-16 --------
 * Insertion sort of a linked list
 *
 * #define DRIVER to compile a test driver
 * Driver must be linked to lsortsub.c (Listing 5-13)
 *------------------------------------------------------------*/

#include <stdlib.h>
#include "lsorthdr.h"

#define DRIVER 1

/* Sort from *ListHead to ListEnd */
void InsertionSortLink ( Node **ListHead, Node *ListEnd,
                    CompFunc Compare )
```

```
{
    Node *newlist;  /* we build up the new list here */
    Node *walk, *save;

    newlist = ListEnd;  /* new list will end with this pointer */
    walk = *ListHead;   /* get ready to walk the list */

    for ( ; walk != ListEnd; walk = save )
    {
        /*
         * Run thru newlist, looking for an element that is
         * greater than walk. Watch the value in pnewlink
         * carefully--it points to the 'next' element of
         * of the structure that points to the structure
         * currently under scrutiny. Thus, pnewlist is
         * the equivalent of the 'last' pointer that is
         * required by linked-list insertion algorithms.
         */
        Node **pnewlink;
        for ( pnewlink = &newlist;
                *pnewlink != ListEnd &&
                  Compare(walk, *pnewlink ) >= 0;
                pnewlink = &((*pnewlink)->next) )
                        ;

        save = walk->next;      /* save this */
        walk->next = *pnewlink; /* and link in */
        *pnewlink = walk;
    }

    *ListHead = newlist;
}

#ifdef DRIVER
#include <stdio.h>
#include <string.h>
#include "lsortsub.h"

/*
 * A comparison function
 */
int Cfunc ( Node *L, Node *R )
{
    return ( strncmp ( L->text, R->text, 5 ));
}
```

```
void main ( int argc, char *argv[] )
{
    Node *ListHead;

    if ( argc != 2 )
    {
        fprintf ( stderr, "Usage: linsert infile\n" );
        return;
    }

    if ( LoadList ( argv[1], &ListHead ) == -1 )
        return; /* Couldn't load file */

    InsertionSortLink ( &ListHead, NULL, (CompFunc) Cfunc );
    ShowArray ( ListHead, (CompFunc) Cfunc );
}
#endif
```

Quicksort on a Linked List

Our second linked-list sort is Quicksort. Shellsort could be modified to sort linked lists, but a large number of list traversals would be required. Interestingly, adapting Quicksort to linked lists is straightforward. (Note that this discussion will not repeat information that was discussed in the earlier section on Quicksort. You may want to refer to that discussion while reading this section.) Our first implementation is shown in *lquick1.c* (Listing 5-17). Using the same interface as used by `InsertionSortLink()` in *linsert.c,* we proceed in a fashion that is strongly reminiscent of the approach in *quick3.c*. Because implementing median-of-three would be tricky (not to mention time-consuming), the code simply takes the first element as the pivot. The partitioning loop walks through the remaining elements of the lists and puts them into one of two new linked lists. The two lists and the pivot are linked together, and then the sublists are sorted by a combination of recursion and looping. As with *quick3.c*, small sublists are sorted by use of insertion sort. Unlike *quick3.c*, however, insertion sort performs poorly on forward-ordered lists (see Table 5-2), and therefore it must be performed individually on the small unsorted sublists rather than all at once on the entire nearly sorted list.

You could predict that this routine would not do well on either forward- or reverse-ordered lists, and the data in Table 5-2 bears this out. It is interesting to note, however, that the elimination of tail recursion makes the worst-case maximum stack depth only one call. Despite this failing, the implementation does have one very interesting property: stability. This pleasant surprise comes about due to the way the partitioning is performed. As elements are split off into one of the two sublists, the new element is always placed after all the old elements. Thus, elements with the same key maintain the same relative order. Achieving this effect also requires that items that are less than the pivot be placed in the left sublist, while those that are greater than or equal to the pivot are placed on the right. As noted earlier, this type of partitioning can produce degenerate performance when sorting data that contains large numbers of records with the same key.

Listing 5-17.   The code for Quicksort of linked lists.

```
/*--- lquick1.c ------------------------- Listing 5-17 --------
 * Quicksort for linked lists. Uses an insertion
 * sort on small subfiles and eliminates tail
 * recursion to minimize stack usage.
 *
 * Uses InsertionSortLink() from linsert.c (Listing 5-16)
 *
 * Adapted from an article by Jeff Taylor in
 * C Gazette, Vol 5, No. 6, 1991.
 *
 * #define DRIVER to compile a test driver
 * Driver must be linked to lsortsub.c (Listing 5-13)
 *------------------------------------------------------------*/

#include "lsorthdr.h"

#define DRIVER 1

static CompFunc StoredCompare;
void InsertionSortLink ( Node **, Node *, CompFunc );

static void xQuickSortL1 ( Node **Head, Node *End )
{
    int left_count, right_count, count;
    Node **left_walk, *pivot, *old;
    Node **right_walk, *right;

    if ( *Head != End )
    do {
        pivot = *Head;        /* Take first element as pivot */
        left_walk = Head;     /* Set up left & right halves */
        right_walk = &right;
        left_count = right_count = 0;
```

```
/* Now, walk the list */
for ( old = (*Head)->next; old != End; old = old->next )
{
    if ( StoredCompare ( old, pivot ) < 0 )
    {
        /* Less than pivot, so goes on left */
        left_count += 1;
        *left_walk = old;
        left_walk = &(old->next);
    }
    else
    {
        /* greater than or equal, so goes on right */
        right_count += 1;
        *right_walk = old;
        right_walk = &(old->next);
    }
}

/* Now glue the halves together... */
*right_walk = End;    /* Terminate right list */
*left_walk = pivot;  /* Put pivot after things on left */
pivot->next = right; /* And right list after that */

/* Now sort the halves in more detail */
if ( left_count > right_count )
{
    /*
     * Recursively sort (smaller) right half and then
     * reset local pointers so that when we loop we
     * will see the left half as the entire list. Also,
     * if the right half has fewer than 10 elements,
     * sort it by insertion rather than by quicksort.
     */
    if ( right_count >= 9 )
        xQuickSortL1 ( &(pivot->next), End );
    else
        InsertionSortLink ( &(pivot->next), End,
                            StoredCompare );
    End = pivot;
    count = left_count;
}
else
{
    /* Converse case */
    if ( left_count >= 9 )
        xQuickSortL1 ( Head, pivot );
    else
```

```
                    InsertionSortLink ( Head, pivot, StoredCompare );
            Head = &(pivot->next);
            count = right_count;
        }
    }
    while ( count > 1 );      /* end of do-while */
}

void QuickSortLink ( Node **Head, Node *End, CompFunc Compare )
{

    /* Save address of comparison function */
    StoredCompare = Compare;

    /* Quicksort the list */
    xQuickSortL1 ( Head, End );
}

#ifdef DRIVER
#include <stdio.h>
#include <string.h>
#include "lsortsub.h"

/*
 * A comparison function
 */
int Cfunc ( Node *L, Node *R )
{
    return ( strncmp ( L->text, R->text, 5 ));
}

void main ( int argc, char *argv[] )
{
    Node *ListHead;

    if ( argc != 2 )
    {
        fprintf ( stderr, "Usage: lquick1 infile\n" );
        return;
    }

    if ( LoadList ( argv[1], &ListHead ) == -1 )
        return; /* Couldn't load file */

    QuickSortLink ( &ListHead, NULL, (CompFunc) Cfunc );
    ShowArray ( ListHead, (CompFunc) Cfunc );
}
#endif
```

Degenerate worst-case behavior with a common type of input is not acceptable, so a simple approach to solving this problem is shown in *lquick2.c* (Listing 5-18). Here, rather than use the first element as a pivot, we use a randomly selected pivot. This entails (1) counting the list prior to the first call to xQuickSortL2() and (2) scanning the list to find the randomly selected pivot. These changes render the sort unstable, but as the data in Table 5-2 show, the new sort is speedy for all types of input.

Listing 5-18.   The code for Quicksort of linked lists with a randomly selected pivot.

```
/*--- lquick2.c ------------------------ Listing 5-18 --------
 * Quicksort for linked lists. Uses an insertion
 * sort on small subfiles, eliminates tail
 * recursion to minimize stack usage, and uses
 * a randomly selected pivot to avoid problems
 * with ordered input files.
 *
 * Uses InsertionSortLink() from linsert.c (Listing 5-16)
 *
 * Adapted from an article by Jeff Taylor in
 * C Gazette, Vol 5, No. 6, 1991.
 *
 * #define DRIVER to compile a test driver
 * Driver must be linked to lsortsub.c (Listing 5-13)
 *------------------------------------------------------------*/

#include <stdlib.h>
#include "lsorthdr.h"

#define DRIVER 1

static CompFunc StoredCompare;
void InsertionSortLink ( Node **, Node *, CompFunc );

static void xQuickSortL2 ( Node **Head, Node *End, int N )
{
    int left_count, right_count, npivot;
    Node **left_walk, *pivot, *old;
    Node **right_walk, *right;

    while ( N > 1 )
    {
        if ( N <= 9 )  /* Insertion sort small lists */
        {
            InsertionSortLink ( Head, End, StoredCompare );
            break;
        }
```

```
/* Select a pivot, but not at either end! */
npivot = abs ( rand() ) % N;
if ( npivot < 2 || npivot > N - 2 )
    npivot = 2;

/* Run thru the list to the randomly selected point */
old = *Head;
while ( npivot-- )
    old = old->next;
pivot = old->next;          /* Take as pivot */
old->next = pivot->next; /* Cut from chain */

/* Logic is now basically the same as lquick1.c */
left_walk = Head;       /* Set up left & right halves */
right_walk = &right;
left_count = right_count = 0;

/* Now walk the list */
for ( old = *Head; old != End; old = old->next )
{
    if ( StoredCompare ( old, pivot ) < 0 )
    {
        /* Less than pivot, so goes on left */
        left_count += 1;
        *left_walk = old;
        left_walk = &(old->next);
    }
    else
    {
        /* Greater than or equal to, so goes on right */
        right_count += 1;
        *right_walk = old;
        right_walk = &(old->next);
    }
}

/* Now glue the halves together... */
*right_walk = End;    /* Terminate right list */
*left_walk = pivot;   /* Put pivot after things on left */
pivot->next = right; /* And right list after that */

/* Now sort the halves in more detail */
if ( left_count > right_count )
{
    /*
     * Recursively sort (smaller) right half and then
     * reset local pointers so that when we loop, we
```

```
                 * will see the left half as the entire list,
                 */
                xQuickSortL2 ( &(pivot->next), End, right_count );
                End = pivot;
                N = left_count;
            }
            else
            {
                /* Converse case */
                xQuickSortL2 ( Head, pivot, left_count );
                Head = &(pivot->next);
                N = right_count;
            }
        }
    }
}

void QuickSortLink ( Node **Head, Node *End, CompFunc Compare )
{
    Node *walk;
    int count = 0;
    /* Save address of comparison function */
    StoredCompare = Compare;

    /* Count the list */
    for ( walk = *Head; walk != End; walk = walk->next )
        count += 1;

    /* Quicksort the list */
    xQuickSortL2 ( Head, End, count );
}

#ifdef DRIVER
#include <stdio.h>
#include <string.h>
#include "lsortsub.h"

/*
 * A comparison function
 */
int Cfunc ( Node *L, Node *R )
{
    return ( strncmp ( L->text, R->text, 5 ));
}

void main ( int argc, char *argv[] )
{
    Node *ListHead;
```

```
    if ( argc != 2 )
    {
        fprintf ( stderr, "Usage: lquick2 infile\n" );
        return;
    }

    if ( LoadList ( argv[1], &ListHead ) == -1 )
        return; /* Couldn't load file */

    QuickSortLink ( &ListHead, NULL, (CompFunc) Cfunc );
    ShowArray ( ListHead, (CompFunc) Cfunc );
}
#endif
```

Sorting on Multiple Keys—A Fix for Unstable Sorts

It is unfortunate that our three best algorithms—Quicksort, Heapsort, and Shellsort—are unstable (see Table 5-1). While there is no universal fix for this problem, it is still possible to use these sorts successfully on records that contain multiple keys. The trick is to work with compound keys. Suppose we have a set of records that describe transactions:

```
struct Tr {
    long date;
    long cust_id;
    /* more stuff here */
} ;
```

If we have an array of such transactions already sorted by date, it would be desirable if a second sort by cust_id maintained each customer's records in order by date. To use Shellsort or Quicksort to produce an array sorted by cust_id and then subsorted by date, we need to use a compound key. To implement a compound key we change only the comparison function. For example, this function correctly sorts our transaction records:

```
int compare(struct Tr *left, struct Tr *right)
{
    long diff;
    /* look at customer id first */
    diff = right->cust_id - left->cust_id;
    if (diff != 0)
        return diff < 0 ? -1 : 1;
    /* the id's match, so now check date */
    diff = right->date - left->date;
```

```
        if (diff < 0)
            diff = diff < 0 ? -1 : 1;
        return (int) diff;
}
```

Except that this approach requires some manipulations to avoid possible problems with `int` and `long` conversions, this comparison routine is very simple. It first compares the `cust_id` field. If the two are different, a nonzero comparison value is returned. If they are the same, we have a pair of transactions from the same customer. These transactions are then compared by examining the `date` field.

Thus, it could be said that we have used a **logical** compound key. A physical key consisting of `cust_id` concatenated with `date` was never created. Instead, our comparison function created the logical key by sequentially examining different fields within each record. And while we still have not made Quicksort or Shellsort stable, using this comparison function does allow us to produce a list sorted first by `cust_id` and then by `date`.

Network Sorts

As a counterpoint to the sorts discussed previously, let's now examine a special type of sort known as a **network** sort. In all the sorts we have seen so far, the data to be sorted has an impact on the running time of any given implementation, because different numbers of comparisons and swaps are performed for different inputs. A network sort, however, is completely prewired. All comparisons are predetermined, and all of them are always performed. To make this clear, let's consider a sorting network for four elements, as shown in Figure 5-2.

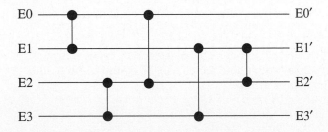

Figure 5-2.   Sorting a network of four elements.

We provide this network with four elements to be sorted (E0 through E3). Each element moves along its horizontal line, and when it encounters a vertical connection, that element is compared (and possibly swapped) with the element at the other end of the connection, with the final output appearing as E0' through E3'. (Take a moment to prove to yourself that it really does sort correctly under all circumstances.) There are two intriguing features of such sorting networks. First, they always require the same amount of time to execute. In the example shown in the figure, five comparisons-swaps are always performed. Second, if the comparison-swap pairs are suitable, some comparison-swaps can be performed simultaneously. In the figure, for example, the first two comparison-swaps are completely independent and could be performed in either order or simultaneously. The same thing is true of the second pair of comparison-swaps. This implies that the four-element sorting network could run in the time required to do only three comparison-swaps.

The problem becomes one of determining an optimal set of swap pairs. While it is known that the absolute minimum number of comparison-swaps required to sort n elements is $ceil(log_2 n!)$, and sorting networks that use this minimum number of comparison-swaps are known for certain values of n, there is no general way of deriving what is the optimal set of comparison-swap pairs for any value of n. One good approach to this problem is the Bose-Nelson algorithm for generating comparison-sort pairs. We will not go into the details of why this algorithm works (see the original article by Bose and Nelson [Bose 1962] as well as Knuth's more general discussion of other sorting networks [Knuth 1973]), but we will look at an implementation (based on the improved sort-pair generation algorithm devised by Hibbard [Hibbard 1963]) of the algorithm as *bose-nel.c* in Listing 5-19.

Listing 5-19.   The code for generating swap pairs.

```
/*--- bose-nel.c ------------------------- Listing 5-19 --------
 * Generate swap pairs based on the Bose-Nelson
 * technique, using the algorithm described by T. N.
 * Hibbard in A Simple Sorting Algorithm, Journal of
 * the ACM 10:142-50, 1963. The code is a direct
 * translation of Hibbard's pseudocode into C, and
 * retains his variable names, line labels, and use
 * of goto statements.
 *
 * Has built-in driver
 *-----------------------------------------------------------*/

#include <stdio.h>
#include <stdlib.h>
#include <math.h>
#include <limits.h>
```

```
/* common variables */
int SwapPairs = 0; /* running total of number of swap pairs */
FILE *OutFile;       /* write swap pairs to this file */

/* Bit access macros */
#define SetBit(x,b) ((x) |=  (1 << (b)))
#define ClrBit(x,b) ((x) &= ~(1 << (b)))
#define TstBit(x,b) ((x) &   (1 << (b)))

void BoseSort ( int N )
{
    unsigned int x, xj, y, yj, j, L;

    fprintf ( OutFile,
            "{ /* Bose-Nelson sort for %d elements */\n", N );

    /* L = ceil(log2(N-1)) */
    L = sizeof(int) * CHAR_BIT - 1;
    for ( ; ! TstBit(N - 1, L); L-- )
              ;
    L += 1;

    /* starting values */
    x = 0;
    y = 1;

  /* Top of loop - x and y are a swap pair */
  A:                        /*--- goto target ---*/
    fprintf ( OutFile, "    swap(%d, %d);\n", x, y );
    SwapPairs += 1;

    j = 0;

  C:                        /*--- goto target ---*/
    xj = TstBit(x, j);
    yj = TstBit(y, j);

    if ( xj == 0 && yj == 0 )
        goto zero;
    else if ( xj && yj )
        goto one;
    else if ( xj == 0 )
        goto first_two;
    else
        goto two;

   zero:                        /*--- goto target ---*/
```

```
        SetBit(x, j);
        SetBit(y, j);
        if ( y <= N - 1 )
            goto A;

    one:                            /*--- goto target ---*/
        ClrBit(y, j);
        goto A;

    two:                            /*--- goto target ---*/
        ClrBit(x, j);
        j += 1;
        goto C;

    first_two:                      /*--- goto target ---*/
        ClrBit(x, j);
        ClrBit(y, j);
        if ( j == L )
            return;
        j += 1;
        if ( TstBit(y, j) )
            goto D;
        SetBit(x, j);
        SetBit(y, j);
        if ( y > N - 1 )
            goto first_two;
        if ( y < N - 1 )
            j = 0;

    D:                              /*--- goto target ---*/
        ClrBit(x, j);
        SetBit(y, j);
        goto A;
}

int main ( int argc, char *argv[] )
{
    int i, n;
    double optimal = 0.0;

    if ( argc != 3 || ( n = atoi ( argv[1] )) <= 1 )
    {
        fprintf ( stderr,
                  "Usage: bose-nel N outfile, where N > 1\n" );
        return ( EXIT_FAILURE );
    }

    if (( OutFile = fopen ( argv[2], "w" )) == NULL)
```

```
    {
        fprintf ( stderr, "Can't open %s\n", argv[2] );
        return ( EXIT_FAILURE );
    }

    BoseSort ( n );

    fprintf ( OutFile,
                " } /* There are %d swaps */\n", SwapPairs );
    fclose ( OutFile );

    printf ( "There were %d swaps generated.\n", SwapPairs );

    /*
     * Report theoretical optimum.
     * Start by computing log10(n!)
     */
    for ( i = 1; i <= n; i++ )
        optimal += log10 ( i );

    /*
     * Convert to ceil(log2(n!)) using
     * fact that log10(2) = .30103
     */
    optimal = ceil ( optimal / 0.30103 );

    printf ( "The best theoretical sort uses %.0f swaps.\n",
            (float) optimal );

    return ( EXIT_SUCCESS );
}
```

The *bose-nel.c* program does not actually perform a sort. Instead, it produces a C-code fragment that is meant to be placed into another program. For example, if we ask *bose-nel.c* to generate a Bose-Nelson sort for four elements, we get the following:

```
{ /* Bose-Nelson sort for 4 elements */
    swap(0, 1);
    swap(2, 3);
    swap(0, 2);
    swap(1, 3);
    swap(1, 2);
} /* There are 5 swaps */
```

The actual work is done by swap( ). It must examine the two items passed to it and swap them if appropriate. Note how this sequence of swap pairs corresponds to the network sort shown earlier in Figure 5-2.

The main advantage of a network sort like the Bose-Nelson sort is that, if you can arrange to perform some of the comparison-swaps simultaneously, a network sort may be faster than any other sort you can devise. Network sorts also lend themselves well to hardware implementations. There are, however, substantial disadvantages. Any given network sort is good only for a certain value of n, and as the number of comparison-swaps increases, so does the size of the program; a Bose-Nelson sort of 100 items makes 1,511 calls to swap( ) (Table 5-6)! Thus, network sorts are not good general-purpose sorts but rather are best reserved for fixed-size sorts of small numbers of items that must be performed often and very quickly.

Table 5-6.   Number of swap pairs generated by the Bose-Nelson algorithm for various *N*

N	Number of Swap Pairs
10	32
50	487
100	1,511
1,000	57,158

Summary: Choosing a Sort

As we have seen, all implementations of a given sort represent a compromise of some kind. There is no single best sort. However, some algorithms are generally better than others. Choosing between Shellsort, Heapsort, and Quicksort for small numbers of records (fewer than a thousand) is really a coin toss, as you can see from Figure 5-3. The advantages of Heapsort's and Quicksort's $N \lg N$ order over Shellsort's $N^{1.25}$ order do not become obvious until several thousand records are sorted. If Quicksort is implemented badly, it should be avoided, but we have seen ways to implement it well. While both Shellsort and Heapsort have the advantage of being largely independent of their input—they really do not have a degenerate worst case—a well-implemented Quicksort that is unlikely to encounter a degenerate case, is faster than Heapsort and Shellsort, and is generally the method of choice.

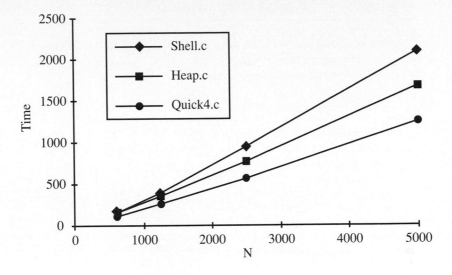

Figure 5-3. **Running times of *shell.c*, *heap.c*, and *quick4.c* on random-ordered data sets of various sizes.**

These considerations aside, you would probably do best to use ANSI C's `qsort()` unless you need to sort a linked list. It is advisable, however, to test your compiler's version against a few data sets to make sure it is well behaved. Try forward-ordered, reverse-ordered, and increasing-decreasing records. Also try data sets that contain many duplicate keys; a data set in which all the keys are either 0 or 1 provides a good test. If your compiler's `qsort()` performs well on all four types of data sets, you can feel comfortable using it. A simple routine for this purpose is shown in Listing 5-20 (*qstest.c*), along with a routine to generate test data sets that are presorted in a variety of ways (Listing 5-21, *makedata.c*). At the time of this writing, three popular IBM PC–based C compilers were from Borland, Microsoft, and Watcom. Of the three, only Borland C++'s `qsort()` gave equally speedy performances on all types of data sets. Surprisingly, the `qsort()` provided by both Microsoft and Watcom deteriorated when given reverse-ordered data sets or data sets with many duplicate keys. The situation with the compiler libraries available to you may be equally varied, and you should definitely investigate it before releasing any applications. If you find that your compiler's `qsort()` is deficient, a well-behaved `qsort()` replacement is provided as *quick5.c* (see Listing 5-11). Both programs were used during the preparation of this chapter.

Listing 5-20. A routine to test qsort().

```
/*--- qstest.c --------------------------- Listing 5-20 --------
 * Test compiler's qsort()
 * Link with sortsub.c (Listing 5-1)
 *
 * Has built-in driver
 *-------------------------------------------------------------*/
#include <stdio.h>
#include <string.h>
#include <stdlib.h>
#include <time.h>
#include "sorthdr.h"
#include "sortsub.h"

/*
 * A comparison function
 */
int pCfunc ( Element **L, Element **R )
{
    return ( strncmp ( (*L)->text, (*R)->text, 5 ));
}


void main ( int argc, char *argv[] )
{
    Element **Array;
    int Items = 2000;
    time_t a, b;

    if ( argc != 2 && argc != 3 )
    {
        fprintf ( stderr, "Usage: qstest infile [maxitems]\n" );
        return;
    }

    if ( argc == 3 )
        Items = atoi ( argv[2] );

    if (( Items = LoadArray ( argv[1], Items, &Array )) == -1 )
        return; /* Couldn't load file */

    time ( &a );
    qsort( Array, Items, sizeof(Element *),
           (int (*) (const void *, const void*))pCfunc );
    time ( &b );
    printf ( "Sorted %d items in %.0lf seconds.\n",
                Items, difftime ( b, a ));
}
```

Usage of the next program is explained in `main()`:

Listing 5-21.   A data generator to test sorts.

```c
/*--- makedata.c ------------------------ Listing 5-21 --------
 * Generate data for sort tests
 *
 * For usage, see main()
 *-----------------------------------------------------------*/

#include <stdio.h>
#include <stdlib.h>
#include <ctype.h>
#include <string.h>

void main ( int argc, char *argv[] )
{
    int i, from, to, step;

    if ( argc != 3 || strchr ( "fFrRbBuU?", *argv[1] ) == NULL)
    {
        printf ( "usage: makedata [f|r|b|?] n > outfile\n"
                 "    f = forward-ordered\n"
                 "    r = reverse-ordered\n"
                 "    u = up and down-ordererd\n"
                 "    b = binary (mixed ones and zeros)\n"
                 "    ? = random-ordered\n" );

        return;
    }

    if ( *argv[1] == '?' )
    {
        to = atoi ( argv[2] );

        for ( i = 0; i != to; i++ )
            printf ( "%05d\n", abs ( rand() ));

        return;
    }

    if ( tolower ( *argv[1] ) == 'b' )
    {
        to = atoi ( argv[2] );

        for ( i = 0; i != to; i++ )
            printf ( "%05d\n", abs(rand()) % 2 );
```

```
        return;
    }

    if ( tolower ( *argv[1] ) == 'u' )
    {
        to = atoi ( argv[2] ) / 2;
        for ( i = 0; i < to; i++ )
            printf ( "%05d\n", i );
        for ( i = to; i >= 0; i-- )
            printf ( "%05d\n", i );

        return;
    }

    if ( tolower ( *argv[1]) == 'f' )
        step = 1;
    else
        step = -1;

    i = atoi ( argv[2] );

    if ( step == 1 )
    {
        from = 0;
        to = i;
    }
    else
    {
        from = i;
        to = 0;
    }

    for ( i = from; i != to; i += step )
        printf ( "%05d\n", i );
}
```

Resources and References

Bose, R. C., and R. J. Nelson. "A Sorting Problem." *Journal ACM*, Vol. 9, pp. 282–296, 1962. This book presents the basis for the network sorting algorithm discussed in this chapter.

Hibbard, T. N. "A Simple Sorting Algorithm." *Journal ACM*, Vol. 10, pp. 142–50, 1963. This article presents the improved Bose-Nelson sort-pair generator that is used in *bose-nel.c*.

Hoare, C. A. R. "Quicksort." *Computer Journal*, Vol. 5, pp. 10–15, 1962. This article summarizes and analyzes in substantial detail the author's previous very short descriptions of the underlying algorithm.

Knuth, D. E. *The Art of Computer Programming*. Vol. 3. *Sorting and Searching*. Reading, MA: Addison-Wesley, 1973. This book is one of the two key references for this chapter. Knuth provides detailed mathematical analyses of the running times of each algorithm, along with many interesting historical details. He includes a substantial amount of extra material that is useful if you are interested in (1) other methods of calculating h for Shellsort and (2) additional approaches to sorting networks.

Sedgewick, R. *Algorithms in C*. Reading, MA: Addison-Wesley, 1990. This book is the other key reference for this chapter. Sedgewick is the undisputed master of Quicksort, and his text is an approachable source for details on its optimization. He also explores a number of other sorts that we do not describe in this text, including external sorting. The only weakness of Sedgewick's text is that the code examples have not always been converted correctly to use C's zero-based arrays and, as discussed in the beginning of this chapter, would thus need to be modified for use in any actual application.

Shell, D. L. *Communications of the ACM*. Vol. 2, pp. 30–32, 1959. This is the original description of Shellsort and is the source of its name.

Taylor, J. "Quicksorting Linked Lists." *C Gazette*, Vol. 5, No. 6, pp. 17–20, 1991. This is a good discussion of Quicksort for linked lists, and the code in this chapter follows Taylor's implementation. Note, however, that the code published with Taylor's article does not correctly implement a stable Quicksort. To fix his code, the comparisons in the inner loops must be altered to use *less than* rather than *less than or equal to*.

Chapter 6

Trees

A critical problem in many applications is the ability to locate a specific stored item quickly. The hash table techniques discussed in Chapter 3 represent one group of algorithms that address this problem, while the string-searching techniques described in Chapter 4 are another such group. A third general class of algorithms consists of tree algorithms. While more complex in their implementation than the other two techniques, they offer offsetting advantages that make them attractive under certain circumstances. Of particular interest is the relative ease with which you can adapt trees so that they store large amounts of data in secondary storage. In this chapter we discuss four tree algorithms. The first three (binary trees, red-black trees, and splay trees) are suited primarily to in-memory work, while the fourth (B-trees) is meant to be used with secondary storage such as a hard disk.

Binary Trees

Binary trees are the simplest tree algorithm, but they form the basis for the other algorithms. Their strengths and weaknesses also provide insights into the other tree algorithms. As shown in Figure 6-1, a binary tree is composed of nodes that contain at least three items: two pointers to other nodes and some user data. In this case, the tree contains four nodes. Node 2 contains data (its name) and pointers to nodes 1 and 3, while Node 3 points to Node 4.

Descriptions of trees make frequent use of family-oriented terminology such as *child*, *parent*, *grandparent*, and *great-grandparent*. We would thus call Node 1 the left child of Node 2, Node 3 the parent of node 4, and Node 4 the grandchild of Node 2. It should be apparent that a node may have zero, one, or two children. This definition is recursive in that either or both children of a given node can themselves be a binary tree.

The **root** of the binary tree is the one node that lacks a parent, and we normally draw trees so that this node appears as the topmost node in a diagram. The **height** or **depth** of any given node is the number of nodes that separate it from the root. The height (depth) of the tree is the same as the height (depth) of the highest (deepest) node. For example, in Figure 6-1, Node 2 has a height of zero, Nodes 1 and 3 have a height of one, Node 4 has a height of two, and the tree has an overall height of two.

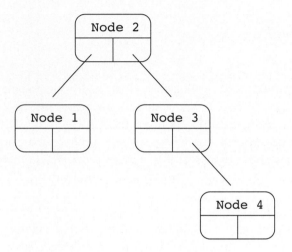

Figure 6-1.   A simple binary tree.

In addition to its topology, another important characteristic of a binary tree is its **traversal order**. You will frequently want to visit all the nodes in a tree, ensuring that you visit each node only once and in some consistent order. There are three possible traversal orders, all of which are recursive:

Preorder: Visit (1) the node, (2) the left child, and (3) the right child.
Inorder: Visit (1) the left child, (2) the node, and (3) the right child.
Postorder: Visit (1) the left child, (2) the right child, and (3) the node.

Of great importance, visiting a child implies that we recursively visit all of the child's children. Thus, even though the definitions are simple, all three traversal orders ultimately include visits to all the nodes in a tree. The three traversal orders may be used for various purposes at various times.

Consider Figure 6-2. Here, the expression 2+(6*7) has been parsed and stored in a binary tree. (Empty pointers and boxes around the nodes have been eliminated.) If we wanted to print the expression in its natural form, we would use an inorder traversal. However, by traversing the tree in postorder, the expression is converted to RPN (Reverse Polish Notation) and is easily evaluated.

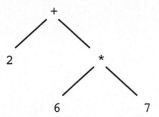

Figure 6-2. Binary tree for the expression 2+(6*7).

Note carefully that a tree's traversal order must be followed strictly and that you should not let empty subtrees fool your eye. Figure 6-3 shows a tall, skinny binary tree. The tree has been redrawn on the right with the empty subtrees so that the order is easier to see. It is important to realize that an inorder traversal visits the nodes in the order 1-2-3-4, even though the lack of many subtrees may make you think you are seeing a different order. Adding the empty subtrees makes the correct order somewhat easier to see.

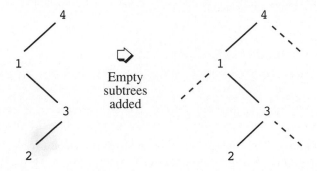

Figure 6-3. A tall, skinny tree with many empty subtrees.

When you want to use a binary tree to store large amounts of data, just follow a simple rule: the keys of the data stored at each node are in increasing order when the inorder traversal is used. By following this rule, you can now think of binary trees as having the form shown in Figure 6-4. This type of tree is often called a **binary search tree**. In this figure, all the left children have keys that precede the key of the parent. The right children have keys at least equal to the key of the parent.

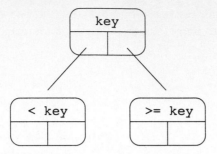

Figure 6-4.   A binary search tree.

Let's now examine a binary tree implementation. The complete source code for the binary tree routine is found in Listings 6-1 and 6-2 as *bintree.c* and *bintree.h*. This code can be compiled in three distinct ways. We will first examine it as compiled without either the REDBLACK or SPLAY switches defined. We start building the definition for a tree node in *bintree.h* with the following code. (Ignore the text inside the RBONLY macro for now; it will not be used for our binary search tree.)

```
#define BINTREE_STUFF(x) struct x *link[2] RBONLY(;int red)
typedef struct sBnode {
    BINTREE_STUFF(sBnode);
} Bnode;
```

In effect, then, a Bnode has the following form:

```
typedef struct sBnode {
    struct sBnode *link[2];
} Bnode;
```

This provides the two child pointers that are required for building the tree. All generic tree routines that we implement will manipulate Bnodes. However, a node without any data in it is not very useful. The approach to defining a node with data is found in *bintree.c* in the test driver:

```
typedef struct sMynode {
    BINTREE_STUFF(sMynode);
    char text[20];
} Mynode;
```

This will expand into the following:

```
typedef struct sMynode {
    struct sMynode *link[2];
    char text[20];
} Mynode;
```

In other words, a `Mynode` begins with two pointers in the same way that a `Bnode` does. If we were programming in C++, we would simply inherit `Bnode` into `Mynode`. In C, we do by hand what a C++ compiler does automatically: we define the structures so that they begin identically, and then we tack extra bytes onto the end of one of the structures. Because ANSI C guarantees that data pointers are of a common size, it is safe to interconvert pointers to `Bnode`s and `Mynode`s freely. We can now define a structure that holds all the information necessary for describing the root of a tree:

```
typedef struct sBintree {
    Bnode *DummyHead; /* points to node above the root */
    CompFunc Compare; /* compares two nodes */
    int DuplicatesOk; /* does tree take duplicates? */
    size_t NodeSize;  /* size (bytes) of a node */
} Bintree;
```

We will use `DummyHead` to point to a node whose right child is the actual tree root. Many tree operations are simplified if the root has a parent. `Compare` is a pointer to a user-defined function that compares two nodes and returns a negative value, zero, or a positive value, depending on their relative order (in a fashion identical to the return values from `strcmp()`). `DuplicatesOk` tells the tree routines whether items with duplicate keys are allowed in the tree. We store the size of a user node in `NodeSize` because `sizeof(Bnode)` will not take the user's data area into account.

Listing 6-1. Fundamental routines for binary trees.

```
/*--- bintree.c --------------------------- Listing 6-1 ---------
 * Binary tree routines. Provides plain binary search,
 * red-black, and self-adjusting (splay) trees.
 *
 * Switches:      REDBLACK - Use red-black variant
 *                SPLAY    - Use splay tree variant
 *                TEST     - Include a test driver
 *                ALTDRAW  - Use only standard drawing symbols
 *                           when drawing tree diagrams
 *-------------------------------------------------------------*/

#define TEST

#include <stdlib.h>
#include <stdio.h>
```

```c
#include <string.h>
#include <ctype.h>
#include "bintree.h"

/* A safe malloc() */
static void * tmalloc(size_t size)
{
    void *p;
    if ((p = malloc(size)) == NULL) {
        printf("Out of memory\n");
        exit(1);
    }

    return p;
}

/*
 * Create and initialize a node for the user. 'size' both can
 * and should be greater than sizeof(Bnode) to allow for a
 * data area for the user.
 */
Bnode *InitBintreeNode(size_t size)
{
    Bnode *n;

    n = tmalloc(size);
    n -> link[LEFT] = n -> link[RIGHT]  = NULL;
    RBONLY(n -> red = 0;)

    return n;
}

/* Create an empty tree */
Bintree *NewBintree (Bnode *dummy,
    CompFunc cf,
    int dup_ok,
    size_t node_size)
{
    Bintree *t;

    t = tmalloc(sizeof(Bintree));
    t -> DummyHead = dummy;
    t -> Compare = cf;
    t -> DuplicatesOk = dup_ok;
    t -> NodeSize = node_size;

    return t;
}
```

```
#if defined(SPLAY)

/*
 * During a top-down splay, we build up the future left and right
 * sub-trees in trees whose roots are stored in the array LR[].
 * LRwalk[] retains a current pointer into each of these trees.
 * We are always interested in finding the bottom left node of
 * the right tree or the bottom right node of the left tree.
 * Thus, PUSH(LEFT) starts at LRwalk[LEFT], steps down and to
 * the right until it hits bottom, and then stores the new
 * location in LRwalk[LEFT].
 */
#define PUSH(x) {                                       \
                    Bnode *w;                           \
                    for (w = LRwalk[x];                 \
                        w -> link[!(x)];                \
                        w = w -> link[!(x)]);           \
                    LRwalk[x] = w;                      \
                }

int splay(Bintree *t, Bnode *n)
{
    Bnode *s, *ch, *gch;
    Bnode LR[2], *LRwalk[2];
    int s_comp, ch_comp, dir, dir2;

    s = t -> DummyHead -> link[RIGHT];
    if (s == NULL) /* empty tree */
        return 1; /* no match */

    /*
     * Create two empty trees: we place portions of the initial
     * tree onto these two trees as we "splay down" the tree.
     */
    LR[LEFT].link[RIGHT] = NULL;
    LR[RIGHT].link[LEFT] = NULL;

    LRwalk[LEFT]  = &LR[LEFT];
    LRwalk[RIGHT] = &LR[RIGHT];

    /* not really needed */
    LR[LEFT].link[LEFT] = NULL;
    LR[RIGHT].link[RIGHT] = NULL;

    for (;;) {
        /* We are at s. Which way now? First, find s's child */
        s_comp = n ? (t -> Compare)(n, s) : 1;
        dir = s_comp < 0;
        ch = s -> link[dir];
        if (s_comp == 0 || ch == NULL)
```

```
            break;

        /* Now, find s's grandchild */
        ch_comp = n ? (t -> Compare)(n, ch) : 1;
        dir2 = ch_comp < 0;
        gch = ch -> link[dir2];

        /*
         * If we've found a match for n (ch_comp==0) or if we've
         * no further to go (gch==NULL), then we're done. ch will
         * be the root of the new tree after reconstruction is
         * complete. This case is the only exit from this loop.
         */
        if (ch_comp == 0 || gch == NULL) {
            s -> link[dir] = NULL; /* break link betw s and ch */
            LRwalk[!dir] -> link[dir] = s; /* hang s on LR */
            PUSH(!dir);  /* and push LRwalk to bottom */

            s = ch; /* advance s to ch */
            s_comp = ch_comp;
            break; /* proceed to tree reconstruction */
        }

        else { /* split up the tree as described in the text */
            if (dir == dir2) { /* zig-zig */
                s -> link[dir] = ch -> link[!dir];
                ch -> link[!dir] = s;
                ch -> link[dir] = NULL;
                LRwalk[!dir] -> link[dir] = ch;
                        PUSH(!dir);
            }

            else { /* zig-zag */
                s -> link[dir] = NULL;
                LRwalk[!dir] -> link[dir] = s;
                PUSH(!dir);
                ch -> link[dir2] = NULL;
                LRwalk[!dir2] -> link[dir2] = ch;
                PUSH(!dir2);
            }
            s = gch;
        }
    }

/* put it all together */
LRwalk[LEFT]  -> link[RIGHT] = s -> link[LEFT];
LRwalk[RIGHT] -> link[LEFT]  = s -> link[RIGHT];
s -> link[LEFT]  = LR[LEFT].link[RIGHT];
s -> link[RIGHT] = LR[RIGHT].link[LEFT];
```

```
    t -> DummyHead -> link[RIGHT] = s;
    return s_comp;
}
#endif

/* Find node n in tree t */
Bnode *FindBintree(Bintree *t, Bnode *n)
{
    #if defined(SPLAY)
    if (splay(t, n))
        return NULL; /* exact match not found */
    else
        return t -> DummyHead -> link[RIGHT];

    #else /* plain or red-black */
    Bnode *s;
    int dir;

    s = t -> DummyHead -> link[RIGHT];
    while (s != NULL) {
        dir = (t -> Compare) (n, s);
        /*
         * If a match, we're done.
         * For Red-Black, must also be a leaf.
         */
        if (dir == 0 RBONLY(&& s -> link[RIGHT] == NULL))
            return s;
        dir = dir < 0;
        s = s -> link[dir];
    }
    return NULL; /* no match */
    #endif
}

#if defined(REDBLACK)
/*
 * Rotate child and grandchild of r along the path
 * specified by searching for n. For example, if n was
 * equal to 3, gc2, or 4, the following rotation occurs:
 *
 *           r                               r
 *           |                               |
 *           c                               gc2
 *        /     \           ==>            /     \
 *     gc1       gc2                     c         4
 *    /   \     /   \                  /   \
 *   1     2   3     4               gc1     3
 *                                  /   \
 *                                 1     2
```

```
 *
 * As r may connect to c via either its left or right
 * link, there are actually four symmetric variants.
 *
 * A pointer to the top of the new rotated nodes (in the
 * case above, to gc2) is returned.
 *
 * This routine is complicated by the fact that the routine
 * uses the value of the node n to decide which direction
 * to rotate. This may or may not be the direction the caller
 * has is mind. Rather than require the caller to specify
 * the direction of the rotation, it seemed easier to allow
 * the caller to specify whether to go in the direction of n
 * or away from it. This is done by the last argument to the
 * function, flip_mode. The caller can indicate that either
 * or both of the directions to child and grandchild should
 * be reversed during the rotation.
 */

#define NO_FLIP   0
#define FLIP_GCH  1
#define FLIP_CH   2
Bnode *rotate(Bintree *t, Bnode *n, Bnode *r, int flip_mode)
{
    Bnode *ch, *gch;
    int ch_dir, gch_dir;

    /* Identify child and grandchild */
    ch_dir = (t -> Compare) (n, r) < 0;
    if (flip_mode & FLIP_CH)
        ch_dir = !ch_dir;
    if (r == t -> DummyHead) /* special condition */
        ch_dir = RIGHT;
    ch = r -> link[ch_dir];

    gch_dir = (t -> Compare) (n, ch) < 0;
    if (flip_mode) {
        if (flip_mode == FLIP_GCH)
            gch_dir = !gch_dir;
        else
            gch_dir = flip_mode & 1;
    }
    gch = ch -> link[gch_dir];

    /* rotate: now move pointers */
    ch -> link[gch_dir] = gch -> link[!gch_dir];
    gch -> link[!gch_dir] = ch;
```

```
      r -> link[ch_dir] = gch;

      return gch;
}


/*
 * Take care of colors and balance. It will color the current
 * location red, the current location's children black, and
 * then look to see if two consecutive red nodes have been
 * created. If so, a single or double rotation will be done
 * to fix the tree.
 */
void split(Bintree *t,   /* tree                  */
           Bnode *n,     /* node being inserted   */
           Bnode **c,    /* current location      */
           Bnode **p,    /* its parent            */
           Bnode *g,     /* its grandparent       */
           Bnode *gg)    /* its great-grandparent */
{
    if (t -> DummyHead -> red) {
        fputs("dummyhead was red!!\n", stdout);
        t -> DummyHead -> red = 0;
    }
    (*c) -> red = 1;
    if ((*c) -> link[LEFT])
        (*c) -> link[LEFT] -> red = 0;
    if ((*c) -> link[RIGHT])
        (*c) -> link[RIGHT] -> red = 0;


    /*
     * Check to make sure we haven't created two red
     * links in a row. If we have, we must rotate.
     */
    if ((*p) -> red) {
        g -> red = 1;
        /*
         * If the red links don't point in the same direction,
         * then will need a double rotation. The lower half
         * is around the grandparent and then the upper half
         * is around the great-grandparent.
         */
        if (((t -> Compare) (n, g) < 0) !=
            ((t -> Compare) (n, *p) < 0))
            *p = rotate(t, n, g, NO_FLIP);

        /* Same for both single and double rotations. */
        *c = rotate(t, n, gg, NO_FLIP);
```

```
            (*c) -> red = 0;
    }


    t -> DummyHead -> link[RIGHT] -> red = 0;
}
#endif

/*
 * Delete node n from tree t. Returns a pointer to the
 * deleted node -- it should then be freed or otherwise
 * destroyed. The versions for the binary tree and the
 * red-black tree are very different, due to the balancing
 * problems that the red-black version must handle.
 */
#if defined(REDBLACK)
Bnode * DelBintree (Bintree *t, Bnode *n)
{
    /*
     * The goal is to arrive at a leaf with a red parent.
     * Thus, we force this by dragging a red node with us
     * down the tree, re-arranging the tree to keep its
     * balance as we go. All the rearrangements keep the tree
     * balanced, so if we cancel the deletion or don't find
     * the specified node to delete, we can just quit.
     */

    Bnode *s, *p, *g;
    int dir, next_dir;

    g = NULL;
    p = t -> DummyHead;
    s = p -> link[RIGHT];
    dir = RIGHT;

    /*
     * First, check on the root. It must exist, have children,
     * and either it or one of its children must be red. We can
     * just paint the root red, if necessary, as this will
     * affect the black height of the entire tree equally.
     */
    if (s == NULL)
        return NULL;

    /* Check to make sure the root isn't an only child. */
    if (s -> link[LEFT] == NULL) {
        if ((t -> Compare)(n, s) == 0) {
            /* deleting the root */
```

```
                p -> link[RIGHT] = NULL;
                return s;
            }
        else
            return NULL;
}


/* Now, either the root or one of its kids must be red */
if (!s -> link[LEFT]  -> red &&
    !s -> link[RIGHT] -> red)
    s -> red = 1; /* Just color the root red */


/*
 * Now, march down the tree, always working to make sure
 * the current node is red. That way, when we do arrive
 * at a leaf, its parent will be red, making the leaf
 * very easy to delete (just drop the leaf, and replace
 * its (red) parent with its (black) sib.)
 */
for (;;) {
    /*
     * If we're at a leaf, we're done.
     */
    if (s -> link[LEFT] == NULL)
        break;

    /*
     * Where are we going next?
     */
    next_dir = (t -> Compare) (n, s) < 0;

    /*
     * If the current node or the next node
     * is red, we can advance.
     */
    if (s -> red || s -> link[next_dir] -> red)
        ;

    /*
     * (If the current node is black)
     * (and the next node is black)
     * but the next node's sib is red ...
     *
     * Then rotate from parent towards the red child. This
     * will lower the current node, and give us a new
     * grandparent (the old parent) and a new
     * parent (the sib that was red). We the paint the
```

```
 * current node red and the new parent is painted black.
 */
else if (s -> link[!next_dir] -> red) {
    g = p;
    p = rotate(t, s -> link[next_dir], p, FLIP_GCH);
    s -> red = 1;
    p -> red = 0;
}


/*
 * (If the current node is black)
 * (and its left child is black)
 * (and its right child is black) ...
 *
 * then (a) the current node's parent must be red (we
 * never advance unless we are leaving a red node),
 * (b) its sib must be black (because the parent is red),
 * and (c) we need to color the current node red. To
 * make this possible, we color the current node red,
 * the parent black and then check for tree imbalances.
 * Two cases exist...
 */
else {
    Bnode *sib;
    if (!p -> red)
        fprintf(stdout, "Parent not red in case 2!\n");
    sib = p -> link[!dir];
    if (sib -> red)
        fprintf(stdout, "Sib not black in case 2!\n");
    if (sib -> link[LEFT] == NULL) {
        fprintf(stdout, "Sib has no kids in case 2!\n");
        return NULL;
    }

    s -> red = 1;
    p -> red = 0;

    /*
     * First case: black sib has two black kids. Just
     * color the sib red. In effect, we are reversing
     * a simple color flip.
     */
    if (!sib -> link[LEFT]  -> red &&
        !sib -> link[RIGHT] -> red)
        sib -> red = 1;

    /*
```

```
                  * Second case: black sib has at least one red kid.
                  * (It makes no difference if both kids are red.)
                  * We need to do either a single or double rotation
                  * in order to re-balance the tree.
                  */
                 else {
                     int redkid_dir;

                     if (sib -> link[LEFT] -> red)
                         redkid_dir = LEFT;
                     else
                         redkid_dir = RIGHT;

                     if (!dir == redkid_dir) {
                         sib -> red = 1;
                         sib -> link[redkid_dir] -> red = 0;
                         g = rotate(t, n, g, FLIP_GCH);
                     }
                     else {
                         rotate(t, n, p, FLIP_CH + redkid_dir);
                         g = rotate(t, n, g, FLIP_GCH);
                     }
                 }
             }
         }

         /* advance pointers */
         dir = next_dir;
         g = p;
         p = s;
         s = s -> link[dir];
     }

     /* Make the root black */
     t -> DummyHead -> link[RIGHT] -> red = 0;

     /* Delete it, if a match. Parent is red. */
     if ((t -> Compare)(s, n) == 0) {
         if (!p -> red && p != t -> DummyHead)
             fprintf(stdout, "Parent not red at delete!\n");
         g -> link[(t -> Compare)(s, g) < 0] =
             p -> link[(t -> Compare)(s, p) >= 0];
         free (p); /* release internal node that we created */
         return s;
     }
     else return NULL;
 }
```

```
#elif defined(SPLAY) /* Splay tree version */
Bnode *DelBintree (Bintree *t, Bnode *n)
{
    Bnode *save, *t2;


    if (splay(t, n))
        save = NULL; /* match not found */
    else {
        save = t -> DummyHead -> link[RIGHT];
        t2 = save -> link[RIGHT];
        if (t -> DummyHead -> link[RIGHT] = save -> link[LEFT])
        {   /* '=' and not '==' is correct on previous line */
            splay(t, NULL);
            t -> DummyHead -> link[RIGHT] -> link[RIGHT] = t2;
        }
        else
            t -> DummyHead -> link[RIGHT] = t2;


    }
    return save;
}

#else /* Binary tree version */
Bnode * DelBintree (Bintree *t, Bnode *n)
{

    Bnode *p, *s, *save;
    int dir, dir_old;

    p = t -> DummyHead;
    s = p -> link[RIGHT];
    dir_old = dir = RIGHT;

    /* Look for a match */
    while (s != NULL && (dir = (t->Compare)(n, s)) != 0) {
        p = s;
        dir = dir < 0;
        dir_old = dir;
        s = p -> link[dir];
    }

    if (s == NULL)
        return NULL; /* no match found */

    save = s;
    /*
     * First case: if s has no right child, then replace s
```

```
     * with s's left child.
     */
    if (s -> link[RIGHT] == NULL)
        s = s -> link[LEFT];
    /*
     * Second case: if s has a right child that lacks a left
     * child, then replace s with s's right child and
     * copy s's left child into the right child's left child.
     */
    else if (s -> link[RIGHT] -> link[LEFT] == NULL) {
        s = s -> link[RIGHT];
        s -> link[LEFT] = save -> link[LEFT];
    }
    /*
     * Final case: find leftmost (smallest) node in s's right
     * subtree. By definition, this node has an empty left
     * link. Free this node by copying its right link to
     * its parent's left link and then give it both of s's
     * links (thus replacing s).
     */
    else {
        Bnode *small;

        small = s -> link[RIGHT];
        while (small -> link[LEFT] -> link[LEFT])
            small = small -> link[LEFT];
        s = small -> link[LEFT];
        small -> link[LEFT] = s -> link[RIGHT];
        s -> link[LEFT] = save -> link[LEFT];
        s -> link[RIGHT] = save -> link[RIGHT];
    }

    p -> link[dir_old] = s;

    RBONLY(s -> red = 0;)

    return save;
}
#endif

/* Insert node n into tree t */
int InsBintree (Bintree *t, Bnode *n)
{
    #if defined(REDBLACK)
    int p_dir;
    Bnode *p, *s;
    Bnode *g   = NULL;
    Bnode *gg  = NULL;
```

```
/* Search until we find a leaf. */
p = t -> DummyHead;
p_dir = RIGHT; /* direction from p to s */
s = p -> link[RIGHT];

if (s) {
    Bnode *temp;
    int dir;

    /* Look for a leaf, splitting nodes on the way down */
    while (s -> link[RIGHT] != NULL) {
        if (s -> link[LEFT]  -> red &&
            s -> link[RIGHT] -> red)
            split(t, n, &s, &p, g, gg);
        gg = g;
        g  = p;
        p  = s;
        p_dir = (t -> Compare) (n, s) < 0;
        s = s -> link[p_dir];
    }

    dir = (t -> Compare) (n, s);
    if (t -> DuplicatesOk == 0 && dir == 0)
        return TREE_FAIL; /* duplicate - not allowed */

    /*
     * Must replace s with a new internal node that has as
     * its children s and n. The new node gets the larger of
     * s and n as its key. The new node gets painted red, its
     * children are black. Coloring is done by split().
     */
    temp = tmalloc(t -> NodeSize);
    dir = dir < 0;
    memcpy(temp, dir ? s : n, t -> NodeSize);
    temp -> link[dir]  = n;
    temp -> link[!dir] = s;
    n = temp;
}

/* Add the new node */
p -> link[p_dir] = n;

/* Color this node red and check red-black balance */
split(t, n, &n, &p, g, gg);
return TREE_OK;

#elif defined(SPLAY)
int dir;
```

```
    Bnode *r;

    dir = splay(t, n);
    if (dir == 0 && t -> DuplicatesOk == 0)
        return TREE_FAIL;
    r = t -> DummyHead -> link[RIGHT];

    if (r == NULL) /* first node? */
        t -> DummyHead -> link[RIGHT] = n;
    else {
        dir = dir < 0;
        n -> link[dir] = r -> link[dir];
        r -> link[dir] = NULL;
        n -> link[!dir] = r;
        t -> DummyHead -> link[RIGHT] = n;
    }
    return TREE_OK;

    #else /* plain binary tree */
    int p_dir;
    Bnode *p, *s;

    /* Search until we find an empty arm. */
    p = t -> DummyHead;
    p_dir = RIGHT; /* direction from p to s */
    s = p -> link[RIGHT];

    while (s != NULL) {
        p = s;
        p_dir = (t -> Compare) (n, s);
        if (p_dir == 0 && t -> DuplicatesOk == 0)
            return TREE_FAIL; /* duplicate */
        p_dir = p_dir < 0;
        s = s -> link[p_dir];
    }

    /* Add the new node */
    p -> link[p_dir] = n;
    return TREE_OK;
    #endif
}

/*
 * Recursive tree walk routines. The entry point is
 * WalkBintree. It will do an inorder traversal of the
 * tree, call df() for each node and leaf.
 */
void rWalk(Bnode *n, int level, DoFunc df)
```

```
{
    if (n != NULL) {
        rWalk(n -> link[LEFT], level + 1, df);
        df(n, level);
        rWalk(n -> link[RIGHT], level + 1, df);
    }
}

int WalkBintree(Bintree *t, DoFunc df)
{
    if (t -> DummyHead -> link[RIGHT] == NULL) {
        fputs("Empty tree\n", stdout);
        return TREE_FAIL;
    }

    rWalk(t -> DummyHead -> link[RIGHT], 0, df);
    return TREE_OK;
}

#if defined(TEST)
/*
 * Test driver
 */

#define BUFLEN 100

/* Our binary tree is made up of these */
typedef struct sMynode {
    /* A copy of the items in a Bnode */
    BINTREE_STUFF(sMynode);

    /*
     * Now for the user's part of the structure. We could put
     * anything here. For these routines, a simple text area.
     */
    char text[20];
} Mynode;

int LoadString(Bintree *t, char *string)
{
    Mynode *m;

    m = (Mynode *) InitBintreeNode(sizeof(Mynode));
    strncpy(m->text, string, sizeof(m->text));
    m->text[sizeof(m->text) - 1] = 0;

    return InsBintree(t, (Bnode *) m);
}
```

```c
void FindString(Bintree *t, char *string)
{
    Mynode m, *r;
    strncpy(m.text, string, sizeof(m.text));
    m.text[sizeof(m.text) - 1] = 0;
    if ((r = (Mynode *) FindBintree(t, (Bnode *) &m)) == NULL)
        puts(" Not found.\n");
    else
        printf(" Found '%s'.\n", r -> text);
}

void DeleteString(Bintree *t, char *string)
{
    Mynode m, *n;
    strncpy(m.text, string, sizeof(m.text));
    m.text[sizeof(m.text) - 1] = 0;
    n = (Mynode *) DelBintree(t, (Bnode *) &m);
    if (n)
        free (n);
    else
        fprintf(stdout, " Did not find '%s'.\n", string);
}

void LoadFile(Bintree *t, char *fname)
{
    FILE *infile;
    char buffer[BUFLEN], *s;
    int i = 0, j = 0;

    if ((infile = fopen(fname, "r")) == NULL) {
        fputs(" Couldn't open the file.\n", stdout);
        return;
    }

    while (fgets(buffer, BUFLEN, infile)) {
        s = buffer + strlen(buffer);
        while(iscntrl(*s))
            *s-- = 0;
        if (buffer[0] == ';') /* a comment */
            ;
        else if (buffer[0] == '-' && buffer[1] != 0) {
            DeleteString(t, buffer+1);
            j++;
        }
        else {
            LoadString(t, buffer);
            i++;
        }
```

```
    }

    fclose(infile);
    printf("Loaded %d items and deleted %d from %s.\n",
        i, j, fname);
}

/*
 * A sample action function: it prints out the data
 * at each node along with the node's level in the tree
 */
int ShowFunc(void *m, int level)
{
    RBONLY(if (((Mynode *)m) -> link[LEFT] == NULL))
        fprintf(stdout, "%s (%d)\n",
        ((Mynode *)m) -> text, level);

    return TREE_OK;
}


/*
 * A pair of functions to print the tree as a diagram.
 */

#if !defined(ALTDRAW)
  #define TOP '+'
  #define BOT '+'
  #define HOR '-'
  #define VRT '|'
#else
  #define TOP '/'
  #define BOT '\\'
  #define HOR '-'
  #define VRT '|'
#endif

#if defined(REDBLACK)
  #if !defined(ALTDRAW)
    #define RTOP '+'
    #define RBOT '+'
    #define RHOR '-'
    #define RVRT '|'
  #else
    #define RTOP '*'
    #define RBOT '*'
    #define RHOR '#'
    #define RVRT '#'
```

```
    #endif
#endif

#define DRAWBUF 100
char draw[DRAWBUF];
char work[DRAWBUF * 2];
int maxdepth;
RBONLY(int blackheight;)
RBONLY(int maxblack;)
FILE *outfile;

void xrWalk(Bnode *n, int level)
{
    int i;

    if (n != NULL) {
        /* Monitor */
        if (level > maxdepth)
            maxdepth = level;
        RBONLY(if (!n -> red) blackheight++;)

        /*
         * Go right
         */
        draw[level * 2] = TOP;
        #if defined(REDBLACK)
        if (n -> link[RIGHT] && n -> link[RIGHT] -> red)
            draw[level * 2] = RTOP;
        #endif
        draw[level * 2 + 1] = ' ';
        xrWalk(n -> link[RIGHT], level + 1);

        /*
         * Show current node
         */
        strncpy(work, draw, level * 2);
        if (level > 0) {
            int c;

            c = work[0];
            for (i = 2; i < level * 2; i += 2)
                #if !defined(REDBLACK)
                if (work[i] == c)
                #else
                if (((c == TOP || c == RTOP) &&
                    (work[i] == TOP || work[i] == RTOP)) ||
                    ((c == BOT || c == RBOT) &&
                    (work[i] == BOT || work[i] == RBOT)))
```

```
            #endif
                work[i - 2] = ' ';
            else
                c = work[i];

    work[level * 2 - 1] =
        RBONLY(((Mynode *)n) -> red ? RHOR :)
        HOR;

    for (i = 0; i < level * 2 - 2; i += 2)
        if (work[i] != ' ') {
            #if !defined(REDBLACK)
            work[i] = VRT;
            #else
            if (work[i] == TOP || work[i] == BOT)
                work[i] = VRT;
            else
                work[i] = RVRT;
            #endif
        }
}

sprintf(work + level * 2, "%s (%d)",
                    ((Mynode *)n)->text, level);
fputs(work, outfile);

#if defined(REDBLACK)
if (n -> link[LEFT] == NULL) { /* leaf */
    if (maxblack < 0)
        maxblack = blackheight;
    else if (maxblack != blackheight)
        fprintf(outfile, "  Leaf has black height %d!",
        blackheight - 1);
}
#endif
fputs("\n", outfile);

/*
 * Go left
 */
draw[level * 2] = BOT;
#if defined(REDBLACK)
if (n -> link[LEFT] && n -> link[LEFT] -> red)
    draw[level * 2] = RBOT;
#endif
draw[level * 2 + 1] = ' ';
xrWalk(n -> link[LEFT], level + 1);
```

```
                RBONLY(if (!n -> red) blackheight--;)
        }
}

int xWalkBintree(Bintree *t, char *name, char *mode)
{
        if (t -> DummyHead -> link[RIGHT] == NULL) {
                fputs("Empty tree\n", stdout);
                return TREE_FAIL;
        }

        maxdepth = -1;
        RBONLY(blackheight = 0;)
        RBONLY(maxblack = -1;)

        outfile = stdout;
        if (name) {
                outfile = fopen(name, mode);
                if (outfile == NULL) {
                        fprintf(stdout, "Can't open %s.\n", name);
                        name = NULL;
                        outfile = stdout;
                }
        }

        xrWalk(t -> DummyHead -> link[RIGHT], 0);
        #if defined(REDBLACK)
        fprintf(outfile, "Max depth %d, black height %d.\n",
                maxdepth, maxblack - 1);
        #else
        fprintf(outfile, "Max depth %d.\n", maxdepth);
        #endif

        if (name)
                fclose(outfile); /* a real file */
        else
                fflush(outfile); /* stdout */

        return TREE_OK;
}

int compare_length = 0;
int CompareFunc(void *n1, void *n2)
{
        if (compare_length)
                return strncmp(((Mynode *)n1)->text,
                ((Mynode *)n2)->text,
                compare_length);
```

```
        else
            return strcmp(((Mynode *)n1)->text,
            ((Mynode *)n2)->text);
}

main(int argc, char **argv)
{
    char inbuf[BUFLEN], *s;
    Bintree *tree;
    Mynode *dummy;
    FILE *logfile = NULL;

#if defined(REDBLACK)
    printf("Red-black binary tree test driver.\n"
        " Lines to red nodes are drawn with %c%c%c lines and\n"
        " lines to black nodes are drawn with %c%c%c lines.\n",
            RHOR, RHOR, RHOR, HOR, HOR, HOR);
#elif defined(SPLAY)
    printf("Splay tree test driver.\n");
#else
    printf("Plain binary tree test driver.\n");
#endif

    /* create a dummy node for the tree algorithms */
    dummy = (Mynode *) InitBintreeNode(sizeof(Mynode));
    dummy->text[0] = 0; /* must contain valid data */

    /* create a tree */
    tree = NewBintree((Bnode *) dummy,
                        CompareFunc, 1, sizeof(Mynode));

    for (;;) {
        fputs("Action (? for help): ", stdout);
        fflush(stdout);
        fgets(inbuf, BUFLEN, stdin);
        s = inbuf + strlen(inbuf);
        while(iscntrl(*s))
            *s-- = 0;

        if (logfile)
            fprintf(logfile, "%s\n", inbuf);

        switch (inbuf[0]) {
            case '?':
                fputs(
                    "@file     - Load strings in file to tree\n"
                    "a string  - Add string to tree\n"
                    "c nn      - Compare only first nn chars\n"
```

```
                "d string   - Delete string from tree\n"
                "dup [0|1] - Disallow/allow duplicates\n"
                "f string   - Find string in tree\n"
                "l file     - Log actions to file\n"
                "l         - Turn off action logging\n"
                "s [file]  - Display tree (overwrite file)\n"
                "S [file]  - Display tree (append to file)\n"
                "w         - Walk tree, running ShowFunc()\n"
                "q         - Quit\n"
                , stdout);
            fflush(stdout);
            break;

    case '@':
            LoadFile(tree, inbuf + 1);
            break;

    case 'a':
            if (inbuf[1] != ' ' || inbuf[2] == 0)
                fputs(" Not a valid command\n", stdout);
            else
                if (LoadString(tree, inbuf + 2)==TREE_FAIL)
                    fputs(" ** Insertion failed\n", stdout);
            break;

    case 'c':
            if (inbuf[1] == ' ' && inbuf[2] != 0) {
                compare_length = atoi(inbuf+2);
                if (compare_length < 0)
                    compare_length  = 0;
            }
            if (compare_length)
                printf("Comparing first %d chars.\n",
                compare_length);
            else
                printf("Comparing entire text.\n");
            break;

    case 'd':
            if (inbuf[1] == 'u' && inbuf[2] == 'p') {
                if (inbuf[3] == ' ' &&
                    (inbuf[4] == '0' || inbuf[4] == '1'))
                    tree -> DuplicatesOk =
                    inbuf[4] == '0' ? 0 : 1;
                fputs("Duplicates are ", stdout);
                if (tree -> DuplicatesOk == 0)
                    fputs("not ", stdout);
                fputs("allowed.\n", stdout);
```

```
            break;
        }

        if (inbuf[1] != ' ' || inbuf[2] == 0)
            fputs(" Not a valid command\n", stdout);


        else
            DeleteString(tree, inbuf + 2);
        break;

case 'f':
    if (inbuf[1] != ' ' || inbuf[2] == 0)
        fputs(" Not a valid command\n", stdout);
    else
        FindString(tree, inbuf + 2);
    break;

case 'l':
    if (inbuf[1] != ' ' || inbuf[2] == 0) {
        if (logfile) {
            fclose(logfile);
            logfile = NULL;
        }
        else
            fputs(" Logfile not open\n", stdout);
    }
    else {
        logfile = fopen(inbuf + 2, "w");
        if (logfile == NULL)
            printf("Can't open %s\n", inbuf + 2);
    }
    break;

case 's': case 'S':
    if (inbuf[1] == ' ' && inbuf[2] != 0)
        xWalkBintree(tree, inbuf + 2,
        inbuf[0] == 's' ? "w" : "a");
    else
        xWalkBintree(tree, NULL, NULL);
    break;

case 'w':
    WalkBintree(tree, ShowFunc);
    break;

case 'q':
    if (logfile)
```

```
                    fclose(logfile);
                return;

            case ';':
                break;   /* comment */

            default:
                fputs(" Not a valid command\n", stdout);
                break;
        }
    }
}
#endif
```

As shown in the following code, we define the prototypes for the five tree primitives—tree creation, tree search, node insertion, node deletion, and tree walking.

```
/* Prototypes */
Bintree *NewBintree (Bnode *dummy, CompFunc cf,
                     int dup_ok, size_t node_size);
Bnode   *FindBintree(Bintree *t, Bnode *n);
int      InsBintree (Bintree *t, Bnode *n);
Bnode   *DelBintree (Bintree *t, Bnode *n);
int      WalkBintree(Bintree *t, DoFunc df);
```

The code for these routines is in *bintree.c*. There is also a test driver that illustrates the uses of the primitives other than the simple processes of creating and walking a tree. Let's examine the three functions.

Tree Search

Searching a binary search tree (Listing 6-1, `FindBinTree`) is straightforward. Look at the following pseudocode:

```
search(node, find) {
    while (node != NULL) {
        if (node->data == find->data)
            return node;
        else if (find->data < node->data)
            node = node -> left;
        else
            node = node -> right;
    }
    return NULL; /* search failed */
}
```

Starting at any given node, we first ask whether the node's data matches the search item. If it does, we quit. If it doesn't, we look to the left if the search item is smaller than the current node, or to the right if it is larger. In the actual code, we take advantage of the fact that we have defined the pointers to the two children as an array of two elements rather than two distinct elements named `left` and `right`. In *bintree.h* we have arbitrarily defined RIGHT as 0 and LEFT as 1. In the code, we store the return value from the comparison function in the variable `dir`. Then, rather than writing

```
if (dir < 0)
    branch to link[1]
else
    branch to link[0]
```

we take advantage of the fact that the expression `dir<0` returns either 0 or 1. Thus, we can simply say the following:

```
examine link[dir < 0]
```

Note how failed searches are handled. If `node` ever becomes NULL, the code knows that the desired item is missing and returns NULL.

Node Insertion

Node insertion is also simple (Listing 6-1, `InsBinTree`). We first descend the tree as if we were searching for the node that we want to insert. When we arrive at a node without a child (that is, when the current node is NULL), we insert the new node as the child of the last node. This type of operation is one reason the structure that defines the tree has a pointer to node that points to the root.

Node Deletion

Deletion is the most difficult of three primitives to implement (Listing 6-1, `DelBinTree`), mainly because we must be certain to maintain the nodes in the correct relative positions so that the key ordering defined in Figure 6-4 will be maintained. Again, we descend the tree, searching for the node that we want to delete. Once we find it, there are three possible cases. In this discussion, we refer to the node to be deleted as *s*.

Case 1: If *s* lacks a right child, replace *s* with *s*'s left child, as shown in Figure 6-5a. This is the simplest case and it also handles the possibility that *s* has no children.

Case 2: If *s*'s right child lacks a left child, then make *s*'s left child into the right child's left child and replace *s* with the right child, as shown in Figure 6-5b.

Case 3: The worst problem arises if *s*'s right child has two children of its own, as shown in Figure 6-5a. We proceed by searching *s*'s *right subtree* for its *leftmost node*. The result is that we find the next largest node after *s*. This node (called "leftmost" in the figure) by definition lacks a left child, so we can easily free it by replacing it with its right child. We then give this new node both of *s*'s children, thus freeing *s*.

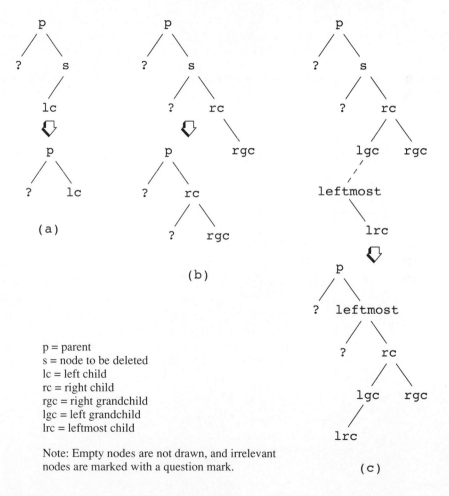

p = parent
s = node to be deleted
lc = left child
rc = right child
rgc = right grandchild
lgc = left grandchild
lrc = leftmost child

Note: Empty nodes are not drawn, and irrelevant nodes are marked with a question mark.

Figure 6-5.   Deletion from a binary tree.

Listing 6-2.   Definitions for binary-tree routines.

```
/*--- bintree.h ------------------------- Listing 6-2 ---------
 * Binary-tree definitions
 *
 *------------------------------------------------------------*/

#define TREE_OK     (0)
#define TREE_FAIL  (-1)
#define LEFT        1
#define RIGHT       0

#if defined(REDBLACK)
    #define RBONLY(x) x
#else
    #define RBONLY(x)
#endif


/*
 * Basic node structure. The actual size of a node is unknown as
 * the user will have appended data bytes on to the end of
 * this structure. The BINTREE_STUFF macro is a convenient way
 * to summarize the items the tree algorithm requires in the
 * node. Its argument is the tag of the structure being defined.
 */
#define BINTREE_STUFF(x)    struct x *link[2] \
                            RBONLY(;int red)
typedef struct sBnode {
    BINTREE_STUFF(sBnode);
} Bnode;

/* Control structure for a binary tree */
typedef int (*CompFunc) (void *node1, void *node2);
typedef int (*DoFunc) (void *node, int level);

typedef struct sBintree {
    Bnode *DummyHead;
    CompFunc Compare;
    int DuplicatesOk;
    size_t NodeSize;
} Bintree;

/* Prototypes */
Bintree *NewBintree (Bnode *dummy, CompFunc cf,
                     int dup_ok, size_t node_size);
Bnode   *FindBintree(Bintree *t, Bnode *n);
int      InsBintree (Bintree *t, Bnode *n);
```

```
Bnode    *DelBintree (Bintree *t, Bnode *n);
int       WalkBintree(Bintree *t, DoFunc df);
Bnode    *InitBintreeNode(size_t size);
```

The Performance of Binary Search Trees

The average performance of a binary search tree is very good. If a tree has N randomly distributed nodes, then it should on average be lg N nodes tall. For example, if we insert the words, "Marry in haste, repent at leisure" into a binary tree, we would get the tree shown in Figure 6-6. The resulting tree is three levels tall and is reasonably well balanced. Could we do better? Certainly, because the tree need be only two levels tall. However, the shape of the binary search tree that results from loading a set of items depends not only on the items but on the order in which they are loaded. This type of tree has no intrinsic mechanism to prevent imbalances between subtrees.

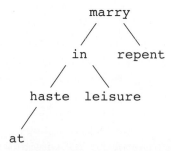

Figure 6-6.   The resulting tree after the phrase "Marry in haste, repent at leisure" has been loaded.

The worst case for a binary tree occurs when its input data is already in order. For example, if we load the same six words in order into a binary tree, the resulting tree is completely unbalanced, as shown in Figure 6-7. In this case, the height of the tree is not lg N, but N. This poor worst-case behavior makes a binary search unacceptable unless you can either (a) guarantee randomly ordered input or (b) study the input before you create the tree. If you know in advance the items to be loaded, it is possible to construct an optimum binary tree by using a straightforward dynamic programming technique. This technique is described in Knuth [Knuth 1973] and will not be discussed here. Instead, we will turn our attention to more complex algorithms that force trees to be balanced at all times.

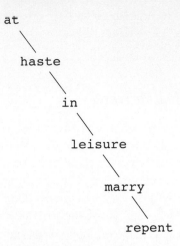

Figure 6-7.   The resulting long, skinny tree after the phrase "at haste in leisure marry repent" has been loaded.

AVL Trees

There are several approaches to creating a balanced tree. For example, if you know how often the items in a tree are used, you can place the more frequently used items higher in the tree, thus creating a **weight-balanced tree**. More generally useful, however, are trees that assume that all items are used with the same frequency. In this case, the tree is forced to be height-balanced; that is, no given subtree is allowed to be too much taller than its siblings. A specific formulation of this idea was first put forth by G. M. Adel'son-Vel'skii and E. M. Landis [Adel'son 1962]. Trees that follow their implementation are often called AVL trees. An **AVL tree** is a binary search tree that obeys the following rule: *The heights of the child trees of any given node differ by at most one.*

This rule requires us to view the tree as a forest of subtrees and to enforce the rule throughout the tree, as shown in Figure 6-8. Note that the rule applies to the small subtrees (a and b) as well as to the two subtrees of the root (c and d). While the rule may sound onerous, it turns out that a balanced tree can be maintained by performing only localized manipulations of the tree. In both cases, node insertion and deletion start identically to the algorithms for binary search trees. After the insertion or deletion, we must rebalance the tree if an imbalance has been introduced.

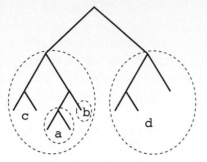

Figure 6-8.   An AVL tree.

To see how this works, consider the tree in Figure 6-9. Here, an insertion or deletion has caused subtree *a* to become too tall. The problem is not with the subtree rooted at *b*, this subtree is balanced. Rather, the imbalance occurs within the entire tree: the right subtree has height *h*, while the left has height *h*+2. (Recall that the root of the tree is said to be of height 0, so the height of the left subtree is *h*+2, not *h*+3). To fix this problem, we apply a *single rotation* to the tree. In effect, we pivot the tree about nodes *b* and *d*; node *b* moves up, and node *d* moves down. Note that there is a symmetric variant of this single rotation in which the right subtree is the one that is too tall. After this exchange, both the left subtree (rooted at *a*) and the right subtree (rooted at *d*) have height *h*+1. Study this figure carefully, because this fundamental operation will appear repeatedly in the remainder of this chapter.

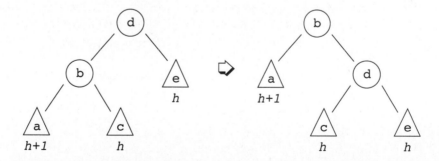

Figure 6-9.   A somewhat abstract AVL tree, in which the actual nodes are drawn as circles, while the triangles represent subtrees of the given height.

A single rotation is useful when the tree that is too tall is an "outside" subtree. However, when the subtree that is too tall is an "inside" subtree, a single rotation will not fix the problem. Consider the situation illustrated in Figure 6-10. The tree starts off unbalanced: the height of the left subtree is

$h+2$ (following the path from f to b to d to c), while the right subtree has height $h+1$. To correct this situation, we perform what is known as a **double rotation**. In effect, node d is drawn up between nodes b and f, and hands off its children to these nodes in the process. The relative heights of subtrees c and e could be reversed, but one tree must have height h and the other height $h-1$. There is a symmetric variant in which the subtree that is too tall is a subtree of node f's right child.

 With these two types of rotations defined, we are now able to repair any type of tree imbalance that we encounter. Due to the importance of these two manipulations to the subsequent discussions, you should take some time to sketch these rotations for yourself and be sure that you fully understand them. Remember also that each configuration has a mirror-image variant in which the out-of-balance subtree is on the other side of the tree.

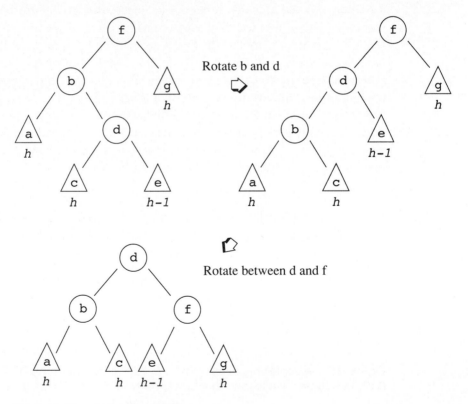

Figure 6-10. A double rotation.

The effect of the AVL rule is to ensure that the tree never becomes substantially imbalanced, and it can be shown that the height of an AVL tree with N nodes will be proportional to lg N. Further, since we can perform insertions and deletions during single top-down traversals of the tree, these operations can be performed in time proportional to lg N. However, actually implementing an AVL tree is troublesome due to the number of special cases which must be considered as well as the possibility that tree restructuring might require multiple rotations to repair new imbalances that develop as a result of prior rotations. This typically means that a backwards traversal of the access path taken during the insertion or deletion must be made. A much better solution that allows rotations to occur during the downward search traversal is presented in the next section.

Red-Black Trees

An easier way to implement AVL trees is by using a concept known as a **red-black tree**. The code in *bintree.c* and *bintree.h* (Listings 6-1 and 6-2) implements a red-black tree when the macro REDBLACK is defined. A red-black tree is, at heart, a binary search tree. However, it makes use of two new concepts.

First, in a red-black tree, data is stored only in the **leaves** of the tree. That is, only the nodes without children contain actual data. Interior nodes are simply for reference.

Second, each node is thought of as being colored red or black. A node's color is determined by these rules:

- All leaves are black.
- Two consecutive red nodes are not allowed along any path from the root.
- All the leaves of the tree must have the same **black depth**, defined as the number of black nodes minus one between the leaf and the root.

A sample red-black tree is shown in Figure 6-11. This tree has a black height of 2, since there are 3 black nodes on the path from the root to any leaf. To emphasize the black height, the tree is drawn so that all the black nodes are at the same level. This tree contains the numbers 1 through 9 in its leaves. Note carefully that the only "real" data is in the leaves. The values in the interior nodes are simply for reference. When we search a red-black tree, the search is not complete until we find a matching node that is also a leaf.

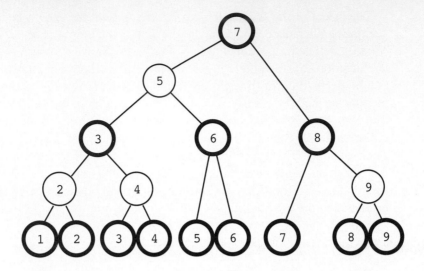

Figure 6-11.   A red-black tree, in which the black nodes are drawn with thick borders.

It is important to understand that the idea of redness and blackness is simply a bookkeeping device that will make it easy to maintain a balanced tree. The way this is done will be discussed in a moment. Nothing else is implied by the redness or blackness of a node, and the tree otherwise behaves exactly like a binary tree. To allow the routines to keep up with node color, we must add a new data item to each node. This new item could, in principle, be as simple as a single bit. In practice, the generic routines will store it as an int. This is demonstrated in *bintree.h* where the variable red is added to the macro BINTREE_STUFF. Thus, our basic node is now of the form

```
typedef struct sBnode {
    struct sBnode *link[2];
    int red;
} Bnode;
```

Figure 6-12 shows insertion into a red-black tree. This procedure is straightforward if you find a leaf with a black parent. The key is that this operation *does not alter the black height of the tree*; the introduction of a red node is a neutral operation as far as black height is concerned. This insertion technique is the reason that a red-black tree can maintain its balance while only localized manipulations of the tree are being performed. The end result is that, in the worst case, our tree consists of alternating red and black nodes. Such a tree with N nodes and black height k would then have an actual height of $2k$, and this height would still be proportional to lg N.

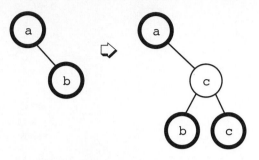

Figure 6-12.   Insertion of "c" into a red-black tree.

To ensure that we arrive at a leaf with a black parent, we perform an operation called the **color flip** during our downward traversal of the tree. This is shown in Figure 6-13, in which node 2 can be either a left or right child of its parent. Every time we encounter a black node with two red children during our downward traversal, we perform a color flip. Again, note that this operation does not alter the black height of the tree and thus can be performed without reference to other parts of the tree.

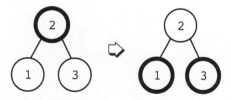

Figure 6-13.   The basic color flip.

It is possible, however, that a color flip might produce two red nodes in a row. As shown in Figure 6-14, this can occur in one of two possible ways. In each case, the tree is still balanced in terms of black height; the problem is to break up the paired red nodes. You do this by performing either a single or a double rotation. If the red nodes go in the same direction, a single rotation is sufficient. If the red nodes zig-zag, then two rotations are required. There is a symmetric variant of each position.

In the code, all the work of rebalancing is handled by `split()`. This routine and a helper routine, `rotate()`, handle all possible cases of doubled-up red nodes.

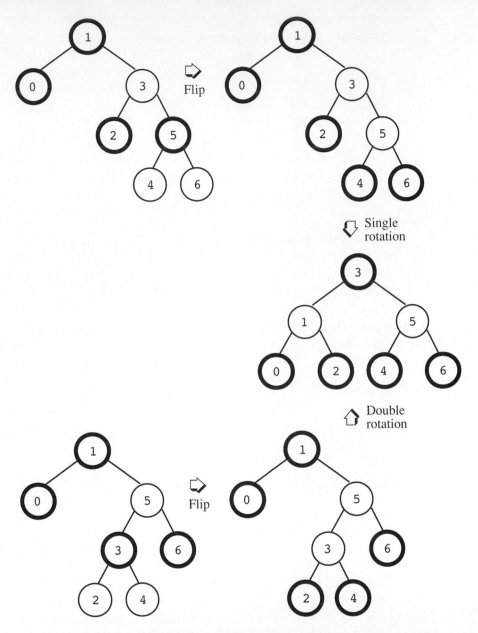

Figure 6-14.   The two patterns of adjacent red nodes formed by color flips.

For the record, it is not always possible to arrive at a leaf with a black parent during insertion. If the final leaf has a red parent with a black sibling, a color flip will not fix the problem. Instead, we insert the node as shown in

Figure 6-12, thus creating two red nodes in a row. We must then rebalance the tree as shown in Figure 6-14.

Figure 6-15 shows an example of this problem. In this case, node 4 is red, and we want to insert node 3. To do so, we perform the standard insertion procedure illustrated in Figure 6-12. This creates a tree that is still balanced with respect to black height, but it has two red nodes in a row. This imbalance is then corrected by (in this case) a double rotation.

An important characteristic of all the preceding manipulations that take place during node insertion is that the tree's black height and balance are preserved at each step along the way. Because of this, the program can stop at any time, even if it has made one or more tree rearrangements.

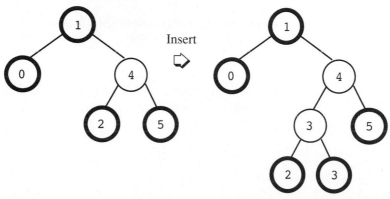

Figure 6-15.   Node insertion when the final leaf has a red parent with a black sibling.

Deletion from red-black trees, like deletion from binary trees, is the most complex operation of all. In theory, deletion should be as simple as reversing the actions shown in Figure 6-12. In other words, we would like to find that the node that is to be deleted has a red parent. Following the idea of insertion, we simply drag a red node down the tree with us. This starts at the root; if neither of its children are red, we color the root red. Then, at each node along the path to the node-to-be-deleted, we force the node to become red by one of the following processes:

- If the current node is red or if the next node along the traversal path is red, we advance.
- If the current node is black and the next node is black, the current node must have a red parent, because we would not have otherwise advanced. If the next node has a red sibling, we can escape by performing the operation shown in Figure 6-16.

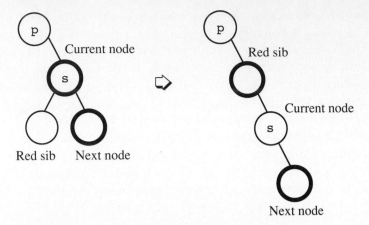

Figure 6-16. The operation to perform if the current node and the next node are black but the next node's sibling is red.

- The current node is black, the next node is black, the current node's sibling is black, and the current node's parent is red. If the current node's sibling has two black children, then the solution is simple: just color the sibling red. In effect, this is a reverse color flip, as shown in Figure 6-17.

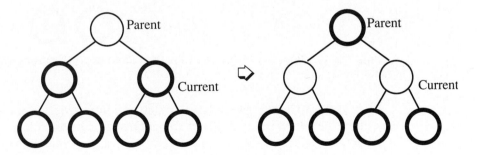

Figure 6-17. A reverse color flip that colors the current node red.

- This is the most complex case. The conditions are the same as for the preceding case, except that the current node's sibling has one or more red children. If we simply color the current node red and its parent black, a single or double rotation will balance the tree. In the case of the single rotation, a small amount of recoloring is necessary, as shown in Figure 6-18.

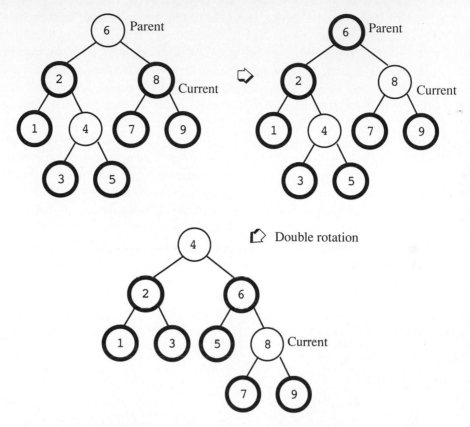

Figure 6-18. Coloring the current node red and the parent black, and then balancing the tree with a single or double rotation.

Like the AVL trees described in the previous section, we can see that the black height of a red-black tree is proportional to lg N. As noted earlier, the effect of the red-black rule is to guarantee that a red-black tree of black height h has a total height of at most $2h$, so the total height of the tree is still proportional to lg N. As with AVL trees, all operations can be performed during a single downward traversal, so searching, deletion, and insertion all occur in time proportional to lg N. In practice, this algorithm performs very well.

Splay Trees

Splay trees are a third binary-tree variant. They use the same structure as the simple binary search tree discussed at the beginning of this chapter. No balancing information or node color information is stored in the nodes. Instead, splay trees are a cross between the "move-to-the-top" approach to linked-list maintenance (discussed in Chapters 2 and 3) and a binary tree. Rather than try to keep the tree in balance as we did with red-black trees, we implement a form of constant rearrangement: each time we access the tree, we use double and single rotations to rearrange the tree so that the accessed node (or space for it) is at the root of the tree. Splay trees "learn" as they are used, and recently used items are accessed more quickly than unused items.

All splay tree operations are related to a special operation called Splay. `Splay(tree, node)` will rearrange `tree` so that `node` is the root of the tree. If `node` is not present in the tree, then the root will be the node that would immediately precede or follow `node` if it were in the tree.

To see how this operation makes searching, insertion, and deletion easier, let's consider these actions before discussing how to implement `Splay()`. Searching is trivial. After `Splay(tree, node)`, we merely examine the root of the tree. If it is identical to `node`, then we have found `node` in the tree. Otherwise, `node` is not in the tree, as shown in Figure 6-19.

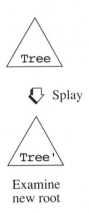

Examine
new root

Figure 6-19.   Completing a search following Splay.

Insertion is almost as simple: after Splay, we cut the tree in half, make the new node the root, and make the two tree halves the right and left children of the new root. This procedure is illustrated in Figure 6-20, where the tree has been redrawn after Splay so that the first two levels of the tree can be seen. The new node is placed to the left or right of node a, depending on the relative ordering of the two nodes. Deletion from a splay tree is simply a matter of reversing these steps after the desired node is located by Splay.

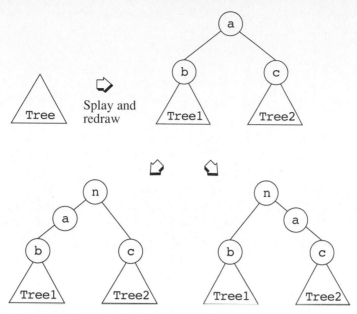

Figure 6-20.   Insertion after Splay.

Implementing a splay is surprisingly straightforward. A bottom-up splay will be described first because it is easier to understand. However, a splay can be more efficiently implemented in a top-down fashion, and that approach is taken in the code.

To implement a bottom-up splay, we first trace a path from the root to the desired node. Then we gradually rotate this node to the root by applying one of the three cases shown in Figure 6-21. In each case, the node labeled 1 is the target node, and the triangles represent unspecified subtrees that may be of any size or may be empty. The trees shown are usually subtrees, and the attachment to the next level of the tree is shown as a vertical dotted line that may be a left or right link. Operation *a* is the terminal case, in which the target node becomes the root of the tree. Operation *b* is the "zig-zig" case and is implemented as two successive single rotations: the first between nodes 3 and 2 and the second between nodes 2 and 1. Operation *c* is also the "zig-zag" case and is implemented as a double rotation. Each case has a symmetric variant. In this figure we apply operations *b* or *c* until the target node either becomes the root, in which case we have finished, or is only one level removed from the root, in which case we apply operation *a* and we have finished.

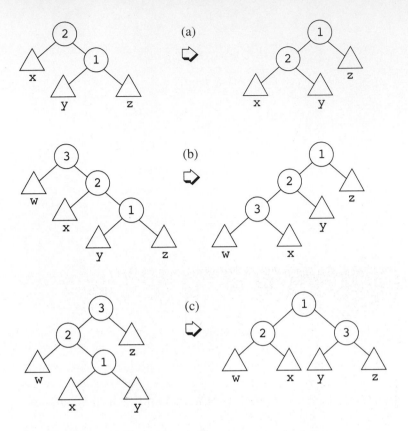

Figure 6-21.   The three operations of a bottom-up Splay.

The code to implement a top-down splay is in Listing 6-1, *bintree.c* and is controlled by the constant SPLAY. The code is a straightforward implementation of the effects shown in Figure 6-22.

In each case shown in the figure, the top node is the root of the current tree, and the search path is taking us toward node 1. The first three operations are identical to those of Figure 6-21: operation *a* is the terminal case, and operations *b* and *c* are the "zig-zig" case and the "zig-zag" case. To perform the splay, we break the tree apart as shown and hang the fragments onto the left and right storage trees, marked L and R. The central fragment becomes the new tree and is reprocessed according to the same rules. Fragments are always placed as far right as possible within the left storage tree and as far left as possible within the right storage tree. When the tree has been reduced to the desired node, we put the pieces back together as shown in operation *d*.

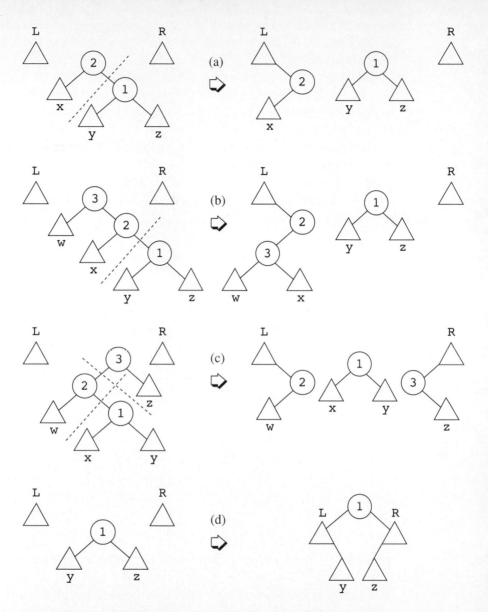

Figure 6-22. The procedure for performing a top-down splay.

As with the other trees, we handle the mirror-image cases as a part of the general case by defining the left and right child pointers as a two-element array. The only tricky aspect of the code is the way in which the left and right storage trees are maintained. The roots of these trees are stored in the array LR, while the array LRwalk holds a pointer to the lower-left node of the right subtree and to the lower-right node of the left subtree. After each addition to a storage tree, we invoke the macro PUSH to advance LRwalk to the bottom of the storage tree.

It is interesting to note the tremendous simplicity of the code for the search, insert, and delete operations for splay trees. This simplicity is especially evident when the code is compared to the code used by the binary tree and red-black tree variants.

The types of tree rearrangements performed by the top-down splay are shown in Figure 6-23. Arrangement *a* is a splay tree after we have inserted the numbers 1 through 10 in order; *b* is the tree after we have searched for node 1; *c* is the tree after we have searched for node 5; and *d* is the tree after we have searched for node 4.

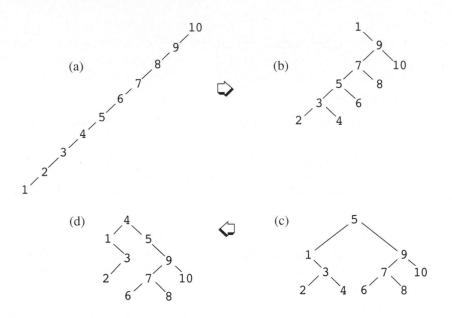

Figure 6-23.   The types of tree arrangements performed by the top-down Splay.

It is important to note several facts about these types of tree arrangements. First, splay trees, like binary trees, will become long and thin if all the elements are inserted in order. However, any access of a lower element quickly has the effect of shuffling the tree. The shuffled tree is shorter, and access to all elements improves. Second, recently used elements remain near the top of the tree. This has obvious advantages in some situations. Finally, the top-down and bottom-up Splay operations do not produce identical trees (although the differences are subtle). However, the effects produced by each are overall the same, and the top-down implementation is both more efficient and easier to implement.

Analyzing the behavior of splay trees is complex, since each operation affects the overall structure and the depth of many other nodes in the tree. For example, it is easy to see that accessing a given node roughly halves the depth of every node along the search path. Although the analysis is complex, Sleator and Tarjan [Sleator 1985] have shown that the time required to make m accesses of a splay tree with n nodes is proportional to $(m + n) \lg (m + n)$. Because of the way that splay trees "learn" from usage, splay tree behavior must be analyzed over many accesses. However, for any sufficiently large number of tree accesses, the behavior of a splay tree is as good as that of any other type of balanced tree.

B-Trees

The tree algorithms described so far in this chapter work well on data that can be maintained entirely in memory. When this is not the case, you need a tree algorithm that is suited to disk storage. Utilizing disk storage has its own special set of constraints:

- Accessing data on a disk is very slow compared to the time required to access data in memory.
- Read/write operations are best performed on fairly large chunks of data. Indeed, the more we read at a time, the better we'll do (within limits). Using blocks of 2,048 to 4,096 bytes is not at all uncommon. (See Chapter 1 for a discussion of disk I/O optimization.)

These limitations of disk storage mean that we must try to make the most efficient use of large blocks of disk storage. Our algorithm should be organized around these blocks, and we should plan to fit multiple pieces of data into each block. The algorithms that solve this problem are collectively known as **B-tree** algorithms. Almost every author implements B-trees a bit differently, but the underlying concepts are the same.

All B-trees utilize two distinct types of blocks: index blocks and data blocks. Data blocks are the leaves of the B-tree, and all data is stored in them. Index blocks are the upper-level blocks, and they contain only enough information to allow the program to trace a path from the root to the desired record in a data block. As an example, consider Figure 6-24, which depicts a B-tree with two levels of index blocks. The key features of a B-tree are as follows:

- All data blocks are at the same level—in this case the third level down.
- All index and data blocks contain some minimal amount of data. This amount may be defined in terms of the number of keys or of the amount of the block's space that is consumed.

- As with our earlier trees, the items in the index blocks are just keys. To find the data record with the key Harrison, we start at the top (root) block, go to the middle block on the second level, and then go to the rightmost child block of this index block. Here we find the actual record.

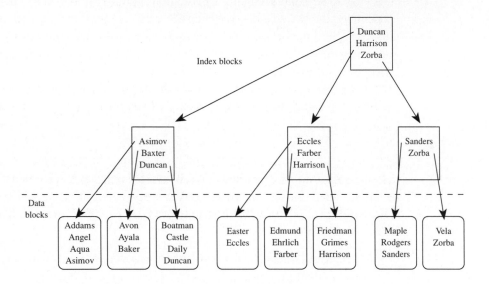

Figure 6-24.   A B-tree with two index levels.

These features taken together mean that a B-tree is balanced in at least some sense of the word. Because all data is at the same depth of the tree, accesses are equally quick for all portions of the tree. In a more rigorous sense, B-trees are usually described as being of **order** d, where each node of the tree contains between d and $2d$ keys or records. A tree with N entries would then be of height $\log_d N$. Note that while order influences tree height, order and height are quite different. This definition of a tree based on its order is really useful, however, only for B-trees where all keys are of fixed length. If variable-length keys are used, then it is more appropriate to require that all blocks contain a certain amount of data. In other words, instead of requiring between d and $2d$ keys per block, we require (for example) that between 15 percent and 85 percent of the bytes in a block be used.

Keeping a B-Tree Balanced

B-trees are easy to describe on paper. The main problems arise when a block becomes either too full or too empty. When it is too full, you must split the block in half and insert an extra key into the block's parent block. This is easy to do, unless of course the parent block is full. In this case, you may need to split the parent block. Ultimately, you may need to split every index block all the way to the root block. And, if the root block needs to be split, the tree must grow in height. Conversely, when a deletion occurs and a block becomes too empty, neighboring blocks on the same level are inspected. If possible, the block that is too empty is merged with either its left or its right sibling. This process may also cascade up the tree, resulting in mergers between many upper-level index blocks. Upper-level index blocks may also be affected even if they aren't merged.

Consider again Figure 6-24. Suppose we were to delete the key Zorba. The Vela/Zorba block is then relatively empty and must be merged with the Maple/Rodgers/Sanders block. Doing so requires the Sanders/Zorba index block to change so that it has only the key Vela, and the root block must be adjusted to have pointers to Duncan/Harrison/Vela. The final product is shown in Figure 6-25. This assumes that the Eccles/Parker/Harrison index block is not large enough to absorb Vela as well. If it were, then the tree would collapse further and have one root block, two second-level index blocks, and seven data blocks.

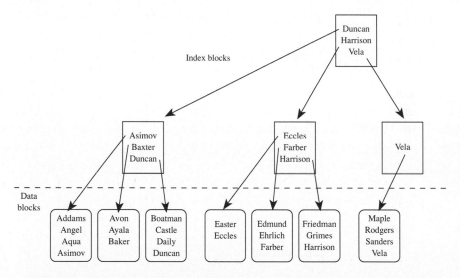

Figure 6-25. **What Figure 6-24 might look like after we have deleted Zorba, merged two data blocks, and propagated a new key upward.**

Implementing a B-Tree Algorithm

Implementing a B-tree is a major undertaking. The work that is required for splitting and merging data and index blocks is complex and full of special cases. However, by making a few simplifying assumptions, we can reduce the complexity substantially while implementing a completely satisfactory B-tree routine. The design goals for this B-tree implementation are as follows:

- Allow variable-length keys.
- Allow variable-length records.
- Keep the index and the data in separate files. These files may use separate fundamental block sizes and have separate split and merge breakpoints, if you prefer. Using a separate index file allows the data file to be reindexed easily if the index becomes corrupt.

To implement these features without being overwhelmed by special cases, you should assume the following:

- A single record with a maximal key must be provided when the data set is created. This record cannot be deleted. The presence of this record means that the tree is never empty.
- The tree will be of fixed height, and this height will be defined at the time that the B-tree is created.

The net effect of these two assumptions is that an empty tree will contain several levels of index blocks and one maximal data record. For example, an empty B-tree with three index levels is shown in Figure 6-26. The record with a key of ∞ cannot be deleted.

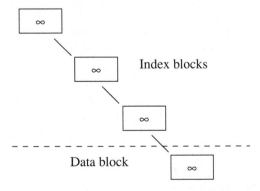

Figure 6-26.   An empty B-tree with three index levels.

These assumptions are actually not very restrictive. Indeed, the requirement for a fixed-height tree is relative rather than absolute; that is, the code could be modified easily to allow the tree to grow or shrink in height. A fixed-height scheme was chosen here because, a we will see later, a tree with a height of four will be more than sufficient for even the most demanding applications.

The Code for B-Tree Implementation

Coding a B-Tree module is an exercise in applied theory and pragmatics. Other than the concepts just presented, little theory will be discussed here; the code and the discussions of its limitations provides ample insight into the design of B-tree modules. The code for our implementation begins with Listing 6-3 (*bt-hdr.h*). Because this is such a large and complex program, a small guide to the source code modules is provided in Table 6-1.

Table 6-1. The source code modules

File	Page	Purpose	Major Entry Points
bt-hdr.h (Listing 6-3)	298	B-tree header file	
bt-new.c (Listing 6-4)	302	Create a B-tree dataset	`bt_new()`
bt-open.c (Listing 6-5)	307	Open an existing dataset	`bt_open()` `bt_close()`
bt-data.c (Listing 6-6)	310	Operate on a dataset	`bt_walk()` `bt_find()` `bt_add()` `bt_delete()`
bt-disk.c (Listing 6-7)	335	Block buffering	`bt_getblock4read()` `bt_getblock4write()` `bt_flush()`
user.h (Listing 6-8)	343	Header for driver	
user.c (Listing 6-9)	344	Sample driver	`main()`

The best place to start a tour of the code is with `main()` in *user.c*. This is a simple driver, much like the one in *bintree.c*. It allows data sets to be created, opened, closed, added to, deleted from, and displayed. It consists mainly of a `switch` statement; to see how to use a particular type of feature, simply examine the relevant `case` statement.

Laying Out a Data Set: `bt_new.c`

Our data sets will consist of two files named *file.ndx* and *file.dat* (see Listing 6-4). The *.ndx* file contains the index; the *.dat* file contains the actual data. The files have a similar layout:

Block 0:   File identification and layout data
Blocks 1-n: Index or data records

Listing 6-3.   Definitions and macros for B-tree routines.

```
/*--- bt_hdr.h --------------------------- Listing 6-3 ---------
 * B-tree header file, to be included by user code
 *
 *---------------------------------------------------------*/

#if !defined(BT_HDR_H)
#define BT_HDR_H

#include <stdio.h>
#include <stdlib.h>
#include <string.h>

/*
 * Some defines
 */
#define MAX_PATH_AND_FILE 100  /* max length of full file name */
#define TREE_OK    (0)
#define TREE_FAIL (-1)

/*
 * Some general typedefs
 */
typedef unsigned BLKSIZE; /* Holds size of disk blocks */
typedef long DISKOFFSET;  /* File offset for fseek */

/*
 * Structure of index files:
 *
 * First block (offset 0L, size is determined by size_struct):
 *    Signature string: SIGNATURE SIG_NDX
 *
 *    Sizes:            Sizes size_struct;
 *
 *      Root block:     DISKOFFSET root_block;
 *      Free block chain: DISKOFFSET free_block;
 *
 *
 * Data blocks
 *    Block control:  BlockControl blockdata;
 *                    If blockstate == sNode, then the
 *                    DISKOFFSETS in this block are pointers
 *                    to additional index blocks.
 *                    If blockstate == sLeaf, then DISKOFFSET
 *                    is a pointer to a data block in the
 *                    .dat file
 *
```

```
*                 key/DISKOFFSET pairs
*
*                     The user-supplied function get_key_size()
*                     is used to step through the block and the
*                     user-supplied functions key2keycmp() and
*                     key2reccmp() are used to compare keys.
*/


/*
 * Structure of data files:
 *
 * First block (offset 0L, size is determined by size_struct):
 *    Signature string: SIGNATURE SIG_DAT
 *
 *    Sizes:             Sizes size_struct;
 *
 *        Root block:     DISKOFFSET root_block;
 *        Free block chain: DISKOFFSET free_block;
 *
 *
 * Data blocks
 *    Block control: BlockControl blockdata;
 *    Data items:    The data records are variable length and are
 *                   just packed in one after another. The user-
 *                   supplied function get_rec_size() is employed
 *                   to step through the records.
 */

/* Signature strings */
#define SIGNATURE "B-Tree File/V1.0/"

/* SIG_DATA and SIG_INDEX must be same length */
#define SIG_DATA  "Dat"
#define SIG_INDEX "Ndx"

typedef struct sSize {
        /* Block sizes and share/split breakpoints */
    BLKSIZE block_size; /* size of blocks */
    BLKSIZE split;      /* split blocks when this # bytes used */
    BLKSIZE merge;      /* merge blocks when this # bytes used */
    unsigned levels;    /* # of index levels (.ndx files only) */
} Sizes;

/* Control structures for disk blocks */
typedef enum eBlockState { sAvail, sNode, sLeaf } BlockState;
typedef struct sBlockControl {
    size_t    bfree;    /* Free data area begins here */
    BlockState blockstate;
```

```
    DISKOFFSET parent;   /* parent of this block */
    DISKOFFSET next;     /* used when block belongs */
                         /* ... to a free chain */
} BlockControl;

/* Control structures for I/O buffer blocks */
typedef enum eBufState { sFree, sClean, sDirty } BufState;
typedef struct sBufferList {
    BufState state;
    DISKOFFSET offset;
    char *buffer;
    struct sBufferList *next;
} BufferList;

/*
 * Master control structure for access to a pair of database
 * files. See code in bt_open.c for example initialization.
 */
#define NDX 0
#define DAT 1
typedef struct sBtree {
    /* Files, file names, and buffers */
    struct {
        char filename[MAX_PATH_AND_FILE];
        int modified;
        FILE *file;
        BufferList *bufferlist;
        Sizes sizes;
        DISKOFFSET root_block;
        DISKOFFSET free_block;
    } fdata[2];

    /*--- Data objects and procedures to manipulate them ---*/

    /* get size of a key */
    unsigned (*getkeysize)(void *);

    /* size of key in a record */
    unsigned (*getkeyNrecsize)(void *);

    /* get size of a record */
    unsigned (*getrecsize)(void *);

    /* compare key to key */
    int (*key2keycmp)(void *, void *);

    /* compare key to record */
    int (*key2reccmp)(void *, void *);
```

```
    /* copy a key from a record */
    void (*rec2keycpy)(void *, void *);

    /* Miscellaneous */
    int error_code;      /* Index into ErrorCode[] */
    int duplicatesOK;    /* Are duplicate keys ok? */

    /* used by insert & delete */
    DISKOFFSET CurrentDataBlock;
    void *SearchKey;
    void *FoundRec;
} Btree;
/* some defines to simplify the code */
#define GETKEYSIZE      (*(bt->getkeysize))
#define GETKEYNRECSIZE  (*(bt->getkeyNrecsize))
#define GETRECSIZE      (*(bt->getrecsize))
#define KEY2KEYCMP      (*(bt->key2keycmp))
#define KEY2RECCMP      (*(bt->key2reccmp))
#define REC2KEYCPY      (*(bt->rec2keycpy))
#define FDATA(x,y)      (bt->fdata[x].y)
#define SIZES(x,y)      (bt->fdata[x].sizes.y)

/* error messages */
extern char *ErrorText[]; /* defined in bt_disk.c */

/* Prototypes */

/* action function used during tree walk */
typedef int (*DoFunc) (Btree *bt, void *rec);


/* bt_new.c */
int  bt_new(Btree *bt, void *maxkey, void *maxrec);

/* bt_disk.c */
char *bt_getblock4read(Btree *bt, int f, DISKOFFSET dof);
char *bt_getblock4write(Btree *bt, int f, DISKOFFSET dof);
BufferList *bt_getnew4write(Btree *bt, int f);
int  bt_flush(Btree *bt);
int  bt_bufinit(Btree *bt, int f);
void bt_bufrelease(Btree *bt, int f);
int  bt_releaseblock(Btree *bt, int f, DISKOFFSET dof);

/* bt_open.c */
int  bt_open(Btree *bt);
int  bt_close(Btree *bt);

/* bt_data.c */
```

```
int  bt_add(Btree *bt, void *rec, void *key);
int  bt_delete(Btree *bt, void *key);
int  bt_find(Btree *bt, void *rec, void *key);
int  bt_walk(Btree *bt, DoFunc df);
#endif
```

The data in block 0 permits the files to be self-identifying, and the
layout of this data is shown in bt_hdr.h. The block contains the
following:

```
"A signature string"        // identifies the file as legitmate
struct sSize {
    unsigned block_size;    // size of blocks in bytes
    unsigned split;         // split blocks using more than this
    unsigned merge;         // merge blocks using less than this
    unsigned levels;        // height of tree (.ndx only)
} sizes;
long root_block;                        // first index block (.ndx only)
long free_block;                        // first block in free-block chain
```

The code in bt_new.c is reached by calling bt_new() and creates two empty
files in a straightforward fashion. For .ndx files, the appropriate number
of index levels are created, while .dat files are created with one data
block that contains the aforementioned record with a maximal key.

Listing 6-4.   Code to create a new B-tree dataset.

```
/*--- bt_new.c -------------------------- Listing 6-4 ---------
 * Create a new, empty B-Tree dataset
 *
 * See user.c (Listing 6-9) for a test driver.
 *-----------------------------------------------------------*/

#include "bt_hdr.h"

/*
 * Create new dataset files. Files are not left open
 *
 * Dataset has one record in it, a record with the maximum key
 * that will ever be used. We populate each index level with
 * this one key and create one data block containing this record.
 */
int bt_new(Btree *bt, void *maxkey, void *maxrec)
{
    char *buffer, *s;
    int i, ret;
    unsigned length, j;
    DISKOFFSET *dof;
    Sizes *sizes;
```

```
BLKSIZE blksize;
BlockControl *bc;

/* Check values, allocate buffers */
ret = TREE_OK;
for (i=0; i < 2; i++) {
    if (SIZES(i,block_size) > 10000) { /* seems unlikely */
        bt -> error_code = 2;
        ret = TREE_FAIL;
        break;
    }

    if (SIZES(i,split) > SIZES(i,block_size) ||
        SIZES(i,merge) > SIZES(i,block_size)) {
        bt -> error_code = 3;
        ret = TREE_FAIL;
        break;
    }

    ret = bt_bufinit(bt, i);
    if (ret)
        break;

    /* Open the file */
    FDATA(i, file) = fopen(FDATA(i, filename), "wb");
    if (FDATA(i, file) == NULL) {
        bt -> error_code = 1;
        ret = TREE_FAIL;
        break;
    }

    /* Steal access to a buffer & initialize file */
    buffer = s = FDATA(i, bufferlist) -> buffer;
    blksize = SIZES(i, block_size);
    memset(buffer, 0, blksize);

    /* Signature string */
    strcpy(s, SIGNATURE);
    strcat(s, i == NDX ? SIG_INDEX : SIG_DATA);
    s += strlen(s) + 1;

    /* Buffer size information */
    sizes = (Sizes *) s;
    *sizes = bt -> fdata[i].sizes;

    /* Offsets to root block and some free blocks */
    s += sizeof(Sizes);
    dof = (DISKOFFSET *) s;
    *dof = blksize;    /* root is first block */
```

```
    *(dof+1) = 0;       /* and the empty block list */

    if (fwrite(buffer, blksize, 1, FDATA(i, file)) != 1) {
        bt -> error_code = 4;
        ret = TREE_FAIL;
        break;
    }

    memset(buffer, 0, blksize);
    bc = (BlockControl *) buffer;
    bc -> bfree = sizeof(BlockControl);
    bc -> next        = 0L;

    if (i == NDX) {
        /* create a block of maxkey/offset */
        bc -> blockstate = sNode;
        s = buffer + bc -> bfree;
        length = GETKEYSIZE(maxkey);
        memcpy(s, maxkey, length);
        s += length;
        bc -> bfree += length + sizeof(DISKOFFSET);

        /* write out levels blocks,
                            each pointing to the next */
        for (j = 1; j <= SIZES(i, levels); j++) {
            bc -> parent = (DISKOFFSET) blksize * (j - 1);
            *((DISKOFFSET *) s) =
                        (DISKOFFSET) blksize * (j + 1);
            /* last block points to data file */
            if (j == SIZES(i, levels)) {
                bc -> blockstate = sLeaf;
                *((DISKOFFSET *) s) =
                            SIZES(DAT, block_size);
            }
            if (fwrite(buffer, blksize, 1,
                        FDATA(i, file)) != 1) {
                bt -> error_code = 4;
                ret = TREE_FAIL;
                break;
            }
        }
    }
    else /* i == DAT */ {
        /* create a block with one entry: maxrec */
        bc -> blockstate = sLeaf;
        bc -> parent = (DISKOFFSET) SIZES(NDX, block_size) *
                            SIZES(NDX, levels);
        s = buffer + bc -> bfree;
        length = GETRECSIZE(maxrec);
```

```
        memcpy(s, maxrec, length);
        bc -> bfree += length;
        if (fwrite(buffer, blksize, 1,
                            FDATA(i, file)) != 1) {
            bt -> error_code = 4;
            ret = TREE_FAIL;
            break;
        }
    }
    fclose(FDATA(i, file));
    FDATA(i, file) = NULL;

    if (ret)
        break;
}

bt_bufrelease(bt, NDX);
bt_bufrelease(bt, DAT);
return ret;
}
```

The data in block 0 permits the files to be self-identifying, and the layout of this data is shown in *bt_hdr.h*. The block contains the following:

```
"A signature string"     // identifies the file as legitimate
struct sSize {
    unsigned block_size; // size of blocks in bytes
    unsigned split;      // split blocks using more than this
    unsigned merge;      // merge blocks using less than this
    unsigned levels;     // height of tree (.ndx only)
} sizes;
long root_block;         // first index block (.ndx only)
long free_block;         // first block in free-block chain
```

The code in *bt_new.c* is reached when bt_new() is called, and this code creates two empty files in a straightforward fashion. For *.ndx* files, the appropriate number of index levels are created, while *.dat* files are created with one data block that contains the aforementioned record with a maximal key.

The parameters to bt_new() include a pointer to a Btree structure. This is a structure that will be used by every routine in the B-tree module. It contains all the information required for accessing the *.ndx* and *.dat* files that make up a data set. Its layout is found in sBtree in *bt_hdr.h*.

A B-tree starts with an array of two substructures: one for the associated *.ndx* file and one for the *.dat* file. The internal data elements of these structures are straightforward, except perhaps for the BufferList object. The index and data files for a given data set have an independent set of buffers that are maintained in a linked list, and this pointer is the head of the list. The buffers are managed by the code in *bt_disk.c*. The values for the sizes of disk blocks, split points, merge points, and so forth are defined at the time of the call to bt_new(). Thereafter, whenever a data set is opened by bt_open(), these values are loaded from the data files themselves.

Access to these two structures is simplified by a pair of macros (#define NDX 0 and #define DAT 1) that provide symbolic subscripts. To further simplify the code, an additional pair of macros is defined that shortens the code required to access a member of the structure:

```
#define FDATA(x,y)      (bt->fdata[x].y)
#define SIZES(x,y)      (bt->fdata[x].sizes.y)
```

Assuming that bt is a pointer to a Btree, these two macros make it easy to access the relevant data for each file. For example, FDATA (NDX,root_block) accesses the disk offset of the root index block. All modules follow the convention of using bt as the name of the pointer to the local Btree structure, so these macros can be used freely.

After this pair of structures comes a set of six pointers to routines that must be supplied by the user. These pointers are pivotal in allowing the B-tree module to accommodate a wide variety of data types. These routines allow the B-tree module to manipulate records and their keys without actually knowing what is in either. To see how this works, examine the record and key structure used by the sample driver in *user.c*:

```
typedef struct UserRecord {
    char key[11];
    char name[25];
    char addr[25];
} UR;
```

This data structure contains a key and two data items. For simplicity, these are implemented as fixed-length objects, but as we shall see, this is not a requirement of the B-tree module. The sample driver accepts input of the form *x;y* and places the string before the semicolon into name[ ] and the string after the semicolon into addr[ ]. Up to the first ten characters of name[ ] are taken as the key. Thus, asking *user.c* to insert "Holmes;Sherlock" will create a record with a 7-byte key ("Holmes" plus a null terminator).

Now, as an example of implementing the six routines, consider the code that determines the size of a key in a record:

```
unsigned UserGetKeyNRecSize(void *k) {
    return strlen( ((UR *) k) -> key ) + 1;
}
```

This routine is passed a `void` pointer that we can assume points to a valid data record. The code casts this into a pointer to a user record, calls `strlen()` on the key, adds one (for the null terminator), and returns the value.

Note also that this technique does not require that the key be the first data item in a record or even that the key exist in a single location. For example, the key could be the result of concatenating several different items, and this concatenation could be done on the fly whenever a key is needed.

The actual data and index blocks themselves are simple. Each one begins with a `BlockControl` structure of the following form (from *bt_hdr.h*):

```
typedef struct sBlockControl {
    size_t    bfree;      /* Free data area begins here */
    BlockState blockstate;
    DISKOFFSET parent;   /* parent of this block */
    DISKOFFSET next;     /* when block belongs to a free chain */
} BlockControl;
```

The field `bfree` is the offset from the beginning of the block to the next free byte. All the data in the block exists in contiguous bytes immediately following the `BlockControl` structure, so the initial value of `bfree` is `sizeof(BlockControl)`. The possible values for `blockstate` (which is an enum) are relevant only to index blocks and consist of `sAvail`, `sNode`, and `sLeaf`. The value `sAvail` identifies a block as free. Pointers in blocks marked `sNode` point to other index blocks, while those in an `sLeaf` point to data blocks. Finally, `parent` is an upward pointer that allows for traversals from a data block back to the root, while `next` is used to store chains of free blocks. The data in an index block consists of contiguous key/`DISKOFFSET` pairs. As previously stated, a key may be of variable length, while a `DISKOFFSET` is typedef'd as a long integer, the standard data type for `fpos_t`, the type that holds a disk address. The data in a data block consists simply of records written one after the other. For both types of blocks the B-tree module uses user-supplied functions to determine the size of keys and records and thus to step through the data.

Listing 6-5.   The code to open a B-tree dataset.

```
/*--- bt_open.c --------------------------- Listing 6-5 ---------
 * Open a B-Tree dataset
 *
 * See user.c (Listing 6-9) for a test driver.
 *-----------------------------------------------------------*/

#include "bt_hdr.h"
```

```
#if defined(HELP1)
#define SHOW(x) x
#else
#define SHOW(x)
#endif

/* Open files, allocate buffers */
int bt_open(Btree *bt)
{
    int i, ret;
    char buffer[512], *s;

    /* Check values, allocate buffers */
    ret = TREE_OK;
    for (i=0; i < 2; i++) {
        FDATA(i,file) = fopen(FDATA(i,filename), "r+b");
        if (FDATA(i,file) == NULL) {
            bt -> error_code = 6;
            ret = TREE_FAIL;
            break;
        }
        FDATA(i, modified) = 0;
        SHOW(printf("bt_open file: %s, file: %Fp\n",
                       FDATA(i, filename), FDATA(i, file));)

        if (fread(buffer, 512, 1, FDATA(i,file)) != 1) {
            bt -> error_code = 7;
            ret = TREE_FAIL;
            break;
        }

        s = buffer;
        if (strcmp(s, i == NDX ?
                    SIGNATURE SIG_INDEX : SIGNATURE SIG_DATA)) {
            bt -> error_code = 8;
            ret = TREE_FAIL;
            break;
        }

        s += strlen(s) + 1;
        bt -> fdata[i].sizes = *((Sizes *) s);
        s += sizeof(Sizes);
        bt -> fdata[i].root_block = *((DISKOFFSET *) s);
        s += sizeof(DISKOFFSET);
        bt -> fdata[i].free_block = *((DISKOFFSET *) s);

        ret = bt_bufinit(bt, i);
        if (ret)
```

```
            break;
    }

    return ret;
}

/* Flush buffers and shut down */
int bt_close(Btree *bt)
{
    int i, ret;

    ret = bt_flush(bt);
    for (i=0; i<2; i++) {
        if (FDATA(i,file)) {
            if (fclose(FDATA(i,file))) {
                bt -> error_code = 9;
                ret = TREE_FAIL;
            }
            FDATA(i,file) = NULL;
        }
        bt_bufrelease(bt, i);
    }

    return ret;
}
```

Using a Data Set: bt_data.c

The module *bt_data.c* (Listing 6-6) contains the code for performing tree walks, searches, additions, and deletions. The code for walking the tree exhaustively is a good place to start. The entry point is bt_walk(). The routine is passed two parameters: a pointer to the tree to be walked and a function to be executed on each record of the tree. An example of such a function can be found in *user.c* as DisplayFunc(). This function is used by the 'w' option of the sample driver in *user.c* and displays the current record. After performing a small amount of initialization, bt_walk() calls bt_walk_down() to do the real work. This function takes several arguments:

```
btint bt_walk_down(Btree *bt,        /* the tree              */
                   int f,            /* NDX or DAT?           */
                   DISKOFFSET block, /* the block             */
                   DoFunc df,        /* an action function    */
                   int level,        /* depth of search       */
                   int mode)         /* SELECTIVE or EXHAUSTIVE */
```

This function examines the block specified by the combination of f and block. If f is NDX, then block is assumed to be the offset of an index block. Otherwise, block is a data block. The function df is a user-supplied function that is called for each record in the dataset, while level is a counter that indicates the depth of recursion. The mode flag determines whether all possible branches of the tree are to be examined (EXHAUSTIVE) or whether only those branches that are along the path toward finding the key stored in bt->SearchKey are to be examined (SELECTIVE). These two modes are supplied so that the same subroutine can be used to either walk the entire tree or simply search a portion of it.

Listing 6-6. The code to add, remove, and find records.

```
/*--- bt_data.c --------------------------- Listing 6-6 ---------
 * Add, remove, and find records
 *
 * See test driver is in user.c  (Listing 6-9)
 *-------------------------------------------------------------*/

#include "bt_hdr.h"

#if defined(HELP1)
#define SHOW(x) x
#else
#define SHOW(x)
#endif

/*
 * Support routines for find, search, walk
 */

int FindFunc(Btree *bt, void *rec) {
    int compare = KEY2RECCMP(bt->SearchKey, rec);
    if (compare > 0)
        return TREE_OK;
    else if (compare == 0) {
        if (bt->FoundRec)
            /*
             * find calls us with FoundRec = a
             * data area where the round record is
             * to be copied
             */
            memcpy(bt->FoundRec, rec, GETRECSIZE(rec));
        else
            /*
             * delete and add call with FoundRec == NULL. When
```

```
                 * we find the record, we set FoundRec non-NULL
                 * to indicate our success.
                 */
                bt->FoundRec = rec; /* irrelevant, non-NULL value */
        }
        else
            bt->FoundRec = NULL;
        return TREE_FAIL;
}

int LocateFunc(Btree *bt, void *rec) {
        int compare = KEY2RECCMP(bt->SearchKey, rec);
        if (compare > 0)
            return TREE_OK;
        else if (compare == 0)
            bt->FoundRec = rec;
        else
            bt->FoundRec = NULL;
        return TREE_FAIL;
}

/*
 * Walk the tree, calling user function df for each data record
 */
#define SELECTIVE   0   /* modes for bt_walk_down */
#define EXHAUSTIVE 1
int bt_walk_down(Btree *bt,        /* the tree                */
                 int f,            /* NDX or DAT?             */
                 DISKOFFSET block, /* the block               */
                 DoFunc df,        /* an action function      */
                 int level,        /* depth of search         */
                 int mode)         /* SELECTIVE or EXHAUSTIVE */
{
    char *s;
    BlockControl *bc;
    unsigned offset, keysize;
    int retval;
    DISKOFFSET datablock;

    s = bt_getblock4read(bt, f, block);
    if (!s) {
        bt->error_code = 7;
        return TREE_FAIL;
    }

    bc = (BlockControl *) s;
    retval = TREE_OK;
```

```
    if (f == NDX) {
        offset = sizeof(BlockControl);
        while (offset < bc->bfree) {
            keysize = GETKEYSIZE(s + offset);
            datablock = *((DISKOFFSET *) (s + offset + keysize));
            if (mode == SELECTIVE) {
                if (KEY2KEYCMP(bt->SearchKey, s+offset) > 0) {
                    offset += keysize + sizeof(DISKOFFSET);
                    continue;
                }
            }
            retval =  bt_walk_down(bt,
                        bc->blockstate == sLeaf ? DAT : NDX,
                        datablock, df, level + 1, mode);
            if (retval)
                break;

            /* recursive calls may invalidate our buffer */
            s = bt_getblock4read(bt, f, block);
            bc = (BlockControl *) s;
            offset += keysize + sizeof(DISKOFFSET);
        }
    }
    else { /* f == DAT */
        bt->CurrentDataBlock = block;
        offset = sizeof(BlockControl);
        while (offset < bc->bfree) {
            retval = df(bt, s + offset); /* do user's bidding */
            if (retval)
                break;
            offset += GETRECSIZE(s + offset);
        }
    }

    return retval;
}

/*
 * Systematically walk the tree
 */
int bt_walk(Btree *bt, DoFunc df) {
    bt->CurrentDataBlock = 0L;
    return bt_walk_down(
        bt, NDX, FDATA(NDX, root_block), df, 0, EXHAUSTIVE);
}

/*
 * Search for a record
```

```
    */
int bt_find(Btree *bt, void *rec, void *key) {
    int retval;

    bt->SearchKey = key;
    bt->FoundRec = rec;
    retval = bt_walk_down(
        bt, NDX, FDATA(NDX, root_block), FindFunc, 0, SELECTIVE);
    if (retval && bt->FoundRec)
        return TREE_OK; /* found it */
    else
        return TREE_FAIL;
}


/*
 * update index blocks
 */
DISKOFFSET bt_fix_index (Btree *bt,
                         void *replacekey,
                         DISKOFFSET fixblock,
                         DISKOFFSET oldblock,
                         void *newkey,
                         DISKOFFSET newblock)
{
    /*
     * This is a very heavily used routine that performs
     * major updates to index blocks. It can insert a new
     * index pointer, replace a pointer, or delete a pointer.
     * It will split the block if it overflows.
     *
     * If replacekey == NULL: (inserting a new key)
     *   In index block fixblock, find the key/DISKOFFSET pair
     *   that has oldblock for its DISKOFFSET. Then,
     *   1) update this key/DOF pair so that DOF is newblock
     *   2) insert newkey/oldblock as a new pair just in front
     *   3) split index block if now too big
     *
     * If replacekey != NULL (replacing an existing key)
     *   In index block fixblock, find the key/DISKOFFSET pair
     *   that has oldblock for its DISKOFFSET This pair will
     *   actually be replacekey/oldblock. The value of replacekey
     *   is used both as a flag and to allow the routine to see
     *   quickly if it will need to split the block. Then,
     *   1) update this key/DOF pair so that key is newkey (**)
     *   2) split index block if now too big
     *   3) promulgate key replacement upwards if key/DOF pair
     *        is the last key/DOF pair in the block
     *
```

```
 *    (**) If newkey is NULL, then the key/DISKOFFSET pair is
 *         simply deleted and not replaced.
 *
 * Note that we do not actually do these operations in this
 * order. We proceed by first determining if we need to split
 * the index block. If so, we allocate a new block and then
 * recursively call ourself to place the new entry into the
 * next level up. Only if this succeeds do we actually commit
 * a change to the database.
 *
 * We return the DISKOFFSET of oldblock and newblock's new
 * parent.
 */

char *pblock,              /* current index block (fixblock) */
     *pblock1 = NULL;      /* added index block, if we need one */
char *keycopy;
BlockControl *bc, *bc1 = NULL;
DISKOFFSET newindexblock = 0, newparent;
BufferList *bl = NULL;
unsigned keysize, newsize, previous;
unsigned offset, lastoffset, replacesize;
int delta;
int bt_merger(Btree *, int, DISKOFFSET);

SHOW(printf("bt_fix_index/a: %Fp, %d, %ld\n",
                                        bt, NDX, fixblock);)
pblock = bt_getblock4write(bt, NDX, fixblock);
if (!pblock)
    return 0L;
bc = (BlockControl *) pblock;
newsize = -sizeof(DISKOFFSET);
if (newkey)
    newsize = GETKEYSIZE(newkey);
replacesize = 0;
if (replacekey)
    replacesize = GETKEYSIZE(replacekey) + sizeof(DISKOFFSET);
delta = (int) newsize + (int) sizeof(DISKOFFSET) -
                                        (int) replacesize;
if (bc->bfree + delta > SIZES(NDX,split)) {
    int oldblockseen = 0;

    if (bc->parent == 0) {
        /*
         * We're trying to split the root block!
         * Complain & abort.
         */
        bt->error_code = 17;
```

```
        return 0L;
    }

    /* allocate a new index block */
    bl = bt_getnew4write(bt,NDX);
    if (!bl)
        return 0L;
    pblock1 = bl -> buffer;
    newindexblock = bl -> offset;
    bc1 = (BlockControl *) pblock1;
    bc1 -> blockstate = sNode;

    /* locate the break point */
    offset = sizeof(BlockControl);
    previous = 0;
    while (offset < bc->bfree/2) {
        previous = offset;
        keysize = GETKEYSIZE(pblock + offset);
        if (*((DISKOFFSET *)(pblock + offset + keysize)) ==
                                          oldblock)
            oldblockseen = 1;
        offset += keysize + sizeof(DISKOFFSET);
    }
    if (previous == 0) {
        /*
         * Major problem. there is one key that it so large
         * we can't divide the block. This should never
         * happen, as keys should be small relative to the
         * size of the block. Complain and abort. The index
         * may now be corrupt.
         */
        bt->error_code=18;
        return 0L;
    }
    keysize = GETKEYSIZE(pblock + previous);
    keycopy = malloc(keysize);
    memcpy(keycopy, pblock + previous, keysize);

    /* make sure we can alter our parent */
    newparent =
        bt_fix_index(bt,
                     NULL,
                     bc->parent,
                     fixblock,
                     keycopy,
                     newindexblock);
    free (keycopy);
    if (!newparent)
```

```
        return 0L;

/* refresh our pointers */
SHOW(printf("bt_fix_index/b: %Fp, %d, %ld\n",
                              bt, NDX, fixblock);)
pblock  = bt_getblock4write(bt,NDX,fixblock);
SHOW(printf("bt_fix_index/c: %Fp, %d, %ld\n",
                              bt, NDX, newindexblock);)
pblock1 = bt_getblock4write(bt,NDX,newindexblock);
if (!pblock || !pblock1)
    return 0L;
bc  = (BlockControl *) pblock;
bc1 = (BlockControl *) pblock1;
bc -> parent = bc1 -> parent = newparent;

/* divide'em up */
memcpy(pblock1 + bc1->bfree, pblock + offset,
                                bc->bfree - offset);
bc1 -> bfree += bc -> bfree - offset;
bc  -> bfree = offset;

/* common parent */
bc1 -> parent = bc -> parent = newparent;

/* same level, same use */
bc1 -> blockstate = bc -> blockstate;

/* tell children of new index block */
/* ... about their new parent */
offset = sizeof(BlockControl);
while(offset < bc1 -> bfree) {
    char *pblock2;
    BlockControl *bc2;
    DISKOFFSET goal;

    keysize = GETKEYSIZE(pblock1 + offset);
    goal = *((DISKOFFSET *)(pblock1 + offset + keysize));
    SHOW(printf("bt_fix_index/d: %Fp, %d, %ld\n",
        bt, bc1->blockstate == sLeaf ? DAT : NDX,
        goal);)
    pblock2 = bt_getblock4write(bt,
            bc1->blockstate == sLeaf ? DAT : NDX,
            goal);
    if (!pblock2)
        return TREE_FAIL;
    bc2 = (BlockControl *) pblock2;
    bc2 -> parent = newindexblock;
```

```
        /* freshen our pointers */
        SHOW(printf("bt_fix_index/e: %Fp, %d, %ld\n",
            bt, NDX, newindexblock);)
        pblock1 = bt_getblock4write(bt, NDX, newindexblock);
        bc1 = (BlockControl *) pblock1;
        offset += keysize + sizeof(DISKOFFSET);
    }

    /* transfer our attention to new index block */
    if (!oldblockseen)
        fixblock = newindexblock;
}

/*
 * Now, after many struggles, it is safe to insert our new
 * pointer into the block pointed to by pblock. We start by
 * locating the key/DISKOFFSET pair that has oldblock for
 * its DISKOFFSET...
 */
pblock =
    bt_getblock4write(bt, NDX, fixblock); /* fresh pointer */
if (!pblock)
    return 0L;
bc = (BlockControl *) pblock;

offset = sizeof(BlockControl);
lastoffset = 0;
keysize = GETKEYSIZE(pblock + offset);
while (offset < bc ->bfree) {
    keysize = GETKEYSIZE(pblock + offset);
    if (*((DISKOFFSET *)(pblock + offset + keysize)) ==
                                                oldblock)
        break;

    lastoffset = offset;
    offset += keysize + sizeof(DISKOFFSET);
}
if (*((DISKOFFSET *)(pblock + offset + keysize)) !=
                                            oldblock) {
    /* something is very wrong */
    bt -> error_code = 19;
    return 0L;
}

if (replacekey) { /* change keys but not DISKOFFSETs */
    DISKOFFSET saveblock;

    /* move remaining data up */
```

```
        memmove(pblock + offset + replacesize + delta,
                pblock + offset + replacesize,
                bc->bfree - offset - replacesize);

/* insert newkey/oldblock */
if (newkey) { /* if NULL, we are actually deleting */
    memmove(pblock + offset, newkey, newsize);
    *((DISKOFFSET *)(pblock + offset + newsize)) =
                                            oldblock;

}
bc->bfree += delta;

/*
 * Is this the last pointer in the block? If so, must
 * update our parent so that it knows about the change
 */
saveblock = fixblock;
if (offset + newsize + sizeof(DISKOFFSET) >=
                                            bc->bfree) {
    int delete_newkey = 0;
    if (!newkey && lastoffset) {
        /*
         * We are deleting the last key of a non-empty
         * block. We must promote a new last key.
         */
        newkey =
            malloc(GETKEYNRECSIZE(pblock + lastoffset));
        if (!newkey) {
                bt->error_code=16;
                return 0L;
        }
        REC2KEYCPY(pblock + lastoffset, newkey);
        delete_newkey = 1;
    }
    fixblock = bt_fix_index(bt, replacekey, bc->parent,
                            fixblock, newkey, 0L);

    if (delete_newkey)
        free(newkey);

    /* is the block empty? if so, delete it. */
    if (bc->bfree == sizeof(BlockControl)) {
        if (bt_releaseblock(bt, NDX, saveblock))
            fixblock = 0L;
    }
    else { /* should we merge the block? */
        if (bc->bfree < SIZES(NDX, merge))
            if (bt_merger(bt, NDX, saveblock))
```

```
                        fixblock = 0L;
                }
        }

        return fixblock;
    }
    else {
        /* update existing key/DISKOFFSET to point to newblock */
        *((DISKOFFSET *)(pblock + offset + keysize)) = newblock;

        /* insert newkey/oldblock */
        memmove(pblock + offset + newsize + sizeof(DISKOFFSET),
                pblock + offset,
                bc->bfree - offset);
        memmove(pblock + offset, newkey, newsize);
        *((DISKOFFSET *)(pblock + offset + newsize)) = oldblock;
        bc -> bfree += newsize + sizeof(DISKOFFSET);

        return fixblock;
    }
}


/*
 * Add a new record
 *
 * Our general add strategy is:
 *
 *  1) Locate the spot for the insertion
 *  2) Split the data block if necessary (bt_split)
 *  3) Split index blocks if necessary (bt_fix_index)
 *  4) Re-locate the spot for the insertion
 *  5) Insert can now proceed without further splits
 *
 * Note that we actually commit step 3 to the database
 * before step 2--this allows us to abort if step 3
 * fails.
 */

/* split bottom data block in half */
int bt_split(Btree *bt)
{
    char *pblock, *pblock1, *keycopy;
    BufferList *bl;
    DISKOFFSET datablock, datablock1, newparent;
    BlockControl *bc, *bc1;
    unsigned previous, offset;

    datablock = bt->CurrentDataBlock;
```

```
     SHOW(printf("bt_split/a: %Fp, %d, %ld\n",
                              bt, DAT, datablock);)
     pblock = bt_getblock4write(bt, DAT, datablock);
     if (!pblock) {
         bt->error_code = 7;
         return TREE_FAIL;
     }

     bc = (BlockControl *) pblock;
     SHOW(printf("bt_split: parent of %ld is %ld\n",
                              datablock, bc->parent);)

     offset = sizeof(BlockControl);
     previous= 0;
     while (offset < bc->bfree/2) {
         previous = offset;
         offset += GETRECSIZE(pblock + offset);
     }

     if (previous == 0) { /* major problem - can't divide block */
         bt -> error_code = 15;
         return TREE_FAIL;
     }

     /* get a copy of the break record's key */
     keycopy = malloc(GETKEYNRECSIZE(pblock + previous));
     if (!keycopy) {
         bt -> error_code = 16;
         return TREE_FAIL;
     }
     REC2KEYCPY(pblock + previous, keycopy);

     /* get a new block */
     bl = bt_getnew4write(bt, DAT);
     if (!bl) {
         bt->error_code = 7;
         return TREE_FAIL;
     }

     pblock1 = bl -> buffer;
     datablock1 = bl -> offset;
     bc1 = (BlockControl *) pblock1;
     bc1 -> blockstate = sLeaf;

     /*
      * do insert into upper level blocks first. If this fails,
      * we have not committed any changes to the database and we
      * can just abort.
```

```
       */
       SHOW(printf("calling bt_fix_index(%Fp,%s,%ld,%ld,%ld\n",
                       bt,keycopy,bc->parent,datablock,datablock1);)
       newparent =
           bt_fix_index(bt, NULL, bc->parent, datablock,
                       keycopy, datablock1);
       free(keycopy);
       if (!newparent)
           return TREE_FAIL;

       /* Now divide the data */
       SHOW(printf("bt_split/b: %Fp, %d, %ld\n",
                                   bt, DAT, datablock);)
       pblock  = bt_getblock4write(bt, DAT, datablock);

       SHOW(printf("bt_split/c: %Fp, %d, %ld\n",
                                   bt, DAT, datablock1);)
       pblock1 = bt_getblock4write(bt, DAT, datablock1);

       bc  = (BlockControl *) pblock;
       bc1 = (BlockControl *) pblock1;
       memcpy(pblock1 + bc1->bfree, pblock + offset,
                                   bc->bfree - offset);
       bc1 -> bfree += bc -> bfree - offset;
       bc  -> bfree = offset;
       bc1 -> parent = bc -> parent = newparent; /* common parent */

       return TREE_OK;
}

int bt_add_record(Btree *bt, void *rec, void *key)
{
       char *s;
       BlockControl *bc;
       unsigned offset, datasize;
       DISKOFFSET datablock;
       int retval;

   top:
       datablock = bt->CurrentDataBlock;
       SHOW(printf("bt_add_record: %Fp, %d, %ld\n",
                                   bt, DAT, datablock);)
       s = bt_getblock4write(bt, DAT, datablock);
       if (!s) {
           bt->error_code = 7;
           return TREE_FAIL;
       }
```

```
    bc = (BlockControl *) s;
    datasize = GETRECSIZE(rec);

    if (bc->bfree + datasize > SIZES(DAT,split)) {
        if (bt_split(bt))
            return TREE_FAIL; /* couldn't do it */
        else {
            /* re-locate position for block to insert */
            retval = bt_walk_down(
                bt, NDX, FDATA(NDX, root_block),
                LocateFunc, 0, SELECTIVE);
            if (!retval)
                return retval;
            goto top; /* try again */
        }
    }

    /* looks good. make a space */
    offset = sizeof(BlockControl);
    while (offset < bc->bfree) {
        if (KEY2RECCMP(key, s + offset) < 0)
            break; /* goes before this record */
        offset += GETRECSIZE(s + offset);
    }
    /* make our moves */
    memmove(s + offset + datasize, s + offset,
                            bc->bfree - offset);
    memmove(s + offset, rec, datasize);
    bc->bfree += datasize;
    return TREE_OK;
}

int bt_add(Btree *bt, void *rec, void *key)
{
    int retval = TREE_OK;

    bt->SearchKey = key;
    bt->FoundRec = NULL;
    retval = bt_walk_down(
        bt, NDX, FDATA(NDX, root_block),
        LocateFunc, 0, SELECTIVE);
    if (!retval) {
        bt->error_code = 14;
        return TREE_FAIL; /* should never occur */
    }

    /*
     * Now, if FoundRec == NULL, then the current data record is
```

```
 * the right place for the new record and the new record
 * does not exist.
 *
 * If FoundRec != NULL, then FoundRec points to a data record
 * with the same key as the record to be inserted
 */

    retval = TREE_OK;
    if (bt->FoundRec) {
        if (!bt->duplicatesOK)
            retval = TREE_FAIL;
    }

    if (!retval)
        retval = bt_add_record(bt, rec, key);

    return retval;
}

/*
 * Delete a record
 *
 * Our general delete strategy starts in
 * bt_delete_record() and is:
 *
 *  1) Locate & delete offending record
 *
 *  2) If record was the rightmost record in its block,
 *     update key in parent index block(s). Note that
 *     this process involves removing an old key and
 *     inserting a new one: if the new key is larger
 *     than the old one, the block could potentially
 *     exceed the split limit. This could in turn split
 *     the parent, etc. Alternatively, the parent
 *     could need to merged. All of this is handled by
 *     bt_fix_index().
 *
 *  3) If datablock that held the deleted record is now
 *     smaller than merge, locate and examine the
 *     left and then the right sisters of this block.
 *     If the current block can be combined with
 *     either, then we will merge them. To merge,
 *     we first shift the tree so that the target
 *     datablocks have the same index block as their
 *     parent, we combine the blocks, and then drop
 *     one entry from the parent index block.
 */
```

```
/*
 * Routines to merge blocks
 */
#define LEFT 0
#define RIGHT 1

/* find sister of child in parent at level==0 */
DISKOFFSET bt_find_sister(Btree *bt,
                          DISKOFFSET parent,
                          DISKOFFSET child,
                          int direction,
                          int level) {

    char *pblock;
    BlockControl *bc;
    unsigned offset, lastoffset, keysize;
    DISKOFFSET dof;

    pblock = bt_getblock4read(bt, NDX, parent);
    if (!pblock)
        return 0L;
    bc = (BlockControl *) pblock;

    /* find key/diskoffset with child for its diskoffset */
    lastoffset = 0;
    offset = sizeof(BlockControl);
    dof = 0;
    while (offset < bc -> bfree) {
        keysize = GETKEYSIZE(pblock + offset);
        dof = *((DISKOFFSET *)(pblock + offset + keysize));
        if (dof == child)
            break;
        lastoffset = offset;
        offset += keysize + sizeof(DISKOFFSET);
    }

    if (dof != child) {
        bt->error_code = 22;
        return 0L;
    }

    if (direction == LEFT) {
        if (lastoffset) { /* it is in this block */
            keysize = GETKEYSIZE(pblock + lastoffset);
            dof =
                *((DISKOFFSET *)(pblock + lastoffset + keysize));
            while (level > 0) { /* unwind the chain */
                level--;
```

```
                pblock = bt_getblock4read(bt, NDX, dof);
                if (!pblock)
                    return 0L;
                bc = (BlockControl *) pblock;
                offset = sizeof(BlockControl);

                /* find rightmost entry */
                while (offset < bc -> bfree) {
                    keysize = GETKEYSIZE(pblock + offset);
                    dof = *((DISKOFFSET *)(pblock + offset +
                                                    keysize));
                    offset += keysize + sizeof(DISKOFFSET);
                }
            }
            return dof;
        }
        else if (bc->parent)
            return bt_find_sister(bt, bc->parent, parent,
                            LEFT, level + 1);
        else
            return 0L;
    }
    else { /* direction == RIGHT */
        keysize = GETKEYSIZE(pblock + offset);
        offset += keysize + sizeof(DISKOFFSET);

        if (offset < bc->bfree) { /* it is in this block */
            keysize = GETKEYSIZE(pblock + offset);
            dof = *((DISKOFFSET *)(pblock + offset + keysize));
            while (level > 0) { /* unwind the chain */
                level--;
                pblock = bt_getblock4read(bt, NDX, dof);
                if (!pblock)
                    return 0L;
                bc = (BlockControl *) pblock;
                offset = sizeof(BlockControl);
                keysize = GETKEYSIZE(pblock + offset);
                dof =
                    *((DISKOFFSET *)(pblock + offset + keysize));
            }
            return dof;
        }
        else
        if (bc->parent)
            return bt_find_sister(bt, bc->parent, parent,
                            RIGHT, level + 1);
        else
            return 0L;
```

```
    }
}

/* merge left into right, if possible */
int bt_do_merge(Btree *bt,
                int f,  /* DAT or NDX */
                DISKOFFSET left,
                DISKOFFSET right) {
    char *pleft, *pright;
    BlockControl *bcleft, *bcright;
    void *oldkey;
    unsigned offset, recsize;

    pleft = bt_getblock4read(bt, f, left);
    if (!pleft)
        return TREE_FAIL;
    pright = bt_getblock4read(bt, f, right);
    if (!pright)
        return TREE_FAIL;

    bcleft  = (BlockControl *) pleft;
    bcright = (BlockControl *) pright;

    if (bcleft->bfree + bcright->bfree - sizeof(BlockControl) <
            SIZES(f, split)) { /* let's do it! */
        unsigned moving;

        /* get modifiable copies */
        pleft = bt_getblock4write(bt, f, left);
        if (!pleft)
            return TREE_FAIL;
        pright = bt_getblock4write(bt, f, right);
        if (!pright)
            return TREE_FAIL;

        bcleft  = (BlockControl *) pleft;
        bcright = (BlockControl *) pright;

        /* this many new bytes */
        moving = bcleft->bfree - sizeof(BlockControl);

        /* make room & copy */
        memmove(pright + sizeof(BlockControl) + moving,
                pright + sizeof(BlockControl),
                bcright->bfree);
        memmove(pright + sizeof(BlockControl),
                pleft  + sizeof(BlockControl),
                moving);
```

```
bcright->bfree += moving;

/* now, to discard the left block ... */

/* ... we first find & copy the last record's key */
offset = sizeof(BlockControl);
if (f == NDX)
    recsize = GETKEYSIZE(pleft + offset) +
                              sizeof(DISKOFFSET);
else
    recsize = GETRECSIZE(pleft + offset);
while (offset + recsize < bcleft->bfree) {
    offset += recsize;
    if (f == NDX)
        recsize = GETKEYSIZE(pleft + offset) +
                              sizeof(DISKOFFSET);
    else
        recsize = GETRECSIZE(pleft + offset);
}

if (f == NDX) {
    unsigned keysize;

    keysize = GETKEYSIZE(pleft + offset);
    oldkey = malloc(keysize);
    if (!oldkey) {
            bt->error_code = 16;
            return TREE_FAIL;
    }
    memmove(oldkey, pleft + offset, keysize);
}
else {
    oldkey = malloc(GETKEYNRECSIZE(pleft + offset));
    if (!oldkey) {
        bt->error_code = 16;
        return TREE_FAIL;
    }
    REC2KEYCPY(pleft + offset, oldkey);
}

/* ... and then run up the tree, deleting oldkey */
if (!bt_fix_index(bt, oldkey, bcleft->parent,
                  left, 0L, 0L))
    return TREE_FAIL;
free (oldkey);

/* ... and finally free the block */
if (bt_releaseblock(bt, f, left))
```

```
            return TREE_FAIL;

        /* tell children about their new parent */
        if (f == NDX) {
            pright = bt_getblock4write(bt, f, right);
            if (!pright)
                return TREE_FAIL;

            bcright = (BlockControl *) pright;
            moving += sizeof(BlockControl);
            offset  = sizeof(BlockControl);
            while(offset < moving) {
                char *pblock2;
                BlockControl *bc2;
                DISKOFFSET goal;
                unsigned keysize;

                keysize = GETKEYSIZE(pright + offset);
                goal = *((DISKOFFSET *)(pright + offset +
                                                keysize));
                SHOW(printf("bt_do_merge: %Fp, %d, %ld\n",
                        bt, bcright->blockstate == sLeaf ? DAT :
                        NDX, goal);)
                pblock2 = bt_getblock4write(bt,
                        bcright->blockstate == sLeaf ? DAT :
                        NDX, goal);
                if (!pblock2)
                    return TREE_FAIL;
                bc2 = (BlockControl *) pblock2;
                bc2 -> parent = right;

                /* freshen our pointers */
                pright = bt_getblock4write(bt, NDX, right);
                bcright = (BlockControl *) pright;
                offset += keysize + sizeof(DISKOFFSET);
            }
        }

        return TREE_OK;
    }
    else
        return TREE_FAIL; /* didn't fit */
}

/* main merge routine */
int bt_merger(Btree *bt, int f, DISKOFFSET block)
{
    char *pblock;
```

```
    BlockControl *bc;
    DISKOFFSET sister;

    pblock = bt_getblock4read(bt, f, block);
    if (!pblock)
        return TREE_FAIL;
    bc = (BlockControl *) pblock;

    if (bc->bfree < SIZES(f,merge)) { /* try to do a merge! */
        /* look left */
        sister = bt_find_sister(bt, bc->parent, block, LEFT, 0);
        if (sister && !bt_do_merge(bt, f, sister, block))
            return TREE_OK;

        /* look right */
        sister = bt_find_sister(bt, bc->parent, block, RIGHT, 0);
        if (sister && !bt_do_merge(bt, f, block, sister))
            return TREE_OK;
    }

    if (!bt->error_code)
        return TREE_OK;
    else
        return TREE_FAIL;
}

int bt_delete_record(Btree *bt)
{
    DISKOFFSET block;
    char *pblock;
    BlockControl *bc;
    unsigned offset, recsize, lastoffset;
    int compare, retval = TREE_OK;

    /* target record should be in this block */
    block = bt->CurrentDataBlock;
    pblock = bt_getblock4write(bt, DAT, block);
    if (!pblock)
        return TREE_FAIL;
    bc = (BlockControl *) pblock;

    /* find the record */
    offset = sizeof(BlockControl);
    lastoffset = 0;
    while (offset < bc->bfree) {
        recsize = GETRECSIZE(pblock + offset);
        compare = KEY2RECCMP(bt->SearchKey, pblock + offset);
        if (compare < 0) {
```

```
                bt -> error_code = 20;
                return TREE_FAIL; /* should not happen */
        }
        else if (compare == 0)
                break;
        lastoffset = offset;
        offset += recsize;
}

if (offset >= bc->bfree) {
        bt -> error_code = 20;
        return TREE_FAIL;
}

/* expunge the record */
bc->bfree -= recsize;
if (bc->bfree > offset) { /* not the last record */
        memmove(pblock + offset,
                pblock + offset + recsize,
                bc->bfree - offset);
        retval = bt_merger(bt, DAT, block);
}
else {
        /* deleting the last record in a block. must promulgate
           the key of the new last record upward.
         */
        void *oldkey, *newkey = NULL;
        oldkey = malloc(GETKEYNRECSIZE(pblock + offset));
        if (!oldkey) { bt->error_code=16; return TREE_FAIL; }
        REC2KEYCPY(pblock + offset, oldkey);

        /* is there a new last record? */
        if (lastoffset) {
                newkey = malloc(GETKEYNRECSIZE(pblock + lastoffset));
                if (!newkey) {
                        bt->error_code = 16;
                        return TREE_FAIL;
                }
                REC2KEYCPY(pblock + lastoffset, newkey);
        }

        /* run up the tree, replacing oldkey with newkey */
        if (!bt_fix_index(bt, oldkey, bc->parent, block,
                        newkey, 0L))
                retval = TREE_FAIL;

        if (!retval) {
                if (lastoffset) /* merge if needed */
```

```
                    retval = bt_merger(bt, DAT, block);

            else /* this block is empty */
                    retval = bt_releaseblock(bt, DAT, block);
        }

        free(oldkey);
        if (newkey)
            free(newkey);
    }

    return retval;
}

int bt_delete(Btree *bt, void *key)
{
    int retval;

    bt->SearchKey = key;
    bt->FoundRec = NULL;
    retval = bt_walk_down(
        bt, NDX, FDATA(NDX, root_block), FindFunc, 0, SELECTIVE);
    if (retval && bt->FoundRec)
        return bt_delete_record(bt);
    else
        return TREE_FAIL;
}
```

It should now be easy to understand bt_walk_down(). After retrieving a copy of the specified block, bt_walk_down() either calls itself recursively to handle the next layer of index block or runs through the data records calling the user-supplied action function. The code used for stepping through an index block demonstrates many idioms used elsewhere in the module:

```
offset = sizeof(BlockControl);
while (offset < bc->bfree) {
    keysize = GETKEYSIZE(s + offset);
    datablock = *((DISKOFFSET *) (s + offset + keysize));
    if (mode == SELECTIVE) {
        if (KEY2KEYCMP(bt->SearchKey, s+offset) > 0) {
            offset += keysize + sizeof(DISKOFFSET);
            continue;
        }
    }
    retval =  bt_walk_down(bt,
                bc->blockstate == sLeaf ? DAT : NDX,
                datablock, df, level + 1, mode);
```

```
        if (retval)
            break;

        /* recursive calls may invalidate our buffer */
        s = bt_getblock4read(bt, f, block);
        bc = (BlockControl *) s;
        offset += keysize + sizeof(DISKOFFSET);
    }
```

A counter, `offset`, is initialized to point to the first data byte. Because the data begins immediately following the block's `BlockControl` structure, `offset` needs to be set only to `sizeof(BlockControl)`. Then, as long as `offset` is less than or equal to `bt->bfree`, the code examines the key at the location specified by `offset`. Note that `offset` is truly an offset: it specifies a location relative to `s`, a pointer returned by the call to `bt_getblock4read()` that originally retrieved the block and stored it in memory. This separation is important because, as you will see in a moment, the value of `s` may vary during successive iterations of this loop. You determine the size of the key at `s+offset` by using the macro `GETKEYSIZE`. This macro expands into a call to the function specified by `bt->getkeysize`. The corresponding `DISKOFFSET` is then found at `s+offset+keysize`. Finally, assuming that `mode` isn't `SELECTIVE`, `bt_walk_down()` calls itself again. Once this recursive call is returned, the loop refreshes its pointer to the disk block by again calling `bt_getblock4read()`. This last step is important. Particularly in the higher index blocks, each recursive call to `bt_walk_down()` may entail dozens of other recursive calls, each of which will load an index block. The disk block cache holds a small number of blocks that it discards on a least-recently-used basis. You must always assume that pointers to disk blocks are invalid if other recursive tree accesses are generated.

The code that examines data blocks is similar in structure to the code that is used for scanning an index block. The only additional wrinkle is that this code saves the offset of the current data block in `bt->CurrentDataBlock`. After making a `SELECTIVE` call to `bt_walk_down()`, the caller can use this value to determine the location of the data block that contains the record of interest.

Finding a Record: `bt_find()`

The code for locating a specific record builds on the code that walks the entire tree and starts at `bt_find()`. Here, pointers to the target key and an output area are loaded into the `B-tree` structure and `bt_walk_down()` is called. On this call, however, `mode` is `SELECTIVE` and the action function is `FindFunc()`, a function supplied by the B-tree code at the start of *bt_data.c* (Listing 6-6). Because mode is SELECTIVE, only one index block on each level will be examined. Then, once the correct data block is found, FindFunc() is called for each of its data records. When the correct data record is found, it is copied to the output area and success is signaled. Note that, like many routines in this module, FindFunc() actually has two modes of operation: it can find and copy the data from a given record, or it can determine whether a record with a given key exists in the data set.

Inserting a New Record: bt_add()

Addition and deletion are the two most complex operations. Of the two, addition is easier and we will start with it. The entry point for addition is bt_add() in *bt_data.c* (Listing 6-6). This routine first uses the familiar bt_walk_down() routine to locate the data block where the new record will go. This search also allows the routine to refuse to insert records with duplicate keys, if appropriate. Once the correct location is determined, bt_add_record() is invoked to do the actual work. If the new record fits, it is simply copied into the appropriate location. If not, bt_split() is called to handle the problem. With bt_split() we now encounter the first major tree-manipulation subroutine.

After locating a record that divides the current data block roughly in half, bt_split() calls upon bt_fix_index() to have a pointer to the new block inserted into the parent index block. This routine is the true workhorse of the entire B-tree module. It can insert a new key and pointer combination, update a pointer's key, or delete a key and a pointer. Doing these things for any one index block is simple; the problem comes about when, for example, the insertion of a new key and pointer causes a block to overflow. The routine handles these problems in a straightforward fashion: it recurses toward the root block until it can see that the operation will be successful. Then, all necessary changes are made as the recursive stack is unwound. The actual block manipulations are also straightforward. The reason for the only real complexities is that the routine is used for inserting, modifying, and deleting. However, the segments that perform these operations are independent of each other and can be studied separately.

During an insertion, the only problem that bt_fix_index() faces is the possibility that inserting a new pointer might cause the current index block to contain more than split bytes, thus necessitating a block split. As discussed previously, this breakpoint is determined by the "fullness" of the block rather than by the absolute number of records in the block. This approach allows a data block to contain many small records or just a few larger ones. If the block overflows, a new index block must be obtained and a pointer to it must be inserted into the previous level index block. This might, of course, cause the previous level index block to split, and so on. If the root block overflows, then the tree must grow in height. The current code does not allow this (an error code is returned instead), but it would be trivial to implement: just retrieve a new block, make it the root block, and insert a pointer to the current index block as the only entry. The subsequent code would then propagate the split into this new root block.

Deleting a Record: `bt_delete()`

Deletions are the most challenging part of the B-tree module. After determining that the record of interest exists, `bt_delete()` invokes `bt_delete_record()` to do the actual work. This routine starts by removing the desired record from the data block. This is always safe, even if it leaves the block empty. If, however, the deletion leaves some data in the block, one special case must be handled: if the deleted record is the last record of the block, the index block's key for this block (that is, the key in the block that points to this block) is now in error and must be corrected. An example of this process of promulgating a new terminal key upward is shown earlier in Figure 6-25. It is important to note that this process may require that you modify index blocks on multiple levels. Furthermore, since we allow variable-length keys, the new key may be either smaller or larger than the key it replaces. Thus, the change of keys could actually cause the given index block to be split or to be merged. Again, `bt_fix_index()` handles all these conditions.

While the code for splitting two index blocks is embedded in `bt_fix_index()`, the code for merging two blocks is in a separate routine, `bt_merger()`. If a block needs to be merged, this routine locates first the left sibling block and then the right sibling block and determines whether a merge is possible. If so, `bt_merger()` invokes `bt_do_merge()` to do the following:

1. Pull the data from the left block into the right block.
2. Delete the key of the left block's rightmost entry from the parent index block(s).
3. Place the left block on the free chain.

Finding the left or right sibling is the task of `bt_find_sister()`. As you might imagine, this process can be as simple as looking one index level up to find the previous or succeeding entry. If we need the left sibling of the leftmost entry in a block, we may need to climb and descend several tree levels to find the desired entry. The same situation can occur also when we need to find the right sibling of the rightmost entry in a block. This process is implemented as a recursive search.

Note that bt_fix_index() plays a prominent role in the deletion process. As before, deleting an index key might cause an index block to shrink so that it needs to be merged with its siblings. This would lead to a nested, recursive call to bt_merger(), and so on. To see this diagramatically, consider a calling diagram rooted on bt_delete(), as shown in Figure 6-27.

```
                                    Recursively calls:
bt_delete()
└─>-bt_walk_down()                  [itself]
└─>-bt_delete_record()
    └─>-bt_merger()
    |   └─>-bt_find_sister()        [itself]
    |   └─>-bt_do_merge()
    └─>──────└─>-bt_fix_index()     [itself] [bt_merger()]
```

Figure 6-27.   A calling diagram rooted on bt_delete().

Accessing a Disk: bt_disk.c

Buffered disk access is achieved by the module bt_disk.c (Listing 6-7). A list of disk buffers is maintained for each *.ndx* and *.dat* file. Access to disk blocks is mainly through bt_getblock4read() and bt_getblock4write(). The only difference between these routines is that after bt_getblock4write(), the block is assumed to be "dirty" and will be written to disk before being discarded.

When a disk block is requested, the list of buffers is searched. If the block is not present, the last block in the list is discarded and the new block is read. The most recently used block is always kept at the beginning of the list. During initialization, enough index block buffers are allocated to ensure that, at a minimum, one block from each level of a full-height tree can be present in memory simultaneously.

Listing 6-7.   Disk routines and error messages for B-trees.

```
/*--- bt_disk.c -------------------------- Listing 6-7 ---------
 * Disk-access routines and array of error messages
 *
 *-------------------------------------------------------------*/
```

```
#include "bt_hdr.h"

#if defined(HELP1)
#define SHOW(x) x
#else
#define SHOW(x)
#endif

char *ErrorText[] = {
  /*  0 */ "Not an error",
  /*  1 */ "bt_new: Could not create new data file",
  /*  2 */ "bt_new: Bad block_size value",
  /*  3 */ "bt_new: Bad split or merge values",
  /*  4 */ "bt_new: Could not write to new data file",
  /*  5 */ "bt_disk: Couldn't allocate buffers",
  /*  6 */ "bt_open: Couldn't open data file",
  /*  7 */ "bt_disk: Couldn't read data file",
  /*  8 */ "bt_open: Signature string missing",
  /*  9 */ "bt_close: Couldn't close file",
  /* 10 */ "bt_disk: Couldn't read/write file",
  /* 11 */ "bt_add: Attempted to add duplicate key",
  /* 12 */ "bt_split: Attempted to split block w/ NULL parent",
  /* 13 */ "bt_split: Couldn't find child in parent",
  /* 14 */ "bt_data: Locate failed",
  /* 15 */ "bt_data: couldn't split a block--record too large",
  /* 16 */ "bt: out of memory",
  /* 17 */ "bt_fix_index: trying to split root index block!",
  /* 18 */ "bt_fix_index: couldn't split a block--key too large",
  /* 19 */ "bt_fix_index: lost oldblock--critical error",
  /* 20 */ "bt_delete_record: couldn't find target record",
  /* 21 */ "bt_replacekey: couldn't find target key",
  /* 22 */ "bt_find_sister: couldn't find target key"
};

static int bt_blwrite(Btree *bt, int f, BufferList *bl)
{
    int ret = TREE_OK;

    if (fseek(FDATA(f,file), bl->offset, SEEK_SET))
        ret = TREE_FAIL;
    if (!ret &&
        fwrite(bl->buffer,
        SIZES(f,block_size), 1, FDATA(f,file)) != 1)
            ret = TREE_FAIL;

    if (ret) {
        bt -> error_code = 10;
        SHOW(printf("failing in " __FILE__
```

```
                            " at line %d\n", __LINE__);)
    }
    else
        bl->state = sClean;

    return ret;
}

static int bt_blread(Btree *bt, int f, BufferList *bl)
{
    int ret = TREE_OK;

    SHOW(printf("bt_blread: bt = %Fp, f = %d, bl = %Fp\n",
                        bt, f, bl);)
    SHOW(printf("filename: %s, file: %Fp\n",
                        FDATA(f, filename), FDATA(f, file));)
    SHOW(printf("buffer state=%d, offset=%lx,"
                "buffer=%Fp, next=%Fp\n",
                        bl->state, bl->offset,
                        bl->buffer, bl->next);)
    SHOW(printf("seeking to %ld\n", bl-> offset);)
    SHOW(fflush(stdout);)
    if (fseek(FDATA(f,file), bl->offset, SEEK_SET)) {
        ret = TREE_FAIL;
        SHOW(printf("failing in " __FILE__
                    " at line %d\n", __LINE__);)
    }
    SHOW (else printf(" now at %ld\n", ftell(FDATA(f, file)));)


    if (!ret &&
        fread(bl->buffer,
        SIZES(f,block_size), 1, FDATA(f,file)) != 1) {
          ret = TREE_FAIL;
        SHOW(printf("failing in " __FILE__
                    " at line %d\n", __LINE__);)
    }

    if (ret) {
        bl -> state = sFree;
        bt -> error_code = 10;
        SHOW(printf("failing in " __FILE__
                    " at line %d\n", __LINE__);)
    }
    else
        bl->state = sClean;

    return ret;
```

```
}

/* Load a disk block into a free buffer */
static BufferList *bt_getbuf(Btree *bt, int f, DISKOFFSET dof)
{
    BufferList *bl, *free_b, *free_p, *parent, *gparent;

    /* Already loaded? */
    free_b = free_p = parent = gparent = NULL;
    for (bl = FDATA(f,bufferlist); bl; ) {
        if (bl->state == sFree) {
            free_p = parent;
            free_b = bl;
        }
        else if (bl->offset == dof) {
            if (parent) { /* move to top of list */
                parent->next = bl -> next;
                bl -> next = FDATA(f,bufferlist);
                FDATA(f, bufferlist) = bl;
            }
            return bl;
        }

        gparent = parent;
        parent = bl;
        bl=bl->next;
    }

    if (!free_b) { /* Must free up an active buffer */
        /*
         * parent points to last buffer in list, and
         * gparent is the parent of this buffer. Because we
         * always move the most recently used buffer to the head
         * of the list, the last buffer is the least-recently
         * used buffer and gets tossed out.
         */
        free_b = parent;
        parent = gparent;
        if (free_b->state == sDirty && bt_blwrite(bt, f, free_b))
            free_b = NULL;
    }
    else
        parent = free_p;

    if (free_b) { /* A free buffer */
        SHOW(printf("bt_getbuf: Assigning bl at %Fp"
                    "to offset %ld\n", free_b, dof);)
        free_b -> offset = dof;
```

```
        if (bt_blread(bt, f, free_b)) {
            free_b -> state = sFree;
            free_b = NULL;
        }
        else {
            free_b -> state = sClean;
        }
    }

    if (free_b && parent) { /* Move new buffer to head of list */
        parent -> next = free_b -> next;
        free_b -> next = FDATA(f,bufferlist);
        FDATA(f,bufferlist) = free_b;
    }

    return free_b;
}

/* Get a block for read only */
char *bt_getblock4read(Btree *bt, int f, DISKOFFSET dof)
{
    BufferList *bl;
    SHOW(printf("bt_getblock4read(%Fp, %d, %ld)\n",bt,f,dof);)
    bl = bt_getbuf(bt, f, dof);
    if (bl)
        return bl -> buffer;
    else
        return NULL;
}

/* Get a block for read & write */
char *bt_getblock4write(Btree *bt, int f, DISKOFFSET dof)
{
    BufferList *bl;

    SHOW(printf("bt_getblock4write(%Fp, %d, %ld)\n",bt,f,dof);)
    bl = bt_getbuf(bt, f, dof);
    if (bl) {
        bl -> state = sDirty;
        return bl -> buffer;
    }
    else
        return NULL;
}

/* Get a new block for read & write */
BufferList *bt_getnew4write(Btree *bt, int f)
{
```

```
BufferList *bl;
BlockControl *bc;
DISKOFFSET dof;

/* first, are then any empty blocks already available? */
if ((dof = FDATA(f, free_block)) != 0) {
    SHOW(printf("bt_getnew4write(%Fp, %d, %ld)\n",bt,f,dof);)
    bl = bt_getbuf(bt, f, dof);
    if (!bl)
        return bl;
    bc = (BlockControl *) bl->buffer;
    FDATA(f, free_block) = bc->next;
    FDATA(f, modified) = 1;
}
else {
    /* extend the file */
    if (fseek(FDATA(f,file), 0L, SEEK_END))
        return NULL;
    dof = ftell(FDATA(f, file));

    /* just write something */
    if (fwrite(FDATA(f,bufferlist),
                    SIZES(f,block_size),
                1,
                    FDATA(f, file)) != 1) {
        bt -> error_code = 10;
        SHOW(printf("failing in " __FILE__
                    " at line %d\n", __LINE__);)
        return NULL;
    }
    SHOW(printf("bt_getnew4write #2(%Fp, %d, %ld)\n",
                    bt,f,dof);)
    bl = bt_getbuf(bt, f, dof);
    if (!bl)
        return bl;
}

/* initialize block */
bc = (BlockControl *) bl->buffer;
bc -> bfree = sizeof(BlockControl);
bc -> blockstate = sAvail;
bc -> parent = 0;
bc -> next = 0;

/* and ensure that all is written out */
bt_flush(bt);

bl -> state = sDirty;
```

```
        return bl;
}

int bt_flush(Btree *bt) {
    int i, ret;

    ret = TREE_OK;
    for (i=0; i<2; i++) {
        if (FDATA(i,file) && FDATA(i,bufferlist)) {
            char *p;
            DISKOFFSET *d;
            BufferList *bl;

            /* root block data changed? */
            if (FDATA(i, modified)) {

                /* get 1st block */
                p = bt_getblock4write(bt, i, 0L);
                p += sizeof(SIGNATURE) + sizeof(SIG_INDEX) - 1;
                p += sizeof(Sizes);
                d = (DISKOFFSET *) p;
                *d = FDATA(i, root_block);
                d++;
                *d = FDATA(i, free_block);
                FDATA(i, modified) = 0;
            }

            for (bl = FDATA(i,bufferlist); bl; bl = bl->next) {
                if (bl->state == sDirty)
                    ret = bt_blwrite(bt, i, bl);
            }

            fflush(FDATA(i, file));
        }
    }

    return ret;
}

int bt_bufinit(Btree *bt, int f)
{
    int i, cnt;
    BufferList dummy, *bl;

    if (FDATA(f,bufferlist) == NULL) {
        bl = &dummy;
        if (f == DAT)
            cnt = 5;
```

```
        else
            cnt = (int) SIZES(f,levels) * 3 / 2;
        if (cnt < 3)
            cnt = 3; /* minimum number */

        for (i = 0; i < cnt; i++) {
            bl -> next = malloc(sizeof(BufferList));
            if (bl -> next == NULL) {
                bt -> error_code = 5;
                return TREE_FAIL;
            }
            bl = bl -> next;
            bl -> buffer =
                malloc(SIZES(f,block_size));
            if (bl -> buffer == NULL) {
                bt -> error_code = 5;
                return TREE_FAIL;
            }
            bl -> state = sFree;
            bl -> offset = 0;
            bl -> next = NULL;
        }

        FDATA(f,bufferlist) = dummy.next;
    }
    return TREE_OK;
}

/* Release memory allocated to buffers */
void bt_bufrelease(Btree *bt, int f)
{
    BufferList *bl, *bl2;

    bl = FDATA(f,bufferlist);
    if (bl) {
        while(bl) {
            free(bl -> buffer);
            bl2 = bl -> next;
            free(bl);
            bl = bl2;
        }
        FDATA(f,bufferlist) = NULL;
    }
}

/* put a block on the free chain */
int  bt_releaseblock(Btree *bt, int f, DISKOFFSET dof)
{
```

```
    char *pblock;
    BlockControl *bc;

    pblock = bt_getblock4write(bt, f, dof);
    if (!pblock)
        return TREE_FAIL;
    bc = (BlockControl *) pblock;

    bc -> next = FDATA(f, free_block);
    bc -> blockstate = sAvail;
    FDATA(f, free_block) = dof;
    FDATA(f, modified) = 1;

    return TREE_OK;
}
```

Using the Module: `main()`

The code that does all the previously described work is heavily commented, and further details about its behavior can be obtained by examining the code directly and running the sample application. As we have already discussed, this application loads a pair of strings into a structure and computes a key based on the value of the first string. The sample driver can be used to insert, delete, and find records. The contents of the tree, as well as its internal structure, can be dumped at any time. In addition, a map of disk-block usage can be generated.

To further simplify testing, the driver normally compiles with very small cut-offs for `split` and `merge`. This causes the data and index blocks to fill quickly, thus allowing the behavior of the tree to be examined in detail with a minimum of data.

Listing 6-8.   Definition of sample data for *user.c*.

```
/*--- user.h ----------------------------- Listing 6-8 ---------
 * Sample data record definition
 *-----------------------------------------------------------*/

/* example data records */
typedef struct UserRecord {
    char key[11];
    char name[25];
    char addr[25];
} UR;

/* a record with a maximal key. initialized in user.c */
extern UR MaxRec;
```

```
/* The routines */
unsigned UserGetKeySize ( void *r );
unsigned UserGetRecSize ( void *r );
int UserKey2KeyCmp ( void *k1, void *k2 );
int UserKey2RecCmp ( void *k, void *r );
void UserRec2KeyCpy ( void *k, void *r );
```

Listing 6-9. Support routines and test driver for B-tree code.

```
/*--- user.c ----------------------------- Listing 6-9 ---------
 *Sample support routines and a driver
 *-----------------------------------------------------------*/

#include "bt_hdr.h"
#include <ctype.h>
#include "user.h"

#define TESTSIZES /* use small block limits to force splits */

/*
 * A record with a maximal key
 */
UR MaxRec = { "\xff\xff\xff\xff\xff\xff\xff\xff\xff\xff",
              "Maximal", "record" };

/*
 * The support routines that the btree routines call
 */
unsigned UserGetKeySize(void *k) {
    return strlen( (char *) k ) + 1;
}

unsigned UserGetKeyNRecSize(void *k) {
    return strlen( ((UR *) k) -> key ) + 1;
}

unsigned UserGetRecSize(void *r) {
    return sizeof(UR);
}

int UserKey2KeyCmp(void *k1, void *k2) {
    return strcmp((char *) k1, (char *) k2);
}

int UserKey2RecCmp(void *k, void *r) {
    return strcmp((char *) k, ((UR *) r)->key);
}
```

```
void UserRec2KeyCpy(void *rec, void *key) {
        strcpy((char *) key, ((UR *) rec) -> key);
}

/*
 * Some tree display routines
 */
char *BlockStates[] = { "sAvail", "sNode", "sLeaf" };
BLKSIZE index_blksize;
FILE *outfile;

void show_basic(Btree *bt, int f) {
    DISKOFFSET length, blkcount;
    BLKSIZE blksize;

    fprintf(outfile, "File: %s\n", FDATA(f,filename));

    blksize = SIZES(f, block_size);
    fprintf(outfile, "  Block size: %d, split: %d, merge: %d\n",
            blksize,
            SIZES(f, split),
            SIZES(f, merge));

    if (f == NDX)
        fprintf(outfile, "  Index has %d levels\n",
                SIZES(f, levels));

    fseek(FDATA(f, file), 0L, SEEK_END);
    length = ftell(FDATA(f,file));
    blkcount = length/blksize;
    fprintf(outfile, "  File length %ld (%ld blocks)\n",
                length, blkcount);

    if (f == NDX)
        fprintf(outfile, "  Root index block at %ld"
                            " (block no. %ld)\n",
                FDATA(f, root_block),
                FDATA(f, root_block)/blksize);

    fprintf(outfile,
            " First free block at %ld (block no. %ld)\n",
            FDATA(f, free_block),
            FDATA(f, free_block)/blksize);
}

/*
 * Given index block is at given level. Display contents
 * and then recursively examine the children.
 */
```

```
void prefix(int level) {
    for (; level; level--) fprintf(outfile, " * ");
}

void walk_down(Btree *bt, int f, DISKOFFSET block,
               int level, int mode) {
    char *s, *key;
    BlockControl *bc;
    unsigned offset, keysize, keycount = 0;
    DISKOFFSET *pDof;

    prefix(level);
    if (f == NDX)
        fprintf(outfile,
                "Level %d index block %ld at offset %ld.",
                level, block/index_blksize, block);
    else
        fprintf(outfile, "Data block %ld at offset %ld.",
                         block/SIZES(DAT, block_size), block);

    if (mode)
        fprintf(outfile, "\n");

    s = bt_getblock4read(bt, f, block);
    if (!s) {
        bt->error_code = 7;
        return;
    }

    bc = (BlockControl *) s;

    if (mode) {
        prefix(level);
        fprintf(outfile,
            "blockstate: %s, free data: "
            "%d, parent: %ld, next: %ld\n",
            BlockStates[bc->blockstate],
            bc->bfree,
            bc->parent,
            bc->next);
    }

    if (f == NDX) {
        offset = sizeof(BlockControl);
        while (offset < bc->bfree) {
            keysize = GETKEYSIZE(s + offset);
            key = s + offset;
            pDof = (DISKOFFSET *) (key + keysize);
```

```
        if (mode) {
            prefix(level);
            fprintf(outfile,
                "Offset %d: key '%s', DISKOFFSET %ld\n",
                offset, key, *pDof);
        }
        offset += keysize + sizeof(DISKOFFSET);
        keycount++;
    }
    if (!mode)
        fprintf(outfile, " %u entries\n", keycount);

    offset = sizeof(BlockControl);
    while (offset < bc->bfree) {
        keysize = GETKEYSIZE(s + offset);
        walk_down(bt,
            bc->blockstate == sLeaf ? DAT : NDX,
            *((DISKOFFSET *) (s + offset + keysize)),
            level + 1, mode);

        /* recursive calls may invalidate our buffer */
        s = bt_getblock4read(bt, f, block);
        bc = (BlockControl *) s;
        offset += keysize + sizeof(DISKOFFSET);
    }
}
else { /* f == DAT */
    offset = sizeof(BlockControl);
    while (offset < bc->bfree) {
        keysize = GETRECSIZE(s + offset);
        if (mode) {
            prefix(level);
            fprintf(outfile,
                "Offset %d: key '%s', name: %s, addr: %s\n",
                offset,
                ((UR *) (s + offset))->key,
                ((UR *) (s + offset))->name,
                ((UR *) (s + offset))->addr);
        }
        offset += keysize;
        keycount++;
    }
    if (!mode)
        fprintf(outfile, " %u entries\n", keycount);
    }
}

/*
 *display contents of data files
```

```
 *
 * mode = 0: just display number of pointers at each level
 * mode = 1: display all data
 */
void show_btree(Btree *bt, FILE *f, int mode) {
    outfile = f;
    if (mode) {
        show_basic(bt, NDX);
        show_basic(bt, DAT);
    }

    index_blksize = SIZES(NDX, block_size);
    walk_down(bt, NDX, FDATA(NDX, root_block), 0, mode);
}


/*
 * Block mapping routines
 *
 * Map is built up in map[] with these codes:
 *   C = control block (always block 0)
 *   N = index block
 *   D = data block
 *   . = lost block
 */
struct MapData {
    long length;
    unsigned blkcount;
    char *map;
} mapdata[2];

void show_btree_mapr(Btree *bt, DISKOFFSET iblock)
{
    char *pblock;
    BlockControl *bc;
    unsigned offset;
    DISKOFFSET dof;

    /* say we've been here */
    mapdata[NDX].map[iblock/SIZES(NDX,block_size)] = 'N';

    /* get the block */
    pblock = bt_getblock4read(bt, NDX, iblock);
    if (!pblock)
        return;
    bc = (BlockControl *)pblock;

    /* scan it */
    offset = sizeof(BlockControl);
    while (offset < bc->bfree) {
```

```
            offset += GETKEYSIZE(pblock + offset);
            dof = *((DISKOFFSET *) (pblock + offset));
            offset += sizeof(DISKOFFSET);
            if (bc->blockstate == sNode) {
                show_btree_mapr(bt, dof);
                pblock = bt_getblock4read(bt, NDX, iblock);
                if (!pblock)
                    return;
                bc = (BlockControl *)pblock;
            }
            else
                mapdata[DAT].map[dof/SIZES(DAT,block_size)] = 'D';
        }
}

void show_btree_map(Btree *bt, FILE *file) {
    int i, j;

    /* setup maps */
    for (i=0; i < 2; i++) {
        fseek(FDATA(i, file), 0L, SEEK_END);
        mapdata[i].length = ftell(FDATA(i, file));
        mapdata[i].blkcount =
                    mapdata[i].length/SIZES(i, block_size);
        mapdata[i].map = malloc(mapdata[i].blkcount);
        for (j=0; j < mapdata[i].blkcount; j++)
            mapdata[i].map[j] = '.';
        mapdata[i].map[0] = 'C';
    }

    /* walk the tree */
    show_btree_mapr(bt, FDATA(NDX, root_block));

    /* trace the free blocks */
    for (i=0; i < 2; i++) {
        DISKOFFSET block;
        char *pblock;
        BlockControl *bc;

        block = FDATA(i, free_block);
        while(block) {
            pblock = bt_getblock4read(bt, i, block);
            if (!pblock)
                break;
            mapdata[i].map[block/SIZES(i, block_size)] = 'f';
            bc = (BlockControl *) pblock;
            block = bc -> next;
        }
    }
```

```c
    /* display the map */
    for (i=0; i < 2; i++) {
        fprintf(file, "%s Block Map:\n        ",
                   i == 0 ? "Index" : "Data");
        for (j=0; j < 10; j++)
            fprintf(file, " %d", j);

        for (j=0; j < mapdata[i].blkcount; j++) {
            if (j % 10 == 0) {
                fprintf(file,"\n%4d: ", j);
            }
            fprintf(file, " %c", mapdata[i].map[j]);
        }
        fprintf(file, "\n");
        free(mapdata[i].map);
    }

}


/*
 * Sample display function
 */
int DataCount = 0;
int DisplayFunc(Btree *bt, void *rec) {
    UR *ur;
    ur = (UR *) rec;
    fprintf(outfile, "k:'%-10s', n:'%-24s', a:'%-24s'\n",
                   ur->key, ur->name, ur->addr);
    DataCount++;
    return TREE_OK;
}


/*
 * Make a new dataset
 */
int make_dataset(char *name)
{
    Btree bt;
    int retval;

    /*
     * Fill in parts of the structure. For the sizes, we
     * give what we want. The only real restriction is that
     * block_size - split must leave enough room to insert
     * the largest possible record or key.
     */
    strcpy(bt.fdata[NDX].filename, name);
    strcat(bt.fdata[NDX].filename, ".ndx");
```

```
    bt.fdata[NDX].modified = 0;
    bt.fdata[NDX].bufferlist = NULL;
    bt.fdata[NDX].sizes.block_size = 2048;
    #if defined(TESTSIZES)
    bt.fdata[NDX].sizes.split    = 80;
    bt.fdata[NDX].sizes.merge    = 45;
    #else
    bt.fdata[NDX].sizes.split    = 2000; /* room for one key */
    bt.fdata[NDX].sizes.merge    = 1024;
    #endif
    bt.fdata[NDX].sizes.levels   = 4;

    strcpy(bt.fdata[DAT].filename, name);
    strcat(bt.fdata[DAT].filename, ".dat");
    bt.fdata[DAT].modified = 0;
    bt.fdata[DAT].bufferlist = NULL;
    bt.fdata[DAT].sizes.block_size  = 4096;
    #if defined(TESTSIZES)
    bt.fdata[DAT].sizes.split    = 500;
    bt.fdata[DAT].sizes.merge    = 300;
    #else
    bt.fdata[DAT].sizes.split    = 3950; /* room for a rec */
    bt.fdata[DAT].sizes.merge    = 2048;
    #endif
    bt.fdata[DAT].sizes.levels   = 0; /* any value is OK */

    bt.getkeysize      = UserGetKeySize; /* user.c */
    bt.getkeyNrecsize  = UserGetKeyNRecSize;
    bt.getrecsize      = UserGetRecSize;
    bt.key2keycmp      = UserKey2KeyCmp;
    bt.key2reccmp      = UserKey2RecCmp;
    bt.rec2keycpy      = UserRec2KeyCpy;

    bt.error_code   = 0;
    bt.duplicatesOK = 1;

    retval = bt_new(&bt, MaxRec.key, &MaxRec);
    if(retval == TREE_OK)
        printf("Data files created.\n");
    else
        printf("Create failed: %s.\n",
                ErrorText[bt.error_code]);

    return retval;
}

/*
 * Open a dataset
```

```
        */
Btree *open_dataset(char *name)
{
        Btree *bt;

        bt = malloc(sizeof(Btree));
        if (!bt)
                return NULL;

        strcpy(bt->fdata[NDX].filename, name);
        strcat(bt->fdata[NDX].filename, ".ndx");
        bt->fdata[NDX].bufferlist = NULL;

        strcpy(bt->fdata[DAT].filename, name);
        strcat(bt->fdata[DAT].filename, ".dat");
        bt->fdata[DAT].bufferlist = NULL;

    bt->getkeysize      = UserGetKeySize; /* user.c */
    bt->getkeyNrecsize  = UserGetKeyNRecSize;
    bt->getrecsize      = UserGetRecSize;
    bt->key2keycmp      = UserKey2KeyCmp;
    bt->key2reccmp      = UserKey2RecCmp;
    bt->rec2keycpy      = UserRec2KeyCpy;

        bt->error_code = 0;
        bt->duplicatesOK = 1;

        if (bt_open(bt)) {
         printf("Open failed: %s.\n",
                                ErrorText[bt->error_code]);
                free(bt);
                bt = NULL;
        }
    else
        fprintf(stdout, "Opened\n");
        return bt;
}


/*
 * A sample driver
 */
int DoData(Btree *bt, char *buffer, int mode) {
    UR ur;
    char *s;
    s = strchr(buffer, ';');
    if (!s) {
        if (mode == 0)
```

```
                s = ""; /* don't need address for deletes */
            else
                return TREE_FAIL; /* trying to add partial data */
        }
        else
            *s++ = '\0';

        strncpy(ur.key, buffer, 10); /* key is first 10 characters */
        ur.key[10] = '\0';
        strncpy(ur.name, buffer, 24);
        ur.name[25] = '\0';
        strncpy(ur.addr, s, 24);
        ur.addr[25] = '\0';

        if (mode == 0)
            return bt_delete(bt, ur.key);
        else
            return bt_add(bt, &ur, ur.key);
}

#define BUFLEN 100
void LoadFile(Btree *bt, char *fname)
{
    FILE *infile;
    char buffer[BUFLEN], *s;
    int i = 0, j = 0, retval = TREE_OK;

    if ((infile = fopen(fname, "r")) == NULL) {
        fputs(" Couldn't open the file.\n", stdout);
        return;
    }

    while (fgets(buffer, BUFLEN, infile)) {
        s = buffer + strlen(buffer);
        while(iscntrl(*s))
            *s-- = 0;

        printf("Loading %s\n", buffer);
        if (buffer[0] == ';') /* a comment */
            ;
        else if (buffer[0] == '-' && buffer[1] != 0) {
            retval = DoData(bt, buffer+1, 0);
            if (retval) {
                printf("  --delete failed\n");
                retval = 0;
            }
            else
                j++;
```

```
        }
        else {
            retval = DoData(bt, buffer, 1);
            if (retval)
                break;
            i++;
        }
    }

    if (retval)
        printf("Failed at line %s\n", buffer);

    fclose(infile);
    printf("Loaded %d items and deleted %d from %s.\n",
        i, j, fname);
}


main(int argc, char **argv)
{
    char inbuf[BUFLEN], *s;
    Btree *bt = NULL;
    FILE *logfile = NULL;

    for (;;) {
        fflush(stdout);
        fputs("Action (? for help): ", stdout);
        fflush(stdout);
        fgets(inbuf, BUFLEN, stdin);
        s = inbuf + strlen(inbuf);
        while(iscntrl(*s))
            *s-- = 0;

        if (logfile)
            fprintf(logfile, "%s\n", inbuf);

        if (!bt && strchr("@adfkKmMsSwW", inbuf[0])) {
            fputs(" **no open dataset\n", stdout);
            continue;
        }

        switch (inbuf[0]) {
            case '?':
                fputs(
        "@file      - load strings in file into tree\n"
        "a string   - add name;addr to tree\n"
        "d string   - delete name;addr from tree\n"
```

```
"dup [0|1]  - disallow/allow duplicates\n"
"f string   - find name;addr in tree\n"
"k/K [file] - display key counts (K = overwrite file)\n"
"l file     - log actions to file\n"
"l          - turn off action logging\n"
"m/M [file] - display block usage map\n"
"n file     - make a new dataset\n"
"o file     - open an existing dataset\n"
"s/S [file] - display tree (S = overwrite file)\n"
"w/W [file] - walk tree, (W = overwrite file)\n"
"q          - quit\n"
, stdout);
        fflush(stdout);
        break;

    case '@':
        LoadFile(bt, inbuf + 1);
        break;

    case 'a':
        if (inbuf[1] != ' ' ||
            !inbuf[2]        ||
            !strchr(inbuf,';'))
            fputs(" Not a valid command\n", stdout);
        else
            if (DoData(bt, inbuf + 2, 1) == TREE_FAIL)
                fputs(" ** Insertion failed\n", stdout);
        break;

    case 'd':
        if (inbuf[1] == 'u' && inbuf[2] == 'p') {
            if (inbuf[3] == ' ' &&
                (inbuf[4] == '0' || inbuf[4] == '1'))
                bt -> duplicatesOK =
                inbuf[4] == '0' ? 0 : 1;
            fputs("duplicates are ", stdout);
            if (bt -> duplicatesOK == 0)
                fputs("not ", stdout);
            fputs("allowed.\n", stdout);
            break;
        }

        if (inbuf[1] != ' ' || inbuf[2] == 0)
            fputs(" Not a valid command\n", stdout);


        else {
            if (DoData(bt, inbuf + 2, 0) == TREE_FAIL)
```

```
                fputs(" ** Delete failed\n", stdout);
        }
        break;

case 'f':
        if (inbuf[1] != ' ' || inbuf[2] == 0)
            fputs(" Not a valid command\n", stdout);
        else {
            UR record;
            inbuf[12] = '\0';
            if (bt_find(bt, &record, inbuf+2) ==
                                          TREE_FAIL)
                fputs(" ** Find failed\n", stdout);
            else
                fprintf(stdout, "found %s;%s\n",
                        record.name, record.addr);
        }
        break;

case 'k': case 'K': {
            FILE *out;

            if (inbuf[1] == ' ' && inbuf[2] != 0) {
                out = fopen(inbuf+2,
                            inbuf[0] == 'k' ? "w" : "a");
                if (!out)
                    printf("Can't open %s\n", inbuf + 2);
                else {
                    show_btree(bt, out, 0);
                    fclose(out);
                }
            }
            else
                show_btree(bt, stdout, 0);
        }
        break;

case 'l':
        if (inbuf[1] != ' ' || inbuf[2] == 0) {
            if (logfile) {
                fclose(logfile);
                logfile = NULL;
            }
            else
                fputs(" Logfile not open\n", stdout);
        }
        else {
            logfile = fopen(inbuf + 2, "w");
```

```
            if (logfile == NULL)
                printf("Can't open %s\n", inbuf + 2);
        }
        break;

    case 'm': case 'M': {
            FILE *out;

            if (inbuf[1] == ' ' && inbuf[2] != 0) {
                out = fopen(inbuf+2, inbuf[0] ==
                                       'm' ? "w" : "a");
                if (!out)
                    printf("Can't open %s\n", inbuf + 2);
                else {
                    show_btree_map(bt, out);
                    fclose(out);
                }
            }
            else
                show_btree_map(bt, stdout);
        }
        break;

    case 'n':
        if (inbuf[1] != ' ' || inbuf[2] == 0)
            fputs(" Not a valid command\n", stdout);
        else
            make_dataset(inbuf+2);
        break;

    case 'o':
                if (inbuf[1] != ' ' || inbuf[2] == 0)
            fputs(" Not a valid command\n", stdout);
        else {
            if (bt) {
                if (bt_close(bt))
                    printf("\nClose failed: %s\n",
                            ErrorText[bt->error_code]);
                else
                    printf("\nData files closed.\n");

                bt = NULL;
            }
                        bt = open_dataset(inbuf+2);
        }
        break;

    case 'q':
```

```
        if (logfile)
            fclose(logfile);

        if (bt) {
            if (bt_close(bt))
                printf("\nClose failed: %s\n",
                        ErrorText[bt->error_code]);
            else
                printf("\nData files closed.\n");
        }
        return;

    case 's': case 'S': {
            FILE *out;

            if (inbuf[1] == ' ' && inbuf[2] != 0) {
                out = fopen(inbuf+2, inbuf[0] ==
                                        's' ? "w" : "a");
                if (!out)
                    printf("Can't open %s\n", inbuf + 2);
                else {
                    show_btree(bt, out, 1);
                    fclose(out);
                }
            }
            else
                show_btree(bt, stdout, 1);
        }
        break;

    case 'w': case 'W': {
            if (inbuf[1] == ' ' && inbuf[2] != 0) {
                outfile = fopen(inbuf+2, inbuf[0] ==
                                        'w' ? "w" : "a");
                if (!outfile)
                    printf("Can't open %s\n", inbuf + 2);
                else {
                    DataCount = 0;
                    bt_walk(bt, DisplayFunc);
                    fprintf(outfile, "%d items\n",
                            DataCount);
                    fclose(outfile);
                    outfile = NULL;
                }
            }
            else {
                DataCount = 0;
                outfile = stdout;
```

```
            bt_walk(bt, DisplayFunc);
            fprintf(outfile, "%d items\n",
                    DataCount);
            outfile = NULL;
        }
    }
    break;

case ';':
    break;   /* comment */

default:
    fputs(" Not a valid command\n", stdout);
    break;
}
if (bt && bt->error_code) {
    printf("ERROR: %s\n", ErrorText[bt->error_code]);
    bt->error_code = 0;
}
    }
}
}
```

Determining the Height of a Tree

The capacity of a tree is determined by its height and its block size. Look at the example shown in Table 6-2. Suppose we decide to use index blocks of 2,048 bytes and we estimate that our average key size is 10 bytes. If a `diskoffset` is 4 bytes, then a key plus `diskoffset` is 14 bytes. With 12 bytes used by the `BlockControl` structure, this leaves room for (2048–12)/14 = 145 keys per index block. We further decide to use 4,096-byte data blocks, and we estimate that our average record size is 100 bytes. There will then be (4096–12)/100 = 40 records per data block. Our tree's capacity is then given as $145^{height-1}$x40.

Table 6-2. An example in which the capacity of a tree is determined by its height and block size.

Height	Maximum number of records
1	5,800
2	841,000
3	121,945,000
4	17,682,025,000

While the actual capacity will be slightly less since we never allow the blocks to become completely full, a tree with a height of four looks like it would store a lot of data. Note also that the decision to create a tree with a fixed height of four has very little performance impact. Because of the block-buffering system, the relevant upper-level index blocks are likely to always be available in memory for small trees. Therefore, accessing them does not require a disk access, and little overhead is incurred. It was for these reasons that a fixed-height scheme was chosen.

Additional Modifications

The B-tree code in Listings 6-3 through 6-9 is really only a beginning, and commercial B-tree packages provide many more features than are implemented here. However, this module is certainly functional, it performs well, and it is a good demonstration of the types of problems that must be solved. Features that could be added include the following:

- The tree could be allowed to grow and shrink in height. This would involve adding a new root block when `bt_fix_index()` finds that the root block must be split. Conversely, code for removing the root block would need to be added to the deletion routines. However, in reality this would have very little impact on performance.
- It would be useful to have `next()` and `previous()` functions that, given one record, will return the next or previous record. The example code does not provide this ability directly. Rather, the tree-walk routines will call a user-defined function to operate on each record in succession. These functions could, however, be built easily using the code in `bt_find_sister()`.
- Improved disaster protection could be provided. For example, if the user were to terminate a session in the middle of a tree update, the data base would likely become corrupt. You can best handle this type of problem by keeping a "before image" of the files. Each time a block is modified, a "before" copy is written to a "before image" file. Then, at user-definable intervals, all files are flushed to a disk and, as a last step, the "before image" file is cleared. This approach allows recovery from many types of disasters.
- Additional maintance tools could be created—particularly, tools for reindexing a *.dat* file and tools for repairing a corrupt index.

Can You See the Forest?

This chapter has covered a lot of ground. Staring with a simple binary tree, we have examined height-balanced trees (red-black trees) and usage-balanced trees (splay trees). Each of these trees could easily be used for an in-memory tree. Then, to solve the problem of larger data sets, we created an on-disk B-tree module. Common to all these trees, however, is the idea of keys and records in steadily increasing order. While different in detail, the algorithms for tree traversal are conceptually similar for each: start at the top, descend to the left, go to the middle, and then go to the right. Even insertion and deletion have a similar feel throughout.

These are some of the most complex routines in this book, and there is no substitute for running the actual code in order to see how it all works. Each routine has an extensive test driver to simplify this process, and each tree can print itself in a diagrammatic form for study.

Resources and References

Adel'son-Vel'skii, G. M., and E. M. Landis. "An Algorithm for the Organization of Information." *Soviet Math*, Vol. 3, pp. 1259–1263, 1962. This is the original AVL paper. The discussions in Knuth and Melhorn are easier to follow.

Bayer, R., and E. McCreight. "Organization and Maintenance of Large Ordered Indexes." *Acta Informatica*, Vol. 1, pp. 173–189, 1972. This is the basic B-tree paper.

Comer, Douglas. "The Ubiquitous B-tree." *Computing Surveys*, Vol. II, pp. 121–137, 1979. This article contains an interesting section on the history of B-trees, including a discussion of the origin of the term *B-tree*.

Knuth, Donald E. *The Art of Computer Programming. Vol. 3: Sorting and Searching*. Reading, MA: Addison-Wesley, 1973. This is one of the two key general resources for this chapter and is encyclopedic in format. See especially Section 6.22 for the material described in this chapter under the heading "The Performance of Binary Trees."

Melhorn, K. *Data Structures and Algorithms 1: Sorting and Searching*. Berlin: Springer-Verlag, 1984. This book is the other key general resource for this chapter. It discusses a number of interesting subtopics that Knuth passes over. In particular, Melhorn's discussion of splay trees is excellent, although the interested reader should actually consult the original article by Sleator and Tarjan.

Sleator, D. D., and R. E. Tarjan. "Self-Adjusting Binary Search Trees." *Journal ACM*, Vol. 32, pp. 652–686, 1985. This is the original paper on splay trees. The top-down Splay operation demonstrated in *bintree.c* is taken from this article.

Tarjan, Robert E., and Christopher J. Van Wyk. "An O(n log log n)-Time Algorithm for Triangulating a Simple Polygon." *Siam J. Comput*, Vol. 17, pp. 143–178, 1988. This article contains a helpful discussion of red-black trees.

Chapter 7

Date and Time

The challenges presented by date and time routines are not typical of those you find in traditional algorithms. Rather, the challenges focus on handling the vagaries of human history as they are reflected in the calendar. To understand how date and time routines work, you need to understand how calendars have evolved to their current state.

The Julian calendar, first implemented by Julius Caesar (hence its name) in 46 B.C., defined a year as having an average length of 365¼ days. The extra day (called a **leap day**) that occurred every four years was recognized by establishing that every fourth year (the **leap year**) would comprise 366 days while the remaining years (the **common years**) would comprise 365 days. This arrangement resulted in inaccuracies. By setting the year at 365¼ days, the calendar was setting the duration of a single revolution of the earth around the sun at 365 days, 6 hours. In fact, a single revolution takes 365 days, 5 hours, 49 minutes, and 12 seconds. The defined calendar year was 10 minutes and 48 seconds (or 10.8 minutes) too long. Over the course of 400 years, this difference resulted in the calendar being 3 days ahead of itself.

As time passed, the problem worsened, and by the sixteenth century (nearly 1600 years after the Julian calendar was instituted), the calendar was 12 days ahead. This had serious implications for the Catholic Church, which had the responsibility for setting Easter. Easter, the Church found, was losing the feel of the end of winter, all the while compressing the holy year whose major holy days—with the exception of Christmas—are defined in relation to Easter.

In 1582, Pope Gregory XIII decided to trim the extra days the Julian calendar had added, and to redefine which years were leap years, so that they better reflected the astronomical reality. He cut ten days from October:

October 4, 1582, was followed by October 15, 1582. In addition, he mandated that from then on all years evenly divisible by four would be leap years except those that were evenly divisible by 100 and not divisible by 400. For example, in the period 1599 to 1999, all years that are evenly divisible by 4 are leap years except for 1700, 1800, and 1900. Years 1600 and 2000 are leap years. The effect of this change is that 3 century years out of every 400 years are not leap years. This step corrects the Julian calendar error of 3 extra days every 400 years. The new calendar was named the Gregorian calendar after the pope and is used almost universally today.

The modifications proclaimed by Pope Gregory applied only to lands over which the Catholic Church had dominion. Protestant countries, such as England, refused on principle to go along with any papal edict and hence moved to the Gregorian calendar at separate times. While most Protestant countries adopted the new calendar in the 1699–1701 time frame, England (and hence the American colonies) did not switch over until 1752. By the time they made this move, another spurious day from the Julian calendar had crept into the error between the two calendars. So, in September 1752, England cut eleven days from the calendar: September 2, 1752, was immediately followed by September 14, 1752. After 1752, most major Western countries were on the Gregorian calendar. However, smaller nations held out much longer for all sorts of political reasons. Romania did not convert until 1919; Turkey not until 1927. Even today, countries under the dominion of the Eastern Orthodox Church use a variant of the Gregorian calendar to formulate their own dating system. Hence, when discussing historical dates, it is not sufficient to know when the event occurred but also *where*.

In the routines presented in this chapter, we use the year 1582 as the change-over date. We could have used the English/American year, 1752, but the important dates in the intervening period of 1582 to 1752 were very much attached to continental European events rather than to events in England or the American colonies. Our choice is the one commonly made, although UNIX chooses the American date of 1752 as its change-over point. Therefore, when you use any calendars prior to 1752, it is imperative that you establish whether you are working with the Julian or the Gregorian calendar.

The Gregorian calendar made one additional change: it set the starting date of the new year as January 1. Previously, individual countries celebrated the new year on different days—some as early as December 25 and others as late as March 25. Before 1752, England and the American colonies used March 25 as New Year's Day. That is, March 24, 1701, was followed by March 25, 1702. Because of this change, George Washington's birthday, which today is given as February 22, 1732, was actually recorded on that day as February 11, 1731. Hence, if you need to talk exactly about any date prior to 1752, you must know where the event was recorded and whether the date has been converted to a Gregorian calendar. Dates prior to the modern age are tricky business.

Most calendar systems use the conventions adopted by the routines presented in this chapter: 1582 is used as the switch-over point, and the current calendar convention of starting the new year on January 1 is projected backward over previous years. It is commonly understood that this projection means that the dates will occasionally be at odds with the dates as they would have been recorded on the given day. If you need to know the exact day as it was recorded for an event prior to 1582, these routines will not work for you, nor will just about any routines you can lay hold of. Most calendars used on computers today seek to do one thing: to give every day a unique, identifying sequential code that allows the user to compute dates relative to the current period. Beyond that, all bets are off. These routines will tell you whether in their scheme June 1, A.D. 848 was a Saturday, but there is no assurance that the answer will jibe with the reality had you been alive that day. Calendars such as these that project the current calendrical scheme backward are termed **proleptic** calendars. For dates prior to the switch-over date, they should be used with care.

A Library of Date Routines

If people did not need to know what year they were in, a simple way to account for all days is to choose one day and call it day 1, and then consecutively number all days from that day on. This scheme was first proposed by a monk who named these numbered days **Julian days** after his father, Julius. (Julian days should not be confused with the Julian calendar.) Because the monk believed an unusual confluence of calendrical cycles had occurred on January 1, 4713 B.C., he used this date as his starting point. (The likelihood that this day was in any way close to any discernible event is extremely low.) Nonetheless, days numbered from that day forward are called Julian days. By convention, the fateful day of October 15, 1582 (the first day of the Gregorian calendar), is generally accepted as Julian date 2,299,161.

In the routines presented shortly, we count days from January 1, A.D. 1, the theoretical first day of the Christian era. (By convention, there is no year 0.) Since our dates use a different starting point from the Julian counting, they cannot be called Julian dates; hence, in this chapter we simply call them day numbers.

All our routines hold the dates (and times) in the structure of form `struct tm` as defined in the ANSI C header *time.h*, shown in Figure 7-1. This structure has room for the year, month, day, hour, minute, second, and a host of other data.

Figure 7-1.   The ANSI `tm` structure in *time.h*.

```
struct tm {
          int tm_sec;              /* seconds, 0-based */
          int tm_min;              /* minutes, 0-based */
          int tm_hour;             /* hours,   0-based */
          int tm_mday;             /* day of the month, 1-based */
          int tm_mon;              /* month, note: 0-based! */
          int tm_year;             /* year since 1900 */
          int tm_wday;             /* weekday: Sun = 0, Sat = 6 */
          int tm_yday;             /* day of the year, 0-based */
          int tm_isdst;            /* daylight savings time flag */
};
```

This structure has several unfortunate aspects: months are zero-based, meaning that January is counter-intuitively numbered 0; also, most functions that use this structure expect the year to be between 0 and 99. The routines add 1900 to the year. In our work, we respect the use of zero-based months; however, our years go all the way back to year A.D. 1. In our routines, therefore, it is imperative to always use the full year when computing dates. Otherwise, 94 will be interpreted as A.D. 94 rather than as 1994.

Only the three date and three time fields are used by the routines presented in this chapter. The other fields are ignored or computed separately.

To move a date into a `tm` structure, use the function `LoadDateStruct`, as shown in Figure 7-2. This function should be used as the entry point for all date routines in this library.

Figure 7-2.   `LoadDateStruct()` loads a date into a `tm` structure.

```
/*------------------------------------------------------------
 * Loads a date passed as three integers into a tm structure.
 * Returns 0 on success, -1 on error.
 *------------------------------------------------------------*/
int LoadDateStruct ( struct tm *date, int yy, int mm, int dd )
{
    date->tm_year = yy;
    date->tm_mon  = mm - 1; /* for compatibility w/ ANSI C */
    date->tm_mday = dd;

    if ( IsDateValid ( date ) == NO )
        return ( -1 );
    else
        return ( 0 );
}
```

The function `LoadDateStruct()` expects to be handed a pointer to the `tm` structure and three integers to load: one each for the year, month, and day. These should be the actual values (the function will make the month zero-based). Because `LoadDateStruct()` is generally called before other date functions are used, it also checks the validity of the date by calling `IsDateValid()`, the function shown in Figure 7-3.

Figure 7-3. `IsDateValid()` determines whether a given date is valid.

```
/*-------------------------------------------------------------
 * Returns YES if date is valid, otherwise returns NO.
 *-------------------------------------------------------*/
int IsDateValid ( struct tm *date )
{
    if ( date->tm_mon < 0 || date->tm_mon > 11 )    /* per ANSI */
        return ( NO );

    if ( date->tm_year < 1 )
        return ( NO );

    if ( IsYearLeap ( date->tm_year ) == NO )
        if ( date->tm_mday < 1 ||
            date->tm_mday > Days_in_month[ date->tm_mon + 1] )
          return ( NO );
        else
        if ( date->tm_mday < 1 ||
            date->tm_mday >
                    Days_in_month_leap[ date->tm_mon + 1] )
          return ( NO );

    return ( YES );
}
```

`IsDateValid()` checks that all parameters are within range. For example, our earliest date is in the year A.D. 1, so all dates must have years greater than 0. It also checks the number of days in the month by looking up the days in a table. This table is one of several data tables that are accessed by the date functions. As a result, these tables are declared as static data elements at the global level for the date routines. This means that all date routines can access these tables, but no other code can do so. These tables are shown in Figure 7-4.

Figure 7-4. Global static data accessed by the date routines.

```
static const int Days_in_month [13] = {
    0,
    31, 28, 31,      /* Jan, Feb, Mar */
    30, 31, 30,      /* Apr, May, Jun */
    31, 31, 30,      /* Jul, Aug, Sep */
    31, 30, 31       /* Oct, Nov, Dec */
};

/* same as above but for a leap year */

static const int Days_in_month_leap [13] = {
    0,
    31, 29, 31,      /* Jan, Feb, Mar */
    30, 31, 30,      /* Apr, May, Jun */
    31, 31, 30,      /* Jul, Aug, Sep */
    31, 30, 31       /* Oct, Nov, Dec */
};

static const char *Day_name[7] = {
    "Sunday",    "Monday",
    "Tuesday",   "Wednesday",
    "Thursday",  "Friday",
    "Saturday"
};

static const char *Day_name_abbrev[7] = {
    "Sun",   "Mon",
    "Tue",   "Wed",
    "Thu",   "Fri",
    "Sat"
};

static const char *Month_name[13] = {
    "",
    "January",   "February",  "March",
    "April",     "May",       "June",
    "July",      "August",    "September",
    "October",   "November",  "December"
};

static const char *Month_name_abbrev[13] = {
    "",
    "Jan",   "Feb",   "Mar",
    "Apr",   "May",   "Jun",
    "Jul",   "Aug",   "Sep",
    "Oct",   "Nov",   "Dec"
};
```

IsDateValid() accesses the arrays of integers Days_in_month and Days_in_month_leap. These arrays are identical except for the values in element 2 (February), which predictably are 28 and 29 respectively. If necessary, these two tables could be folded into one and the value of February's entry could be calculated each time. However, this requires that you either keep track of the element's value or constantly reset it at the start of every date calculation. Changing the values of small tables of constants is not a good practice, and it opens the door to subtle bugs. Because memory is generally inexpensive and plentiful, using several tables is a better choice. In addition, it allows the tables to be defined as const, which serves as another safety measure.

For IsDateValid() to know which table to use, it must first determine whether the current year is leap. To do this, it calls IsYearLeap(), shown in Figure 7-5. It passes the function an integer containing the year to be examined, and returns YES or NO, depending on whether the year is leap.

Figure 7-5. IsYearLeap() determines whether a given year is leap.

```
/*-------------------------------------------------------------
 * Returns YES or NO depending on whether a year is leap or not
 *-----------------------------------------------------------*/
int IsYearLeap ( int year )
{
    if ( year % 4 != 0 )     /* if year not divisible by 4... */
        return ( NO );       /* it's not leap */

    if ( year < 1582 )       /* all years divisible by 4 were */
        return ( YES );      /* leap prior to 1582           */

    if ( year % 100 != 0 )   /* if year divisible by 4, */
        return ( YES );      /* but not by 100, it's leap */

    if ( year % 400 != 0 )   /* if year divisible by 100, */
        return ( NO );       /* but not by 400, it's not leap */
    else
        return ( YES );      /* if divisible by 400, it's leap */
}
```

Note the comments that explain how leap years are determined. According to the explanations presented earlier, in the Gregorian calendar (that is, since 1582), all years that are evenly divisible by 4 are leap years *unless* they are evenly divisible by 100 and not evenly divisible by 400. Hence, 1900 was not a leap year (evenly divisible by 100 but not by 400), while 2000 will be leap (evenly divisible by 100 and 400). Prior to 1582, all years that were evenly divisible by 4 were leap years. (There is some dispute as to exactly when this rule was first applied. It is possible that the years A.D. 4 and A.D. 8 were not leap years simply because this rule was not yet observed. However, since no definitive evidence exists, it is conveniently assumed that both these years were leap years.)

Knowing how dates were calculated also allows us to convert dates to day numbers. Day numbers start at some chosen date and assign that date a value of 1. Every day thereafter is assigned a successive integer; that is, the next day is day 2, followed by day 3, and so on. The Julian day numbers discussed earlier use January 1, 4713 B.C. as the starting date. The routines presented here use January 1, A.D. 1, the first day of the Christian era. The function `DateToDayNumber()` in Figure 7-6 accepts a pointer to a `tm` date structure and converts the date to a day number. Note that the returned day number is a long integer. If the date is discovered to be invalid, the function returns a long integer of value −1L.

Figure 7-6. `DateToDayNumber()` converts a date to a day number.

```
/*-------------------------------------------------------------
 * Returns a long which contains the number of days since
 * Jan 1, AD 1; returns -1L on error. See text for observations
 * on the use of this function.
 *-----------------------------------------------------------*/
long DateToDayNumber ( struct tm * date )
{
    long day_num;
    int  mm, yy;

    if ( IsDateValid ( date ) == NO )
        return ( -1L );

    yy = date->tm_year;
    mm = date->tm_mon + 1;

    /* get all the regular days in preceding years */

    day_num =  ( yy - 1 ) * 365L;

    /* now get the leap years */

    day_num += ( yy - 1 ) / 4L;

    /*
     * now back out the century years that are not leap:
```

```
 * this would be all century years that are
 * not evenly divisible by 400: 1700, 1800, 1900, 2100...
 */

day_num -= ( yy - 1 ) / 100L;
day_num += ( yy - 1 ) / 400L;

/*
 * before 1582 all century years were leap, so adjust for
 * this. If year is > 1582, then just add 12 days for years
 * 100, 200, 300, 500, 600, 700, 900, 1000, 1100, 1300, 1400
 * and 1500. Otherwise, calculate it.
 */

if ( yy - 1 > 1582L )
    day_num += 12L;
else
{
    day_num += ( yy - 1 ) / 100L;
    day_num -= ( yy - 1 ) / 400L;
}

/* now, add the days elapsed in the year so far */

if ( IsYearLeap ( date->tm_year ) == NO )
    while ( --mm )
        day_num += Days_in_month[ mm ];
else
    while ( --mm )
        day_num += Days_in_month_leap[ mm ];

/* add days in current month for the year being evaluated */

day_num += date->tm_mday;

/*
 * now adjust for the 10 days cut out of the calendar when
 * the change was made to the Gregorian calendar. This change
 * reflects the jump from October 4 to October 15, 1582, a
 * deletion of 10 days.
 */

if ( day_num > 577737L )
    day_num -= 10L;

return ( day_num );
}
```

The code for this function is extensively commented so that it might be self-explanatory. The only really unusual code appears at the end of the function, once the day number has been computed. The code reads as follows:

```
if ( day_num > 577737L )
        day_num -= 10L;
```

Up to this point in the function, the day-number calculation has not taken into account that October 4, 1582, is succeeded by October 15. This test determines whether the computed date comes after October 4, 1582 (which would be day 577,737 from January 1, A.D. 1). If the date is past this point, the function subtracts the 10 days that mark the start of the Gregorian calendar from the day number.

The day number is a cornerstone of all date and calendar functions. For example, to identify the day of the week, you get the day number and then use the modulus function. Any given day number modulo 7 will return a unique value of 0 through 6 that can be used to indicate the day of the week. For example, `DayOfWeek()` in Figure 7-7 accepts a `tm` structure and returns an integer from 0 to 6, where 0 signifies Sunday.

Figure 7-7. `DayOfWeek()` calculates the day of a given week.

```
/*-------------------------------------------------------------
 * Returns an integer from 0-6 signifying the day of the week,
 * where 0 = Sunday and 6 = Saturday. Returns -1 on error.
 *-----------------------------------------------------------*/
int DayOfWeek ( struct tm *date )
{
    long day_num = DateToDayNumber ( date );

    if ( day_num < 0 )
        return ( -1 );

    return ( (int) (( day_num % 7 ) + 5 ) % 7 );
}
```

By convention, western calendars begin each week with Sunday, so Sunday is generally assigned the value of 0 and Saturday the value 6. Once `DayOfWeek` accepts a `tm` structure containing a date, it calculates the day number. This day number is then divided by 7 and the remainder is obtained (using the modulo operator). Because our counting system did not start on a Sunday, the modulo result must have 5 added to it in order to obtain results consistent with a Sunday value of 0 and a Saturday value of 6. Adding 5 to the modulo result, however, may generate a result greater than 6; therefore, the modulo 7 operation is performed a second time. The final value is then returned as the day of the week.

A similar useful piece of information (that we will need shortly) is what day of the year it is—that February 25, for example, is the 56th day of the year. The function `DayOfYear()` in Figure 7-8 accepts a date structure and converts it to a day number. It then computes the day number for January 1 of that year. It returns the difference between the two day numbers as the day of the year.

Figure 7-8. `DayOfYear()` identifies the day of the year for a given date. Returns –1 on error.

```
/*-----------------------------------------  ----------------
 * Returns an integer from 1-366 signifying the day of the year.
 * where 1 is Jan 1, 365 or 366 is Dec 31, and -1 is an error.
 *---------------------------------------------------------*/
int DayOfYear ( struct tm *date )
{
    struct tm jan1;

    if ( LoadDateStruct ( &jan1, date->tm_year, 1, 1 ) == -1 )
        return ( -1 );

    return ((int) ( DateDiff ( date, &jan1 ) + 1 ));
}
```

Another useful application of the day number is a function that tells you how far apart two dates are. This function, `DateDiff()`, as shown in Figure 7-9, merely computes the day numbers for the two separate dates and then subtracts the second day number from the first one.

Figure 7-9. `DateDiff()` calculates the number of days between two given dates. No error code is returned.

```
/*----------------------------------------------------------
 * Accepts pointers to two date structures and returns the
 * difference in days between them as a long int. Negative if
 * the first date is earlier, positive if it is later. No error
 * return is possible, so programmers must make sure the dates
 * are valid.
 *---------------------------------------------------------*/
long DateDiff ( struct tm *d1, struct tm *d2 )
{
    return ( DateToDayNumber ( d1 ) - DateToDayNumber ( d2 ));
}
```

Because any long integer value can be returned, the function cannot return an error code. You must make sure that the dates are valid before calling the function; otherwise the results may be unreliable.

Converting a day number back to a valid date is clearly necessary at some point after you have invoked almost any of the preceding functions. The function `DayNumberToDate()` in Figure 7-10 accepts a long integer containing the day number and a pointer to a `tm` structure where it will place the resulting date.

Figure 7-10. `DayNumberToDate()` converts a number back to a valid date. Returns –1 on error.

```c
/*------------------------------------------------------------
 * Converts a day number into an actual date.
 *--------------------------------------------------------*/
int DayNumberToDate ( long int day_num, struct tm *date )
{
    int     dd, mm, yy, i;
    long    days_left;

    if ( day_num > 577737L )
        day_num += 10L;

    yy = (int) ( day_num / 365 );
    days_left = day_num % 365L;

    /* prior to 1700, all years evenly divisible by 4 are leap */

    if ( yy < 1700 )
        days_left -= ( yy / 4 );
    else
    {
        days_left -= ( yy / 4 );      /* deduct leap years */
        days_left += ( yy / 100 );    /* add in century years */
        days_left -= ( yy / 400 );    /* deduct years / 400 */
        days_left -= 12;              /* deduct century years that
                                         were leap before 1700 */
    }

    /* make sure days left is > 0 */

    while ( days_left <= 0 )
    {
        if ( IsYearLeap ( yy ) == YES )
        {
            yy -= 1;
```

```
                days_left += 366;
        }
        else
        {
            yy -= 1;
            days_left += 365;
        }
    }

    /*
     * yy holds the number of elapsed years.
     * So, add 1 for the current year.
     */

    yy += 1;

    /*
     * now deduct the days in each month, starting
     * from January to find month and day of month.
     * adjust for leap year, of course.
     */

    dd = (int) days_left;
    mm = 0;

    if ( IsYearLeap ( yy ) == YES )
        for ( i = 1; i <= 12; i++ )
        {
            mm = i;
            if ( dd <= Days_in_month_leap[i] )
                break;
            else
                dd -= Days_in_month_leap[i];
        }
    else
        for ( i = 1; i <= 12; i++ )
        {
            mm = i;
            if ( dd <= Days_in_month[i] )
                break;
            else
                dd -= Days_in_month[i];
        }

    if ( LoadDateStruct ( date, yy, mm, dd ) == -1 )
        return ( -1 );
    else
        return ( 0 );
}
```

The preceding code is somewhat more complicated than the routine that converts dates to day numbers. The code first adjusts for days after the beginning of the Gregorian calendar. It then divides the day number by 365 and stores the quotient in yy, the tentative guess as to which year it is. The remainder from the division is stored in days_left. The routine then tries to subtract from days_left all the leap days that occurred prior to yy. If days_left drops below 0, a year is deducted from yy and either 365 or 366 days are added to days_left until it is greater than 0. At this point, yy holds the correct number of completed years. The value of days_left will tell us the month and day. Since the month and day will occur in the year after the completed years, yy is incremented before month and day calculations begin. These last calculations are easy to perform and are fully explained in the code.

An example of how to use the routines presented so far in this chapter appears in Listing 7-1, *lilcal.c*. This program performs a subset of the duties done by the UNIX *cal* utility. When *lilcal* is called with no arguments, it prints a calendar for the current month. If it is called with the month and year, it prints the calendar for that month. An example of the latter command line is lilcal 7 1776. This command would print the calendar for the fateful month of July 1776.

Listing 7-1.   *lilcal.c* is a program that performs much of the calendar printing capability of the UNIX *cal* utility.

```
/*--- lilcal.c -------------------------------------------------
 * lilcal works similarly to the UNIX cal program.
 * If you type lilcal with no arguments, it prints the calendar
 * for the current month; otherwise, provide it with two argu-
 * ments: the month and year. Hence, lilcal 9 56 will print the
 * calendar for September 1956. October 1582 is hardwired as
 * a special case. UNIX cal allows you to print the calendar for
 * a whole year. Since this code is cosmetic rather than algo-
 * rithmic, it is not included here.
 *-------------------------------------------------------------*/

#include <stdio.h>
#include <stdlib.h>
#include <time.h>

#include "datelib.h"

void PrintCalendar ( int, int );
void PrintOct1582 ( void );

int main ( int argc, char *argv[] )
```

```
{
    int start_yy, start_mm;

    time_t timer;
    struct tm *tms;

    if ( argc != 1 && argc != 3 )
    {
        fprintf ( stderr, "lilcal requires 0 or 2 arguments\n" );
        return ( EXIT_FAILURE );
    }

    if ( argc == 1 )     /* current month */
    {
        timer = time ( NULL );
        tms   = localtime ( &timer );
        tms->tm_mon += 1;

        start_mm = tms->tm_mon;
        start_yy = tms->tm_year;
        start_yy += 1900;
    }
    else
    if ( argc == 3 )
    {
        start_mm = atoi ( argv[1] );
        start_yy = atoi ( argv[2] );
    }

    /*
     * due to the calendar change, October 1582 is a unique
     * month and must be provided for specially.
     */

    if ( start_yy == 1582 && start_mm == 10 )
        PrintOct1582();
    else
        PrintCalendar ( start_yy, start_mm );

    return ( EXIT_SUCCESS );
}

void PrintCalendar ( int cal_yy, int cal_mm )
{
    char       buffer [40];
    struct tm date;
    int        day_of_week;
    int        days_in_month;
```

```
int        days_to_print[42];
int         i, j, rows;

if ( LoadDateStruct ( &date, cal_yy, cal_mm, 1 ) == -1 )
{
    fprintf ( stderr, "Illegal month: %02d-%02d\n",
                cal_yy, cal_mm );
    return;
}

/* get the day of the week for the 1st of month */

day_of_week = DayOfWeek ( &date );

/* find out how many days in the month */

switch ( cal_mm )
{
    case  1:
    case  3:
    case  5:
    case  7:
    case  8:
    case 10:
    case 12:
        days_in_month = 31;
        break;

    case  4:
    case  6:
    case  9:
    case 11:
        days_in_month = 30;
        break;

    case  2:
        days_in_month = 28;
        if ( IsYearLeap ( cal_yy ) == YES )
            days_in_month += 1;
        break;
}

/* load up the days to print */

for ( i = 0; i < 42; i++ )
    days_to_print[i] = 0;

for ( i = day_of_week, j = 1; j <= days_in_month; i++, j++ )
```

```
        days_to_print[i] = j;

    /* now print the calendar */

    TimeSprintf ( buffer, 40, "    %B %Y", &date );
    printf ( "%s\n", buffer );
    printf ( "  S  M Tu  W Th  F  S\n" );

    for ( rows = 0; rows < 6; rows++ )   /* print up to 6 rows */
    {                                    /* of 7 days.         */
        for ( i = 0; i < 7; i++ )
            if ( days_to_print[(rows * 7) + i] == 0 )
                printf ( "   " );
            else
                printf ( " %2d",
                          days_to_print[(rows * 7) + i] );
        printf ( "\n" );
    }
}

void PrintOct1582 ( void )
{
    printf ( "     October 1582\n" );
    printf ( "  S  M Tu  W Th  F  S\n" );
    printf ( "        1  2  3  4 15 16\n" );
    printf ( " 17 18 19 20 21 22 23\n" );
    printf ( " 24 25 26 27 28 29 30\n" );
    printf ( " 31\n" );
}
```

The program loads the month and year into a tm structure, specifying the first day of that month. It then calls DayOfWeek() to find out on which day the month began. Next, it verifies how many days occurred in the month. It then moves the days of the month into the appropriate calendar slots (using the array days_to_print). Finally, it prints the array, seven entries (that is, one calendar row) at a time. Note that October 1582 is explicitly tested for and a hard-coded solution is provided for this month. The program also calls TimeSprintf(), a date-formatting routine presented later, in Listing 7-14.

The code in *lilcal.c* calls *datelib.h*, which contains the prototypes for the library functions. This file appears in Listing 7-2.

Listing 7-2.   *datelib.h* contains the prototypes for the date and time routines.

```
/*----------------------------------------------------------
 * Prototypes for datelib.c
 *--------------------------------------------------------*/

long    DateDiff ( struct tm *, struct tm * );
long    DateToDayNumber ( struct tm * );
int     DayNumberToDate ( long int, struct tm * );
int     DayOfWeek ( struct tm * );
int     DayOfYear ( struct tm * );
int     IsDateValid ( struct tm * );
int     IsTimeValid ( struct tm * );
int     IsYearLeap ( int );
int     LoadDateStruct ( struct tm *, int, int, int );
int     LoadTimeStruct ( struct tm *, int, int, int );
double  TimeDiff ( struct tm *, struct tm * );
int     TimeSprintf ( char *, int, char *, struct tm * );

#ifndef YES
#define YES    1
#define NO     0
#endif
```

Note that the prototypes include time functions. These functions are discussed in the next section, along with the central routine for printing dates and times in a multitude of formats.

Time Routines

The preceding discussion of calendars shows that calendars historically have been fairly inadequate at keeping track of days and years in a predictable and sequential manner. Today, we use a calendar system that is essentially universal and predictable. As long as we use dates taken from the Gregorian calendar, we can compute dates in the recent past and in the distant future with full accuracy. Moving into pre-Gregorian calendars, however, injects elements of doubt and confusion into the date manipulations.

The measurement of time suffers from some equally nettlesome issues. Recall that time is measured in reference to astronomical events such as the earth's rotation (a day) or the earth's rotation around the sun (a year). As a result, subdivisions of the day (seconds, minutes, and hours) relate precisely to the day's length—that is, 60 seconds per minute, 60 minutes per hour, 24 hours per day. The earth, however, undergoes very slight variations in its rotation, requiring periodically that seconds (known as **leap seconds**) be added to compensate for these irregularities. Leap seconds (whose number varies from 0 to 2) are generally announced every quarter by worldwide standards organizations and are added on the last day of the quarter. Leap seconds are explicitly accounted for in the ANSI C standard: the `tm` structure may hold seconds values in `tm_sec` of 0 to 61. Because there is no way of predicting when or how many leap seconds will be added, it is impossible to measure *exactly* the time intervals to specific future events. The following routines make no concession for leap seconds and assume 60-second minutes.

Most time routines extract the current time from the system and manipulate it either to print it or to use it as the basis for timing events. The ANSI C library presents numerous functions that perform these tasks well. These functions will not be duplicated here. Rather, we present functions for loading time into a `tm` structure, validating the time, measuring in seconds the distance between two events, and then printing time in a wide variety of formats.

Loading time into a `tm` structure has none of the oddities of loading a day. Therefore, the code for this function, shown in Figure 7-11, is completely straightforward.

Figure 7-11. `LoadTimeStruct()` accepts a pointer to a `tm` structure into which it loads integers that have been passed for hours, minutes, and seconds.

```
/*-------------------------------------------------------------
 * Loads time into an existing tm structure.
 * Returns 0 on success, -1 on error
 *-----------------------------------------------------------*/
int LoadTimeStruct ( struct tm *date, int hh, int mm, int ss )
{
    date->tm_hour = hh;
    date->tm_min  = mm;
    date->tm_sec  = ss;

    if ( IsTimeValid ( date ) == NO )
        return ( -1 );
    else
        return ( 0 );
}
```

Note that the function makes no use of the date fields in the `tm` structure. Hence, if the date is important to you, you can load it into the structure (using `LoadDateStruct()`) either before or after you have loaded the time.

LoadTimeStruct() validates the time by calling IsTimeValid() and passing it a pointer to the tm structure, as shown in Figure 7-12. The function returns YES if the components of time are in the correct ranges (using a 24-hour clock and a 60-second minute); otherwise it returns NO.

Figure 7-12. IsTimeValid() verifies the time fields in a tm struct.

```
/*-----------------------------------------------------------
 * Returns YES if time is valid; otherwise returns NO.
 *---------------------------------------------------------*/
int IsTimeValid ( struct tm * date )
{
    if ( date->tm_hour < 0 || date->tm_hour > 23 )
        return ( NO );

    if ( date->tm_min < 0 || date->tm_min > 59 )
        return ( NO );

    /*
     * Technically speaking, ANSI allows for minutes with
     * 61 or 62 seconds for leap seconds that are added
     * with little warning by astronomical societies to
     * reflect slight changes in the earth's rotation.
     * For reasons discussed in the text, however, we
     * observe only the 60-second minute.
     */

    if ( date->tm_sec < 0 || date->tm_sec > 59 )
        return ( NO );

    return ( YES );
}
```

The function TimeDiff() is similar to the ANSI C function difftime(). It accepts two tm structures into which time *and date* information has been loaded, as shown in Figure 7-13. It then subtracts the first time from the second and returns the number of seconds in a double. Because any double value, both positive and negative, could be correct, no error code is returned. Therefore, be sure that the data you hand this function is valid.

The benefit of TimeDiff() over the ANSI difftime() arises from difftime()'s limitation that all times must occur on dates starting in 1900 or later. Our function accepts all dates and times since January 1, A.D. 1.

Figure 7-13. `TimeDiff()` **is handed two** `tm` **structures loaded with valid date and time data, and then returns the time in seconds between the two events. Note the return type is a double.**

```
/*-----------------------------------------------------------
 * TimeDiff() operates like difftime(); however, it can accept
 * times before Jan 1, 1900. No error return.
 *-------------------------------------------------------------*/
double TimeDiff ( struct tm *t1, struct tm *t2 )
{
    long day_num;
    double d1, d2;

    day_num = DateToDayNumber ( t1 );
    d1 = day_num * 86400.0 + t1->tm_hour * 3600.0 +
        t1->tm_min * 60.0 + t1->tm_sec;

    day_num = DateToDayNumber ( t2 );
    d2 = day_num * 86400.0 + t2->tm_hour * 3600.0 +
        t2->tm_min * 60.0 + t2->tm_sec;

    return ( d1 - d2 );
}
```

Formats for Date and Time Data

Virtually all the date and time routines examined previously will appear in applications that need to print or display the date or time in a programmer-selected format. Because these formats vary tremendously by locale (there is a multitude of incompatible international formats) and by user preference, the ANSI C library provides a `sprintf()`-like function that allows you to design the format of the information. This function, `strftime()`, like `sprintf()`, accepts an output buffer and a format string. It also accepts a variable that indicates the maximum size of the output string, and it accepts a pointer to the `tm` structure whose data is to be formatted.

The format string uses a set of format characters that are different from those of `sprintf()`. The format characters for `strftime()` are listed in Table 7-1.

Table 7-1. The format characters used in ANSI C's `strftime()`

Format Character	Description	Sample Output
`%a`	Weekday name (3 chars)	`Mon`
`%A`	Weekday name (full)	`Monday`
`%b`	Month name (3 chars)	`Oct`
`%B`	Month name (full)	`October`
`%c`	Date and time (UNIX style)	`Oct  3 10:11:12 1994`
`%d`	2-digit day of month (01–31)	`03`
`%H`	2-digit hour (01–23)	`22`
`%I`	2-digit hour (01–12)	`10`
`%j`	3-digit day of year (001–366)	`309`
`%m`	2-digit month (01–12)	`10`
`%M`	2-digit minute (00–59)	`11`
`%p`	A.M. or P.M.	`AM`
`%S`	2-digit second (00–59)	`12`
`%U`	2-digit week number where Sunday begins the week and week 1 is the first full week of the year (00–53)	`37`
`%w`	Weekday (0–6, 0 = Sunday)	`1`
`%W`	2-digit week number where Monday begins the week and week 1 is the first full week of the year (00–53)	`7`
`%x`	Date string (11 chars)	`Oct   3 1994`
`%y`	2-digit year without century	`94`
`%Y`	4-digit year with century	`1994`
`%Z`	Time zone characters, or none if no time zone is in use	`EST`
`%%`	Like `printf()`'s % sign	`%`

Using the formatting options in `strftime()`, you can represent time and date in a wide range of formats, including international formats. However, `strftime()` works only on years that begin with 1900. Because of this limitation, we have provided in `TimeSprintf()`, shown in Figure 7-14. This function works the same way as `strftime()`—accepting the same arguments and generating the same output—with the sole exception that `TimeSprintf()` outputs an error message if an invalid format character is found. The code in `TimeSprintf()` makes heavy use of the date and time routines presented earlier in this chapter and is a good illustration of how to use the functions. One small note: some parameters, such as `%c` (print date and time), call `TimeSprintf()` recursively, since their output is really a series of formatted fields that `TimeSprintf()` can generate individually.

Figure 7-14. `TimeSprintf()` **prints dates and times in a variety of formats.**

```
/*-------------------------------------------------------------
 * Operates like strftime() except:
 *   a) it returns -1 on error;
 *   b) strftime() expects tm_year to be 2 digits and so always
 *      adds 1900 to the year, while TimeSprintf() believes the
 *      year to be the actual year: 94 is AD 94 and so does not
 *      add 1900.
 *-------------------------------------------------------------*/
int TimeSprintf ( char *string, int max_size,
                  char *format, struct tm *ptm )
{
    char *pf;
    int   i, j;

    int   yy;        /* scratch variable for year */
    int   mon;       /* our internal use of the month is 1-12 */
    char *buffer;    /* where the output string goes */

    mon = ptm->tm_mon + 1;

    buffer = malloc ( 1024 );   /* largest likely output string */
    if ( buffer == NULL )
        return ( -1 );

    i = 0;     /* where we are in the output string */


    for ( pf = format; *pf != '\0' && i < 1024; pf++ )
    {
        if ( *pf != '%' )
            buffer[i++] = *pf;
        else
            switch ( *(++pf) )
            {
                /*--- day of the week: Sunday, Monday...---*/

                case 'a':                 /* 3-letter weekday */
                    j = DayOfWeek ( ptm );
                    strncpy ( buffer + i,
                            Day_name_abbrev[j], 3 );
                    i += 3;
                    break;
```

```
    case 'A':                  /* full weekday */
        j = DayOfWeek ( ptm );
        strcpy ( buffer + i, Day_name[j] );
        while ( *(buffer + i) != '\0' )
            i++;
        break;

    case 'w':                  /* weekday as a digit */
        j = DayOfWeek ( ptm );
        buffer[i++] = j + '0';
        break;

        /*--- day of the month: 1, 2, 3...---*/

    case 'd':                  /* day as a number */
        buffer[i++] = ptm->tm_mday / 10 + '0';
        buffer[i++] = ptm->tm_mday % 10 + '0';
        break;

    case 'm':                  /* month as a number */
        buffer[i++] =  mon  / 10 + '0';
        buffer[i++] =  mon  % 10 + '0';
        break;

        /*--- month ---*/

    case 'b':                  /* 3-letter month */
        strncpy ( buffer + i,
                Month_name_abbrev[mon], 3 );
        i += 3;
        break;

    case 'B':                   /* full month name */
        strcpy ( buffer + i, Month_name[mon] );
        while ( *(buffer + i) != '\0' )
            i++;
        break;

        /*--- year ---*/

    case 'Y':                  /* year with century: 1994 */
        yy = ptm->tm_year;

        if ( yy < 0 )
        {
            buffer[i++] = '-';
            yy = -yy;
        }
```

```
        if ( yy > 9999 )
        {
            buffer[i++] = yy / 10000 + '0';
            yy %= 10000;
        }

        if ( yy > 999 )
        {
            buffer[i++] = yy / 1000 + '0';
            yy %= 1000;
        }

        if ( yy > 99 )
        {
            buffer[i++] = yy / 100 + '0';
            yy %= 100;
        }

        buffer[i++] = yy / 10 + '0';
        buffer[i++] = yy % 10 + '0';
        break;

case 'y':                   /* year without century: 94 */
        yy = ptm->tm_year;

        if ( yy < 0 )
        {
            buffer[i++] = '-';
            yy = -yy;
        }

        if ( yy > 100 )
            yy %= 100;

        buffer[i++] = yy / 10 + '0';
        buffer[i++] = yy % 10 + '0';
        break;

case 'x':                   /* locale-specific date */
{
    char s[18];

    TimeSprintf ( s, 18, "%a, %b %d, %Y", ptm );
    strcpy ( buffer + i, s );
    i += strlen ( s );
}
        break;
```

```
        /*--- time in numbers ---*/

    case 'I':                   /* hour on 12-hr clock */
    {
        int hour;

        if ( ptm->tm_hour > 12 )
            hour = ptm->tm_hour - 12;
        else
            hour = ptm->tm_hour;

        buffer[i++] = hour / 10 + '0';
        buffer[i++] = hour % 10 + '0';
    }
        break;

    case 'H':                   /* hour on 24-hr clock */
        buffer[i++] = ptm->tm_hour / 10 + '0';
        buffer[i++] = ptm->tm_hour % 10 + '0';
        break;

    case 'M':                   /* minute as a number */
        buffer[i++] = ptm->tm_min / 10 + '0';
        buffer[i++] = ptm->tm_min % 10 + '0';
        break;

    case 'S':                   /* seconds as a number */
        buffer[i++] = ptm->tm_sec / 10 + '0';
        buffer[i++] = ptm->tm_sec % 10 + '0';
        break;

    case 'X':                   /* time string: hh:mm:ss */
    {
        char s[9];

        TimeSprintf ( s, 9, "%H:%M:%S", ptm );
        strcpy ( buffer + i, s );
        i += 8;
    }
        break;

        /*--- miscellaneous ---*/

    case 'c':                   /* date and time */
    {
        char s[28];

        TimeSprintf ( s, 28, "%b %d %H:%M:%S %Y", ptm );
```

```
        strcpy ( buffer + i, s );
        i += strlen ( s );
    }
        break;

    case 'j':              /* day of the year: 1-366 */
    {
        int day_of_year;

        day_of_year = DayOfYear ( ptm );

        if ( day_of_year < 10 )
            buffer[i++] = day_of_year + '0';
        else
        {
            if ( day_of_year > 99 )
            {
                buffer[i++] = day_of_year / 100 + '0';
                day_of_year %= 100;
            }

            buffer[i++] = day_of_year / 10 + '0';
            buffer[i++] = day_of_year % 10 + '0';
        }
    }
        break;

    case 'p':              /* AM or PM */
        if ( ptm->tm_hour < 12 )
            buffer[i++] = 'A';
        else
            buffer[i++] = 'P';
        buffer[i++] = 'M';
        break;

    case 'U':              /* Sunday week of year */
    case 'W':              /* Monday week of year */
    {
        int day_of_year,
            day_of_week,
            sunday_week;

        struct tm jan1;

        int jan1_dow;      /* jan 1 day of week */

        day_of_year = DayOfYear ( ptm );
        day_of_week = DayOfWeek ( ptm );
```

```
        LoadDateStruct ( &jan1, ptm->tm_year, 1, 1 );
        jan1_dow = DayOfWeek ( &jan1 );

        if ( jan1_dow != 0 )
            day_of_year -= ( 7 - jan1_dow );

        if ( day_of_year < 1 )
            sunday_week = 0;
        else
        {
            sunday_week = 1;
            sunday_week += ( day_of_year - 1 ) / 7;
        }

        if ( *pf == 'W' )    /* if Monday week */
            if ( day_of_week < 1 )
                sunday_week -= 1;

        if ( sunday_week > 9 )
        {
            buffer[i++] = ( sunday_week / 10 ) + '0';
            sunday_week %= 10;
        }

        buffer[i++] = sunday_week + '0';
    }
        break;

case 'Z':                /* the time zone */
    {
        char *temp;

        temp = setlocale ( LC_TIME, NULL );
        if ( temp == NULL )
            buffer[i++] = 'C';
        else
        {
            strcpy ( buffer + i, temp );
            i += strlen ( temp );
        }
    }
        break;

case '%':                /* the percent sign */
        buffer[i++] = '%';
        break;

default:
```

```
            strcpy ( buffer + i, "Error in TimeSprintf() " );
            i += 23;
        }
    }
    buffer[i] = '\0';

    strncpy ( string, buffer, max_size );
    free ( buffer );

    if ( i <= max_size )
        return ( i );
    else
        return ( 0 );
}
```

A Final Reminder

The routines presented in this chapter give you all the basic functionality that you would need for doing almost any calendar programming. Just be sure that if you use dates prior to 1753, you decide carefully in what year you will recognize the switch to the Gregorian calendar (1752, the U.S. date; or 1582, the date that is used in this chapter and by much of Europe). Note that all dates prior to the switch-over year have a fairly good chance of being bogus. They are assigned their value by convention more than as a direct reflection of what a calendar on any given day would have stated.

Resources and References

Meyer, Peter. "Julian and Gregorian Calendars." *Dr. Dobb's Journal,* March 1993 (#198). This article is the best recent discussion of computing calendars. The explanations are lucid, but it is difficult to match the prose to their code implementation. The code also contains some quirky aspects.

The history of the Western calendar has been written up many times. A good synopsis appears in most every almanac. Other reference books give varying levels of detail on this intriguing topic.

Chapter 8

Arbitrary-Precision Arithmetic

Arbitrary-precision arithmetic allows users to perform arithmetic operations with results that are accurate to as many places as desired. The routines presented in this chapter perform addition, subtraction, multiplication, and division to a precision that is limited in practice by the user's stack space and absolutely to the size of a short integer. The absolute limit of 32,768 digits should serve the needs of almost every conceivable application.

There are two primary purposes for using arbitrary-precision arithmetic. The first purpose is to manipulate numbers larger than those supported directly by the native platform—generally about 18 digits in the mantissa and roughly 300 orders of magnitude in the exponent. The second purpose is to avoid rounding errors in all numbers, regardless of size.

In many situations it is beneficial to use numbers that exceed the range of doubles and floating-point numbers available in C and in other programming languages. Number theory, random-number generation, and other types of mathematical research often require the ability to handle very large numbers beyond the scope of standard hardware processors. However, the primary use of arbitrary-precision arithmetic is to resolve troublesome rounding errors generated by the manner in which numbers are stored in memory. The use of binary digits to emulate decimal numbers introduces a series of complications especially when fractional numbers need to be represented. To see how difficult this task is, you need only be aware of the difficulty of storing ordinary fractions in binary form. When you consider how a number such as 1/10 would be stored in conventional binary terms, it becomes clear that the process of mapping decimal fractions to binary form is rife with opportunities for errors in representation.

These errors take two forms: floating-point numbers do not sum to an exact total, and very small adjacent numbers tend to become equivalent. The accumulation of these two forms of errors make floating-point numbers unsuitable for accounting purposes. Because the largest integer available on a standard 32-bit chip allows integers up to $\pm 2 \times 10^9$, accounting software for amounts over $20 million cannot keep track of pennies—an unacceptable limitation.

For scientific purposes, the inability to distinguish very small numbers is a serious compromise. Nakamura [Nakamura 1993] shows how small a number has to be before it becomes indistinguishable. As you can see in Table 8-1, an investigation into this question shows that the number, generally called the **machine epsilon,** varies little when you exclude supercomputers such as the Cray.

Table 8-1.   The machine epsilon for several popular platforms

Precision	IBM PC	IBM 370	VAX 11	Cray XMP
Single	1.19E-7	9.53E-7	1.19E-7	3.55E-15
Double	2.77E-17	2.22E-16	2.77E-17	1.26E-29

Between the inability to handle numbers smaller than 10^{-17} or dollar sums larger than $21 million, there are convincing reasons for abandoning floating-point calculations in favor of arbitrary-precision arithmetic. The approach used in this chapter is to store integers as arrays of digits with each digit in occupying a single byte.

Building a Calculator

The arbitrary-precision routines presented in this chapter can be used in a stand-alone fashion. However, for the purpose of demonstrating their use, they have been bundled with three front ends: a calculator, a high-precision computation of square roots using Newton's method, and a generator of amortization tables. The calculator is discussed in this section; the other two applications are discussed at the end of the chapter.

The calculator presented here can be used interactively or in batch mode. If the calculator is run from the command line with no arguments, it queries the user to enter the two terms and asks for the operation to be performed on them. It then displays the answer on the screen and exits. If a single argument is provided, the calculator expects that argument to be a script that lists the terms and the operations to be performed. The program writes the terms to a file named *longmath.out*, unless a second command-line argument is provided, in which case that argument is used as the output file name.

The input file consists of a regular text file with one entry per line. The entries are listed in the same way that they would be entered on a normal calculator: the first term, followed by an operator, followed by a second term. The result of the calculation is then carried forward as the first term of the next operation. To begin a new operation, the user specifies an operator of C or c (for *clear*), which resets all terms to zero. Figure 8-1 shows a sample script file, followed by the resulting output file in Figure 8-2. In the answer file, the precision is set to 20 digits.

Figure 8-1.   A sample script file for the arbitrary-precision calculator.

```
12
/
7
–
1.0
*
2
+
16
/
8
C
123456.789012
/
3.141592653589793
```

Figure 8-2.   The answer file resulting from the script in Figure 8-1.

```
12
/
7
=
1.7142857142857142857
–
1.0
=
0.7142857142857142857
*
2
=
1.4285714285714285714
```

(continued)

Figure 8-2 *(continued).*

```
+
16
=
17.428571428571428571
/
8
=
2.1785714285714285714
C
123456.789012
/
3.141592653589793
=
39297.516459025981773
```

The code for the calculator, presented in Listing 8-1 (*calcmain.c*), first creates three data structures: two to hold the terms that will be entered and a third to hold the result of the calculation. Next, the program checks to see whether it was called interactively and then gets input from either the user or the input script. It converts the terms of the calculation to an internal form, loads them into the foregoing data structures, performs the operation, and displays the answer on the screen or writes it to an output file. If the program is running a script, it repeats the process until the end of the script.

Listing 8-1. `calcmain()` handles input and output for the calculator and executes the specified calculations.

```
/*--- calcmain.c ------------------------- Listing 8-1 --------
 * Calculator main line for longmath routines.
 *
 * If the program is invoked without any arguments, it responds
 * as an interactive command-line calculator, with all necessary
 * prompts on the screen. Otherwise:
 *
 * If one argument is supplied, it is taken to be a filename,
 * for a calculator script that may contain the following:
 * terms in the prescribed form,
 * the arithemetic operators: +, -, *, /
 * the directive 'C' which clears and resets the calculator to 0
```

```
 *
 * In the absence of a clear command, the result of the previous
 * operation is carried over into the first term.
 *
 * If a second file is specified, all terms and operations and
 * their results are written to it; otherwise, the output file
 * is longmath.out
 *------------------------------------------------------------*/

#include <stdio.h>
#include <stdlib.h>
#include <string.h>

#include "longmath.h"

int main ( int argc, char *argv[] )
{
    struct TermData *term1,       /* two terms and the solution */
                    *term2,
                    *solution;

    int operator;
    int format  - NORMAL;         /* default to NORMAL notation */

    char buffer [2*MAX_SIZE];     /* buffer for user input */

    /*--- allocate and initialize the terms ---*/

    term1    = TermCreate();
    term2    = TermCreate();
    solution = TermCreate();

    if ( term1 == NULL || term2 == NULL || solution == NULL )
    {
        fprintf ( stderr, "Cannot allocate memory\n" );
        return ( EXIT_FAILURE );
    }

    /*--- the interactive calculator ---*/

    if ( argc < 2 )     /* no input file specified, hence  */
    {                   /*  it must be interactive.        */

        printf ( "Arbitrary-Precision Math. Press Q to Quit\n" );

        /* get the first term */

        printf ( "Type first term and press <Enter>\n" );
```

```
gets ( buffer );
if ( *buffer == 'q' || *buffer == 'Q' )
    return ( EXIT_SUCCESS );
else
{
    format = AsciiToTerm ( buffer, term1 );
    if ( ! format )
    {
        printf ( "Invalid term; aborting!\n" );
        exit ( EXIT_FAILURE );
    }
}

/* get the second term */

printf ( "Type second term and press <Enter>\n" );
gets ( buffer );
if ( *buffer == 'q' || *buffer == 'Q' )
    return ( EXIT_SUCCESS );
else
{
    format = AsciiToTerm ( buffer, term2 );
    if ( ! format )
    {
        printf ( "Invalid term; aborting!\n" );
        exit ( EXIT_FAILURE );
    }
}

/* get the desired operation */

printf (
  "Type operation ( + - * / ) and press <Enter>\n" );

operator = getchar();
if ( operator == 'q' || operator == 'Q' )
    return ( EXIT_SUCCESS );

if ( operator != '+' && operator != '-' &&
     operator != '*' && operator != '/' )
{
    printf ( "Invalid operator; aborting!\n" );
    exit ( EXIT_FAILURE );
}

/*--- compute the result --- */
```

```
        if ( ! ComputeResult (
                    term1, operator, term2, solution ))
         return ( EXIT_FAILURE );

        /*--- print the answer ---*/

        TermToAscii ( solution, buffer, format );

        printf ( "%s\n", buffer );

        return ( EXIT_SUCCESS );
    }
    else    /* calculator operations in a file */
    {
        FILE *fin, * fout;          /* file handles */
        char fin_name[64],          /* file names */
             fout_name[64];

        strcpy ( fin_name, argv[1] );
        if ( argc > 2 )
            strcpy ( fout_name, argv[2] );
        else
            strcpy ( fout_name, "longmath.out" );

        fin = fopen ( fin_name, "rt" );
        if ( fin == NULL )
        {
            fprintf ( stderr, "Error opening: %s\n", fin_name );
            return ( EXIT_FAILURE );
        }

        fout = fopen ( fout_name, "wt" );
        if ( fout == NULL )
        {
            fprintf ( stderr, "Error opening: %s\n", fout_name );
            return ( EXIT_FAILURE );
        }

        while ( ! feof ( fin ))
        {
            /* get the first term */

            format =  GetFileTerm ( term1, fin, fout );
            if ( ! format )
                break;

            /* get the operator */
```

```
if ( ! GetFileOperator ( &operator, fin, fout ))
    break;

continuing:  /* we'll jump to here if further ops */

/* get next term */

format =  GetFileTerm ( term2, fin, fout );
if ( ! format )
    break;

/*
 * if an error occurs in computing, abort *unless*
 * the next operation is a 'clear,' which starts
 * a new calculation.
 */

if ( ! ComputeResult (
            term1, operator, term2, solution ))
{
    fprintf ( stderr, "Error in Computing.\n" );
    fprintf ( fout, "Error in Computing.\n" );

    if ( ! GetFileOperator ( &operator, fin, fout ))
    {
        fprintf ( fout, "Aborting...\n" );
        return ( EXIT_FAILURE );
    }
    else
    if ( operator != 'C')
    {
        fprintf ( fout, "Aborting...\n" );
        return ( EXIT_FAILURE );
    }
    else    /* next operation was 'clear' */
    {
        TermInit ( term1 );
        TermInit ( term2 );
        TermInit ( solution );
        continue;
    }
}
else
{
    /* if no error, print the solution */

    TermToAscii ( solution, buffer, format );
    fprintf ( fout, "=\n%s\n", buffer );
```

```
                /* get the next operation */

                if ( ! GetFileOperator ( &operator, fin, fout ))
                    break;

                if ( operator == 'C' )   /* clear = reinit */
                {
                    TermInit ( term1 );
                    TermInit ( term2 );
                    TermInit ( solution );
                    continue;
                }
                else                    /* keep going */
                {
                    TermCopy ( term1, solution );
                    TermInit ( term2 );
                    TermInit ( solution );
                    goto continuing;
                }
            }
        }
        fclose ( fin );
        fclose ( fout );
    }
    return ( EXIT_SUCCESS );
}


/*-----------------------------------------------------------
 * Get an operator from the input file and check it for errors;
 * write a copy of it to outfile. Returns 0 on error, else 1.
 *-----------------------------------------------------------*/
int GetFileOperator ( int *operator,
                      FILE * infile, FILE *outfile )
{
    char buffer [ MAX_SIZE + 4 ];
    char *p;

    if ( fgets ( buffer, MAX_SIZE + 4, infile ) == NULL )
        return ( 0 );

    /* replace the CR/LF with a null; check length */

    p = strchr ( buffer, '\n' );
    if ( p == NULL )
    {
        printf ( "Error: invalid operator :\n%s\n", buffer );
        fprintf ( outfile,
```

```
                           "Error: invalid operator :\n%s\n", buffer );
        return ( 0 );
    }
    else
        *p = '\0';

    *operator = *buffer;

    if ( *( buffer + 1 ) != '\0' ||
            ( *operator != '+' &&
              *operator != '-' &&
              *operator != '*' &&
              *operator != '/' &&
              *operator != 'c' &&
              *operator != 'C' ))
    {
        printf ( "Error: Invalid operator %c\n", *operator );
        fprintf ( outfile,
                  "Error: invalid operator :\n%s\n", buffer );
        return ( 0 );
    }

    if ( *operator == 'c' )
        *operator = 'C';

    fprintf ( outfile, "%c\n", *operator );

    return ( 1 );
}


/*-------------------------------------------------------------
 * Get a term from the input file and check it for errors;
 * write a copy of it to outfile. Returns 0 on error, else
 * returns SCIENTIFIC or NORMAL, indicating the number format.
 *-----------------------------------------------------------*/
int GetFileTerm ( struct TermData * t,
                  FILE * infile, FILE *outfile )
{
    char buffer [ MAX_SIZE + 4 ];
    char *p;
    int  format = NORMAL;

    if ( fgets ( buffer, MAX_SIZE + 4, infile ) == NULL )
        return ( 0 );    /* EOF */

    /* replace the CR/LF with a null; check length */

    p = strchr ( buffer, '\n' );
```

```
if ( p == NULL )
{
    printf ( "Error: term too long:\n%s\n", buffer );
    fprintf ( outfile,
            "Error: term too long:\n%s\n", buffer );
    return ( 0 );
}
else
    *p = '\0';

/* convert to term and check length and errors */

format = AsciiToTerm ( buffer, t );
if ( t->sign == 0 ||
    ( t->places_before + t->places_after > MAX_SIZE ))
{
    printf ( "Error: term too long or invalid:\n%s\n",
            buffer );
    fprintf ( outfile,
            "Error: term too long or invalid:\n%s\n",
            buffer );
    return ( 0 );
}

fprintf ( outfile, "%s\n", buffer );
return ( format );
}
```

Representing the Numbers

The numbers used in the arithmetic operations, known as **terms**, need to be stored in a manner that makes them accessible to all routines that perform computations on them. In this chapter, they are represented in a structure of the following form:

```
struct TermData {
        char *term;
        int  sign;
        int  digits_before;
        int  digits_after;
}
```

The field `term` is an array of characters, each of which contains a single digit. The size of the array is $2*MAX\_SIZE + 1$, where `MAX_SIZE` is a preprocessor constant that stipulates the maximum size of a term. In other words, `MAX_SIZE` represents the precision to be used in the arithmetic operations. When you want to change the precision, you change the value of this constant and recompile the routines. (`TermData` and `MAX_SIZE` are found in *longmath.h*, in Listing 8-20.)

The internal representation of `term` is set up so that the first digit after the decimal point (if any) is at the midpoint of the array (that is, at `term[MAX_SIZE]`). This allows `MAX_SIZE` digits to exist on either side of the decimal point. It is important to note that this format is used only for the internal representation of the numbers. The external representation of the result of any calculation will be limited to a total of `MAX_SIZE` digits. If necessary, low-order digits (after the decimal point) are truncated. If the result is still wider than the maximum number of digits, an overflow occurs. If the overflow is of significant digits (left of the decimal point), the overflow results in an error. If the overflow occurs in digits right of the decimal point, rounding occurs and the excess digits are truncated. It may appear wasteful to discard right-hand digits that exceed the maximum specification (established by `MAX_SIZE`), but saving them is an inexact practice. For example, in some multiplication it is possible to have `2*MAX_SIZE` digits left over, while in other calculations there are none at all. Moreover, these routines are based on the model offered by most calculators, which have a fixed-size window. They show an overflow error when an overflow occurs to the right; and they round and truncate when an overflow occurs to the left.

We chose this method of representing the terms so that interim results could be stored with maximum precision. The internal representation with `MAX_SIZE` digits on either side of the decimal point allows us to conveniently know at all times where the decimal point is located.

In the structure `TermData`, the integer `sign` is set to +1 or –1, depending on the sign of the term. The fields `digits_before` and `digits_after` specify the number of digits before and after the decimal point, respectively. A term containing the value of 12.34 when `MAX_SIZE` equals 5 would be stored as shown in Figure 8-3. In the figure, `DEC_LOC` points to the first digit after the decimal point.

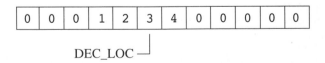

Figure 8-3.   A normalized view of 12.34 stored in a term of `MAX_SIZE` = 5.

To place a number in the format used by `TermData`, you call the function `AsciiToTerm()`, passing it a string that consists of the number to be converted. The function `AsciiToTerm()` expects the string it is passed will use one of two formats: normal format or scientific notation. Normal format is the way numbers are generally written by most people. In normal format, the term has an optional leading sign (trailing signs are not recognized). If the number has no digits to the left of the decimal point, a leading zero may optionally be prepended. In the grammar used for specifying regular expressions, the terms must use the following format in order to be accepted by `AsciiToTerm()`:

```
[+|-]?[0-9]*[.[0-9]+]
```

where * indicates zero or more occurrences of the preceding bracketed expression; + indicates one or more occurrences, and ? indicates zero or one occurrence.

Scientific notation is familiar to most C programmers as the format used to express floating-point numbers. These numbers consist of three parts: the **mantissa**, the letter 'e' or 'E' (which acts as a separator), and the **exponent**. Both the mantissa and the exponent consists of one or more digits optionally preceded by a + or −. Only the mantissa can use a decimal point. In our implementation, if there is a decimal point in the mantissa, it can be preceded by one digit at most. Numbers given to the calculator can use either scientific or normal notation. The notation used on the last term entered determines the format of the result.

If `AsciiToTerm()` encounters a number in scientific notation, it returns the manifest constant `SCIENTIFIC`; otherwise it returns `NORMAL`. In the case of error, it returns 0 and sets the `sign` variable in `TermData` to zero. Because all functions deal with the `TermData` data structures, common sense suggests including an error code in the structure itself, so that functions can independently establish the validity of the term rather than depend on flags or error codes passed between functions. Since the only legal values for `sign` are +1 or −1, the 0 makes an effective error flag. In Listing 8-2, `AsciiToTerm()` normalizes a term for the arithmetic functions.

Listing 8-2.   The function `AsciiToTerm()` normalizes a term for the arithmetic functions.

```
/*--------------------------------------------------------------
 * Converts a null-terminated ASCII number in either normal or
 * scientific notation to a term.
 *
 * If the first character is a sign or a decimal point, we
 * process it and replace it with a 0, so as to enable
 * processing of a string of digits. However, to maintain the
```

```
 * integrity of the ASCII string, we save the original first
 * character in first_char and restore it before returning.
 * This is of use only when the calculator is reading input
 * from a file.
 *
 * Returns NORMAL, SCIENTIFIC depending on format of string,
 *  or returns 0 on error.
 *-------------------------------------------------------------*/
int AsciiToTerm ( char *buffer, struct TermData *t )
{
    char * dec_pt,
         * p;
    int    i, exponent, len, notation;
    char * new_term;
    char   first_char;
    char * exp;            /* where the exponent flag is */

    new_term = t->term;    /* point new_term to where it'll go */

    /* is it scientific notation? */

    exp = strpbrk ( buffer, "eE" );
    notation = ( exp == NULL ? NORMAL : SCIENTIFIC );

    first_char = *buffer;

    if ( isdigit ( *buffer ))        /* get the sign */
        t->sign = +1;
    else
    {
        if ( *buffer == '-' )
            t->sign = -1;
        else
        if ( *buffer == '+' )
            t->sign = +1;
        else
        if ( *buffer != '.' )
        {
            t->sign = 0;    /* flag error */
            return ( 0 );
        }

        /* replace any leading sign by a zero */

        if ( *buffer != '.' )
            *buffer = '0';
    }
```

```
dec_pt = strchr ( buffer, '.' );
len = strlen ( buffer );

/*
 * load the digits after the decimal point. The first
 * digit goes at term[DEC_LOC], subsequent digits
 * go to the right up to MAX_SIZE digits.
 */

if ( dec_pt != NULL )   /* Only if there's a decimal point */
{
    p = dec_pt + 1;
    for ( i = DEC_LOC; *p && i != 2*MAX_SIZE; i++, p++ )
    {
        if ( ! isdigit ( *p ))  /* check that it's a digit */
        {
            if ( notation == NORMAL )
            {
                t->sign = 0;    /* if not, show an error */
                break;
            }
            else   /* if it's scientific notation... */
            {
                if ( *p == 'e' || *p == 'E' )
                    break;
                else
                {
                    t->sign = 0;    /* show an error */
                    break;
                }
            }
        }
        else
            new_term[i] = *p - '0';
    }
}

if ( notation == SCIENTIFIC )
{
    p = exp + 1;
    exponent = atoi ( p );
}

if ( t->sign == 0 )     /* any error so far ? */
    return ( 0 );

/*
 * load the digits before the decimal point. You load at
```

```
 * the first place right of buffer[DEC_LOC] and add digits
 * to the left up to MAX_SIZE digits.
 */

if ( dec_pt == NULL )
{
    if ( notation == NORMAL )
        p = buffer + len - 1;
    else
        p = exp - 1;
}
else
    p = dec_pt - 1;


for ( i = DEC_LOC - 1; p >= buffer && i >= 0; i--, p-- )
{
    if ( ! isdigit ( *p ))  /* check that it's a digit */
    {
        t->sign = 0;        /* if not, indicate an error */
        break;
    }
    else
    {
        new_term[i] = *p - '0';
        if ( p == buffer ) /* this test for pointer wrap- */
            break;            /* around on Intel segments    */
    }
}

/*
 * if it's scientific notation, shift the term right or left
 * depending on the exponent. If the exponent is > 0, shift
 * left exponent number of places; if it's < 0, shift right.
 */

if ( notation == SCIENTIFIC )
{
    if ( exponent > 0 )
    {
        while ( exponent-- )    /* shift left */
        {
            if ( *new_term > 0 )
            {
                printf ( "Error: %s too large\n", buffer );
                return ( 0 );
            }
```

```
                memmove ( new_term, new_term + 1,
                                       2*MAX_SIZE - 1 );
                new_term[2*MAX_SIZE - 1] = 0;
            }
        }
    else
    if ( exponent < 0 )          /* shift right */
    {
        int warning = 0;

        while ( exponent++ )
        {
            if ( new_term[2*MAX_SIZE - 1] > 0 )
                warning += 1;

            memmove ( new_term + 1, new_term,
                                        2*MAX_SIZE - 1 );
            *new_term = 0;
        }

        if ( warning )
            printf ( "Low order truncation of % digits.\n",
                        warning );
    }
}       /* note: if exponent = 0, no shift occurs */


/*
 * find out how many places before decimal point:
 * start at new_term[0] and move left until you encounter
 * the first non-zero digit or the decimal point.
 * Minimum places_before = 1.
 */

for ( p = new_term;
      *p == '\0' &&  p < new_term + DEC_LOC; p++ )
        ;          /* just loop to the first non-zero digit */

t->places_before = ( new_term + DEC_LOC ) - p;

/*
 * find out how many places after decimal point:
 * if there was a decimal point, then start at right end
 * of new_term and go left until you encounter the first
 * non-zero digit or the decimal point. If there was no
 * decimal point, then places_after = 0.
 */
```

```
        if ( dec_pt == NULL )
            t->places_after = 0;
        else
        {
            for ( p = new_term + 2*MAX_SIZE;
                    *p == '\0' && p >= new_term + DEC_LOC;
                    p-- )
                    ;    /* just loop to the first non-zero digit */

                t->places_after = ( p - ( new_term + DEC_LOC ) + 1 );
        }

        *buffer = first_char;

        return ( notation );
}
```

You will note in Listing 8-2 that the digits are stored as their actual values rather than as characters. For example, the digit zero is stored as 0x00, not as '0' (which would be 0x30 in the ASCII alphabet). This means that operations on the array of digits cannot use C's string functions, since these functions treat 0x00 as a special character.

You will note also that the location of the decimal point in the array is referred to as `term[DEC_LOC]` (for *dec*imal *loc*ation). Previously, we indicated that the first decimal digit is located at `term[MAX_SIZE]`. The preprocessor constant `DEC_LOC` is defined as a synonym for `MAX_SIZE`. The use of `DEC_LOC` is simply for purposes of readability. The last point to note is that the array is padded with zeros to the left of the leading digit and to the right of the last digit.

A complimentary function, `TermToAscii()`, converts a normalized term into an ASCII string, as shown in Listing 8-3. It is used for printing the solution to the screen or to a file; the former by the simple use of `printf()`. The function generates a normalized term by using the same format used for input: a leading sign if negative, and a leading zero if there are no digits left of the decimal point. It will print a maximum of `MAX_SIZE` significant digits.

Listing 8-3. The function `TermToAscii()` converts a normalized term to a printable string.

```
/*-------------------------------------------------------------
 * Converts a normalized term into an ASCII string
 *-----------------------------------------------------------*/
void TermToAscii ( struct TermData * t, char *ascii,
                   int notation )
```

```
{
        char *first,        /* first printing digit */
             *last,         /* last printing digit */
             *output;       /* where the ascii string is built */

        first = t->term;
        output = ascii;

        /* skip leading zeros */

        while ( *first == '\0' && first < t->term + 2*MAX_SIZE )
            first++;

        /* if at end, print answer of 0 and exit */

        if ( first == t->term + 2*MAX_SIZE )
        {
            *output++ = '0';
            *output = '\0';
            return;
        }
        else    /* if past decimal point, start at dec. pt. */
        {
            if ( first >= t->term + DEC_LOC )
                first  = t->term + DEC_LOC;
        }

        /* find last non-zero digit up to decimal point */

        last = t->term + 2*MAX_SIZE;

        while ( last > first &&
                last >= t->term + DEC_LOC &&
              *last == '\0' )
                    last--;

        /* before beginning printing, check the sign */

        if ( t->sign == -1 )
            *output++ = '-';

        /* if we start at the decimal point, print leading 0 */
        if ( first == t->term + DEC_LOC )
            *output++ = '0';

        while ( first <= last )
        {
            if ( first == t->term + DEC_LOC )
```

```
          *output++ = '.';

      *output++ = *first + '0';
      first += 1;
  }

  *output = '\0';

if ( notation == SCIENTIFIC )
    AsciiToScientific ( ascii );


}
```

The function is passed a flag stating in what format the result should appear. If the desired format is scientific notation, the string is then passed to `AsciiToScientific()`, which does the final touch-up to put the string into scientific notation. (See Listing 8-4.) Note that this function trims trailing zeros such that 1.6000000e4 will appear as 1.6e4. Users who prefer to retain the trailing zeros can comment out the indicated section.

Listing 8-4.   The function `AsciiToScientific()` converts a number in normal format to scientific notation.

```
/*---------------------------------------------------------------
 * Takes a string in normal notation and converts it to
 * scientific notation of the form:
 *                    [-](0-9).(0-9)*e[+|-](0-9)*
 * The final string overlays the original string. This could be
 * dangerous since the new form is conceivably longer than the
 * original form. However, we know the input string is twice
 * MAX_SIZE, so there should always be enough room to fit. This
 * routine would have to modify this aspect if it were to be
 * used as a generic format conversion function.
 *---------------------------------------------------------------
 */
int AsciiToScientific ( char *ascii )
{
    char * buffer,
         * dec_pt,       /* location of the decimal pt, if any */
         * first_digit;  /* where the first non-zero digit is */

    char str_exp[8];      /* will hold exponent string */


    int i, j, ascii_len, exponent;
```

```
i = j = exponent = 0;

ascii_len = strlen ( ascii );

buffer = malloc ( ascii_len + 6 );
if ( ascii_len < 1 || buffer == NULL )
    return ( 0 );

/* process the sign */

if ( ! isdigit ( *ascii ))
{
    if ( *ascii == '-' )
        buffer[i++] = ascii[j++];
    else
    if ( *ascii != '+' )
    {
        printf (
            "Invalid number for scientific format\n" );
        return ( 0 );
    }
}

/* now process the digits. First check for decimal point. */

dec_pt = strchr ( ascii, '.' );

/* skip to the first non-zero digit */

while ( ascii[j] == '.' || ascii[j] == '0' )
{
    j +=1;
    if ( ascii[j] == '\0' )     /* end of string */
    {
        printf (
            "Invalid number for scientific format\n" );
        return ( 0 );
    }
}

first_digit = &ascii[j];

buffer[i++] = ascii[j++];
buffer[i++] = '.';
if ( ! ascii[j] )        /* e.g. 6 = 6.0e1 */
    buffer[i++] = '0';
else
    while ( ascii[j] )
```

```
            if ( ascii[j] == '.' )
                j += 1;
            else
                buffer[i++] = ascii[j++];

    /* do we have trailing zeros? Trim 1.600e4 to 1.6e4 */

    j = i - 1;
    while ( j > 1 && buffer[j - 1] != '.' )
    {
        if ( buffer[j--] == '0' )
            i -= 1;
        else
            break;
    }

    /* compute the exponent */

    if ( dec_pt )
    {
        if ( first_digit > dec_pt ) /* e.g., 0.0065  */
            exponent = ( first_digit - dec_pt ) * -1;
        else                        /* e.g., 650.2   */
            exponent = dec_pt - first_digit - 1;
    }
    else  /* no decimal point */
    {
        exponent = ascii_len - 1;
        if ( ! isdigit ( *ascii ))  /* was there a + or - ? */
            exponent -= 1;
    }

    /* output the exponent */

    buffer[i++] = 'e';

    memset ( str_exp, '\0', 8 );
    sprintf ( str_exp, "%d", exponent );
    strcpy ( buffer + i, str_exp );

    /* overlay the original string */

    strcpy ( ascii, buffer );
    free ( buffer );
    return ( 1 );
}
```

To create terms, you use `TermCreate()`, which allocates the data structure, and `TermInit()`, which initializes a term to zero. (See Listings 8-5 and 8-6.) You will note that `TermInit()` initializes the sign to +1. A sign of 0 could not be used, since this value is an error flag, as discussed previously. You call `TermInit()` to initialize terms at creation and to clear them and reset them to zero.

Listing 8-5.   A program in which `TermCreate()` allocates a term and calls `TermInit()`.

```
/*-------------------------------------------------------------
 * Creates a TermData structure and initializes it to
 * a value of zero. Returns NULL on error.
 *-----------------------------------------------------------*/
struct TermData * TermCreate ( void )
{
    struct TermData *t;

    t = malloc ( sizeof ( struct TermData ));
    if ( t == NULL )
        return ( NULL );

    t->term = (char *) malloc ( 2*MAX_SIZE + 1 );
    TermInit ( t );

    return ( t );
}
```

Listing 8-6.   `TermInit()` initializes a term to zero.

```
/*-------------------------------------------------------------
 * Initialize a term to zero.
 *-----------------------------------------------------------*/
void TermInit ( struct TermData *t )
{
    t->places_before = 0;
    t->places_after  = 0;
    t->sign          = 1;
    memset ( t->term, '\0', 2*MAX_SIZE + 1 );
}
```

The final function for handling terms is `TermCopy()`, which simply copies a term from one data structure to another, as shown in Listing 8-7.

Listing 8-7. The function `TermCopy()` copies a term.

```
/*---------------------------------------------------------------
 * Copy a term from the second argument to the first.
 * Returns a pointer to the copied string.
 *---------------------------------------------------------------*/
struct TermData * TermCopy ( struct TermData * dest,
                             struct TermData * src )
{
    dest->sign          = src->sign;
    dest->places_before = src->places_before;
    dest->places_after  = src->places_after;

    memcpy ( dest->term, src->term, 2*MAX_SIZE + 1 );

    return ( dest );
}
```

The Calculation

The function `ComputeResult()` oversees the arithmetic operations, as shown in Listing 8-8. It is passed four arguments: a character containing the operation that should be performed (valid choices are +, −, *, and /, for addition, subtraction, multiplication, and division, respectively) and three pointers to `TermData` structures. The first two structures contain the terms upon which the arithmetic operation will be performed, and the third structure will hold the normalized result.

Listing 8-8. The function `ComputeResult()` supervises the arithmetic operations.

```
/*---------------------------------------------------------------
 * This function handles the signs and invokes the correct
 * arithmetic operation.
 *---------------------------------------------------------------*/
int ComputeResult ( struct TermData *t1, int operator,
            struct TermData *t2, struct TermData *sol )
{
    int cmp;

    TermInit ( sol );    /* just good practice */

    switch ( operator )
    {
        case '+':
```

```
/*
 * addition really occurs only when the signs
 * are the same. If signs differ, the operation
 * is really subtraction. In that case, we call
 * subtraction routines. Before calling
 * NormalSubtract(), we make sure the terms are
 * in the right order. See the comments in the
 * subtraction section below for more info on this.
 */

if ( t1->sign == t2->sign ) /* a + b or -a + -b */
{
    if ( ! NormalAdd ( t1, t2, sol ))
    {
        fprintf ( stderr,
            "Overflow on addition\n" );
        return ( 0 );
    }
    sol->sign = t1->sign;
}
else
if ( t1->sign == -1 )   /* -a + b */
{
    sol->sign = -1;

    cmp = NormAbsCmp ( t1, t2 );
    if ( cmp < 0 ) /* t2 larger than t1 */
    {
        sol->sign = -sol->sign;
        NormalSubtract ( t2, t1, sol );
    }
    else
    if ( cmp > 0 ) /* t1 larger than t2 */
        NormalSubtract ( t1, t2, sol );
    else
    {                  /*  t1 = t2, so sol = 0 */
        TermInit ( sol );
        return ( 1 );
    }
}
else                        /* a + -b */
{
    sol->sign = +1;

    cmp = NormAbsCmp ( t1, t2 );
    if ( cmp < 0 ) /* t2 larger than t1 */
    {
        sol->sign = -sol->sign;
```

```
                 NormalSubtract ( t2, t1, sol );
          }
          else
          if ( cmp > 0 ) /* t1 larger than t2 */
               NormalSubtract ( t1, t2, sol );
          else
          {                   /*  t1 = t2, so sol = 0 */
               TermInit ( sol );
               return ( 1 );
          }
     }
     break;

case '-':
     /*
      * there are four possible cases for subtraction,
      * and each is treated differently:
      *  a - b          subtract a from b
      *  a - -b         add a and b
      * -a - b          add a and b, multiply by -1
      * -a - -b         subtract a from b, multiply by -1
      *
      * multiplying by -1 is accomplished simply
      * by flipping the sign of the result.
      *
      * Moreover, subtraction is set up so that we always
      * subtract the smaller term from the larger. If t2
      * is larger than t1, however, then we flip the
      * sign of the solution and reverse the terms. This
      * approach works because x - y = -1( y - x ). That
      * is, you can flip the terms in subtraction if you
      * flip the sign of the difference:
      *              3 - 7 = -1 * ( 7 - 3 )
      */

     if ( t1->sign == +1 )
     {
          if ( t2->sign == +1 )  /* a - b */
          {
               sol->sign = +1;

               cmp = NormAbsCmp ( t1, t2 );
               if ( cmp < 0 ) /* t2 larger than t1 */
               {
                    sol->sign = -sol->sign;
                    NormalSubtract ( t2, t1, sol );
               }
               else
```

```
                if ( cmp > 0 ) /* t1 larger than t2 */
                    NormalSubtract ( t1, t2, sol );
                else
                {                 /*  t1 = t2, so sol = 0 */
                    TermInit ( sol );
                    return ( 1 );
                }
            }
        }
        else
        {                         /* a - -b */
            if ( ! NormalAdd ( t1, t2, sol ))
            {
                fprintf ( stderr,
                    "Overflow on addition\n" );
                return ( 0 );
            }
            sol->sign = +1;
        }
    }
    else
    {                             /* -a - b */
        if ( t2->sign == +1 )
        {
            if ( ! NormalAdd ( t1, t2, sol ))
            {
                fprintf ( stderr,
                    "Overflow on addition\n" );
                return ( 0 );
            }
            sol->sign = -1;
        }
        else                      /* -a - -b */
        {
            sol->sign = -1;

            cmp = NormAbsCmp ( t1, t2 );
            if ( cmp < 0 ) /* t2 larger than t1 */
            {
                sol->sign = -sol->sign;
                NormalSubtract ( t2, t1, sol );
            }
            else
            if ( cmp > 0 ) /* t1 larger than t2 */
                NormalSubtract ( t1, t2, sol );
            else
            {                 /*  t1 = t2, so sol = 0 */
                TermInit ( sol );
                return ( 1 );
```

```
                                }
                            }
                        }
                        break;

                case '*':
                    /*
                     * multiplication sign issues are straightforward.
                     * just multiply and set the sign, depending on
                     * whether the terms have the same sign.
                     */

                    if ( ! NormalMultiply ( t1, t2, sol ))
                    {
                        fprintf ( stderr, "Overflow on mulitply\n" );
                        return ( 0 );
                    }
                    if ( t1->sign == t2->sign )
                        sol->sign = +1;
                    else
                        sol->sign = -1;
                    break;


                case '/':
                    /* likewise for division */

                    if ( ! NormalDivide ( t1, t2, sol ))
                        return ( 0 );

                    if ( t1->sign == t2->sign )
                        sol->sign = +1;
                    else
                        sol->sign = -1;
                    break;

                default:
                    fprintf ( stderr, "Unsupported operation %c\n",
                                operator );
                    return ( 0 );
            }

        return ( 1 );
    }
```

The function `ComputeResult()` normalizes the two arithmetic terms and checks for errors in the terms by examining the sign field in the term's data structure, as explained previously. The function then initializes the term that will hold the solution. Finally, there comes the processing of the character `operation`, which indicates what arithmetic function should be performed. Note that this process requires some manipulation of the terms' signs. Why this is needed will soon become apparent.

Addition

Addition is customarily thought of as those operations that can be represented mathematically by a plus. For example, where a and b are positive numbers, $a + b$ is clearly an addition. However, in the case of $a + (-b)$ it is less clear that this is an additive operation. Technically it still is an addition, even though it is implemented by the use of subtraction: $a - b$. This sort of movement between addition and subtraction is handled in `ComputeResult()`. When the function detects that an addition has been requested, it inspects the signs and calls the addition function, `NormalAdd()` (so named for the addition of normalized terms) only if the two terms have the same sign; otherwise, it passes off the operation to the subtraction function `NormalSubtract()`. The function `ComputeResult()` sets the sign of the result (called a **sum**) depending on whether the terms being added are both positive or negative.

The addition operation in `NormalAdd()` is straightforward, as you can see in Listing 8-9. The function is handed two terms that have been normalized and decimal-aligned. The function adds the numbers together starting at the rightmost significant digit. If there are no significant digits right of the decimal point, the addition process begins at the first digit left of the decimal point.

Listing 8-9. The function `NormalAdd()` adds two normalized terms.

```
/*------------------------------------------------------------
 * We start at the rightmost digit of the terms, but no farther
 * left than the decimal point. We work our way left, adding as
 * we go until we reach the leftmost digit, and then go one digit
 * farther, in case of any carry.
 *------------------------------------------------------------*/
int NormalAdd ( struct TermData *t1, struct TermData *t2,
                struct TermData *sum )
{
    int i, j, start, stop;

    start = DEC_LOC +
              max ( t1->places_after, t2->places_after );
    stop  = DEC_LOC - 1 -
              max ( t1->places_before, t2->places_before );
```

```c
for ( i = start; i >= stop; i-- )
{
    sum->term[i] += ( t1->term[i] + t2->term[i] );
    if ( sum->term[i] > 9 )
    {
        sum->term[i] -= 10;
        sum->term[i-1] += 1;
    }
}

sum->places_after = start - DEC_LOC;

for ( i = 0; i < DEC_LOC; i++ )
    if ( (sum->term)[i] != 0 )
        break;
sum->places_before = DEC_LOC - i;

/* make sure that the sum is within MAX_SIZE digits */

i = sum->places_before + sum->places_after - MAX_SIZE;

if ( i > 0 )     /* sum is larger than MAX_SIZE */
{
    int carry = 0;

    if ( i > sum->places_after )
        return ( 0 );    /* high-order truncation will occur*/

    sum->places_after -= i;     /* adjust sum */

    j = DEC_LOC + sum->places_after;     /* do rounding */
    if ( (sum->term)[j] > 4 )
        carry = 1;

    if ( carry )
        while ( 1 )
        {
            j--;

            if ( j == 0 && (sum->term)[j] > 8 )
                return ( 0 );

            (sum->term)[j] += carry;

            if ( (sum->term)[j] > 9 )
                (sum->term)[j] -= 10;
            else
                break;
        }
```

```
    while ( i-- )          /* do low-order truncation */
    {
        (sum->term)[DEC_LOC +
                sum->places_after + i ] = 0;
    }
}

return ( 1 );
}
```

Subtraction

As with addition, the function `ComputeResult()` checks the signs of the terms whenever subtraction is called for, to make sure that subtraction is really required. Operations such as $a - (-b)$ are handed to `NormalAdd()` for addition. Only subtractions in which the terms have similar signs ($a - b$ and $-a - (-b)$) are processed by `NormalSubtract()`.

The function `NormalSubtract()` benefits from a simple algebraic equality: $a - b = -1 * (b - a)$. This rule states that we can flip the order of the terms in the subtraction, as long as we multiply the result by -1. Since multiplication by -1 is the same as toggling the sign, the rule can be concisely stated as follows: you can flip the terms in subtraction, provided that you flip the sign of the result (the result of a subtraction is called the **difference**). We can understand this rule intuitively in the way we subtract manually: if we are asked to subtract 25 from 11, we actually subtract 11 from 25 and then reverse the sign of the difference, which gives us -14. Because it is far easier to subtract smaller absolute values from larger ones, `NormalSubtract()` applies the same principle. Before `NormalSubtract()` is invoked, `ComputeResult()` examines the absolute value of the two terms to see whether they need to be flipped. It does this by calling `NormAbsCmp()` and handing it pointers to two `TermData` structures, as shown in Listing 8-10. `NormAbsCmp()` returns the same values as `strcmp()` does in the standard ANSI C library.

Listing 8-10.   The function `NormAbsCmp()` compares the absolute value of two terms and returns values in the same manner as `strcmp()`.

```
/*-------------------------------------------------------------
 * NormAbsCmp() works similar to strcmp(). The return value is
 * < 0, = 0, > 0 depending on whether the *absolute value* of
 * the first term is less than, equal to, or greater than the
 * second term, respectively.
 *-----------------------------------------------------------*/
int NormAbsCmp ( struct TermData * t1, struct TermData * t2 )
```

```
{
    int memcmp_result;

    /* first check the digits before the decimal point */

    if ( t1->places_before > t2->places_before )
        return ( 1 );

    if ( t2->places_before > t1->places_before )
        return ( -1 );

    /*
     * same number of digits before decimal point,
     * so compare character by character
     */

    memcmp_result =
        memcmp ( t1->term + DEC_LOC - t1->places_before,
                 t2->term + DEC_LOC - t2->places_before,
                 t1->places_before +
                     max ( t1->places_after, t2->places_after ));

    if ( memcmp_result > 0 )
        return ( 1 );
    else
    if ( memcmp_result < 0 )
        return ( -1 );
    else
        return ( 0 );
}
```

The function `NormAbsComp()` determines which term is greater by examining how many leading digits each term. (Leading digits occur to the left of the decimal point.) If both terms have the same number of leading digits, the function compares the terms, digit by digit, until it finds one that is larger.

Once the terms have been set up correctly by size, a loop in `NormalSubtract()` steps through the terms, starting with the rightmost digit, and performs the subtraction. As with addition, if there are no digits to the right of the decimal point, the subtraction starts at the first digit to the left of the decimal point.

An interesting detail is how the carry is performed. Traditionally, in the United States, if you have to subtract a large digit from a smaller one, you do it this way:

```
    234    becomes    1 12 14
=    89             =     8  9
   ---               ----------
   145                1  4  5
```

The rightmost 9 of the bottom term (technically, this term is called a **subtrahend**) is subtracted from the 4 of the top term (the **minuend**), the 4 is expanded to 14, and the next digit on the left in the minuend (the 3) is decremented to indicate that 10 has been added to the 4. You repeat the process in order to subtract the 8: the 2 (in the minuend where the 3 used to be) is expanded to 12, and the leading 2 is decreased to a 1. This generates the subtraction shown on the right in the example.

The method used in `NormalSubtract()` is one that is used in other parts of the world. Rather than subtract from the minuend digits to the left when the need occurs, this system adds one digit to the subtrahend. The previous example would look like this:

```
    234     becomes    2 13 14
  =  89               = 1  9  9
    145                 1  4  5
```

When the 9 is initially subtracted from the 4, the 4 is expanded to 14 as usual. But then, rather than decrementing the 3 in the minuend, we increment the 8 in the subtrahend, which gives us 9. We then subtract this 9 from the 3 by first expanding the 3 to 13. Expanding the 3 to 13 causes us to repeat the previous steps: we increment the next digit in the subtrahend. In this case, the hundreds digit is incremented from 0 to 1. Subtracting this 1 from the 2 in the minuend is the final step in the subtraction. Note that both methods give exactly the same result. Listing 8-11 shows a sample program in which `NormalSubtract()` uses the second method to subtract two normalized terms.

Listing 8-11. A program in which `NormalSubtract()` subtracts two normalized terms.

```c
/*------------------------------------------------------------
 * subtraction: We first determine where to start the process
 * of subtraction. It is the rightmost digit of the two terms,
 * that is to the right of the decimal point, else it is
 * at the first digit left of the decimal point. We then
 * proceed from that digit (the least significant digit) and
 * move to the left until we reach the leftmost digit of the
 * two terms. Because of the possibility of a carry, we go one
 * digit more to the left. This duplicates manual subtraction.
 *------------------------------------------------------------*/
int NormalSubtract ( struct TermData * t1, struct TermData * t2,
                     struct TermData * diff )
{
    /*
     * The result of a subtraction is called a difference,
```

```
 * hence we named the variable containing the answer diff.
 */

int carry, i, j;
int max_after, max_before;
char *p1, *p2, *pd;

/*
 * we'll copy the terms to scratch since we'll be altering
 * them with any carries and borrows that we do.
 */

char scratch1 [2*MAX_SIZE + 1],
     scratch2 [2*MAX_SIZE + 2];

memcpy ( scratch1, t1->term, 2*MAX_SIZE + 1 );
memcpy ( scratch2, t2->term, 2*MAX_SIZE + 1 );

/* where to start subtracting? */

max_before = max( t1->places_before, t2->places_before );
max_after  = max( t1->places_after,  t2->places_after );

j =  max_before + max_after;

/*
 * at worst, the rightmost digit is the last digit left of
 * the decimal point. So, start no further left than there.
 */

p1 = scratch1   + DEC_LOC + max_after - 1;
p2 = scratch2   + DEC_LOC + max_after - 1;
pd = diff->term + DEC_LOC + max_after - 1;

while ( j >= 0 )
{
    /*
     * if there is a carry, borrow 10 and
     * add 1 to the next higher digit in t2
     */

    if ( *p2 > *p1 )
    {
        *p1  += 10;
        *( p2 - 1 ) += 1;
    }

    *pd = *p1 - *p2;   /* the actual subtraction */
```

```
        pd--; p1--; p2--; /* move to the next higher digit */
        j--;
}

for ( j = 0, pd = diff->term;
        pd < diff->term + DEC_LOC; j++, pd++ )
          if ( *pd != 0 )
              break;

diff->places_before = DEC_LOC - j;

/*
 * to get the number of places after, start at max_after,
 * the maximum number of places after, and move left
 * until the first nonzero digit right of the decimal pt.
 */

pd = diff->term + DEC_LOC + max_after - 1;
while ( pd >= diff->term + DEC_LOC )
    if ( *pd == 0 )
    {
        max_after -= 1;
        pd -= 1;
    }
    else
        break;

diff->places_after  = max_after;

/*
 * There can be too many digits in the result: subtract
 * MAX_SIZE digits right of the decimal pt from MAX_SIZE
 * digits left of the decimal point. If this occurs, we
 * round and truncate.
 */

i = diff->places_before + diff->places_after - MAX_SIZE;

if ( i > 0 )     /* overflow */
{
    diff->places_after = MAX_SIZE - diff->places_before;
    i = DEC_LOC + diff->places_after;
    if ( (diff->term)[i] > 4 )  /* round up if > 4 */
        carry = 1;
    else
        carry = 0;

    j = i;
```

```
        i -= 1;

        /* add carry (the rounding) */

        while ( carry )
        {
            if ( i == 0 && (diff->term)[i] > 8 )
            {
                printf ( "Overflow on subtraction\n" );
                return ( 0 );
            }

            (diff->term)[i] += carry;

            if ( (diff->term)[i] > 9 )
            {
                (diff->term)[i] -= 10;
                carry = 1;
                i--;
            }
            else
                carry = 0;
        }

        /* now zero out the digits we have truncated */

        while ( j < 2*MAX_SIZE )
            (diff->term)[j++] = 0;
    }

    return ( 1 );
}
```

The second method of subtraction is favored because it requires no special processing. The first method does have a special case: subtracting a carry when the next digit to the left in the minuend is a zero. Suppose, for example, that you want to subtract 99 from 201. After you have expanded the 1 to 11, you find that the 0 cannot simply be decremented. Instead, you must test for and replace the 0 with a 9, and you must propagate the carry to the next digit to the left. If the next digit is a 0, you must repeat the process and again propagate the carry to the next digit to the left. If the digits left consist of a string of 0's, the carry and propagation must be performed for each 0 before any further subtraction can occur. This problem does not occur using the second method. By incrementing the subtrahend, you limit the processing of the carry to the next digit to the left. Even in the worst case, where a 9 is incremented by a carry to a 10, the 10 can wait its turn to be subtracted without requiring that the carry be immediately propagated all the way up the number. This difference between the two methods makes the second method far easier to code in C.

Multiplication

Like addition and subtraction, multiplication is a straightforward operation. Before the computation actually begins, `ComputeResult()` examines the signs of the two terms. If they are the same, the result of the multiplication (termed the **product**) is positive; otherwise the result is negative. The two terms are then passed to `NormalMultiply()`, where the multiplication is performed.

To see how the multiplication is performed, we need to examine a multiplication problem as it is performed manually. Here is an illustrative example, which we hope will look familiar:

```
      3 1 8 7    the multiplicand
  x     4 6 9    the multiplier
    2 8 6 8 3    intermediate products
  1 9 1 2 2 ·        "           "
  1 2 7 4 8 · ·      "           "
1 4 9 4 7 0 3    the product
```

For each digit of the multiplier, a separate intermediate product is generated. To minimize the number of passes of multiplication (one pass through the multiplicand for every digit in the multiplier) and of addition, we make the multiplier the shorter of the two terms.

The multiplication then loops through each digit of the multiplicand for every digit in the multiplier. The operation is a fair copy of the manual approach to multiplication, with the exception of two details: the intermediate products are totaled as they are generated, and the multiplication of the individual digits is performed in a lookup table.

The latter modification is done for the sake of speed. If we were to emulate manual calculations, every digit of the multiplier and the multiplicand would have to be multiplied, and the modulo function (which is performed as a division) would have to be applied to the result, in order to ascertain what digit to place in the intermediate product. Because there are only one hundred possible combinations of digits, their products are stored in a table of integers and are simply looked up rather than calculated. Notice the format of the table (thoughtfully called `table[]` in the code); the result of 4×7, for example, is not 28, but 0x0208. Essentially, a table entry is loaded with two bytes: one that contains the low-order digit (8), and one that contains the high-order digit (2). If the result had been entered in the table as 28, a separate operation would have been necessary to separate the 8—which is added to the intermediate result—from the 2 (or 20), which is carried over.

The architecture of the table itself requires a little explanation because the table was designed so that access to it would not require a multiplication (after all, this is the purpose of the table to begin with). The most pragmatic approach would have been to build a two-dimensional table. Then we would access `table[4,7]` to determine the product of 4×7. However, the subscripts of two-dimensional tables are often converted into pointer addresses by multiplication. To avoid this multiplication, the table was designed as a one-dimensional table. Subscripts are computed as $10 *$ the first digit plus the second digit. Therefore, the previous access would be computed as $10*4+7$ or `table[47]`. The value there is the same as that of `table[74]`, namely 0x0208. You will probably notice that multiplication is used to ascertain this subscript. But, in fact, the computation of the first part of this subscript ($4*10$) is done by lookup in a small table of ten entries called `mults_of_10`. Hence, with these two tables that occupy the size of 110 integers, we have eliminated a multiplication (and a division) for every digit that is multiplied.

A point to note about multiplication is that, unlike the other functions, `NormalMultiply()` uses buffers that are `4*MAX_SIZE` rather than `2*MAX_SIZE`. This allows us to have `2*MAX_SIZE` digits to the right of the decimal point. This change is brought about by multiplications such as $0.001 * 0.999$. Supposing that `MAX_SIZE` is 3, if we did not have `2*MAX_SIZE` digits after the internal decimal point, we could not perform this multiplication, because the rightmost digit of the result will be placed six places to the right of the decimal point. While it is true that the maximum possible number of digits that will appear in the product is only `MAX_SIZE`, we need to compute the full length of the product in order to round correctly before truncating the excess digits. In our example, 0.001×0.999 gives an internal representation of 0.000999. Since `MAX_SIZE` is 3, rounding and truncation will convert this to 0.001. Notice that if we did not have `2*MAX_SIZE` digits to the right of the decimal point, the rounding would be incorrect and the result would be 0. In Listing 8-12, `NormalMultiply()` performs the multiplication of two normalized terms.

Listing 8-12.   The function `NormalMultiply()` performs the multiplication of two normalized terms.

```
/*----------------------------------------------------------------
 *   Multiplication of normalized terms.
 *   In the expression c = a * b, a is called the multiplicand,
 *   b the multiplier, and c the product.
 *----------------------------------------------------------------*/
```

```
int NormalMultiply ( struct TermData * t1,
          struct TermData * t2, struct TermData * prod )
{
    /*
     * Each digit of the multiplier will require the generation
     * of an intermediate result, which is added to previous
     * intermediate results, to produce the product. Hence,
     * we'll make the multiplier the shorter of the two terms.
     */

    char *mcand,      /* the multiplicand */
         *mier,       /* the multiplier   */
         *temp;       /* temporary hold area for product */

    int  mcand_curr,  /* where we are in the muliplicand */
         mier_curr,   /* where we are in the multiplier */
         temp_curr,   /* where we are in the temp product */
         temp_here;

    int  mcand_len,   /* number of digits in multiplicand */
         mier_len;    /* number of digits in multiplier */

    int  carry;       /* the carry digit when adding the
                         intermediate results */
    int  i, j, from, to;

    static int table [100] =
    {
     /*          0*0     0*1     0*2     0*3     0*4   */
     /* 0 */ 0x0000,0x0000,0x0000,0x0000,0x0000,
     /*          0*5     0*6     0*7     0*8     0*9   */
            0x0000,0x0000,0x0000,0x0000,0x0000,
     /*          1*0     1*1     1*2     1*3     1*4   */
     /* 1 */ 0x0000,0x0001,0x0002,0x0003,0x0004,
     /*          1*5     1*6     1*7     1*8     1*9   */
            0x0005,0x0006,0x0007,0x0008,0x0009,
     /*          2*0     2*1     2*2     2*3     2*4   */
     /* 2 */ 0x0000,0x0002,0x0004,0x0006,0x0008,
     /*          2*5     2*6     2*7     2*8     2*9   */
            0x0100,0x0102,0x0104,0x0106,0x0108,
     /*          3*0     3*1     3*2     3*3     3*4   */
     /* 3 */ 0x0000,0x0003,0x0006,0x0009,0x0102,
     /*          3*5     3*6     3*7     3*8     3*9   */
            0x0105,0x0108,0x0201,0x0204,0x0207,
     /*          4*0     4*1     4*2     4*3     4*4   */
     /* 4 */ 0x0000,0x0004,0x0008,0x0102,0x0106,
     /*          4*5     4*6     4*7     4*8     4*9   */
            0x0200,0x0204,0x0208,0x0302,0x0306,
```

```
/*            5*0     5*1     5*2     5*3     5*4   */
/* 5 */ 0x0000,0x0005,0x0100,0x0105,0x0200,
/*            5*5     5*6     5*7     5*8     5*9   */
        0x0205,0x0300,0x0305,0x0400,0x0405,
/*            6*0     6*1     6*2     6*3     6*4   */
/* 6 */ 0x0000,0x0006,0x0102,0x0108,0x0204,
/*            6*5     6*6     6*7     6*8     6*9   */
        0x0300,0x0306,0x0402,0x0408,0x0504,
/*            7*0     7*1     7*2     7*3     7*4   */
/* 7 */ 0x0000,0x0007,0x0104,0x0201,0x0208,
/*            7*5     7*6     7*7     7*8     7*9   */
        0x0305,0x0402,0x0409,0x0506,0x0603,
/*            8*0     8*1     8*2     8*3     8*4   */
/* 8 */ 0x0000,0x0008,0x0106,0x0204,0x0208,
/*            8*5     8*6     8*7     8*8     8*9   */
        0x0400,0x0408,0x0506,0x0604,0x0702,
/*            9*0     9*1     9*2     9*3     9*4   */
/* 9 */ 0x0000,0x0009,0x0108,0x0207,0x0306,
/*            9*5     9*6     9*7     9*8     9*9   */
        0x0405,0x0504,0x0603,0x0702,0x0801
};

static int mults_of_ten [10] =
    { 0, 10, 20, 30, 40, 50, 60, 70, 80, 90 };

mcand_len = mier_len = 0;

/*
 * products can overflow a term, since the number of
 * digits left of the decimal pt in the product is the
 * sum of the digits left of the decimal pt in the
 * multiplier and multiplicand - 1. Likewise, the number
 * of digits right of the decimal point is the sum of
 * these digits in the multiplier and multiplicand.
 *
 * Hence, our internal representation of the product,
 * temp, has 2*MAX_SIZE digits on either side of the
 * decimal point. We will round and truncate as necessary
 * when we load the digits into prod.
 */

temp = calloc ( 1, 4*MAX_SIZE + 1 );
if ( temp == NULL )
{
    printf ( "Out of memory in multiplication.\n" );
    return ( 0 );
}
```

```
/*
 * the following test avoids guaranteed high-order
 * truncation and saves having to do the multiplication
 * only to discover the overflow at end.
 */

if ( t1->places_before + t2->places_before - 1 >
     MAX_SIZE )
{
    free ( temp );
    return ( 0 );
}

if (( t1->places_before + t1->places_after ) >
( t2->places_before + t2->places_after ))
{
    mcand = t1->term;
    mier  = t2->term;

    mcand_len = t1->places_before + t1->places_after;
    mier_len  = t2->places_before + t2->places_after;

    mcand_curr = DEC_LOC + t1->places_after - 1;
    mier_curr  = DEC_LOC + t2->places_after - 1;
}
else
{
    mcand = t2->term;
    mier  = t1->term;

    mcand_len = t2->places_before + t2->places_after;
    mier_len  = t1->places_before + t1->places_after;

    mcand_curr = DEC_LOC + t2->places_after - 1;
    mier_curr  = DEC_LOC + t1->places_after - 1;
}

/*
 * The number of digits after the decimal points in a
 * product is the sum of the number of decimal digits
 * in  each term: 12.6 * 1.2 = 15.12.
 * Hence, we start putting digits into prod, using the
 * following formulation:
 */

temp_curr = 2*DEC_LOC +
            t1->places_after + t2->places_after - 1;
```

```
carry = 0;
while ( mier_len > 0 )   /* the multiplication loop */
{                        /* for each digit of multiplier */
    int j, a, b, val;

    i = mcand_len;
    j = mcand_curr;
    temp_here = temp_curr;

    while ( i >= 0 )      /* process the whole multiplicand */
    {
        if ( mier [ mier_curr ] == 0 )
            break;

        a = mier [ mier_curr ];
        b = mcand [ j ];
        a += mults_of_ten [ b ];

        val = table [ a ];
        temp[ temp_here ] += carry + val & 0x00FF;
        carry = val >> 8;
        if ( temp[temp_here] > 9 )
        {
            carry += temp[temp_here] / 10;
            temp[ temp_here ] %= 10;
        }
        j--;            /* move up the multiplicand */
        i--;            /* one less iteration to do */
        temp_here--; /* move one product digit to the left */
    }
    mier_curr--;    /* move up the multiplier */
    mier_len--;     /* one less multiplier digit */
    temp_curr--;    /* move up the solution by one digit */
}

if ( carry > 0 )
    temp[temp_curr] = carry;

for ( i = 0; i < 2*DEC_LOC; i++ )
    if ( temp[i] != 0 )
        break;

/* did we overflow anyway? */

if (( 2*DEC_LOC - i ) > MAX_SIZE )
{
    free ( temp );
    return ( 0 );
```

```
}
else
    prod->places_before = 2*DEC_LOC - i;

/* copy the digits before the dec pt from temp to prod */

from = 2*DEC_LOC - 1;
to   = DEC_LOC - 1;

i = prod->places_before;
while ( i-- )
    (prod->term)[to--] = temp[from--];

/*
 * now examine the digits after the decimal point
 * and perform rounding and truncation as necessary
 */

for ( i = 4*MAX_SIZE - 1; i >= 2*DEC_LOC; i-- )
      if ( temp[i] != 0 )
        break;

prod->places_after = i - 2*DEC_LOC + 1;

/* j = maximum places after */

j = MAX_SIZE - prod->places_before;

/* do we have to round and truncate? */

if ( j < prod->places_after )
{
    prod->places_after = j;
    if ( temp[2*DEC_LOC + j] > 4 )   /* we round up if > 4 */
        carry = 1;
    else
        carry = 0;

    /* copy the digits over */

    from = 2*DEC_LOC + j - 1;
    to   = DEC_LOC + j - 1;

    while ( j-- )
        (prod->term)[to--] = temp[from--];

    /* now do the rounding */
```

```
        if ( carry )
        {
            i = DEC_LOC + prod->places_after - 1;
            while ( 1 )
            {
                /*
                 * we now add carry (the rounding). If
                 * the current digit is 9, the carry will
                 * generate a 10, meaning that we have to
                 * carry to the next digit left. If this
                 * occurs at the leftmost digit, it can
                 * cause an overflow, so this possibility
                 * is checked for first.
                 */

                if ( i == 0 &&                /* overflow */
                     (prod->term)[i] > 8 )
                {
                    free ( temp );
                    return ( 0 );
                }

                (prod->term)[i] += carry;

                if ( (prod->term)[i] > 9 )
                {
                    (prod->term)[i] -= 10;
                    i--;
                }
                else
                    break;
            }
        }
    }
    else    /* no truncation so just copy the digits */
    {
        j = prod->places_after;

        from = 2*DEC_LOC + j - 1;
        to   = DEC_LOC + j - 1;

        while ( j-- )
            (prod->term)[to--] = temp[from--];
    }

    free ( temp );
    return ( 1 );
}
```

Division

Division is the most difficult of the four basic arithmetic operations. It requires far more work than the other operations, and the nature of the work is considerably more complex. In the calculator presented here, three times more code is used for division than for multiplication, which itself is twice the size of subtraction. Before examining these complexities, we need to examine the process of division itself. We use the approach taught in modern U.S. schools, as shown in Figure 8-4.

```
          3  1  7
2  8  1 | 8  9  0  7  7
          8  4  3
             4  7  7
             2  8  1
             1  9  6  7
             1  9  6  7
                      0
```

Figure 8-4.   Manual division as taught in U.S. schools.

In the figure, 281 is the **divisor**, 89077 is the **dividend**, and 317 is the **quotient**. The numbers 843, 477, and 1967 are intermediate dividends. This kind of figure probably looks familiar to you, or at least you can transpose a different system into this one.

Several factors contribute to the complexity of division:

- Unlike the other operations, division requires guessing. Each quotient digit is first guessed and then tested to see whether it is too large or too small.
- The dividend is constantly changing. As we proceed through the division and bring down digits, the dividend becomes a series of various intermediate dividends.
- For large numbers, we cannot deal with the number in its entirety. Instead, we have to take the first few digits of the divisor and the first few digits of the dividend in order to guess the next quotient digit.

These three aspects of division make it a dynamic operation; that is, the values of the terms keep changing. As a result, we spend considerable effort in keeping track of where we are in the division process. To minimize the difficulty of keeping track of terms, their lengths and their values, the division function, NormalDivide(), does not store the terms as a series of individual digits, but rather as a true string where, for example, 0 is stored as '0'(0x30) rather than as 0 (0x00). This approach, while creating overhead, allows the C string functions to manipulate the terms easily. It also makes the code far less complex. Consult Listing 8-13.

Listing 8-13.   The function `NormalDivide()` performs the division of two normalized terms.

```
/*-------------------------------------------------------------
 * Division is accomplished by turning the term data into an
 * array of characters rather than bytes holding the numeric
 * value of each digit--the latter format is used in the other
 * arithmetic operations. However, in division, it becomes a
 * cumbersome format. (See text.)
 *-----------------------------------------------------------*/
int NormalDivide  ( struct TermData * dvend_arg,
                    struct TermData * dvsor_arg,
                    struct TermData * quot )
{
#define ASCII_VAL ( '0' ) /* the difference between 0 and '0' */

    unsigned int
         leading_zeros = 0,
         divend_len,
         divsor_len,
         idivend_len;

    int  strcmp_return,
         strncmp_return;

    char *answer,
         *dividend,
         *divisor,
         *interim,
         *new_interim,
         *product;

    unsigned int
         quo_guess,

         next_dvend_digit = 0,

         answer_idx = 0,

         dvsor_len,
         idvend_len;
```

```
int  dvend_order, /* order of magnitude of divisor and   */
     dvsor_order; /* dividend. Used for locating decimal */
                  /* point in quotient.                  */

char *pc;    /* generic variables */
int  i, j;


dividend     = calloc ( 1, 2*MAX_SIZE + 1 );
divisor      = calloc ( 1, MAX_SIZE + 1 );
interim      = calloc ( 1, 2*MAX_SIZE + 1 );
new_interim  = calloc ( 1, 2*MAX_SIZE + 1 );
product      = calloc ( 2, 2*MAX_SIZE + 1 );
answer       = calloc ( 2, MAX_SIZE + 1 );

if ( dividend == NULL || divisor == NULL   ||
     interim  == NULL || new_interim == NULL ||
     product  == NULL || answer == NULL )
{
    printf ( "Error allocating memory in division\n" );
    return  ( 0 );
}

/* load dividend with the digits as character values */
i = 0;
for ( pc  = dvend_arg->term +
            DEC_LOC - dvend_arg->places_before;
      pc <= dvend_arg->term +
            DEC_LOC + dvend_arg->places_after - 1;
      pc++, i++ )
        dividend[i] = *pc + ASCII_VAL;

/* remove leading zeros */

while ( *dividend == '0' )
    DivShiftArrayLeft ( dividend );


/* likewise, for the divisor */
i = 0;
for ( pc  = dvsor_arg->term +
            DEC_LOC - dvsor_arg->places_before;
      pc <= dvsor_arg->term +
            DEC_LOC + dvsor_arg->places_after - 1;
      pc++, i++ )
        divisor[i] = *pc + ASCII_VAL;

while ( *divisor == '0' )
    DivShiftSmallArrayLeft ( divisor );
```

```
/* If divisor is zero, signal error and abort */

if ( DivCheckZeroOnly ( divisor ))
{
    printf ( "Error: Division by Zero\n" );
    return ( 0 );
}

/* If dividend is zero, set quotient to zero and exit */

if ( DivCheckZeroOnly ( dividend ))
{
    TermInit ( quot );
    return ( 1 );
}

divend_len = strlen ( dividend );
divsor_len = strlen ( divisor );

/*
 * If dividend is < divisor,
 * add zeros to end of dividend
 * an add leading zeros to quotient
 */

while ( divend_len < divsor_len )
{
    *( dividend + divend_len ) = '0';
    leading_zeros += 1;
    divend_len += 1;
}

if ( divend_len == divsor_len )
{
    strcmp_return = strcmp ( dividend, divisor );
    if ( strcmp_return < 0 )    /* dividend is lesser */
    {
        *( dividend + divend_len ) = '0';
        leading_zeros += 1;
        divend_len += 1;
    }
    else
    if ( strcmp_return == 0 )    /* they're the same */
    {
        answer[answer_idx++] = '1';
        goto wrapup;
    };                           /* otherwise, divisor is lesser */
}
```

```
/* load the dividend into interim */

strcpy ( interim, dividend );
idivend_len = strlen ( interim );

loop:                        /*--- main loop ---*/

if ( divsor_len > 3 )
    dvsor_len = idvend_len = 4;
else
if ( divsor_len < idivend_len )
{
    if ( strcmp ( divisor, interim ) > 0 )
    {
        dvsor_len = divsor_len;
        idvend_len = divsor_len + 1;
    }
    else
        dvsor_len = idvend_len = divsor_len;
}
else /* can only be the terms are equal length */
{
    dvsor_len  = divsor_len;
    idvend_len = idivend_len;
}

if ( dvsor_len == idvend_len && dvsor_len > 1 )
    if ( DivAtoin ( divisor, dvsor_len ) >
         DivAtoin ( interim, dvsor_len ))
            dvsor_len -= 1;

quo_guess = DivAtoin ( interim, idvend_len ) /
            DivAtoin ( divisor, dvsor_len );

if ( quo_guess > 9 )
    quo_guess /= 10;

try_quo_guess:       /*--- try_quo_guess goto ---*/

DivQuickMult ( divisor, quo_guess, product );

strncmp_return =
    strncmp ( product, interim, strlen ( product ));

if ( strncmp_return > 0 )   /* if product > interim */
{
    if ( quo_guess == 1 )
    {
```

```
                     /*
                      * a quo_guess of 1 can be a special case:
                      * try 9 and bring down another digit
                      */

                     if ( DivSpecialCase ( divisor, interim ))
                     {
                         quo_guess = 9;

                         /*
                          * did we already pad the dividend ?
                          * if so, then add a zero to interim dividend,
                          * if not, then bring down another digit.
                          */

                         if ( leading_zeros )
                             interim[idvend_len++] = '0';
                         else
                         if ( next_dvend_digit < divend_len )
                             interim[idvend_len++] =
                                 dividend[next_dvend_digit++];

                         /* and try again */

                         goto try_quo_guess;
                     }
                     else            /* not special case */
                         DivShiftArrayRight ( product );
                 }
                 else

                 /* quo_guess != 1, so check whether array needs shift */

                 if ( strlen ( product ) < idivend_len )
                     DivShiftArrayRight ( product );
                 else
                 {              /* guess was just too high so try again */
                     quo_guess -= 1;
                     goto try_quo_guess;
                 }
        }

        /* load the correct digit */

        answer[answer_idx++] = quo_guess + ASCII_VAL;

        /*
```

```
 * if no next digit to bring down has been ascertained,
 * the next operation sets which digit to start bringing
 * down. Only done the first time through here.
 */

if ( ! next_dvend_digit )
    next_dvend_digit = strlen ( product );

/* new_interim = interim - product */

DivQuickSub ( interim, product, new_interim );

if (( DivCheckZeroOnly ( new_interim )
    && next_dvend_digit  >= divend_len )
    || answer_idx >= MAX_SIZE )         /* are we done? */
        goto wrapup;

while ( *new_interim == '0' )
    DivShiftArrayLeft ( new_interim );

memset ( interim, '\0', 2*MAX_SIZE + 1 );
strcpy ( interim, new_interim );
idivend_len = strlen ( interim );

get_next_digit:      /*--- loop for get next digit ---*/

if ( next_dvend_digit < divend_len )
    interim[idivend_len++] = dividend[next_dvend_digit++];
else
{                      /* if beyond EO dividend, bring down 0 */
    interim [ idivend_len++] = '0';
}

if ( idivend_len < divsor_len )    /* if interim < divisor */
{
    answer[answer_idx++] = '0';
    if ( answer_idx >= MAX_SIZE )
        goto wrapup;
    goto get_next_digit;
}
else
if ( idivend_len == divsor_len )    /* same length */
{
    if ( strcmp ( divisor, interim ) > 0 )
    {                               /* but divisor is greater */
        answer[answer_idx++] = '0';
        if ( answer_idx >= MAX_SIZE )
            goto wrapup;
```

```
            goto get_next_digit;
        }
    }

goto loop;

wrapup:

/*
 * Now take result from answer and place it in quot. We
 * compare the order of magnitudes of the dividend and the
 * divisor to determine where the decimal point goes.
 * The rule is:
 *
 *    Places  =       Order       -  Order       + 1
 *                    (dvend)        (divisor)
 *
 *        where strcmp ( dividend, divisor ) > 0
 *        otherwise, don't add 1.
 *
 * A positive number is the number of places left of
 * the decimal point. From this, we subtract any leading
 * zeros.
 */

/* get the order for the dividend */

if ( dvend_arg->places_before != 0 )
    dvend_order = dvend_arg->places_before;
else
{
    i = 0;
    pc = dvend_arg->term + DEC_LOC;
    while ( pc < dvend_arg->term + 2*MAX_SIZE )
    {
        if ( *pc != 0 )
            break;
        else
        {
            i  += 1;
            pc += 1;
        }
    }
    dvend_order = -i;
}

/* get the order for the divisor */
```

```
if ( dvsor_arg->places_before != 0 )
    dvsor_order = dvsor_arg->places_before;
else
{
    i = 0;
    pc = dvsor_arg->term + DEC_LOC;
    while ( pc < dvsor_arg->term + 2*MAX_SIZE )
    {
        if ( *pc != 0 )
            break;
        else
        {
            i   += 1;
            pc += 1;
        }
    }
    dvsor_order = -i;
}

i = dvend_order - dvsor_order;

if  ( strcmp ( dividend, divisor ) >= 0 )
    i += 1;

j = DEC_LOC - i;

 /*
  * quot has already been intialized to zeros,
  * so we can start moving in the digits.
  */

for ( i = 0; i < answer_idx && j < 2*MAX_SIZE; i++, j++ )
    (quot->term)[j] = answer[i] - ASCII_VAL;

/* compute the number of places before and after */

for ( i = 0; i < DEC_LOC; i++ )
    if ( (quot->term)[i] != 0 )
        break;

quot->places_before = DEC_LOC - i;

for ( i = 2*MAX_SIZE - 1; i >= DEC_LOC; i-- )
    if ( (quot->term)[i] != 0 )
        break;

quot->places_after = i - DEC_LOC + 1;
```

```
        /* free the terms we created on the heap */

        free ( dividend );
        free ( divisor );
        free ( interim );
        free ( new_interim );
        free ( product );
        free ( answer );

        return ( 1 );
}
```

The first item in this function is #define ASCII_VAL ('0'), which defines the difference between '0' and 0. It is the ASCII character value (hence, ASCII_VAL) that transforms a value into its corresponding character. It is used to convert terms into characters. The code next allocates the variables that are needed to hold the interim values generated by division. The terms handed to the function are then loaded into the character arrays dividend and divisor. Any leading zeros (such as those that might occur if one term were 0.009) are stripped away by the functions DivShiftArrayLeft() and DivShiftSmallArrayLeft(), as shown in Listing 8-14. The functions differ only by the size of the array that they shift. (Note: Functions that are called only by the division routines bear the prefix Div).

Listing 8-14.   The functions `DivShiftArrayLeft()` and `DivShiftSmallArrayLeft()` shift an array of characters left one byte, dropping the first character. Used in division to truncate leading zeros.

```
/*----------------------------------------------------------------
 * Shifts an array of chars left by one character, truncating
 * the leftmost char. Called by division only when the leading
 * character is a '0'. The small version works on MAX_SIZE
 * arrays, the regular version on 2*MAX_SIZE.
 *----------------------------------------------------------------*/
void DivShiftArrayLeft ( char *array )
{
    char buffer [ 2*MAX_SIZE + 1 ];
    memset ( buffer, '\0', 2*MAX_SIZE + 1);
    strcpy ( buffer, array );
    strcpy ( array, buffer + 1 );
}
```

```
void DivShiftSmallArrayLeft ( char *array )
{
    char buffer [ MAX_SIZE + 1 ];
    memset ( buffer, '\0', MAX_SIZE + 1);
    strcpy ( buffer, array );
    strcpy ( array, buffer + 1 );
}
```

The leading zeros can be truncated with impunity because they are not needed. The later calculation that locates the decimal point will not need to retain this information. As shown in Listing 8-15, the arrays are then examined by the function `DivCheckZeroOnly()` to see whether either array contains a zero value. This function returns a 1 if the array passed to it contains only zeros; otherwise it returns 0.

Listing 8-15.   The function `DivCheckZeroOnly()` checks an array of char-acters for values other than zero.

```
/*-------------------------------------------------------------
 * This function checks a division term for a zero value.
 * Called only by division operation.
 *-----------------------------------------------------------*/
int DivCheckZeroOnly ( const char *array )
{
    while ( *array )
    {
        if ( *array != '0' )
            return ( 0 );
        array += 1;
    }

    return ( 1 );
}
```

If the divisor is 0, an error occurs, a message is displayed on the screen (even if the program is running from a script), and the division terminates with an error code of 0. If the dividend is 0, `NormalDivide()` sets the quotient to 0 and returns. (0 divided by any legal number is 0.)

If the divisor is longer than the dividend (since leading zeros have been stripped away, a longer number will mean that it has a greater value), the dividend is padded with zeros until it is the length of the divisor. Hence, 15 into 6 is converted to 15 into 60. This operation will affect the location of the decimal point, so the number of zeros added to the dividend is recorded in the variable `leading_zeros` (so named because it indicates how many leading zeros must be added to the final quotient). In the previous example, 6 is converted into 60, and `leading_zeros` is set to 1. Later, when we format the quotient, we will know that the correct answer is not 4, but 4 with a leading zero—that is, 0.4.

By padding the dividend with zeros, we now know that it is either longer than or the same length as the divisor. If the dividend and divisor are the same length, we compare them. If the divisor is greater (such as 60 into 50), we again pad the dividend with a zero (making it 60 into 500) and we augment `leading_zeros`. Because all divisions but the first one are performed with the use of intermediate dividends (see Figure 8-4), we simply load the initial dividend into the intermediate dividend, `interim`, now so that we can use the same code for all divisions.

We are now ready to enter the cycle of division. It begins at the `goto` destination, `loop`. The first task is to figure out how many digits of the divisor and the dividend we can use to make our first guess of the quotient digit. We try to take as many digits as possible, since the more digits we use, the more likely the guessed digit will be correct. The maximum number of digits we can use is four. This is because of the size limitation of 16-bit integers. Their maximum value is 65,535—meaning that four-digit numbers are the maximum size where all such numbers can be held in an integer. If both divisor and dividend are longer than four digits, we use the first four digits of each. We then compare these two values. If the divisor value is greater than the dividend value, we take only three digits of the divisor. For example, if we divide 98985 (the divisor) into 676774 (the dividend), we would start with four-digit "stubs": 9898 and 6767. Because 9898 is greater than 6767, we scale back the divisor stub to three digits, 989, and divide it into 6767 to get our first guess at a quotient digit.

The conversion of the stubs into an integer is performed by the function `DivAtoin()`, as shown in Listing 8-16. This function works just like the ANSI C function `atoi()`, but it is passed a second parameter that indicates the maximum number of digits to convert from the passed string.

If the divisor and the dividend do not each have four or more digits, every attempt is made to make sure that the stubs have the same number of digits (with the divisor stub being the lesser) or that the divisor stub has one fewer digit.

Finally, once the stubs have been ascertained, the dividend stub is divided by the divisor stub, resulting in a guess at the quotient digit. This digit is stored in `quo_guess`. In the preceding example, 6767 would be divided by 989, resulting in a (correct) guess of 6.

Listing 8-16. The function `DivAtoin()` converts a passed string into an integer, with a limit on the maximum number of characters to use.

```c
/*------------------------------------------------------------
 * Performs atoi for length number of characters. Called by
 * division to establish the stubs of the divisor and dividend
 * we will use to try guessing the next quotient digit.
 *------------------------------------------------------------*/
int DivAtoin ( const char *string, int length )
{           /* usual tests for sign and white space omitted */
    int i, n;
    n = 0;

    for ( i = 0;
        i < length && ( string[i] >= '0' && string[i] <= '9'
);
        i++ )
            n = 10 * n + string[i] - '0';

    return ( n );
}
```

We now ascertain whether the guess is correct. First, if it is greater than 10 (such as stubs of 49 divided by 2, giving us 24), we divide it by 10 (giving us a guess of 2). Next, we multiply the guessed digit by the divisor and store the result in `product`. As you can see in Listing 8-17, we perform this multiplication by using `DivQuickMult()`, which is an abbreviated form of multiplication, since it always multiplies a string by only a single digit.

Listing 8-17. The function `DivQuickMult()` multiplies an array of characters by a single digit.

```c
/*------------------------------------------------------------
 * This function multiplies an array of digits as characters
 * by a single-digit integer. Called by division only.
 *------------------------------------------------------------*/
void DivQuickMult ( const char *long_term, int digit,
                    char *result )
{
    int from, to; /* array subscripts */
    int new_carry, old_carry, hold;

    new_carry = old_carry = hold = to = 0;

    memset ( result, '\0', 2*MAX_SIZE + 1 );
    for ( from = strlen ( long_term ) - 1;
```

```
            from >= 0; from--, to++ )
    {
        hold = ( long_term[from] - ASCII_VAL ) * digit;
        new_carry = hold / 10;
        result[to] = hold % 10 + old_carry;
        if ( result[to] > 9 )
        {
            new_carry += 1;
            result[to] -= 10;
        }
        result[to] += ASCII_VAL;
        old_carry = new_carry;
    }

    if ( old_carry )           /* if any left over */
        result[to] = old_carry + ASCII_VAL;

    strrev ( result );
}
```

If product is larger (ascertained by strcmp()) than the interim dividend, our guess was too high. We need to explore several possibilities before taking action. The first is that the strcmp function has provided an inaccurate comparison. For example, if we were dividing 7 into 12, the correct guess would be 1 and the product would be 7. However, when the comparison of the strings 7 and 12 occurred, 7 would appear to be greater than 12, because 7 is greater than the initial 1 in 12. In this case, we check the length of the product. If it is less than the length of the intermediate dividend, we know that we have a smaller number, regardless of the result of strcmp(). To normalize the product for the later subtraction, however, we shift the product to the right and prepend one (or more) leading zeros until it is the same length as the intermediate dividend. This operation is performed by DivShiftArrayRight(), whose operation is self-explanatory. Consult Listing 8-18.

Listing 8-18.   The function DivShiftArrayRight() shifts an array of characters to the right and prepends a zero.

```
/*-------------------------------------------------------------
 * Shifts an array of characters right one character and
 * prepends a zero. Called only by division.
 *-----------------------------------------------------------*/
void DivShiftArrayRight ( char *array )
{
    memmove ( array + 1, array, strlen ( array ));
    array[0] = '0';
}
```

The alternative case is that the guessed digit was too big. If it has a value of anything other than 1, we decrement it by 1 and try the verification of the guess once again. To do this, we jump to `try_quo_guess`.

If the guess is 1, however, we cannot blithely decrement the guess, since a guess of 0 is always an error. We check to see whether we should set the guess to 9. To do this, we call the function `DivSpecialCase()`, as shown in Listing 8-19. This function checks to see whether or not a 9 will work.

Listing 8-19.   The function `DivSpecialCase()` multiplies the divisor by 9 and compares the product to the intermediate dividend in order to test whether a guess of 9 will work.

```
/*----------------------------------------------------------------
 * If the division guesses a quotient digit that is too high,
 * we normally would decrement the guess by 1 and try again.
 * However, if the guessed digit is a 1, we have to be careful,
 * because the decrement should give us a 9, not a 0. This
 * function tests whether the correct digit is in fact a 9, or
 * whether we have misapprehended the dividend on our guess.
 * Called only by division.
 *----------------------------------------------------------------*/
int DivSpecialCase ( const char *divisor,
                     const char *curr_dividend )
{
    char test_result [2*MAX_SIZE + 1];

    DivQuickMult ( divisor, 9, test_result );

    if ( strcmp ( curr_dividend, test_result ) > 0 )
        return ( 1 );
    else
        return ( 0 );
}
```

The need for this test arises from the following circumstance. If we divide 88,888 into 888,867 the two stubs are both 8,888, giving us a guess of 1. Before we can tell whether a 9 will work, we test it with this function. The other possibility is the one articulated earlier ($12/7 = 1$ that `strcmp()` compares erroneously). One way or the other, we either decrement to 9 or retain our current guess.

If we decrement to 9, however, we cannot simply retry our guess, since if a guess of 1 was too high, 9 will always fail. We must bring down the next digit from the dividend. We know from our previous work that if `leading_zeros` is greater than zero, then we have already had to pad the dividend, because the dividend was originally shorter than the divisor. In this case, we simply add another zero to the intermediate dividend. We then try our guess of 9.

Having ascertained a correct guess digit, we store it in the array `answer`. We then make a note of where we are in the dividend, so that when we bring down the next dividend digit, we are aware of how far we have proceeded through the dividend. This location is tracked by `next_dvend_digit`.

Next, we subtract the product of the guessed digit and the divisor from the intermediate dividend using `DivQuickSub()`, as shown in Listing 8-20. The result is the new intermediate dividend, termed `new_interim`.

Listing 8-20.   The function `DivQuickSub()` subtracts one array of characters from another.

```
/*--------------------------------------------------------------
 * Subtracts one array of chars (the subtrahend) from another
 * array (the minuend), generating a difference. Called only
 * by division.
 *------------------------------------------------------------*/
void DivQuickSub ( char *minuend, char *subtrahend,
                   char *diff )
{
    int sub, to;     /* indices to various arrays */

    sub = to = strlen ( subtrahend ) - 1; /* start at right   */
    diff[to + 1] = '\0';          /* after setting end of string */

    while ( sub >= 0 )
    {
        if ( minuend[sub] < subtrahend[sub] )
        {
            minuend[sub] += 10;
            subtrahend[sub - 1] += 1;
        }
        diff[to--] = minuend[sub] - subtrahend[sub] + CV;
        sub -= 1;
    }
}
```

We check the new interim dividend to see whether it is zero. If it is, we have finished, if and only if we have brought down every digit of the dividend or our answer has exceeded the maximum number of digits. If we have finished, we jump to `wrapup`, where the answer is formatted appropriately.

If we have not finished, we lop off any leading zeros in the new intermediate dividend and bring down another digit from the original dividend. If we have already gone past the end of the dividend, then we bring down a zero, simply by appending it to the end of the new interim dividend.

After we bring down this digit, we compare the new interim dividend to the divisor. If it is less than the divisor, there is no point in guessing a quotient digit; we know that the guess will be zero. So we simply add a zero to the answer, bring down another digit and try the comparison again. Only when our interim dividend is greater than the divisor do we loop back to the beginning of the division process and try again.

Finally, we have a complete solution. Our only remaining task is to locate the decimal point. The rule for this is to compare the orders of magnitude of the divisor and the dividend. The first digit of the answer is x number of places from the decimal point, where a positive x is to the left of the decimal point and a negative x is to the right. The formula is:

$$x = \text{order (dividend)} - \text{order (divisor)} + y$$

where y is 1 when `strcmp(dividend, divisor)` is > 0; otherwise, $y = 0$. For example, $12/5 = 2.4$. Order(dividend) = 2, order(divisor) = 1, and $y = 0$. Hence, $x = 1$, and there is 1 digit to the left of the decimal point. Contrast this with $75/5 = 15$; the orders are the same as the previous example, but $y = 1$, so $x = 2$, and there are two digits to the left of the decimal point.

Knowing the location of the decimal point, we then load the digits into the `TermData` structure, carefully subtracting the `ASCII_VALUE` value, and we return from the division function.

There are certainly other approaches to the division operation. Some authors use a method of converting the numbers to base 256 and then applying a fast Fourier transform to help ascertain the next quotient guess.

We selected the current approach because it is intuitive and understandable. It allows readers who might want to optimize it to do so. Possible optimizations include not using character strings but instead using binary values, as we did in the other operations. The quick multiplication and subtraction functions could also be optimized by using the treatments shown when those operations were presented in detail. You can make the shifting of arrays to the right and left into in-line code rather than calling a function each time. Of these optimizations, the most challenging is certainly the conversion of character strings. If you retain the strings, a simple optimization is not to add and subtract `ASCII_VALUE` each time, but to put the values in a lookup table, similar to what we did in the multiplication section.

The code in Listing 8-21 shows the function declarations and the defined constants.

Listing 8-21.   The header file *longmath.h,* which shows the function declarations and globals for the calculator.

```
/*--- longmath.h -------------------------- Listing 8-20 ------
 *  Header file for arbitrary-precision arithmetic routines
 *  in longmath.c
 *-------------------------------------------------------------*/

#ifndef LONGMATH_H              /* avoid multiple inclusions */
#define LONGMATH_H   1

struct TermData {               /* the data for each term */
        char    *term;              /* the term */
        int     sign;               /* pos or neg; 0 = error */
        int     places_before;      /* before decimal point */
        int     places_after;       /* after decimal point */
};

#ifndef MAX_SIZE
#define MAX_SIZE     20         /* maximum length of a term. */
#endif                          /* Can be changed freely.    */


#define NORMAL        1         /* formats of terms */
#define SCIENTIFIC    2

#ifndef min
#define min(a,b) ((a) < (b) ? (a) : (b))
#define max(c,d) ((c) > (d) ? (c) : (d))
#endif


int  AsciiToTerm    ( char *, struct TermData * );
int  AsciiToScientific ( char * );
int  ComputeResult  ( struct TermData *, int,
                        struct TermData *, struct TermData * );
int  DivAtoin       ( const char *, int );
int  DivCheckZeroOnly   ( const char * );
void DivQuickMult   ( const char *, int, char * );
void DivQuickSub    ( char *, char *, char * );
void DivShiftArrayLeft      ( char * );
void DivShiftSmallArrayLeft ( char * );
void DivShiftArrayRight     ( char * );
int  DivSpecialCase ( const char *, const char * );
int  GetFileOperator( int *, FILE *, FILE * );
int  GetFileTerm    ( struct TermData * , FILE *, FILE * );
int  NormalAdd      ( struct TermData *, struct TermData *,
                        struct TermData * );
int  NormAbsCmp     ( struct TermData *, struct TermData * );
```

```
int   NormalDivide   ( struct TermData *, struct TermData *,
                                 struct TermData * );
int   NormalMultiply ( struct TermData *, struct TermData *,
                                 struct TermData * );
int   NormalSubtract ( struct TermData *, struct TermData *,
                                 struct TermData * );
char * strrev         ( char * ); /* for portability */
void TermInit         ( struct TermData * );
struct TermData *
      TermCopy        ( struct TermData *, struct TermData * );
struct TermData *
      TermCreate      ( void );
void TermToAscii      ( struct TermData *, char *, int );


#define DEC_LOC      MAX_SIZE     /* location of decimal point */

#endif
```

Final Notes about the Calculator

The calculator presented in this chapter is an application that is intended to demonstrate the use of arbitrary-precision arithmetic. It is not intended to be a production calculator. To make it into a full-fledged production calculator, even for only the arithmetic functions, a few enhancements should be considered:

- Any overflow should be detected. Currently, this implementation burdens the user to know the maximum width of the generated result. It does not check whether the width specified by the user is sufficient. Consider that if a number that is of order 10^{-20} is divided by a number of order 10^{20}, the resulting quotient will have at least 40 digits. A safe way to avoid this problem is to compile the routines with MAX_SIZE set to some value much larger than will ever be needed, such as 100 digits, for example.
- Some routines place terms on the stack. If you anticipate using more than 250 digits, these routines should place the terms on the heap rather than risk overflowing the stack. The trade-off, as ever, is performance.
- The scripting facility should allow for variables and for comments.
- The scripting facility as currently implemented shows error messages to the screen and simply notes in the output script that an error occurred.
- A good calculator would extend these routines by adding memory save/ restore, reciprocals, and exponentiation. It would also insert commas in the result to improve legibility, and would offer built-in constants such as π and e to the maximum precision available.

- It would be helpful to have some way of stating the needed number of digits after the decimal point. This feature is particularly desirable in calculations involving money.

Newton's Algorithm for Square Roots

As mentioned at the beginning of this chapter, one compelling reason for using arbitrary-precision routines is to obtain answers that are more accurate than the floating-point support offered by most C compilers and their standard libraries. A demonstration of the preceding routines is offered here to show their comparative accuracy.

The program presented in this section computes square roots by using an algorithm made famous by Isaac Newton in the eighteenth century. The program also calculates the square root generated by calling `sqrt()` from the standard C library—and compares the two results.

Newton's algorithm is derived from his work on solving polynomial equations [Knuth 1981]. The equation he proposes, taken from Robert Seeley's book *Calculus of One Variable* [Seeley 1972], is for a constant, c, where $c > 0$:

$$x_{n+1} = \frac{c + x^2_n}{2x_n}$$

The equation performs a series of approximations of the square root of c. Each approximation builds on the previous one. Once x_{n+1} is computed, it becomes x in the next iteration. The first value of x is a guess at the square root. In our implementation, this first guess is always $c/3$. You can perform the approximations as many times as necessary; whenever the user terminates the iterations, x_{n+1} is the then-computed square root of c.

In actual practice, the approximations should stop at one of two points. The first is when two successive iterations produce the same value of x_{n+1}. This value is the best square root that the method can approximate. The second occasion for stopping is when Newton's method starts to ping-pong back and forth between two values. For certain numbers—the method gets very close (generally slightly too small), then it iterates again and obtains a value that is slightly too large, and in the next iteration it obtains the previous number that was too small. At this point it enters a cycle that will always generate the same pair of values. In our implementation, we trap this condition by not allowing more than fifty approximations. Because almost all values that converge on a single square root do so long before fifty approximations, we arbitrarily set this limit as the point for breaking off further calculations. Listing 8-22 shows the driver for Newton's approximation of square roots.

Listing 8-22.   The driver for Newton's approximation of square roots.

```
/*--- sqrtmain.c ------------------------ Listing 8-22 -------
 * Uses the longmath routines to perform Newton's algorithm for
 * finding square roots. Compares the result to the C floating-
 * point function sqrt(). This implementation keeps approximating
 * until Newton's method no longer generates a difference
 * or until 50 iterations have been performed. Beyond 50
 * iterations, it is assumed that the algorithm is ping-ponging
 * around the final number. Square root of 525 with MAX_SIZE
 * = 20 is an example of this problem.
 *-----------------------------------------------------------*/

#include <stdio.h>
#include <stdlib.h>
#include <math.h>

#include "longmath.h"

main ( int argc, char *argv[] )
{

    int i;
    char buffer[2*MAX_SIZE];


    struct TermData *square;     /* the original number */

    struct TermData *xn,         /* variables in equation */
                    *xn1,
                    *product;

    struct TermData *two,        /* constants */
                    *three;

    struct TermData *temp1,      /* intermediate results */
                    *temp2,
                    *temp3,
                    *z;

    float fsquare, fsqrt;        /* the floats we'll compare to */

    square  = TermCreate();
    xn      = TermCreate();
    xn1     = TermCreate();
    product = TermCreate();
```

```
two      = TermCreate();
three    = TermCreate();

temp1    = TermCreate();
temp2    = TermCreate();
temp3    = TermCreate();
z        = TermCreate();


if ( argc < 2 )
{
    printf ( "Usage: sqrtmain number\n" );
    return;
}

AsciiToTerm ( argv[1], square );

/* no imaginary numbers in this version */

if ( square->sign == -1 )
{
    printf ( "Square cannot be negative\n" );
    return;
}

/* square root of zero is zero */

if ( square->places_before + square->places_after == 0 )
{
    printf ( "0\n" );
    return;
}

/*
 * We start with a guess of dividing square by 3, hence
 *          xn = square / 3.0
 */

AsciiToTerm ( "3.0", three );

if ( ! ComputeResult ( square, '/', three, xn ))
{
    printf ( "error 1\n" );
    return;
}


printf ( "Square root of %s\n", argv[1] );
```

```
TermToAscii ( xn, buffer, NORMAL );
printf ( "First guess is %s\n", buffer );

AsciiToTerm ( "2.0", two );

for ( i = 0; ; i++ ) /* repeat until root or max 50 loops */
{

    /* Newton's approach keeps approximating using
     * this formula:
     *  xn1 = ( square + ( xn * xn )) / ( 2.0 * xn )
     */

    TermCopy ( z, xn );
    if ( ! ComputeResult ( z, '*', xn, temp2 ))
    {
        printf ( "error 2\n" );
        return;
    }

    if ( ! ComputeResult ( square, '+', temp2, temp1 ))
    {
        printf ( "error 3\n" );
        return;
    }


    if ( ! ComputeResult ( two, '*', xn, temp3 ))
    {
        printf ( "error 4\n" );
        return;
    }

    if ( ! ComputeResult ( temp1, '/', temp3, xn1 ))
    {
        printf ( "error 5\n" );
        return;
    }

    TermToAscii ( xn1, buffer, NORMAL );
    printf ( "%2d %s\n", i, buffer );

    /* Are we done ? */

    if ( ! NormAbsCmp ( xn, xn1 ))
        break;

    if ( i > 49 )
    {
```

```
            printf ( "\nLast entry is the closest approxima"
                     "tion. Algorithm no longer converging\n" );
            break;
        }

        /* The current xn1 becomes the next xn */

        TermCopy ( xn, xn1 );
    }

    /* print the square root */

    TermToAscii ( xn1, buffer, NORMAL );
    printf ( "\nSquare root: %s\n", buffer );

    /* print the square of the square root */

    TermCopy ( xn, xn1 );
    if ( ! ComputeResult ( xn, '*', xn1, product ))
    {
        printf ( "error 6\n" );
        return;
    }

    TermToAscii ( product, buffer, NORMAL );
    printf ( "Computed square: %s\n", buffer );

    /* print the difference */

    if ( ! ComputeResult ( square, '-', product, xn ))
    {
        printf ( "error 7\n" );
        return;
    }
    TermToAscii ( xn, buffer, NORMAL );

    printf ( "Delta: %s\n", buffer );

    /* now test the built-in floating-point routines */

    fsquare = atof ( argv[1] );
    fsqrt = sqrt ( fsquare );

    printf ( "\n\nMath lib root: %4.12f, square: %4.12f\n",
             fsqrt, fsqrt * fsqrt );

    return;
}
```

The program expects the number whose root is to be found to be passed as a command-line argument. For example, to find the square root of 12, you enter the following:

```
sqrtmain 12
```

Figure 8-5 shows the output to the screen.

Figure 8-5.   Newton's approximations for the square root of 12.

```
Square root of 12
First guess is 4
 0 3.5
 1 3.4642857142857142857142857142857142857142857142857
 2 3.4641010369360827092728123598226633278121937855802
 3 3.4641016151378022584665807763904663020846013532384
 4 3.4641016151377487557588609078878572990155080515546
 5 3.4641016151377545287424513512372517455841129689613
 6 3.4641016151377545869965803058235924441288312523805
 7 3.4641016151377545864717683280006138189726781337505
 8 3.4641016151377545864717688527952736637176592254
 9 3.4641016151377545864717688469866020306341908931645
10 3.4641016151377545864717688469860189068623093018019
11 3.4641016151377545864717688469860188485441008817557
12 3.4641016151377545864717688469860188426603820170627
13 3.4641016151377545864717688469860188427186938175414
14 3.4641016151377545864717688469860188427186360824566
15 3.4641016151377545864717688469860188427186360877048
16 3.4641016151377545864717688469860188427186360877048

Square root: 3.4641016151377545864717688469860188427186360877048
Delta: 0.0000000000000000008080000888081608968096096768097


Math lib root: 3.464101552963, square: 11.999999569242
```

It took sixteen approximations for the algorithm to settle on a square root of 12. After listing the approximations, the program prints the square of the computed root and shows as `Delta` the difference between the computed square and the original square. On the last line is shown the square root and square of the root as obtained by using `sqrt(12)` from the standard C library.

This example shows that Newton's results are far more accurate than the standard math library. The preceding results use the library in Borland's C/C++ compiler, version 4.0. Values from other libraries show comparable disparities in accuracy. On a purely empirical basis, we have found that the standard math library routines are more accurate for values greater than ten million. Below that threshold, Newton's approximations are generally more accurate; however, every once in a while the standard math function will attain marginally better results. For an excellent discussion of Newton's algorithm, including how it works and how it can be optimized, see column 14 of Bentley [Bentley 1988].

An Amortization Table

The final listing of this chapter, Listing 8-23 shows an application that computes what amount of a given mortgage payment is applied to principal and interest on any given loan. It lists month by month the distribution of each payment (down to the fraction of a cent) for every payment until the loan is paid off. To apply the program for your own uses, pass the command-line arguments as explained in the comment box at the top of the listing. Note that interest is marked as a decimal, so that 12% is 0.12, 8½ is 0.085, and so forth. For best results the program should be compiled with that of MAX_SIZE defined as 10.

Listing 8-23.   The main line for a mortgage interest/principal calculator.

```
/*--- amrtmain.c ------------------------- Listing 8-23 -------
 * Loan amortization calculator. Enter the values for principal,
 * interest rate, and loan payment on the command line, where
 * -$ = principal, -r = rate, -p =payment. For example, a loan
 * of $250,000 at 7.5% with payments of $2900 is entered as:
 *
 *    amrtmain -r0.075  -$250000 -p2900
 *
 * Careful: minimal checking is done for entry errors. Under
 * UNIX the $ command line switch must be escaped: -\$5000
 * The program output consists of a table that shows the
 * outstanding principal, the amount of interest, and the
 * principal paid for each month of the loan.
 *-----------------------------------------------------------*/

#include <stdio.h>
#include <stdlib.h>
#include <string.h>

#include "longmath.h"

void ShowUsage ( void );
```

```
int main ( int argc, char *argv[] )
{
    struct TermData *principal, *rate, *payment;
    struct TermData *interest, *temp, *temp2;

    char buffer [7*MAX_SIZE];    /* buffer for output */

    int i, month;

    month      = 0;
    principal  = TermCreate();
    rate       = TermCreate();
    payment    = TermCreate();
    interest   = TermCreate();
    temp       = TermCreate();
    temp2      = TermCreate();

    /* try out various values */

    if ( argc != 4 )
    {
        ShowUsage();
        return ( EXIT_FAILURE );
    }

    for ( i = 1; i < argc; i++ )
    {
        char *p;
        if ( *argv[i] != '-' )
        {
            ShowUsage();
            return ( EXIT_FAILURE );
        }
        else
        {
            p = &argv[i][1];
            switch ( *p )
            {
                case '$':
                    AsciiToTerm ( p + 1, principal );
                    break;
                case 'p':
                    AsciiToTerm ( p + 1, payment );
                    break;
                case 'r':
                    AsciiToTerm ( p + 1, rate );
                    break;
                default:
```

```
                    fprintf ( stderr,
                             "Invalid switch: -%c\n", *p );
                    ShowUsage();
                    return ( EXIT_FAILURE );
            }
        }
    }

    /*
     * divide rate by 12 to get monthly rate,
     * then copy back to rate.
     */

    AsciiToTerm ( "12", temp );
    if ( ! ComputeResult ( rate, '/', temp, temp2 ))
    {
        printf ( "error 1\n" );
        return ( EXIT_FAILURE );
    }
    TermCopy ( rate, temp2 );

    /* print principal and monthly rate */

    memset ( buffer, ' ', MAX_SIZE * 7 );
    TermToAscii ( principal, buffer, NORMAL );

    buffer [strlen ( buffer )] = ' ';
    TermToAscii ( rate, buffer + MAX_SIZE * 2 + 3, NORMAL );
    buffer[strlen ( buffer )] = ' ';
    TermToAscii ( payment, buffer + MAX_SIZE * 4 + 3, NORMAL );

    printf (
        "Original Principal     Monthly Rate        Payment\n" );
    printf ( "%s\n\n", buffer );

    printf ( "Mnth Principal Left     Interest Paid" );
    printf ( "        Principal Paid\n" );

    /* print payments while principal > 0 */

    while ( principal->sign > 0 )
    {

        /* interest = principal * rate */

        if ( ! ComputeResult ( principal, '*', rate, interest ))
        {
            printf ( "error 2\n" );
```

```
            return ( EXIT_FAILURE );
        }

        /* temp = payment - interest */

        if ( ! ComputeResult ( payment, '-', interest, temp ))
        {
            printf ( "error 3\n" );
            return ( EXIT_FAILURE );
        }

        if ( temp->sign < 0 )
        {
            printf (
                "Monthly interest is > than monthly payment"
                "\nLoan will never be paid off\n" );
            return ( EXIT_FAILURE );
        }

        /* print month (same as payment number) */

        if (( month % 12 ) == 0 )
            printf ( "\n" );
        printf ( "%4d ", ++month );

        /* print: principal  interest  temp */

        memset ( buffer, ' ', MAX_SIZE * 7 );
        TermToAscii ( principal, buffer, NORMAL );
        buffer[strlen ( buffer )] = ' ';
        TermToAscii ( interest, buffer + MAX_SIZE * 2, NORMAL );
        buffer[strlen ( buffer )] = ' ';
        TermToAscii ( temp, buffer + MAX_SIZE * 4, NORMAL );
        printf ( "%s\n", buffer );

        /* principal = principal - temp */

        if ( ! ComputeResult ( principal, '-', temp, temp2 ))
        {
            printf ( "error 4\n" );
            return ( EXIT_FAILURE );
        }
        TermCopy ( principal, temp2 );
    }

    return ( EXIT_SUCCESS );
}
```

```
void ShowUsage ( void )
{
    printf (

  "Loan amortization calculator. Enter the principal,\n"
  "interest rate, and loan payment on the command line,\n"
  "where -$ = principal, -r = rate, -p =payment. For example,\n"
  "a loan of $250,000 at 7.5%% with payments of $2900 enter:\n\n"
  "    amrtmain -r0.075  -$250000 -p2900\n\n"
  "Note: UNIX users should enter the principal as -\\$250000\n" );
}
```

Resources and References

Bentley, Jon. *More Programming Pearls: Confessions of a Coder*. Reading, MA: Addison-Wesley, 1988. This is a true classic in the literature of algorithms. It is the second volume of Bentley's re-presentation of his "Programming Pearls" column in *Communications of the ACM*.

Knuth, Donald E. *The Art of Computer Programming*. Vol. 2: *Semi-Numerical Algorithms*, 2d ed. Reading, MA: Addison-Wesley, 1981. See pp. 250–312 for a discussion of arbitrary-precision arithmetic. Several other approaches have emerged since Knuth's treatment of this topic.

Nakamura, Shoichiro. *Applied Numerical Methods in C*. Englewood Cliffs, NJ: Prentice Hall, 1993. This is a textbook about numerical methods, with good explanations and several solutions in C.

Seeley, Robert. *Calculus of One Variable*. Glenview, IL: Scott, Foresman & Co., 1972. This is a college-level calculus textbook that cannot be recommended for pedagogical purposes.

Chapter 9

Data Compression

Data compression attempts to transform data so that it occupies less space. Two kinds of data compression exist today: **lossless** compression, in which no loss of data occurs during compression, and **lossy** compression, in which some data is lost and is not incorporated into the compressed data. With lossy compression, uncompression of the compressed file will not yield all the data of the original file. Lossy compression is used primarily to compress certain kinds of graphics files, where the need for very high compression is greater than the need to retain all the original data. For example, a high-resolution image compressed for shipment to a site with low resolution displays might sacrifice some detail for greater compression. Audio files can make similar trade-offs. In this chapter, only lossless algorithms are presented. That is, the algorithms guarantee that an uncompressed file will have the same data as the original file.

All data-compression techniques rely on the presence of data redundancy. They all examine the data to be compressed in order to find recurring characters or patterns of characters that can be represented by shorter symbols. The process of converting recurring characters or patterns into shorter symbols, known as **codes**, is called **encoding**; the process of translating codes back into the original characters or patterns is called **decoding**. A simple form of encoding is used by text editors that encode a sequence of spaces into the tab character. The tab character is the symbol that encodes the number of spaces necessary to reach the next tab stop.

If the compression algorithm can find no patterns to encode, no data compression will occur. At best, the output file in such cases will be the same size as the original; at worst (and more commonly the case), the compressed file will be larger than the original. This principle is inviolable: for all compression algorithms and each input file there exists a compressed version that cannot be further compressed. If this were not so, you could compress a file over and over until it shrank to a single character.

Other factors can make output files grow larger than the original file. One chief cause is housekeeping overhead. For an uncompression program to work properly, it often needs to have information about how the file was encoded. This information is generally passed in a header section at the beginning of the output file. In the previous example of converting spaces to tabs, an uncompression program must know where tab stops occur (every 4 columns, every 8 columns, and so on). The absence of this information in source files has often led programmers to manually realign code when a destination machine used different tab stops from those of the original machine. If the space-to-tab compression were part of a true data compression package, the compressed file would have the overhead of the tab-stop size.

There are other causes of expansion. Continuing with the previous example, we would run into difficulty in files where tabs should not be expanded to spaces. For example, certain entries in UNIX makefiles require tabs. To show that it should not be expanded, a tab would have to bear some kind of flag. The presence and meaning of this flag would have to be communicated to the uncompression program, incurring additional overhead.

Because the effectiveness of data compression (expressed as the ratio of encoded bytes to bytes of uncompressed data) is intimately tied to the patterns in the original data, it follows that the more you know about the data itself, the more efficiently you can compress it. As a result, ad hoc data-compression schemes can be developed that are extremely efficient for their intended data set, even though they may be unsatisfactory when applied in a different context. The algorithms presented in this chapter are all general-purpose compression schemes. Despite their universal nature, it will become clear that certain algorithms are far better than others on certain kinds of data.

Run-Length Encoding

Run-length encoding (RLE) is sometimes referred to as **recurrence coding**. Both names suggest the approach that this algorithm takes. It looks for sequences of recurring characters and collapses them into a single character, followed by a count showing how often that character occurs in the run.

For example, the string *AAAAAABBBBCCCC* could be compressed into a string that shows each character immediately followed by the number of times the character occurs: *A6B4C5*. This compressed string contains three codes (here, a letter-count combination) that are easily decoded into the original string. The encoded string occupies 6 bytes, while the original occupied 15. The compression efficiency of this one example is 40 percent. That is, the ratio of the compressed data's size to the original data's size, 6/15, is 0.4. The entropy is likewise 0.40; it takes 48 bits to encode 120 bits of data.

The limitation of this example is that it does not compress short runs of characters very well. Because a code requires two bytes, runs of two bytes are encoded but they save no space, and runs of a single letter are expanded if encoded. Hence, the string *AABCD* becomes *A2B1C1D1*. The encoded string is 8 bytes long, while the original string is only 5 bytes. Compression has not been effective.

To remedy this problem, we could encode sequences only when they contain three or more of the same character. All other characters go through uncompressed. To identify the beginning of a sequence in the compressed file, we use a flag byte that identifies the next two bytes as a compression code. In this manner, the entire code occupies three bytes: a flag byte, the character that forms the sequence, and the count of repetitions. For example, *AAAAABC* becomes [*flag byte*]*A5BC*. This scheme is used in the implementation that follows and is the way that RLE is commonly implemented.

The flag byte, also called a **sentinel**, requires special consideration. If the sentinel occurs naturally within the text being compressed, it has to be treated specially. A simple way of handling it is to encode it and give it a count of 1. Hence, if we were to use a sentinel of 0xFF, we would get the following possibilities:

- Code for the sequence *AAAAA*:
  0xFF, 'A', 5   (regular compression code)
- Code for a naturally occurring byte of 0xFF:
  0xFF, 0xFF, 1   (sentinel in input text)

With this approach, a solitary sentinel byte that occurs in the input expands the resulting output. Hence, the sentinel value should be chosen carefully so that it is not likely to occur frequently in the input file. (Note that every sentinel byte in the input does not necessarily generate a 3-byte code. If two successive sentinels appear, the count in the code is simply changed to a 2; this is true also for 3 or more successive sentinels. Only runs of 1 or 2 sentinel bytes in the input expand the output.) An optimization suggests itself here. Because only the sentinel byte can have counts of 1 or 2, we encode sentinel runs of 1 or 2 by using only two bytes: the sentinel byte followed by a count of either 1 or 2. There is no need to add the value of the byte to be repeated, since we know from the count that the repeating byte can be only the sentinel.

By this scheme, the overhead of processing a solitary sentinel byte in the input file is reduced to just 2 bytes.

In the implementation of RLE shown in Listing 9-1 (*rle1.c*), codes are arranged in a slightly different order: sentinel byte, count, and repeating byte. This order is mandated by the optimization discussed just previously. Note that the maximum count is the maximum value of a byte: 255. Recurring sequences larger than 255 bytes are broken down into a series of codes, each representing a 255-byte segment.

Listing 9-1.   Encoder for run-length encoding compression.

```
/*--- rle1.c --------------------------- Listing 9-1 ---------
 *  Run-Length Encoding for files of all types
 *
 *------------------------------------------------------------*/

#include <stdio.h>
#include <stdlib.h>

#define Sentinel    0xF0    /* the sentinel flag */
#define BUFFER_SIZE 30000

#define WriteCode(a,b,c) \
        fprintf( outfile, "%c%c%c", a, b, c )

FILE *infile,
     *outfile;

int main ( int argc, char *argv[] )
{
    char *buffer;
    char prev_char;
    int  bytes_read,
         count,
         eof,
         first_time,
         i;

    if ( argc != 3 )
    {
        fprintf ( stderr, "Performs standard RLE compression\n"
                          "Usage: rle1 infile outfile\n" );
        return ( EXIT_FAILURE );
    }

    if (( infile = fopen ( argv[1], "rb" )) == NULL )
```

```
{
    fprintf ( stderr, "Error opening %s\n", argv[1] );
    return ( EXIT_FAILURE );
}

if (( outfile = fopen ( argv[2], "wb" )) == NULL )
{
    fprintf ( stderr, "Error opening %s\n", argv[2] );
    return ( EXIT_FAILURE );
}

/* write the header to the output file */

fprintf ( outfile, "%c%c%c%c", 'R', 'L', '1', Sentinel );

/* initialize the necessary variables */

eof       = 0;
first_time = 1;

buffer = (char *) malloc ( BUFFER_SIZE );
if ( buffer == NULL )
{
    fprintf ( stderr, "Unable to allocate %d bytes\n",
              BUFFER_SIZE );
    return ( EXIT_FAILURE );
}

/* process the input file */

while ( ! eof )
{
    bytes_read = fread ( buffer, 1, BUFFER_SIZE, infile );
    if ( bytes_read == 0 )
    {
        eof = 1;
        break;
    }

    for ( i = 0; i < bytes_read; i++ )
    {
        /* first time through is a special case */

        if ( first_time )
        {
            prev_char = buffer[i];
            count = 1;
            first_time = 0;
```

```
            i++;
        }

        if ( buffer[i] == prev_char )    /* repeated char */
        {
            count += 1;
            if ( count == 255 )
            {
                WriteCode ( Sentinel, count, prev_char );
                count = 0;
            }
            continue;
        }
        else    /* a new char, so write out all known data */
        {
            if ( count < 3 )
            {
                if ( prev_char == Sentinel )
                {
                    fprintf ( outfile, "%c%c",
                                    Sentinel, count );
                }
                else
                    do
                    {
                        fputc ( prev_char, outfile );
                    }
                    while ( --count );
            }
            else
                WriteCode ( Sentinel, count, prev_char );

            prev_char = buffer[i];
            count = 1;
        }
    }

    /* we're at end of bytes_read, is it EOF? */

    if ( bytes_read < BUFFER_SIZE )
        eof = 1;
}

/* at EOF, so flush out any remaining bytes to be written */

if ( count < 3 )
{
    if ( prev_char == Sentinel )
```

```
    {
        fprintf ( outfile, "%c%c",
                        Sentinel, count );
    }
    else
        do
        {
            fputc ( prev_char, outfile );
        }
        while ( --count );
}
else
    WriteCode ( Sentinel, count, prev_char );

fclose ( infile );
fclose ( outfile );

return ( EXIT_SUCCESS );
}
```

The program in Listing 9-1 is straightforward. Data is read in, byte by byte. If the current byte is different from the previous byte, the previous byte is written to the output file, and the current byte is saved. If the current byte is the same as the previous byte, a counter is incremented. If the counter gets past 3 (the minimum length to make encoding efficient), then the next different byte will force the compression code to be formulated and written to the output file. Sentinels (here chosen quite arbitrarily as 0xF0) that occur naturally in text are also monitored and handled as previously discussed.

One detail to note is that before writing any compressed data, the program writes header information to the output file. This header consists of four bytes: the first three bytes contain the letters RL1, and the last byte contains the sentinel value. At minimum, a header of one byte is needed to identify the sentinel-byte value. The string RL1 is used to confirm that the uncompression program is being applied to the correct kind of compressed file. There is nothing magic about the letters RL1; any sufficiently informative value would work.

The RLE implementation could be enhanced regarding the selection of the sentinel value. Previous discussion showed that single sentinel bytes occurring naturally in the input file could expand in the output file. Therefore, it makes sense to monitor the frequency of naturally occurring sentinels in the input file. If they pass a preestablished threshold, it makes sense to change sentinels. We can do this by using a code value that is not defined: a code containing a sentinel byte followed by a count of zero. Hence, to change the sentinel from 0xF0 to 0xF4, the following code could be issued: 0xF0, 0, 0xF4. Upon detecting the zero-count byte after the sentinel code, the uncompression program would know that the next byte represents the new sentinel.

The ability of a data-compression algorithm to change the way it handles data in order to obtain better efficiency makes the algorithm **adaptive**. Many techniques for data compression are adaptive, especially where compression effectiveness is more important than compression speed. For example, the Huffman algorithm, presented later in this chapter, reads the input file twice: once to establish the frequency of every character in the input file, and a second time to use the character frequencies to obtain maximal compression.

The adaptive dimension suggested here is not implemented in this version of RLE (nor in most versions) because RLE is designed to be fast and simple. The less the overhead, the better. In addition, RLE is almost always used on known data sets (such as databases), where the likelihood of choosing an effective sentinel is high.

The uncompression routines for RLE (see Listing 9-2, *unrle1.c*) read the compressed file, check for the RL1 signature in the header, and use the next byte as the sentinel value. The program then reads through the file, passing any regular characters through to the output file and expanding any codes announced by the sentinel value. Both the compression and uncompression routines use large input buffers (30,000 bytes) to accelerate processing. Much of the code in the uncompression routines handles the problem of a compression code falling across the boundary of a buffer. Other than this housekeeping issue, the code is comparatively straightforward.

Listing 9-2. Decoder for run-length encoding uncompression.

```
/*--- unrle1.c --------------------------- Listing 9-2 --------
 *   Uncompresses rle1 files
 *
 *----------------------------------------------------------*/

#include <stdio.h>
#include <stdlib.h>

#define BUFFER_SIZE 30000

FILE *infile,
     *outfile;

int main ( int argc, char *argv[] )
{
    char *buffer,
         sentinel;
```

```
int  bytes_read,
     count,
     i;

/*--- process files open ---*/

if ( argc != 3 )
{
    fprintf ( stderr, "Uncompresses RLE1-compressed file\n"
                      "Usage: unrle1 infile outfile\n" );
    return ( EXIT_FAILURE );
}

if (( infile = fopen ( argv[1], "rb" )) == NULL )
{
    fprintf ( stderr, "Error opening %s\n", argv[1] );
    return ( EXIT_FAILURE );
}

if (( outfile = fopen ( argv[2], "wb" )) == NULL )
{
    fprintf ( stderr, "Error opening %s\n", argv[2] );
    return ( EXIT_FAILURE );
}

/*--- allocate input buffer ---*/

buffer = (char *) malloc ( BUFFER_SIZE );
if ( buffer == NULL )
{
    fprintf ( stderr, "Unable to allocate %d bytes\n",
              BUFFER_SIZE );
    return ( EXIT_FAILURE );
}

/*--- check the file header ---*/

bytes_read = fread ( buffer, 1, 4, infile );
if ( bytes_read != 4 )
{
    fprintf ( stderr, "Unable to read %s\n", argv[1] );
    return ( EXIT_FAILURE );
}

if ( buffer[0] == 'R' && buffer[1] == 'L' &&
     buffer[2] == '1' )
        sentinel = buffer[3];
else
```

```
{
    fprintf ( stderr, "%s is not an RLE 1 file\n", argv[1] );
    return ( EXIT_FAILURE );
}


/*--- process the file ---*/

while ( 1 )      /* loop until break occurs */
{
    bytes_read = fread ( buffer, 1, BUFFER_SIZE, infile );
    if ( bytes_read == 0 )
        break;

    for ( i = 0; i < bytes_read; i++ )
    {
        if ( buffer[i] != sentinel )
            fputc ( buffer[i], outfile );
        else
        {        /* process sentinel */

            if ( i > bytes_read - 3 ) /* near buffer end */
            {
                if ( i > bytes_read - 2 ) /* no bytes left */
                {
                    bytes_read = fread ( buffer, 1,
                                BUFFER_SIZE, infile );
                    if ( bytes_read < 2 )
                    {
                        fprintf ( stderr,
                                "error in %s\n", argv[1] );
                        fclose ( infile );
                        unlink ( argv[2] );
                        return ( EXIT_FAILURE );
                    }
                    else
                    {
                        i = -1;
                        goto process_count;
                    }
                }
                else                        /* one byte left */
                {
                    if ( buffer[i + 1] < 3 )
                        goto process_count;

                    count = buffer[i + 1];

                    bytes_read = fread ( buffer, 1,
```

```
                            BUFFER_SIZE, infile );
            if ( bytes_read < 1 )
            {
                fprintf ( stderr,
                            "error in %s\n", argv[1] );
                fclose ( infile );
                unlink ( argv[2] );
                return ( EXIT_FAILURE );
            }

            i = 0;
            do
            {
                fputc ( buffer[i], outfile );
            }
                while ( --count );
        }


    }
    else                       /* not end of buffer */
    {
      process_count:

        count = buffer[++i];

        switch ( count )     /* what's the count? */
        {
            case 0:
                fprintf ( stderr,
                            "error in %s\n", argv[1] );
                fclose ( infile );
                unlink ( argv[2] );
                return ( EXIT_FAILURE );
            case 1:
                fputc ( sentinel, outfile );
                break;
            case 2:
                fputc ( sentinel, outfile );
                fputc ( sentinel, outfile );
                break;
            default:
                i += 1;
                do
                {
                    fputc ( buffer[i], outfile );
                }
                    while ( --count );
                break;
```

```
                }
            }
        }
    }

    if ( bytes_read < BUFFER_SIZE )
        break;
}

fclose ( infile );
fclose ( outfile );

return ( EXIT_SUCCESS );
}
```

As currently implemented, the code for both compression and uncompression is surprisingly fast. However, it could be made faster. The output routine must necessarily output characters one at a time (it uses `fputc()`), which makes for slow output. We could increase the speed by writing the bytes to a buffer in memory that is written to disk when it is full and at EOF. In this way, multiple characters are written to disk in one operation rather than one at a time. In actual fact, the writes from `fputc()` are buffered by the compiler library, but these buffers tend to be small—generally 512 bytes or 1,024 bytes.

A further refinement would be to put some sort of checksum into the header of the compressed file. This checksum would be used by the uncompression routine to make sure that the uncompressed file has the same content as the originally compressed file. More information on checksums appears in Chapter 10.

Run-length encoding of the kind examined so far is widely used in business contexts because most databases allocate fixed-length data fields such as customer name, customer address, and the like. In such databases, unused bytes at the end of a field are padded with spaces. Therefore, database records provide an ideal context for run-length compression: sequences of repeating spaces and a low likelihood that a well-chosen sentinel will collide with an actual data byte. When applied to databases, run-length encoding can often obtain compression substantially better than 50 percent, and it is both fast and easy to implement. For these reasons, it has appeared as the default compression scheme for ISAM files on Wang systems, in the pack option of IBM's VM/370 copyfile utility, and by the ARC file compression utility for BBSs.

There are numerous other ways to implement run-length encoding. Microsoft uses run-length encoding in Windows files that bear the .RLE extension. In Microsoft's implementation, the compressed file (a graphics file) contains records that specify the row where the color values are to be displayed, followed by compression codes that specify the color to display and how many pixels should display it. While this method abandons the traditional sentinel-code approach, it retains the use of a code value to indicate a repeating pattern of identical values. For more information on Microsoft's RLE files, consult Tom Swan's book on Windows file formats [Swan 1994].

A natural extension to run-length encoding is a compression scheme that uses codes to indicate repetitions of patterns that are each larger than one byte. An example, is the use of a run-length encoding for entire strings that might recur several times in a file. This family of algorithms is discussed later in this chapter in the section Sliding-Window Compression.

Huffman Compression

Huffman compression, named after a paper by D. A. Huffman [Huffman 1952] tackles the problem of data compression by examining the input files and seeing which characters occur the most frequently. The Huffman algorithm then assigns bit codes to the individual characters, using short bit codes for the most common characters and longer bit codes for less common characters. At the front end of the output file, a header is written, giving the bit equivalents for each character. The bit codes for each input character are then written to the output file. The uncompression algorithm reads the encoded file and reverses the process, translating bit codes back into the original characters according to the translation information in the header.

Huffman's approach uses a binary tree to convert the individual characters to codes. The idea is simple. Consider a binary tree in which the data items reside only in the leaves (or external nodes). The path from the root of the tree to a given leaf can be taken as the binary code for the data in that leaf by recording descent to the left as a 0, and descent to the right as 1.

For example, the tree in Figure 9-1 gives a variable-length coding scheme for three letters: h, a, and t. The code for h is 00, for a is 01, and for t is 1. To obtain these values, proceed from the root of the tree toward the desired letter, keeping track of each path as you descend the tree. If you go left, add a 0 to the code; if you go right, add a 1. Hence, h requires two descents to the left, giving us 00. t requires one descent to the right, giving us 1.

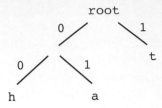

Figure 9-1. A simple binary tree with data stored only in the leaves.

Using this unambiguous scheme to encode a longer message is straight-forward. For example, we could encode *that* as 100011 (from the four codes for the letters—1-00-01-1). To decode these bits, we merely reverse the process. Starting with 1, we go to the right and find that we have arrived at an external node and we write its data, *t*. Likewise, 00 takes us to *h*, 01 takes us to *a*, and finally 1 takes us to the terminal *t*. Note that because this scheme is built on a binary tree, it can guarantee that the codes for each letter are mutually exclusive.

While it is clear that any binary tree that has an external node for each possible character in the input file could be used for this compression scheme, some binary trees are better than others. In particular, we would like commonly used letters to have short bit sequences (that is, to be near the top of the tree), while infrequently used letters should be near the bottom. We did this in Figure 9-1 by placing *t* near the top and giving it a one-bit sequence, while *h* and *a* have two-bit sequences. Huffman's algorithm attacks the construction of the binary tree and its use for creating codes. The algorithm involves the following steps:

1. Scan the input file and tally the number of occurrences of each input character.
2. Consider these symbol/tally pairs as the external nodes of a nascent binary tree. Find the two nodes with the smallest tallies, and create a parent node that joins the two. Set this parent node's tally to the sum of the child node's tallies.
3. Repeat step 2 until all nodes are part of a single binary tree.

To make this concept concrete, consider the 11-character string *abracadabra*. First, we tally the frequency of occurrence of each letter:

Letter	Occurrences
a	5
b	2
c	1
d	1
r	2

Next, we construct the tree as shown in Figure 9-2. In step 1, we put the nodes in order. When two nodes have equal tallies, either node can go first. Then, in step 2, we start the process of constructing parent nodes. Picking the two nodes that have the smallest tallies (*c* and *d*), we construct a new parent and give it a tally of 2 (the sum of the tallies of *c* and *d*). In step 3, we repeat this process with *r* and *b*. At this point, there are three free parent nodes: a, with a tally of 5; the parent of *r* and *b*, with a tally of 4; and the parent of *c* and *d*, with a tally of 2. In step 4, we construct a parent for the smallest of these three, and then finally construct a single parent node to tie the whole tree together.

Encoding is now easy: the bit string for *a* is 0, for *b* is 101, and so on. The final result is as follows:

a	*b*	*r*	*a*	*c*	*a*	*d*	*a*	*b*	*r*	*a*
0	101	100	0	110	0	111	0	101	100	0

Or, grouping the bits into blocks of four bits each and translating the bits into a hexadecimal produces this result:

0101	1000	1100	1110	1011	000
5	8	C	E	B	0

By this approach, we have compressed 11 bytes into 3. While this savings seems fairly impressive, keep in mind that the output file will also need to contain the tree structure in order to allow decoding, and these additional overhead bytes may consume a large portion of our savings.

Notice that this tree places the most common character (*a*) near the top of the tree and assigns it the shortest possible bit string. All other codes are 3 bits long.

Step 1: Put the nodes in order.

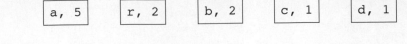

Step 2: Construct a new parent node for the two
nodes that have the smallest tallies.

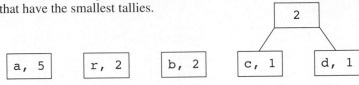

Step 3: Again, construct a new parent node for the two nodes that have
the smallest tallies.

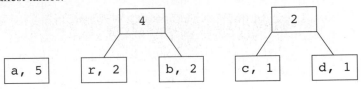

Step 4: Twice more, construct a parent node.

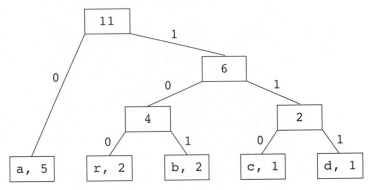

Figure 9-2.   Constructing a Huffman tree for *abracadabra*.

The Code

The code required to implement Huffman encoding is straightforward, and is
shown as *huffenc.c*, *huffdec.c*, and *huffman.h* in Listings 9-3 through 9-5
respectively. Each program contains a test driver so that usage is clear. The
test driver also displays various internal statistics and tables when the appropriate variables are defined.

Looking at the compression routine, shown in Listing 9-3, the principal routine is HuffEncode(). This routine initializes the array in which the tallies are kept, and then calls HuffScan() to accumulate tallies, HuffBuild() to build the tree, and HuffCompress() to generate the output file. The Huffman tree is built into the array HuffTree[], which is actually an array of structures. Interestingly, we can determine in advance the maximum size of this array. With a little thought, it becomes obvious to us that a tree with *N* external nodes (or leaves) must have had *N-1* internal nodes. For example, a two-leaf tree needs one parent. Thus, in *huffman.h*, we define MAXSYMBOLS as 256 (one for each possible character) and MAXNODES as MAXSYMBOLS*2-1. Then, in our array, the first 256 structures are used as the leaf nodes of the tree, with the *i*'th entry corresponding to the character with the ASCII code equal to *i*. We then build the structures for the parent (internal) nodes by using the remaining structures in the array. The links between nodes can then be simply indexes into the array.

Listing 9-3. Routines for Huffman encoding, including a sample driver.

```
/*--- huffenc.c ------------------------- Listing 9-3 ---------
 * Purpose:        Compress an input file, using the Huffman
 *                 encoding technique
 *
 * Entry point:    int HuffEncode (FILE *infile, FILE *outfile)
 *
 *                 Will compress infile into outfile. Both files
 *                 should already be open in binary mode. They
 *                 will be closed by HuffEncode().
 *
 *                 HuffEncode() returns:
 *                     0: success
 *                     1: error while reading in
 *                     2: no data in input file
 *                     3: malloc() failed
 *                     4: error while writing out
 *
 * Switches:       DRIVER - compiles a test driver
 *                 DUMP - dumps Huffman tree at various points
 *                 SHOWSTATS - provides compression statistics
 *-------------------------------------------------------------*/
#define DRIVER
#define SHOWSTATS
#define DUMP

#include <stdio.h>
#include <stdlib.h>
```

```
#include <string.h>
#include <ctype.h>
#include "huffman.h"

#if defined(SHOWSTATS)
#define STATS(x) x
CountType HuffBytesHdr; /* no. header bytes in output file */
CountType HuffBytesOut; /* no. data bytes in output file */
#else
#define STATS(x)
#endif

CountType HuffBytesIn; /* count of bytes in input file */

/*
 * The Huffman tree is built in this array. The ith entry
 * coresponds to the symbol i, so we do not explicitly store
 * the corresponding symbol in the array. The child and parent
 * links are also indexes into the array.
 */
struct _HuffTree {
    CountType count;
    LinkType child[2];
    LinkType parent;
    char *hcode;          /* points to bit code */
    int bitcount;         /* number of bits in bit code */
} HuffTree[MAXNODES];

LinkType HuffRoot;        /* tree's root */
LinkType HuffCount;       /* number of internal nodes */
char *HuffTable = NULL;   /* table of bit codes */
char *HuffTablePtr;       /* points to free space in table */
unsigned HuffBytes;       /* size of bit code table */

#ifdef DUMP
static void HuffDump ( LinkType n )
{
    LinkType i;

    printf ( "root is %d\n", HuffRoot );
    printf ( "No.  Sym   Count  Parent   "
             "Left  Right  BitNo  Bits\n" );
    for ( i = 0; i <= n; i++ )
    {
        if ( HuffTree[i].count )
        {
            printf( "%3d. ", i );
            if ( i < MAXSYMBOLS )
```

```
                {
                    if ( isprint ( i ))
                        printf ( " %c ", i );
                    else
                        printf ( "x%.2X", i );
                }
                else
                    printf ( "n/a" );
                printf ( " %7ld   %5d  %5d  %5d",
                        HuffTree[i].count,
                        HuffTree[i].parent,
                        HuffTree[i].child[LEFT],
                        HuffTree[i].child[RIGHT] );

                if ( HuffTree[i].hcode )
                {
                    int j, k;
                    int byte, bit;

                    j = HuffTree[i].bitcount;
                    printf ( "  %5d  ", j );
                    for ( k = 0; k < j; k++ )
                    {
                        byte = k / 8;
                        bit = k - byte * 8;
                        if ( HuffTree[i].hcode[byte] &
                                        ( 1 << ( 7-bit )))
                            printf ( "1" );
                        else
                            printf ( "0" );
                    }
                }
                printf ( "\n" );
            }
        }
    printf( "\n" );
}


#define DUMPTREE(x) HuffDump(x)
#else
#define DUMPTREE(x)
#endif

/* scan the input file and acquire statistics */

static int HuffScan ( FILE *infile )
{
    int c;
```

```
    HuffBytesIn =  0;
    while (( c = fgetc ( infile )) != EOF )
    {
        HuffTree[c].count++;
        HuffBytesIn++;
    }

    if ( ferror ( infile ))
        return ( 1 );
    else
    {
        rewind ( infile );
        return ( 0 );
    }
}

/* walk the tree, either to get statistics or build bit table */
static void HuffWalk ( LinkType k, int depth )
{
    int dir, bitno, set, byte, bit;
    LinkType w, trace;

    for ( dir = 0; dir < 2; dir++ )
    {
        if ( HuffTree[k].child[dir] == -1 )
        {
            if (dir == LEFT)  /* Left and right are same */
            {
                if ( ! HuffTablePtr )
                    HuffBytes += ( depth + 7 ) / 8;
                else
                {
                    /* second pass, build the codes */
                    HuffTree[k].bitcount = depth;
                    HuffTree[k].hcode = HuffTablePtr;
                    bitno = depth - 1;

                    /* run up the parent links */
                    for ( trace = k, w = HuffTree[k].parent;
                          w;
                          trace = w, w = HuffTree[w].parent )
                    {

                        /* which way did we come? */
                        if ( HuffTree[w].child[LEFT] == trace )
                            set = LEFT;
                        else
                            set = RIGHT;
```

```
                        /* record the bit */
                        if ( set )
                        {
                            byte = bitno / 8;
                            bit = bitno - byte * 8;
                            HuffTablePtr[byte] |=
                                        1 << ( 7 - bit );
                        }
                        bitno--;
                    }
                    HuffTablePtr += ( depth + 7 ) / 8;
                }
            }
        }
        else
            HuffWalk ( HuffTree[k].child[dir], depth + 1 );
    }
}

/* build the internal nodes */
static int HuffBuild ( void )
{

    LinkType i, k, lo1, lo2;

    /* count active nodes */
    for ( i = 0; i < MAXSYMBOLS; i++ )
        if ( HuffTree[i].count )
            HuffCount++;

    /* ensure we have at least two active nodes */
    if ( HuffCount < 1 )
        return ( 2 );
    if ( HuffCount == 1 )
    {
        for ( i = 0; i < MAXSYMBOLS; i++ )
            if ( HuffTree[i].count == 0 )
            {
                HuffTree[i].count++;
                HuffCount++;
                break;
            }
    }

    HuffRoot = MAXSYMBOLS + HuffCount - 2;

    /* build the internal nodes */
    for ( i = MAXSYMBOLS; i <= HuffRoot; i++ )
```

```
{
    /* first, find two smallest nodes */
    for ( k = 0; k < i; k++ )
    {
        if ( HuffTree[k].count && !HuffTree[k].parent )
        {
            lo1 = k;
            k++;
            break;
        }
    }

    for ( ; k < i; k++ )
    {
        if ( HuffTree[k].count && !HuffTree[k].parent )
        {
            lo2 = k;
            k++;
            break;
        }
    }

    for ( ; k < i; k++ )
    {
        if ( HuffTree[k].count && !HuffTree[k].parent )
        {
            if ( HuffTree[k].count < HuffTree[lo1].count )
                lo1 = k;
            else
            if ( HuffTree[k].count < HuffTree[lo2].count )
                lo2 = k;
        }
    }

    /* now, build the new node and update the tree */
    HuffTree[i].count = HuffTree[lo1].count +
                        HuffTree[lo2].count;
    HuffTree[i].child[LEFT]  = lo1;
    HuffTree[i].child[RIGHT] = lo2;
    HuffTree[lo1].parent = HuffTree[lo2].parent = i;
}

/* build the bit codes */
HuffBytes = 0;
HuffTablePtr = NULL;
HuffWalk ( HuffRoot, 0 );

HuffTable = (char *) malloc ( HuffBytes );
```

```
    memset ( HuffTable, 0, HuffBytes );
    if (! HuffTable )
        return ( 3 );
    HuffTablePtr = HuffTable;
    HuffWalk ( HuffRoot, 0 );

    return ( 0 );
}

/* create the output file */
static int HuffCompress ( FILE *infile, FILE *outfile )
{
    LinkType i;
    struct _Header header;
    int outchar, outbit, c;
    char sig[] = SIGNATURE;

    STATS ( HuffBytesHdr = 0 );
    STATS ( HuffBytesOut = 0 );

    /* signature bytes */
    fwrite ( sig, strlen ( sig ) + 1, 1, outfile );
    STATS ( HuffBytesHdr += strlen ( sig ) + 1 );

    /* the root pointer */
    fwrite ( &HuffRoot, sizeof ( HuffRoot ), 1, outfile );
    STATS ( HuffBytesHdr += sizeof ( HuffRoot ));

    /* the number of internal nodes */
    fwrite ( &HuffCount, sizeof ( HuffCount ), 1, outfile );
    STATS ( HuffBytesHdr += sizeof ( HuffCount ));

    /* the character count */
    fwrite ( &HuffBytesIn, sizeof ( HuffBytesIn ), 1, outfile );
    STATS ( HuffBytesHdr += sizeof ( HuffBytesIn ));

    /* the active nodes */
    for ( i = 0; i <= HuffRoot; i++ )
    {
        if ( HuffTree[i].count )
        {
            header.index = i;
            header.child[0] = HuffTree[i].child[0];
            header.child[1] = HuffTree[i].child[1];
            fwrite ( &header, sizeof ( header ), 1, outfile );
            STATS( HuffBytesHdr += sizeof ( header ));
        }
    }
```

```
/* now, compress the input file */
outchar = 0; /* build up output bytes here */
outbit = 0;
while (( c = fgetc ( infile )) != EOF )
{
    char *s;
    int k, count, byte, bit, set;

    s = HuffTree[c].hcode;
    count = HuffTree[c].bitcount;

    /* translate character into bit codes */
    for ( k = 0; k < count; k++ )
    {
        byte = k / 8;
        bit = k - byte * 8;
        if ( s[byte] & ( 1 << ( 7-bit )))
            set = 1;
        else
            set = 0;

        if ( set )
            outchar |= 1 << ( 7 - outbit );
        outbit++;
        if ( outbit == 8 )
        {
            fputc ( outchar, outfile );
            outchar = 0;
            outbit = 0;
            STATS ( HuffBytesOut++ );
        }
    }
}

/* do the last byte, if necessary */
if ( outbit )
{
    fputc ( outchar, outfile );
    STATS ( HuffBytesOut++ );
}

if ( ferror ( infile ))
    return ( 1 );
if ( ferror ( outfile ))
    return ( 4 );

return ( 0 );
}
```

```c
int HuffEncode ( FILE *infile, FILE *outfile )
{
    int retval;
    LinkType i;

    /* set all counts to zero */

    HuffRoot = 0;
    HuffCount = 0;
    memset ( HuffTree, 0, sizeof ( HuffTree ));
    for ( i = 0; i < MAXSYMBOLS; i++)
    {
        HuffTree[i].child[LEFT]  = -1;
        HuffTree[i].child[RIGHT] = -1;
    }

    /* do frequency counts */
    if ( retval = HuffScan ( infile ))
        goto done;

    /* build the tree */
    if ( retval = HuffBuild() )
        goto done;

    DUMPTREE ( HuffRoot );

    /* compress the data file */
    retval = HuffCompress ( infile, outfile );

    #if defined(SHOWSTATS)
    if ( ! retval )
    {
        printf ( "The input file contained %lu bytes\n",
                    HuffBytesIn );
        printf ( "The output file contained %lu header bytes "
                "and %lu data bytes\n",
                    HuffBytesHdr, HuffBytesOut );
        printf ( "Output file %lu%% the size of input file\n",
                    (( HuffBytesHdr + HuffBytesOut ) * 100 ) /
                    HuffBytesIn );
    }
    #endif

  done:
    fclose ( infile );
    fclose ( outfile );
    return ( retval );
}
```

```
/*------------------------------------------------------------------
 * The following driver for the previous routines is active
 * if DRIVER is defined.
 *----------------------------------------------------------------*/
#ifdef DRIVER
int main ( int argc, char *argv[] )
{
    FILE *infile, *outfile;
    int retval;

    if ( argc != 3 )
    {
        fprintf( stderr, "Usage: huffenc infile outfile\n" );
        return ( EXIT_FAILURE );
    }

    infile = fopen ( argv[1], "r+b" );
    if ( infile == NULL )
    {
        fprintf ( stderr, "can't open %s for input\n", argv[1] );
        return ( EXIT_FAILURE );
    }

    outfile = fopen ( argv[2], "w+b" );
    if ( outfile == NULL )
    {
        fprintf ( stderr, "can't open %s for output\n", argv[2]);
        return ( EXIT_FAILURE );
    }

    if ( retval = HuffEncode ( infile, outfile ))
    {
        printf( "compression failed: " );
        if ( retval == 1 )
            printf ( "input error\n" );
        else
        if ( retval == 2 )
            printf ( "empty tree\n" );
        else
        if ( retval == 3 )
            printf ( "malloc failed\n" );
        else
        if ( retval == 4 )
            printf ( "output error\n" );
        else
            printf("\n");
        return  ( retval );
    }
```

```
    else
    {
        printf ( "%s was compressed into %s\n",
                                      argv[1], argv[2] );
        return ( EXIT_SUCCESS );
    }
}
#endif
```

Looking now at the three workhorse routines, the first, `HuffScan()`, reads the input file and increments the tally for every character it reads. It does this to establish the frequency of each character in the input file in order to have the tallies for building the code tree.

The second routine, `HuffBuild()`, is somewhat more complex. It starts by counting the number of nodes with a nonzero tally. Once this number is ascertained, the number of parent nodes required can be computed directly. Then the routine builds the parent nodes by making multiple passes through the nodes and finding the smallest pair of tallies on each pass. This scan always starts with the external nodes and then goes to the internal (parent) nodes.

The next problem is to compute the bit codes for each character. We start by recursively walking the tree (see `HuffWalk()`) and counting the depth of each external node. This depth is rounded up to the nearest multiple of 8, thus giving the number of bytes required to conveniently encode each character, starting on a byte boundary. Then we walk the tree again, and this time the code for each character is computed and stored in a buffer. This second walk is the reason for the parent link in the tree; it makes it easy for us to unravel the recursive path and compute the needed bit string. The approach of building the code for each character in an appropriately sized buffer is necessary because we cannot predict the length of the longest code sequence in advance. It is tempting to use a 16-bit unsigned integer to store the codes, but this approach fails if the tree assigns a 17-bit sequence to a code. Likewise, the use of an unsigned long can also fail, although it would fail less often. The last routine, `HuffCompress()`, produces an output file by first writing the information required to reconstruct the tree, followed by the bit sequence corresponding to each input character.

Uncompression is implemented in *huffdec.c*, shown in Listing 9-4. After reading the header information, the routine reads bits and traces them to their corresponding external nodes. Note that the number of bytes to be translated is sent as a part of the header information; without this, the decompression routine would not know when to stop. End-of-file cannot be used as a stop command, since the last byte might contain only a few bits of information.

Listing 9-4.   Huffman decoding routines with a sample driver.

```c
/*--- huffdec.c ------------------------- Listing 9-4 ---------
 * Purpose:             Uncompress a Huffman-compressed file
 *
 * Entry point:         int HuffDecode(FILE *infile, FILE *outfile)
 *
 *                      Will uncompress infile into outfile. Both
 *                      files should already be open in binary mode.
 *                      They will be closed by HuffDecode().
 *
 *                      HuffDecode() returns:
 *                          0: success
 *                          1: invalid signature byte
 *                          2: invalid header bytes
 *                          3: invalid data bytes
 *
 *
 * Switches:            DRIVER - compiles a test driver
 *                      DUMP - dump the tree after loading
 *-----------------------------------------------------------*/
#define DRIVER

#include <stdio.h>
#include <stdlib.h>
#include <string.h>
#include <ctype.h>
#include "huffman.h"

/* a simple tree */
struct _HuffTree {
    LinkType child[2];
} HuffTree[MAXNODES];

CountType HuffBytesIn;   /* number of bytes to decode */
LinkType HuffRoot;       /* the tree's root */
LinkType HuffCount;      /* the number of internal nodes */

#ifdef DUMP
static void HuffDump ( LinkType n )
{
    LinkType i;

    printf ( "root is %d\n", HuffRoot );
    printf ( "No.  Sym  Left  Right\n" );
    for ( i = 0; i <= n; i++ )
    {
        printf( "%3d. ", i );
```

```
            if ( i < MAXSYMBOLS )
            {
                if ( isprint ( i ))
                    printf( " %c ", i );
                else
                    printf ( "x%.2X", i );
            }
            else
                printf ( "n/a" );

            printf ( " %5d  %5d",
                    HuffTree[i].child[LEFT],
                    HuffTree[i].child[RIGHT] );

            printf ( "\n" );
        }
        printf ( "\n" );
}
#define DUMPTREE(x) HuffDump(x)
#else
#define DUMPTREE(x)
#endif

/* the actual decompression routine */
int HuffDecode ( FILE *infile, FILE *outfile )
{
    int retval = 0;
    LinkType i;
    char buffer[10];
    struct _Header header;
    CountType bytesout;
    int inbyte, bitno, mask, set;

    /* set all counts to zero and initialize symbols */
    memset ( HuffTree, 0, sizeof ( HuffTree ));

    /* check the signature */
    fgets ( buffer, strlen ( SIGNATURE ) + 2, infile );
    if ( strcmp ( buffer, SIGNATURE ))
    {
        retval = 1;
        goto done;
    }

    /* read in header bytes */

    fread ( &HuffRoot, sizeof ( HuffRoot), 1, infile );
    fread ( &HuffCount, sizeof ( HuffCount), 1, infile );
```

```
fread ( &HuffBytesIn, sizeof ( HuffBytesIn), 1, infile );

for ( i = 0;
        i < HuffCount + ( HuffRoot - MAXSYMBOLS + 1 ); i++)
{
    fread ( &header, sizeof ( header ), 1, infile );
    HuffTree[header.index].child[0] = header.child[0];
    HuffTree[header.index].child[1] = header.child[1];
}

if ( ferror ( infile ))
{
    retval = 2;
    goto done;
}
DUMPTREE ( HuffRoot );

/* now, translate the data bytes */
bitno = 8;
for ( bytesout = 0; bytesout < HuffBytesIn; bytesout++ )
{
    /* walk down the tree */
    i = HuffRoot;
    for ( ;; )
    {
        /* do we need a new input byte? */
        if ( bitno > 7 )
        {
            inbyte = fgetc ( infile );
            if ( inbyte == EOF )
            {
                retval = 3;
                goto done;
            }
            bitno = 0;
            mask = 0x80;
        }

        /* test the current bit */
        if ( inbyte & mask )
            set = 1;
        else
            set = 0;
        bitno++;
        mask >>= 1;

        /* walk down the tree */
        i = HuffTree[i].child[set];
```

```
            /* are we there yet? */
            if ( HuffTree[i].child[0] == -1 )
            {
                /* at the bottom -- write the character */
                fputc ( i, outfile );
                break;
            }
        }
    }

  done:
    fclose ( infile );
    fclose ( outfile );
    return ( retval );
}

#ifdef DRIVER
int main ( int argc, char *argv[] )
{
    FILE *infile, *outfile;
    int retval;

    if ( argc != 3 )
    {
        fprintf ( stderr, "Usage: huffdec infile outfile\n" );
        return ( EXIT_FAILURE );
    }

    infile = fopen ( argv[1], "r+b" );
    if ( infile == NULL )
    {
        fprintf ( stderr, "can't open %s for input\n", argv[1] );
        return ( EXIT_FAILURE );
    }

    outfile = fopen ( argv[2], "w+b" );
    if ( outfile == NULL )
    {
        fprintf ( stderr, "can't open %s for output\n", argv[2]);
        return ( EXIT_FAILURE );
    }

    if ( retval = HuffDecode ( infile, outfile ))
    {
        printf ( "decompression failed: " );
        if ( retval == 1 )
            printf ( "invalid signature byte\n" );
        if ( retval == 2 )
```

```
                printf ( "read error in header\n" );
            if ( retval == 3 )
                printf ( "read error in data\n" );
            else
                printf( "\n" );
            return ( retval );
        }
        else
        {
            printf ( "%s was expanded into %s\n",
                                        argv[1], argv[2]);
            return ( 0 );
        }
    }
    #endif
```

The manifest constants and data structures are defined in the header file *huffman.h*, which appears in Listing 9-5.

Listing 9-5.   Header file for *huffenc.c* and *huffdec.c*.

```
/*--- Listing 9-5 ------------------------- huffman.h ---------*
 * Header file for Huffman compression routines              *
 *-----------------------------------------------------------*/

/* Max number of unique symbols or codes */
#define MAXSYMBOLS 256

/* Total number of external and internal nodes */
#define MAXNODES    (MAXSYMBOLS*2-1)

/* Child directions */
#define LEFT  0
#define RIGHT 1

typedef unsigned long CountType;
typedef int LinkType;

/* Header byte structure */
struct _Header {
    LinkType index;
    LinkType child[2];
};

#define SIGNATURE "Huff1"
```

One cumbersome aspect of the code is the recurring requirement to manipulate bits. If you are going to study the code carefully, be sure you are comfortable with C's bit operations.

Other Issues

Huffman coding is surprisingly effective. For many years after it first appeared, Huffman compression was considered the most effective general-purpose compression algorithm. Today, sliding-window compression techniques, such as those discussed in the next section, have that honor, although there are many circumstances in which Huffman coding still proves superior. Two aspects of Huffman coding detrimentally affect its results. In terms of compression efficiency, the need to include the tree with the file means that Huffman is not very effective on small files; the space consumed by the tree and the related header information dominates compression savings. In terms of performance, Huffman coding must read the input file twice. On small files, this causes few problems. However, when compressing files greater than 1 MB, the difference can be noticeable.

What makes Huffman preferable as a general compression algorithm over run-length encoding is that it does not require runs of the same character in order to compress the file. It simply needs an uneven distribution of characters in the input file. Because this is almost always the case, Huffman does well on just about any file.

The implementation of Huffman in the previous listings could be optimized for better performance. Two tasks take up much of its time: reading the input file twice and building the tree. To improve reading performance, it would be preferable to use buffers. Rather than read the input file twice from a disk, you could read it once into a buffer and process it there. This approach works well especially on systems with considerable memory and little or no penalty for paging. For example, extended-DOS programs can allocate multimegabyte buffers without paging. Such programs should read as much of the file as possible into the buffers.

There are several ways to save work on traversing the tallies to create a tree of bit codes. One way is to have a separate step, such as sorting, to order the tallies before you construct the tree. Bentley [Bentley 1995] discusses some approaches to this problem.

So far, we have discussed two compression algorithms that look at single bytes and use either their repetition (RLE) or their frequency (Huffman) to compress files. The next family of algorithms, sliding-window techniques, use series of bytes such as strings as the unit of compression.

Sliding-Window Compression

In the first section of this chapter, we explained the basis of run-length encoding (RLE), a simple compression technique that detects multiple successive occurrences of the same character and that encodes the repeated characters as a single code. RLE, however, will provide no compression on text such as *invitees were invited with involved invitations*. This example contains three occurrences of the string *invit*. These three strings should be compressible, but they would be neglected by RLE.

A family of algorithms first proposed by Jacob Ziv and Abraham Lempel [Ziv 1977] relies on **dictionary-based** techniques to address this problem. Dictionaries containing strings from the input file are built up as the input file is read for compression. If a string of characters in the input file matches an entry in the dictionary (meaning that the string has already appeared in the input file), a brief code—generally consisting of 2 bytes—that points to the previous entry is written to the compressed file. During uncompression, the decoding engine builds a similar dictionary of strings and writes them to the uncompressed file whenever a compression code is uncovered.

Putting aside the way that the dictionary is constructed, let's examine the compression codes. In all compression mechanisms, considerable effort is spent to make compression codes as short as possible. The longer the compression code, the longer the original data has to be in order to achieve data compression. LZ algorithms generally use 2 bytes to encode the necessary data. Two bytes provide 16 bits of usable data. A typical LZ encoding scheme will use 12 bits to indicate which string in the dictionary is being referenced, and 4 bits to indicate how much of the string is duplicated. A 12-bit reference to a dictionary means that the dictionary can have up to 4,096 entries (numbered 0 to 4095, since 4095 is the largest number that can be encoded in 12 bits). The 4-bit length of the string indicates how many bytes of the dictionary string match the current text. For example, if dictionary entry 33 holds the string *to be or not to* and the current input string is *to be orderly at work*, the two strings will match for the first 8 characters. Hence, the LZ code will use the first 12 bits to contain the dictionary entry (33) and 4 bits to indicate the length of the match (8). By this means, the 2-byte LZ code would represent 8 input characters.

Theoretically, under this implementation, strings cannot match for more than 15 characters, since this is the maximum number that can be represented in 4 bits. Techniques that we will examine shortly allow us to stretch this limit to 18 characters.

Character strings that do not appear in the dictionary are added to the dictionary and are passed through to the output file uncompressed. The decoding mechanism needs some way to know whether the bytes that it is examining are LZ codes or uncompressed data. The traditional approach to this problem is for the encoder to emit a single byte, known as a **flag byte**, at the beginning of every sequence of eight characters or compression codes. The byte, containing 8 bits, has a bit set to 0 if the corresponding element is an LZ code, and a bit set to 1 if the corresponding element is an uncompressed character. Therefore, if a sequence of eight items consists of LZ code, *e*, *l*, *e*, *p*, *h*, LZ code, *!* where italic characters between the commas represent uncompressed letters, the corresponding byte will have a binary value of 01111101. (See Figure 9-3, which illustrates another example of the correspondence between the flag byte and the data elements.)

This information gives us the maximum and minimum compression available under standard LZ compression schemes. If no compression is possible because no string is repeated, the output file will require 9 bits for every character (8 bits for the character itself and 1 bit, set to 1, in the flag byte). Hence, an uncompressible file will grow by 1 bit for every 8 bits of data—effectively to 112.5 percent of the original file's size. Under the best of circumstances, where every 18 bytes of input match the string in the dictionary, it takes 17 bits (16 bits for the LZ code and 1 bit for the flag byte) to encode a string of 18 bytes (144 bits). Therefore, at a ratio of 17 bits per 144 bits of data, the maximum compression that LZ techniques can attain is a file that is 11.8 percent the size of the original. Both figures are extremes and will rarely occur in practice. Note that the best case is not quite as good as shown, because the first time through, the 18-byte string will be written untouched to the output file, since it does not yet exist in the dictionary. The next section of this chapter presents LZ-based dictionary compression.

The implementation of the LZ dictionary has undergone wide variation since it was first proposed. In the original work, it was based on a binary tree that would be searched each time from the root in an attempt to find a match. Later versions of LZ made use of a hash table. Even more recent implementations use no fixed dictionary as such. Instead, they look for matches of strings within the last 4,096 bytes. If a match for the current string is found within the previous 4,096 bytes, the 12-bit field in the code holds the offset to the string rather than a reference to a table entry. This approach simplifies the decoding mechanism because it does not have to build or maintain a dictionary. Instead, it simply keeps the last 4,096 bytes of uncompressed data in memory and refers to that data as it uncompresses the file. With every byte that is uncompressed, the 4,096-byte window is moved forward. That is how this family of algorithms has come to be known as **sliding-window compression**.

Files compressed with sliding-window compression are commonly found on Microsoft distribution diskettes. These files often bear an extension consisting of two characters followed by an underscore (such a file might be *filename.ex_*). To compress these files, you use Microsoft's *compress.exe* utility. You can uncompress them by using either Microsoft's *expand.exe* program or the program that appears in Listing 9-6 (*mslzunc.c*).

Listing 9-6.   A program that uncompresses Microsoft's LZ compressed files.

```
/*--- mslzunc.c ------------------------- Listing 9-6 --------
 *  Uncompress a file compressed with Microsoft's compress.exe
 *  program. compress.exe uses a Microsoft variant of the LZ
 *  family of sliding-window compresssion algorithms.
 *
 *  if DRIVER is #defined a driver mainline is compiled.
 *-----------------------------------------------------------*/

#define DRIVER

#include <stdio.h>
#include <stdlib.h>
#include <string.h>
#include "mslzunc.h"

/* 4KB Uncompression window */
char Window[WINSIZE];

/*-----------------------------------------------------------
 * Principal routine that uncompresses the input data
 * using Microsoft's own implementation of LZ algorithms.
 *-----------------------------------------------------------*/
void UncompressData ( FILE *infile, FILE *outfile,
                             unsigned long uncomp_size )
{

    unsigned char   bit_map, byte1, byte2;
    int             length, counter;
    long            location, curr_pos = 0L;

    /* Init our window to spaces */
    memset ( Window, ' ', WINSIZE );

    /* Go through until done */
    while ( curr_pos < uncomp_size )
    {

        /* Get bit_map of flag indicating codes and bytes */
```

```
bit_map = fgetc ( infile );
if ( feof ( infile ))
    return;

/* Go through and decode data */
for ( counter = 0; counter < 8; counter++ )
{

    /* It's a code, so decode it and copy the data */
    if ( ! BITSET ( bit_map, counter ))
    {
        byte1 = fgetc ( infile );

        /* Shouldn't be EOF, but just in case... */

        if ( feof ( infile ))
            return;

        byte2 = fgetc ( infile );
        length = LENGTH ( byte2 );
        location = OFFSET ( byte1, byte2 );

        /* Copy data from 'window' */
        while ( length != 0 )
        {
            byte1 = Window[WRAPFIX(location)];
            Window[WRAPFIX(curr_pos)] = byte1;
            fputc ( byte1, outfile );
            curr_pos++;
            location++;
            length--;
        }
    }
    else    /* it's just a data byte */
    {
        byte1 = fgetc ( infile );
        Window[WRAPFIX(curr_pos)] = byte1;
        fputc ( byte1, outfile );
        curr_pos++;
    }

    if ( feof ( infile ))
        return;

}
}
}
```

```
/*----------------------------------------------------------
 * Verifies the header of the compressed file looking for the
 * Microsoft signature and the size of the uncompressed file.
 * Returns the latter upon success or 0L upon failure.
 *----------------------------------------------------------*/
unsigned long VerifyHeader ( FILE *infile )
{

    COMPHEADER header;
    unsigned long comp_size;

    fseek ( infile, 0, SEEK_END );
    comp_size = ftell ( infile );
    fseek ( infile, 0, SEEK_SET );
    fread ( &header, sizeof ( header ), 1, infile );
    if (( header.Magic1 != MAGIC1 ) ||
        ( header.Magic2 != MAGIC2 ))
    {
        fprintf ( stderr, "input file is not a valid "
                          "compressed file!\n" );
        return ( 0L );
    }

    printf ( "Uncompressing file from %lu bytes to %lu bytes\n",
             comp_size, header.UncompSize );

    return ( header.UncompSize );
}

#ifdef DRIVER
/*----------------------------------------------------------
 * Driver to exercise previous decompression routines. Accepts
 * exactly two command-line arguments: the name of the compressed
 * file and the name to use for the output compressed file.
 *----------------------------------------------------------*/
int main ( int argc, char *argv[] )
{

    FILE *infile, *outfile;
    unsigned long uncompressed_size;

    if ( argc != 3 )
    {
        fprintf ( stderr, "Usage: mslzunc"
                  "compressed-file uncompressed-file\n" );
        return ( EXIT_FAILURE );
    }
```

```
    if (( infile = fopen ( argv[1], "rb" )) == NULL)
    {
        fprintf( stderr, "Can't open %s for input\n", argv[1] );
        return ( EXIT_FAILURE );
    }

    if (( outfile = fopen ( argv[2], "wb" )) == NULL )
    {
        fprintf ( stderr, "Can't open %s for output\n", argv[2]);
        return ( EXIT_FAILURE );
    }

    uncompressed_size =  VerifyHeader ( infile );
    if ( uncompressed_size != 0L )   /* no error occurred */
        UncompressData ( infile, outfile, uncompressed_size );

    fclose ( infile );
    fclose ( outfile );

    if ( uncompressed_size == 0L )  /* previous error occurred */
        return ( EXIT_FAILURE );
    else
        return ( EXIT_SUCCESS );
}
#endif
```

This program, based on Davis [Davis 1994], shows the ins and outs of the sliding-window compression, along with some of Microsoft's own extensions. The code for this program requires a bit of explanation. The driver routine, `main()`, accepts arguments that are the name of the compressed file and the name of the uncompressed file to be generated. After opening the files, the program verifies the header information in the compressed file by using `VerifyHeader()`. The header is defined in the structure `COMPHEADER`, which is declared in Listing 9-7 (*mslzunc.h*). This header contains a signature that comprises two long integers (32-bit integers) whose values appear in `MAGIC1` and `MAGIC2`, followed by a single byte with the value 0x41. Next comes a byte that contains the character from the original file's name replaced with a _ by the compression program. To reconstitute the original file name, use this character (called `FileFix`) to replace the ultimate underscore in the input file name. The next and final field in the header is `UncompSize`, which is the length in bytes of the original file and which should equal the length of the generated uncompressed file. After the magic values in the header are verified and the size of the output file is noted, `UncompressData()` is called to begin processing the file itself.

The function first reads a flag byte whose eight bits correspond to the status of the next eight elements in the file. In the Microsoft implementation, a bit set to 1 means that the corresponding element is an uncompressed byte whose output should be unchanged. If the bit is set to 0, the corresponding element is a two-byte compression code whose exact contents we will discuss shortly. In a flag byte, the least significant bit (rightmost) gives the status of the next immediate element. Hence, a flag byte with the value 0x93 would be the flags for eight elements: 10010011, which means that (starting from the rightmost flag bits) the next two elements are uncompressed bytes, followed by two compression codes, an uncompressed byte, a compression code, and a final uncompressed byte. Figure 9-3 illustrates this example.

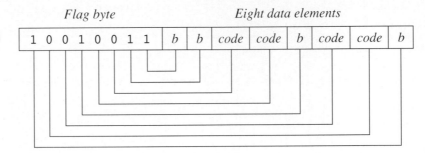

Figure 9-3.   Correspondence between the flag byte and the data elements
(*b* = uncompressed byte; *code* = two-byte compression code).

Testing for these values is done by the BITSET macro in the header file, as shown in Listing 9-7.

The compression codes, as explained previously, occupy 16 bits. Of these 16 bits, the lowest 4 bits of the second byte represent the length of the replacement string, while the upper 12 bits represent the offset from the current position in the uncompressed output file.

The four length bits could hold values from 0 to 15. Because the compression code itself occupies 2 bytes, the minimum sensible value for length is 3 bytes, since strings of less than 3 bytes would not be compressed. Hence, an encoded length of 0 bytes represents the lowest sensible length, 3 bytes. Adding 3 to the length value means that the longest string that can now be represented is 18 bytes. The macro LENGTH in Listing 9-7 shows the length being extracted from a code byte and being adjusted accordingly.

The offset that points to the replacement string is contained in the remaining twelve bits of the compression code. The OFFSET macro in Listing 9-7 extracts the data. Once the location value is established, 16 is added to it. This final

Listing 9-7. Bit operators and header definition of *mslzunc.c*.

```
/*--- mslzunc.h -------------------------- Listing 9-7 --------
 * Values and bit-manipulation macros used in mslzunc.c
 *--------------------------------------------------------*/

typedef struct tagCOMPHEADER {
    long    Magic1;
    long    Magic2;
    char    Is41;    /* 0x41 */
    char    FileFix; /* character saved for -r option */
    long    UncompSize;
} COMPHEADER;

/* Microsoft's magic numbers in header. Magic1 = "SZDD" */

#define MAGIC1 0x44445A53
#define MAGIC2 0x3327F088

/* Constants and macros for uncompression */

#define WINSIZE  4096
#define LENGTH(x) ((((x) & 0x0F)) + 3)
#define OFFSET(x1, x2) \
    (((((x2 & 0xF0) << 4) + x1 + 0x0010) & 0x0FFF)
#define WRAPFIX(x)      ((x) & (WINSIZE - 1))
#define BITSET(byte, bit)  (((byte) & (1<<bit)) > 0)
```

value shows how far into the output window of the last 4,096 bytes you must go to pick up the replacement string.

The Microsoft implementation expects the window to be initialized to spaces. This is important because the window is perceived as a circular queue that is 4,096 bytes long. If, for example, the string that appears in bytes 0–10 were to recur, preceded by 4 spaces, the offset would begin at byte 4,092. By pointing to 4,092, the offset would point to the 4 spaces in bytes 4,092 to 4,095 and the string at locations 0 through 10. Another example is shown in Figure 9-4, where the string `"Who is"` has just been placed in the window. The next string read is `"Who is"`—the same string that exists in bytes 0–5 but preceded by a space. Since the bytes prior to 0 contain spaces and the reference can wrap around (the next byte after 4,095 is byte 0), the reference points to the space in byte 4,095. This wraparound is addressed by the macro WRAPFIX in Listing 9-7.

(Readers who use UNIX or do not have access to Microsoft's compress program will find a source-code implementation on the code diskette that can be obtained for this book.)

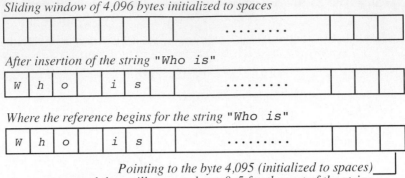

Sliding window of 4,096 bytes initialized to spaces

After insertion of the string "Who is"

Where the reference begins for the string "Who is"

Pointing to the byte 4,095 (initialized to spaces)
and then will wrap to bytes 0–5 for the rest of the string

Figure 9-4.   How Microsoft's sliding window wraps around.

Dictionary-Based Compression (LZW)

The previous section on sliding-window compression contains an introduction to the concepts of dictionary-based compression, especially those articulated by Lempel and Ziv in the LZ family of algorithms. This introduction should be read before proceeding.

Terry Welch, a computer scientist at Unisys, added a significant refinement to the LZ dictionary-based algorithms. He observed that if you preloaded the dictionary with one entry for every character in the character set, several advantages would arise. First, the output from the compression routine could consist solely of codes that correspond to entries into a compression dictionary. Second, the dictionary itself need not be transmitted as part of the compressed file. Instead, the encoding and decoding routines start with the same base dictionary of 256 characters and fill up the dictionary as they go along. We shall shortly see why these advantages are important.

Welch's enhancement to LZ algorithms was named LZW in his honor and is the technique discussed in the remainder of the chapter. Note, however, that before you use this algorithm in your own work, you need to get approval from Unisys. LZW is covered by several patents from Unisys, a company that has repeatedly defended these patents from infringement. Use LZW with care.

The first thing done by both the encoding and decoding mechanisms is to occupy the first 256 slots of the table with one entry each for the respective 256 characters in the machine's character set. As noted previously, this preload of the dictionary means that there is no input character that cannot be translated immediately into a dictionary code. Initially this means replacing an input character of 0 with an output code of 0, which is not terribly impressive. However, the compression routine adds entries to the dictionary based on the sequence of characters seen, and these entries soon allow compression of multicharacter input sequences into single code output sequences. Note that use of a dictionary entry entails use of the entire entry. Unlike sliding windows, there is no provision to use partial entries.

To see how the process works, let's compress the phrase AT AN ATAN (Figure 9-5). Handling of the first character is unremarkable: it is simply output as the corresponding pre-existing code in the dictionary. Likewise, the second character is output as itself. However, even though nothing interesting is happening on the output side (two characters in, two codes out), the dictionary is beginning to take shape. Having now seen the two-character sequence "AT," a new entry is made into the dictionary: code 256 now corresponds to the two-character phrase AT. The handling of the following space, A, and N likewise appears unexciting, but each input character now drives the addition of a new phrase to the dictionary. This phrase is always comprised of the last output phrase with the new character concatenated to it.

Input	Output	Dictionary Action
A	65	No action. Code is in dictionary
T	84	Add code 256 for "AT"
Space	32	Add code 257 for "T "
A	65	Add code 258 for " A"
N	78	Add code 259 for "AN"
Space	see next	
A	258	" A" is entry 258. Add code 260 for "N "
T	84	Add code 261 for " AT"
A	see next	
N	259	"AN" is entry 259. Add code 262 for "TA"

Figure 9-5. Compresson of "AT AN ATAN."

When we get to "A" for the second time, something interesting happens because we have an output code that is not one of the predefined 256 codes. Code 258 was previously defined as "A," and we now use it to replace the "A" of the input string. The remaining compression process is similar, with code 259 being used to replace the terminal "AN" from the input string.

In this sample, we have compressed 10 characters into 8 codes. Because the codes will need to be larger than the 8-bit input characters (12 and 16 bits are common code sizes), it is actually likely that this compression process has increased the size of this very short input file. However, on longer input files,

LZW has a chance to build up much larger phrases in the dictionary and begins to produce very good compression.

LZW Pseudocode

The LZW algorithms are conceptually simple. In pseudocode, the compression algorithm looks like this:

```
OldString = GetFirstCharacter();
while (input exists)
{
     NewChar = GetNewCharacter()
     NewString = OldString + NewChar;
     if (InDictionary(NewString))
          OldString = NewString;
     else
     {
          OutputCode(OldString);
          AddToDictionary(NewString);
          OldString = NewChar;
     }
}
OutputCode(OldString); /* last data code */
OutputCode(EndOfFileCode);
```

Uncompression is likewise simple:

```
OldString = GetACode(); /* first code is itself */
OutputString(OldString);
while ((NewCode = GetACode()) != EndOfFileCode) {
     NewString = Lookup(Newcode);
     OutputString(NewString);
     Append 1st character of NewString to OldString;
     AddToDictionary(OldString);
     OldString = NewString;
}
```

While this appears simple, there is a sneaky problem that can develop during decompression. Let c be a character and let S be any string of length > 0. If the dictionary contains an entry of the form cS as code k, then an input sequence of the form $cScSc$ will cause the compression routine to output code k in response to the initial cS and then internally create code k' for cSc. And, since the next sequence is cSc, the code k' is used prior to clearly defining it for the decompression routine (Figure 9-6)!

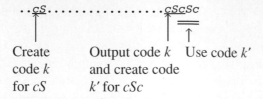

Figure 9-6. **In one case, the LZW compression routine may output a code not known to the decompression routine.**

Fortunately, however, this is the only circumstance under which this can happen, and the decompression routine can easily handle this problem: if an unknown code is seen, it is easily derived as the value of the string corresponding to the previous code with that string's first character appended to the string. While this problem sounds esoteric, it is actually quite common and can be produced with an input string such as "AB ABABA" (Figure 9-7). With these problems identified, however, we are ready to actually implement the LZW algorithm.

Input	Output	Dictionary Action
A	65	No action. Code is in dictionary
B	66	Add code 256 for "AB"
Space	32	Add code 257 for "B "
A		Add code 258 for " A"
B	256	Add code 259 for "ABA"
A		No action
B		No action
A	259	Add code 260 for "ABAx"
x	...	...

Figure 9-7. **Compresson of "AB ABABAx".**

Implementation of LZW Compression

An actual implementation of LZW must grapple with several tricky issues. First, what size code should be used? The answer determines the size of the dictionary that can be used: if we use 12-bit codes, then we will need a dictionary that can hold 2^{12} (4,096) entries. Second, how do we actually store the dictionary? During compression we need to be able to determine quickly whether a given code exists in the dictionary, while during uncompression we need to be able to expand a given code quickly. Third, what do we do when the dictionary fills (as inevitably it will with larger input files)?

An implementation of LZW that addresses these issues is presented in Listings 9-8 (the header file, *lzw.h*), 9-9 (the compression routine, *lzcomp.c*), and 9-10 (the uncompression routine, *lzwunc.c*). While these routines provide two possible codes sizes (12 or 16 bits), the choice of code size is possible only at compile time and is also constrained by the underlying compiler and operating system. Even using a large memory model, there is insufficient memory under MS-DOS for a 16-bit compiler to use 16-bit codes. In effect, 12-bit codes are useful for 16-bit compilers, and 16-bit codes can be used only by 32-bit compilers. Interestingly, however, there is less gain involved in going from 12 to 16 bits than might be expected. This is because the potential for larger phrases in the 16-bit code dictionary is counterbalanced by the need to send four more bits in every code. In either case, the only real changes are in the input/output routines. The text will focus on the 12-bit code case, and the interested reader can examine the listings for details on the implementation changes needed for 16-bit codes.

The header file *lzw.h* (Listing 9-8) defines a number of critical constants. First, we need to reserve several codes for internal use: END_OF_INPUT is reserved as a terminating code, NEW_DICTIONARY will be needed when we deal with the issue of handling a full dictionary, and STARTING_CODE and MAX_CODE tell use the first and last free dictionary codes, respectively. Notice also that while our dictionary will contain at most 4,096 codes, we define the actual dictionary size (DICTIONARY_SIZE) to be a bit larger. As will be described shortly, this will facilitate dictionary searching.

Listing 9-8. Manifest constants for 12- and 16-bit LZW implementations.

```
/*--- lzw.h ----------------------------- Listing 9-8 --------
 * Header file for LZW compression routines                   *
 *-----------------------------------------------------------*/

/* select dictionary size */
#if !defined(BITS)
#define BITS 12
#endif

#if BITS == 12
/* Critical sizes for LZW */
#define PRESET_CODE_MAX 256     /* codes like this are preset */
#define END_OF_INPUT    256     /* this code terminates input */
#define NEW_DICTIONARY  257     /* reinitialize the dictionary */
#define STARTING_CODE   258     /* first code we can use */
```

```
#define MAX_CODE          4096    /* 2 ^ BITS */
#define UNUSED_CODE       4096    /* an invalid code that is never
                                     output. may be >= MAX_CODE if
                                     CodeType can hold it. The
                                     other option is to define
                                     after the fashion of the
                                     code for END_OF_INPUT */
#define DICTIONARY_SIZE 5021      /* a prime # > MAX_CODE * 1.2 */

/* all of these should be unsigned */
typedef unsigned short CodeType;  /* can hold MAX_CODE */
typedef unsigned short IndexType; /* can hold DICTIONARY_SIZE */
typedef unsigned long  CountType; /* used for statistics only */

#define SIGNATURE "LZW12"

#elif BITS == 16 /* requires a 32-bit context */
/* Critical sizes for LZW */
#define PRESET_CODE_MAX 256      /* codes like this are preset */
#define END_OF_INPUT    256      /* this code terminates input */
#define NEW_DICTIONARY  257      /* reinitialize the dictionary */
#define UNUSED_CODE     258      /* an invalid code */
#define STARTING_CODE   259      /* first code we can use */
#define MAX_CODE        65536    /* 2 ^ BITS */
#define DICTIONARY_SIZE 81901L   /* a prime # > MAX_CODE * 1.2 */

typedef unsigned short CodeType;  /* can hold MAX_CODE */
typedef unsigned long IndexType;  /* can hold DICTIONARY_SIZE */
typedef unsigned long CountType;  /* used for statistics only */

#define SIGNATURE "LZW16"

#else
#error Undefined BITS value!
#endif
```

The data required to store the compression dictionary differs slightly between compression and uncompression. In the compression routines, we use a structure of the form

```
struct Dictionary {
    unsigned char c;
    CodeType code;
    CodeType parent;
} dictionary[DICTIONARY_SIZE];
```

where `CodeType` is an unsigned quantity that can hold `MAX_CODE`. Each entry in the table is the terminal node of some string, with the actual string built by *walking backwards* through the linked list defined via the index in `parent`. The other items in this structure are (a) `c`, the character that is the last character of the string that terminates at this node and (b) `code`, the output code for the entry that terminates at this node. Note that the code number for a given string does not correspond to its position in the table, but rather is specified as part of the table entry itself. We do this because of the way that we do table lookups. While it would have been possible to build a tree to hold the dictionary, we would have needed as many as 256 branches at each node of the tree (one for each possible subsequent letter). This structure would be both slow to search and waste memory. Instead, we take advantage of our knowledge of the way the dictionary is accessed, and view the dictionary table as a cross between a hash table and a linked list.

To understand how this works, note that the codes for items in the input dictionary are stored as part of the entry and do not correspond to a physical location in the input dictionary. This last point is important. You may find it useful to think of the entry's location in the dictionary as its physical index and its corresponding code as its logical index. Whenever we need to lookup a string, we always have in hand the (output, or logical) code for the phrase that matches the first n-1 characters of the string along with the n'th character of the target string. We combine these two values in `LZWFind()` to produce a hashed physical index into the input dictionary. That is, suppose we have already scanned the string xy, recorded it as dictionary code 400, and stored it at physical index 500. To find out if the dictionary contains the string xyz, we now combine dictionary code 400 with the code for z to produce a new hashed physical index—perhaps a value of 1200 results. We now examine physical entry 1200 in the dictionary. If it is an entry that (a) has a code letter of z and (b) has a parent code of 400, then we have found what we need. This hashing process will often lead us directly to the node we want. If we don't find a matching node (or an empty node marked with the code `UNUSED_CODE`), then we simply step through the table repeatedly using a prespecified step value until we find one or the other (see Chapter 3 for a review of the hashing concepts). This use of hashing to search the table is the reason that the input dictionary contains more slots than it will ever use: leaving some empty slots allows the table to function much more efficiently. The choice of hashing function for this table can have a significant impact on its performance, and the functions used in the code were selected after experimentation with various alternatives. The efficiency of the hashing function can easily be monitored by defining the `HASHHITS` and `HASHSTATS` variables and inspecting the resulting outcome.

Listing 9-9. **LZW Compression.**

```
/*--- lzwcomp.c -------------------------- Listing 9-9 -------------
 * Compress an input file, using the LZW encoding technique
 *
 * Entry point:      int LZWEncode (FILE *infile, FILE *outfile)
 *
 *                   Will compress infile into outfile. Both
 *                   files should already be open in binary mode.
 *                   They will be closed by LZWEncode().
 *
 *                   LZWEncode() returns:
 *                       0: success
 *                       1: error while reading in
 *                       2: malloc error
 *                       4: error while writing out
 *
 * Switches:         DRIVER    - compiles a test driver
 *                   HASHSTATS - reports on hashing efficiency
 *                   HASHHITS  - show table of hash hits
 *                   SHOWSTATS - provides compression statistics
 *-----------------------------------------------------------*/

#define DRIVER
#define SHOWSTATS

#include <stdio.h>
#include <stdlib.h>
#include <string.h>
#include "lzw.h"

CountType LZWTotBytesIn;    /* no. data bytes in input file */
CountType LZWTotBytesOut;   /* no. data bytes in output file */
CountType LZWCurrBytesIn;   /* no. data bytes in current frame */
CountType LZWCurrBytesOut;  /* no. data bytes in current frame */
unsigned  LZWBestRatio;     /* best ratio we've had */
unsigned  LZWLastRatio;     /* last ratio we saw */

#if defined( HASHHITS ) && !defined( HASHSTATS )
#  define HASHSTATS
#endif

#if defined( HASHSTATS )
#  define SHOWHASH(x) x
CountType HashCount;
CountType HashCollide;
IndexType FreeMax;
#  if defined( HASHHITS )
```

```
unsigned long HashHits[ DICTIONARY_SIZE ];
#  endif
#else
#  define SHOWHASH(x)
#endif

/* structure for the data dictionary */
struct Dictionary {
    unsigned char c;
    CodeType code;
    CodeType parent;
};



/*--- the data storage and output routines ---*/

#if BITS == 12

struct Dictionary dictionary[ DICTIONARY_SIZE ];

/* These are the 12-bit routines */

static int havenibble;
static int olddata;
static void LZWOutInit ( FILE *outfile )
{
    char sig[] = SIGNATURE;
    fwrite ( sig, strlen ( sig ) + 1, 1, outfile );
    havenibble = 0;
    LZWLastRatio = LZWBestRatio = 100;
    SHOWHASH( HashCount = HashCollide = 0; )
#  if defined( HASHHITS )
    SHOWHASH( memset ( HashHits, 0,
             DICTIONARY_SIZE * sizeof ( unsigned long )); )
#  endif
    SHOWHASH( FreeMax = 0; )
}

static int LZWOutFlush ( FILE *outfile )
{
    if ( havenibble )
    {
        if ( fputc ( olddata, outfile ) == EOF )
            return ( 4 );
        LZWTotBytesOut += 1;
        LZWCurrBytesOut += 1;
    }
    return ( 0 );
```

```
}

static int LZWOut ( FILE *outfile, CodeType code )
{
    if ( havenibble )
    {
        olddata |= ( code >> 8 ) & 0xF;
        if ( fputc ( olddata, outfile ) == EOF )
            return ( 4 );
        if ( fputc ( code, outfile ) == EOF )
            return ( 4 );
        LZWTotBytesOut += 2;
        LZWCurrBytesOut += 2;

        havenibble = 0;
    }
    else
    {
        olddata = ( code >> 4 ) & 0xFF;
        if ( fputc ( olddata, outfile ) == EOF )
            return ( 4 );
        LZWTotBytesOut += 1;
        LZWCurrBytesOut += 1;
        olddata = ( code << 4 ) & 0xF0;
        havenibble = 1;
    }
    return ( 0 );
}
#elif BITS == 16
struct Dictionary *dictionary;

/* These are the 16-bit routines */
static void LZWOutInit( FILE *outfile )
{
    SHOWHASH( CountType i; )
    char sig[] = SIGNATURE;

    fwrite ( sig, strlen ( sig ) + 1, 1, outfile );
    SHOWHASH( HashCount = HashCollide = 0; )
#   if defined( HASHHITS )
    SHOWHASH( for ( i = 0; i < DICTIONARY_SIZE; i++ )
                HashHits[ i ] = 0; )
#   endif

    dictionary = malloc ( DICTIONARY_SIZE *
                    sizeof( struct Dictionary ));
}
```

```
static int LZWOutFlush ( FILE *outfile )
{
    return ( 0 );
}

static int LZWOut ( FILE *outfile, CodeType code )
{
    if ( fwrite ( &code, sizeof( CodeType ), 1, outfile ) != 1 )
        return ( 4 );
    LZWTotBytesOut += 2;
    LZWCurrBytesOut += 2;
    return ( 0 );
}
#else
#  error Undefined value for BITS!
#endif

/* our hashing lookup function */
static IndexType LZWFind ( CodeType currcode, int in )
{
    IndexType ndx;
    int step = 11, pastzero = 0;

#if BITS == 12
    ndx = ( currcode << 7 ) ^ in;
#elif BITS == 16
    ndx = ( ( IndexType ) currcode << 8 ) | in;
#endif
    ndx = ndx % DICTIONARY_SIZE;
    SHOWHASH( HashCount++; )
#if defined( HASHHITS )
    SHOWHASH( HashHits[ ndx ] ++; )
#endif
    for ( ;; )
    {
        if ( dictionary[ ndx ].code == UNUSED_CODE )
            break;
        if ( dictionary[ ndx ].parent == currcode &&
             dictionary[ ndx ].c == in )
            break;
        ndx += step;
        if ( ndx >= DICTIONARY_SIZE)
        {
            ndx -= DICTIONARY_SIZE;
            pastzero += 1;

            /*
             * Next is a safety check. If the step
```

```
                    * value and the dictionary size are
                    * relatively prime, there should never
                    * be a problem. However, let's not loop
                    * too many times.
                    */

                   if ( pastzero > 5 )
                       step = 1;
           }
           SHOWHASH( HashCollide++; )

    }
    return ( ndx );
}

int LZWEncode ( FILE *infile, FILE *outfile )
{
    int retval = 0, in;
    CountType i;
    IndexType freecode = STARTING_CODE;
    CodeType currcode;
    IndexType idx;

    LZWTotBytesIn = 0;
    LZWTotBytesOut = 0;
    LZWCurrBytesIn = 0;
    LZWCurrBytesOut = 0;
    LZWOutInit( outfile );
#if BITS == 16
    if ( ! dictionary )
        return ( 2 );
#endif
    for ( i = 0; i < DICTIONARY_SIZE; i++ )
        dictionary[ i ].code = UNUSED_CODE;

    if (( currcode = fgetc ( infile )) == (CodeType) EOF )
        currcode = END_OF_INPUT;
    else
    {
        LZWTotBytesIn += 1;
        LZWCurrBytesIn += 1;
        currcode &= 0xFF; /* make sure we don't sign extend */
        while (( in = fgetc ( infile )) != EOF )
        {
            LZWTotBytesIn += 1;
            LZWCurrBytesIn += 1;
            idx = LZWFind ( currcode, in );
            if ( dictionary[ idx ].code == UNUSED_CODE )
```

```
        {
            /* not a match */
            retval = LZWOut ( outfile, currcode );

            /* now, update the dictionary */
            if ( freecode < MAX_CODE )
            {
                dictionary[ idx ].c = in;
                dictionary[ idx ].code = freecode++;
                dictionary[ idx ].parent = currcode;
            }
            currcode = in;

            /* Had a miss; check compression efficiency */
            if ( LZWCurrBytesIn >= 10000 )
            {
                unsigned ratio;
                ratio = ( LZWCurrBytesOut * 100 ) /
                        LZWCurrBytesIn;
#if defined( HASHSTATS )
                printf( "Input: %lu, "
                        "Output: %lu, "
                        "Overall Ratio; %lu%%, ",
                        LZWTotBytesIn,
                        LZWTotBytesOut,
                        ( LZWTotBytesOut * 100 ) /
                        LZWTotBytesIn );
                printf( "This frame: %u%%\n", ratio );
#endif
                LZWCurrBytesIn = 0;
                LZWCurrBytesOut = 0;
                if ( ratio > LZWBestRatio )
                {
                    if ( ratio > 50 &&
                        ( ratio > 90 ||
                        ratio > LZWLastRatio + 10 ))
                    {
#if defined( HASHSTATS )
                        printf ( "Dictionary reset\n" );
#endif
                        LZWOut ( outfile, NEW_DICTIONARY );
                        for ( i = 0;
                            i < DICTIONARY_SIZE; i++ )
                          dictionary[ i ].code =
                                UNUSED_CODE;
                        SHOWHASH( if (freecode > FreeMax)
                            FreeMax = freecode; )
                        freecode = STARTING_CODE;
```

```
                    }
                }
                else
                    LZWBestRatio = ratio;
                LZWLastRatio = ratio;
            }
        }
        else /* we match so far--keep going */
            currcode = dictionary[ idx ].code;

        if ( retval ) /* make sure no problems so far */
            break;
    }
}

retval = LZWOut ( outfile, currcode );
if ( ! retval )
    retval = LZWOut ( outfile, END_OF_INPUT );
if ( ! retval )
    retval = LZWOutFlush ( outfile );

#if defined( SHOWSTATS )
if ( ! retval )
{
    printf ( "The input file contained %lu bytes\n",
                LZWTotBytesIn );
    printf ( "The output file contained %lu data bytes\n",
                LZWTotBytesOut );
    if ( LZWTotBytesIn != 0 )
        printf ( "Output file is %lu%% "
                    "the size of input file\n",
                    ( LZWTotBytesOut * 100 ) / LZWTotBytesIn );
}
#endif
#if defined( HASHSTATS )
{
    float ratio;
    if ( freecode > FreeMax )
        FreeMax = freecode;
    printf( "The highest code used was %u\n", FreeMax );
    printf( "There were %ld hashes and %ld collisions,\n",
        HashCount, HashCollide );
    ratio = ( float ) HashCollide / ( float ) HashCount;
    printf( "for a ratio of %f\n", ratio );
#  if defined( HASHHITS )
    for ( i = 0; i < min( DICTIONARY_SIZE, 4096 ); i += 8 )
    {
        int j;
```

```
                printf( "%6ld: ", i );
                for ( j = 0; j < 8; j++ )
                {
                    if ( i + j >= DICTIONARY_SIZE )
                        break;
                    printf( "%10ld  ", HashHits[ i + j ] );
                }
                printf( "\n" );
            }
#   endif
        }
#endif

    if ( ferror ( infile ))
        retval = 1;
    if ( ferror ( outfile ))
        retval = 4;
    fclose ( infile );
    fclose ( outfile );
    return ( retval );
}


/*-------------------------------------------------------------
 * The following driver for the previous routines is active
 * if DRIVER is defined.
 *-----------------------------------------------------------*/
#if defined( DRIVER )
int main( int argc, char *argv[] )
{
    FILE * infile, *outfile;
    int retval;

    if ( argc != 3 )
    {
        printf( "Usage: lzwenc infile outfile\n" );
        return ( EXIT_FAILURE );
    }

    infile = fopen( argv[ 1 ], "r+b" );
    if ( infile == NULL )
    {
        fprintf( stderr, "can't open %s for input\n", argv[1] );
        return ( EXIT_FAILURE );
    }

    outfile = fopen( argv[ 2 ], "w+b" );
    if ( outfile == NULL )
    {
```

```
            fprintf( stderr, "can't open %s for output\n", argv[2] );
            return ( EXIT_FAILURE );
        }
    setvbuf ( outfile, NULL, _IOFBF, 8192 );

    retval = LZWEncode ( infile, outfile );

    if ( retval )
    {
        printf( "compression failed: " );
        if ( retval == 1 )
            printf ( "input error\n" );
        else
        if ( retval == 2 )
            printf ( "malloc error\n" );
        else
        if ( retval == 4 )
            printf ( "output error\n" );
        else
            printf ( "\n" );
        return  ( retval );
    }
    else
    {
        printf( "%s was compressed into %s\n",
                                    argv[ 1 ], argv[ 2 ] );
        return ( EXIT_SUCCESS );
    }
}
#endif
```

During uncompression, we can dispense with the code entry and simply store the node in the appropriate position in the table. This works because during compression we never need to search for a phrase in the table: we always have the correct code in hand and can use it to directly as an index into the table. Instead, our problem now is to start at a terminal node and unwind the corresponding phrase. This is easily done by tracing the parent values upward until we reach a node with a code value < 256. At this point, the string must terminate. This process is peformed in *lzwunc.c* (Listing 9-10) by LZWLoadBuffer ( ). This routine uses a simple string buffer to build up the string in reverse order. Note that the nodes with values < 256 are known by the decompression routine to represent themselves and never need to actually be initialized.

Listing 9-10. LZW Uncompression.

```
/*--- lzwunc.c --------------------------- Listing 9-10 -------
 * Decompress an LZW-compressed file
 *
 * Entry point:      int LZWDecode(FILE *infile, FILE *outfile)
 *
 *                   Will decompress infile into outfile. Both
 *                   files should already be open in binary mode.
 *                   They will be closed by LZWDecode().
 *
 *                   LZWDecode() returns:
 *                       0: success
 *                       1: invalid signature byte
 *                       2: bad malloc
 *                       3: read error
 *                       4: write error
 *
 *
 * Switches:         DRIVER - compiles a test driver
 *                   CODES  - displays input codes
 *------------------------------------------------------------*/
#define DRIVER

#include <stdio.h>
#include <stdlib.h>
#include <string.h>
#include "lzw.h"

#if defined( CODES )
unsigned long outcount;
#endif

/* structure for data dictionary */
struct Dictionary {
    unsigned char c;
    CodeType parent;
};

/* decode buffer */
static unsigned char *DecodeBuffer;
static unsigned DecodeBufferSize = 0;
static unsigned LZWLoadBuffer( unsigned, CodeType );

/* the input routines and data storage routines */
#if BITS == 12
/* These are the 12-bit input routines */
/* data dictionary */
```

```
struct Dictionary dictionary[ MAX_CODE ];

static int havenibble;
static int olddata;
static CodeType incode;
static int LZWInInit ( void )
{
    havenibble = 0;
    if ( ! DecodeBufferSize )
    {
        DecodeBufferSize = 1000;
        DecodeBuffer = malloc( DecodeBufferSize );
        if ( DecodeBuffer == NULL )
            return ( 2 );
    }
#   if defined( CODES )
    outcount = 0;
#   endif
    return 0;
}

static int LZWIn ( FILE *infile )
{
    int data;
    if ( havenibble )
    {
        incode = olddata << 8;
        if (( data = fgetc ( infile )) == EOF )
            return ( 4 );
        incode |= ( data & 0xFF );
        havenibble = 0;
#   if defined( CODES )
        {
            unsigned count;
            printf ( "%6ld (1): %4x, \"", outcount, incode );
            count = LZWLoadBuffer ( 0, incode );
            while ( count )
                if ( DecodeBuffer[ --count ] < 32 )
                    printf ( "'0x%X'", DecodeBuffer[ count ] );
                else
                    fputc ( DecodeBuffer[ count ], stdout );
            printf ( "\"\n" );
        }
#   endif
        return ( 0 );
    }
    else
    {
```

```
        if (( data = fgetc ( infile )) == EOF )
            return ( 4 );
        incode = ( data & 0xFF ) << 4;
        if (( data = fgetc ( infile )) == EOF )
            return ( 4 );
        incode |= ( data >> 4 ) & 0xF;
#   if defined( CODES )
        {
            unsigned count;
            printf( "%6ld (0): %4x, \"", outcount, incode );
            count = LZWLoadBuffer ( 0, incode );
            while ( count )
                if ( DecodeBuffer[ --count ] < 32 )
                    printf ( "'0x%X'", DecodeBuffer[ count ] );
                else
                    fputc ( DecodeBuffer[ count ], stdout );
            printf ( "\"\n" );
        }
#   endif
        olddata = data & 0xF;
        havenibble = 1;
        return ( 0 );
    }
}


#elif BITS == 16
/* These are the 16-bit routines */
/* data dictionary */
struct Dictionary *dictionary;

static CodeType incode;
static int LZWInInit( void )
{
#   if defined( CODES )
    outcount = 0;
#   endif
    if (!DecodeBufferSize)
    {
        DecodeBufferSize = 1000;
        DecodeBuffer = malloc ( DecodeBufferSize );
        if ( DecodeBuffer == NULL )
            return ( 2 );
    }
    dictionary = malloc( DICTIONARY_SIZE *
                    sizeof( struct Dictionary ) );
    if ( dictionary == NULL )
        return ( 2 );
```

```
        return ( 0 );
}

static int LZWIn ( FILE *infile )
{
    if ( fread ( &incode, sizeof( CodeType ), 1, infile ) != 1 )
        return ( 4 );
#  if defined( CODES )
    {
        unsigned count;
        printf ( "%6ld (0): %4x, \"", outcount, incode );
        count = LZWLoadBuffer ( 0, incode );
        while ( count )
            if ( DecodeBuffer[ --count ] < 32 )
                printf ( "'0x%X'", DecodeBuffer[ count ] );
            else
                fputc( DecodeBuffer[ count ], stdout );
        printf( "\"\n" );
    }
#  endif
    return ( 0 );
}

#else
#  error Undefined value for BITS!
#endif

/* the actual decompression routine */
static IndexType freecode;
static unsigned LZWLoadBuffer ( unsigned count, CodeType code )
{
    if ( code >= freecode )
    {
        printf( "LZWLoad: code %u out of range!", code );
        return ( 0 );
    }
    while ( code >= PRESET_CODE_MAX )
    {
        DecodeBuffer[ count++ ] = dictionary[ code ].c;
        if ( count == DecodeBufferSize )
        {
            DecodeBuffer =
                realloc ( DecodeBuffer, DecodeBufferSize + 1000 );
            if ( ! DecodeBuffer )
            {
                /* out of memory */
                DecodeBufferSize = 0;
                return ( 0 );
```

```
            }
        else
            DecodeBufferSize += 1000;
        }
        code = dictionary[ code ].parent;
    }
    DecodeBuffer[ count++ ] = code;
    return ( count );
}

int LZWDecode ( FILE *infile, FILE *outfile )
{
    char buffer[ 10 ];
    int retval = 0;
    unsigned int inchar;
    unsigned count;
    CodeType oldcode;

    /* check the signature */
    fgets ( buffer, strlen ( SIGNATURE ) + 2, infile );
    if ( strcmp ( buffer, SIGNATURE ))
    {
        retval = 1;
        goto done;
    }

    /* prime the pump */
    if ( retval = LZWInInit() )
        goto done;
 priming:
    freecode = STARTING_CODE;
    if ( retval = LZWIn ( infile ))
        goto done;
    if ( incode == END_OF_INPUT )
        goto done;

    /* the first character always is itself */
    oldcode = incode;
    inchar = incode;
    if ( fputc( incode, outfile ) == EOF )
    {
        retval = 4;
        goto done;
    }
#if defined( CODES )
    outcount += 1;
#endif
```

```
    while ( ! ( retval = LZWIn ( infile )))
    {
        if ( incode == END_OF_INPUT )
            break;
        if ( incode == NEW_DICTIONARY )
            goto priming;
        if ( incode >= freecode )
        {
            /* We have a code that's not in our dictionary! */
            /* This can happen only one way--see text */

            count = LZWLoadBuffer ( 1, oldcode );

            /* Make last char same as first. Can use either */
            /* inchar or the DecodeBuffer[count-1] */

            DecodeBuffer[ 0 ] = inchar;
        }
        else
            count = LZWLoadBuffer ( 0, incode );

        if ( count == 0 )
            return ( 2 ); /* had a memory problem */

        inchar = DecodeBuffer[ count - 1 ];
        while ( count )
        {
            if ( fputc ( DecodeBuffer[--count], outfile) == EOF )
            {
                retval = 4;
                goto done;
            }
#if defined( CODES )
            outcount += 1;
#endif
        }

        /* now, update the dictionary */
        if ( freecode < MAX_CODE )
        {
            dictionary[ freecode ].parent = oldcode;
            dictionary[ freecode ].c = inchar;
            freecode += 1;

#if defined( CODES )
            {
                unsigned cnt;
                printf( "    just added code %5u: \"",
```

```
                                        freecode - 1 );
                cnt = LZWLoadBuffer ( 0, freecode - 1 );
                while ( cnt )
                    if ( DecodeBuffer[ --cnt ] < 32 )
                        printf ( "'0x%X'", DecodeBuffer[ cnt ] );
                    else
                        fputc ( DecodeBuffer[ cnt ], stdout );
                printf( "\"\n" );
            }
#endif
        }
        oldcode = incode;
    }

 done:
    fclose ( infile );
    fclose ( outfile );
    return ( retval );
}

#if defined( DRIVER )
int main ( int argc, char *argv[] )
{
    FILE * infile, *outfile;
    int retval;

    if ( argc != 3 )
    {
        fprintf ( stderr, "Usage: lzwdec infile outfile\n" );
        return ( EXIT_FAILURE );
    }

    infile = fopen ( argv[ 1 ], "r+b" );
    if ( infile == NULL )
    {
        fprintf ( stderr, "can't open %s for input\n", argv[1] );
        return ( EXIT_FAILURE );
    }

    outfile = fopen ( argv[ 2 ], "w+b" );
    if ( outfile == NULL )
    {
        fprintf( stderr, "can't open %s for output\n", argv[2] );
        return ( EXIT_FAILURE );
    }

    if ( retval = LZWDecode( infile, outfile ))
    {
```

```
            printf( "uncompression failed: " );
            if ( retval == 1 )
                printf ( "invalid signature bytes\n" );
            else
            if ( retval == 2 )
                printf ( "malloc failed\n" );
            else
            if ( retval == 3 )
                printf ( "read error in data\n" );
            else
            if ( retval == 4 )
                printf ( "write error on output\n" );
            else
                printf ( "\n" );
            return ( retval );
        }
        else
        {
            printf ( "%s was expanded into %s\n",
                                        argv[ 1 ], argv[ 2 ] );
            return ( 0 );
        }
    }
#endif
```

Filling the Dictionary

Any reasonably large input file will soon fill the dictionary, and this scenario needs to be considered. One approach is do nothing: just stop recording new codes. Compression will continue to the extent possible. This approach may result in performance deterioration. The algorithm's ability to compress effectively depends strongly on it continuing to see data for which it has codes in its dictionary. If the type of data in the input stream changes significantly, then compression can deteriorate sharply. The demonstration routines handle this problem by monitoring the efficiency of compression. Approximately every 10,000 input bytes, LZWEncode() checks its compression statistics. If the ability to compress appears to be deteriorating, then the dictionary is cleared and phrase addition begins anew. The uncompression routines are notified of this by detecting the reserved code NEW_DICTIONARY in the compressed file.

It is interesting to compare the performance of the 12- and 16-bit versions of these routines. While the 16-bit version sometimes has an advantage for very large files (>1 megabyte), the 12-bit version seems, more often that not, to be slightly superior for the more typical smaller files. To compile the programs with 16-bit processing enabled, define BITS in *lzw.h* as 16. The comparative performance of the two versions is detailed in the following section.

Which Compression Method to Use?

As stated throughout this chapter, various techniques are suited to certain kinds of data. Table 9-1, which follows, shows the compression efficiency of the algorithms presented in this chapter. In all cases, the files used for compression were large. Compression of smaller files will show varying results.

Table 9-1.   The compression performance of algorithms discussed in this chapter showing the size of the output file as a percentage of the input file

Document	RLE	Huffman	Sliding Window[1]	LZW 12 bits	LZW 16 bits
Text: 460 KB	76.6%	48.2%	42.4%	36.9%	32.8%
Binary: 1.9 MB	98.3%	79.7%	54.8%	74.4%	69.8%
Database: 5.3 MB	46.2%	36.2%	32.0%	30.1%	23.6%

[1] Using Microsoft's compress.exe program.

This table shows some interesting patterns. On large files, 16-bit LZW is consistently better than 12-bit LZW. LZW is generally better than sliding window (pure binary files are the exception); sliding window techniques are better than Huffman, and all are better than RLE.

There are factors other than compression efficiency to consider when choosing an algorithm. For example, of all these implementations, sliding window was the slowest—often much slower than the rest—and RLE was the fastest. RLE compresses sufficiently only on databases (as explained earlier). However, it does have a singular advantage: it is the only method that can recover from corruption. The other methods encode bytes as short bit patterns. If any bit is corrupted, all downstream bytes are necessarily corrupted. Whereas, in RLE, the corruption is limited to the corrupted bytes. If a single bit is corrupted, only that data byte or encoded symbol is affected. Uncompression past the point of the corruption will work correctly.

Huffman is the only method that cannot be done on the fly. For Huffman to do its work it must read the entire file twice, so the complete dataset must be known before compression can begin.

LZW, which seems like it should be the favorite under most scenarios, is unfortunately hobbled by the Unisys patents on it. It is not free to use. Undoubtedly, you can create your own version (Welch's addition consisted of preloading the dictionary). However, even these cobbled versions may need to be licensed prior to use.

This means that for most users, the only freely available effective compression routines are Huffman encoding and sliding window. Fortunately, they do an acceptably good job with all types of files.

Resources and References

Bentley, Jon. "Squzng Engl Txt." *UNIX Review*, Vol. 13, No. 2, pp. 61. February 1995.

Davis, Pete. "Microsoft's Compression File Format." *Windows/DOS Developer's Journal*, July 1994, pp. 59–64.

Huffman, D. A. "A Method for the Construction of Minimum-Redundancy Codes." *Proceedings of the IRE*, Vol. 40, No. 9, pp. 1098–1101, September 1952.

Nelson, Mark. *The Data Compression Book.* Redwood City, CA: M&T Books, 1991. If you want to examine data compression in greater depth, this is the best book on the subject by a wide margin. All major algorithms are thoroughly explained with thoughtful illustrations and considerable C source code.

Swan, Tom. *Inside Windows File Formats.* Indianapolis, IN: Howard Sams & Co., 1994.

Ziv, Jacob, and Abraham Lempel. "A Universal Algorithm for Sequential Data Compression." *IEEE Transactions on Information Theory*, Vol. 23, No. 3, pp. 337–343, May 1977. Although Ziv is the lead author, this algorithm, for reasons unknown, is generally referred to as Lempel-Ziv or LZ.

## Chapter 10

Data Integrity and Validation

The first acronym introduced to novice programmers is GIGO—garbage in, garbage out. It is a simple reminder that if data is not accurate, then any results based on that data will be inaccurate as well. The validation of data is an activity found in almost all aspects of computing, but most frequently in data processing and telecommunications. These two domains have the same need for data validation, although they come by this need in very different ways.

In data processing, data is validated as it is entered into an application. Often, the validation process takes place as the data is keyed into an application. For example, it is important to know that a user has typed a valid serial number for an engine part, a claims form, or a personnel record. Validation at the point of entry can take very simple forms. Making sure that a date has four digits in the year, and two each in the month and day fields is one example. Further integrity checks might make sure that the digits correspond to a valid date. Validation of other fields can use a wide variety of means. For example, checksums (discussed in the next section) are often used for making sure that no digits have been reversed within serial numbers.

The field of telecommunications uses data validation for making sure that a site receiving data has received the same data that was sent from the originating site. Telecommunication protocols use all kinds of techniques for establishing data integrity during the transmission itself. These techniques include the use of parity bits for each character and checksums for each packet of transmitted data. The techniques used in telecommunications are examined later in this chapter.

Beyond telecommunications and data processing, data-validation techniques, such as checksums, are used anywhere that a user needs to know whether a file has been modified. For example, virus-protection schemes often work by comparing checksums from current files with checksums on record for those specific files; by so doing, any tampering by a virus can be detected. Internet sites that place a high premium on security use similar checksum schemes to see exactly what has been uploaded or modified on the system. Data validation is commonly used in backup software to make sure that backed-up files are identical to the original files. Anytime you need to establish the integrity of data or binary files, you can find powerful solutions among the algorithms presented in this chapter.

Simple Checksums

The simplest way to validate data is to use a **checksum**. A checksum is a computed value that, when added to some value extracted from the data itself, generates a third value whose integrity can be established.

A simple checksum, called **parity**, is used inside the computer's hardware to verify the integrity of data held in memory. Parity is also widely used in telecommunications, where the technique first gained wide popularity.

When a byte is stored in memory, it typically occupies 8 bits. Transparent to all memory operations, however, for every 8-bit byte, a ninth bit (called the **parity bit**) that cannot be accessed except by the lowest levels of hardware is set in memory. This bit contains a value of either 1 or 0, depending on the value of the byte with which it is associated. In a scheme that uses **odd parity**, the value of the parity bit will be set such that the total number of bits (in the original byte and the parity bit) with the value of 1 is odd. For example, if a byte has the value of 0 (all bits are 0), then in the case of odd parity, the parity bit will have a value of 1. In this manner, between the original byte and the parity bit, there is an odd number of bits with the value of 1; in this case, the total is 1. Likewise, if a byte has a value of 14 (the binary value of 00001110), since the total of bits set to 1 is already odd, the parity bit has a value of 0. In a scheme that uses **even parity**, the total number of bits set to 1 would be even rather than odd. Using parity, the computer memory-management hardware can crudely check that the data in memory was written correctly and has not been corrupted.

The benefit of parity checking is that it can be done very quickly. The drawback is that many errors can go undetected. Single-bit errors will always be detected, but if two bits change value, parity will not notice this. Consider the following example:

```
1111 0111    parity bit (even): 1
1111 1011    parity bit (even): 1
```

Here, a byte has suffered the transposition of two bits but has generated the same parity bit. From this example we see that parity bits will detect transpositions of odd numbers of bits but will not detect transpositions of even numbers of bits.

Telecommunication protocols also use parity. Specifically, asynchronous telecommunication (the kind most frequently employed, except by IBM mainframes) uses parity bits at the end of each character to make sure that it has been transmitted correctly. Anyone who has used a modem has had the experience of setting the protocol needed for dialing into a bulletin board (BBS) or other site. One setting that must be made correctly is the kind of parity used by the destination site. If the parities do not match, the communication protocol will mistakenly believe that transmission errors are occurring. The general choices of parity are odd, even, or none (no parity bits).

CompuServe, for example, defaults to even parity. Most dial-up services today, however, use no parity, primarily because of the reliability issues of parity checking and because sending the parity bit uses up telecommunication bandwidth. In typical asynchronous telecommunications, each byte consumes the following number of bits:

1 start bit (announcing that a byte of data follows)
8 data bits (the byte itself)
0 or 1 parity bits
1 stop bit (announcing the end of the transmission of the byte)

Use of the parity bit, therefore, means that each byte grows from 10 bits to 11 bits, resulting in a 10 percent decrease in throughput. This is substantial enough (especially in view of the limitations of parity checking) that parity bits are rarely used in asynchronous communications any more. Other means of validating data are commonly used; these are discussed later in this chapter.

Parity checking is effective only when a single bit is in error. As soon as two or more bits are corrupted, parity checking will on average be correct only 50 percent of the time. This kind of effectiveness is too low for the transmission of important data. Parity checking is still retained in computer hardware, because the processing of the parity bit is done in firmware and therefore is very quick. In addition, since the parity bit is inaccessible except to the memory-management hardware, the parity bit does not impede data throughput. However, anyone who has bought memory for a computer has surely noticed that RAM chips come in sets of nine (eight chips to hold the data bits, and one to hold the parity bit), meaning that there are costs to maintaining the tradition of parity-checking memory.

Other forms of checksums that are somewhat more effective are used in many applications. For example, the records in object files for Intel processors all have checksums. Object files are generated by a compiler or an assembler. They contain records that hold the program's executable code before it has been linked with the appropriate libraries. The format of object files varies by processor. The Intel processor's object file format specifies that the last byte of each record contain a 1-byte checksum, calculated as specified in an Intel document [Intel 1981]: "The last field in each record is a checksum, which contains the 2's complement of the sum (modulo 256) of all other bytes in the record. Therefore, the sum (modulo 256) of all bytes in the record equals 0."

The Intel example is a classic checksum—a value generated from the data being checked in order to provide a third value (here, 0) whose integrity can be ascertained. The code for this checksum is easy to put together. Add up all the bytes in the data into a single `char` field (excess bits are discarded), and take the negative value of that sum, as shown in Listing 10-1.

Listing 10-1.   Computing an Intel object-file checksum.

```
char IntelCheckSum ( char *data, int length )
{
    char sum;
    int i;

    for ( i = 0, sum = 0; i < length; i++ )
            sum += data[i];

    return (−sum );
}
```

Notice that by making `sum` a `char` (not an `int`), we limit the value of `sum` to a maximum of 8 bits (or a maximum value of 255). Any sum greater than 255 will occupy more than 8 bits, and the overflow bits are truncated. This truncation to a value less than 256 is what the Intel specification means by modulo 256. The final step in the code multiplies the final `sum` by −1, thereby generating the checksum that added to `sum` will result in 0. Notice that we must know the length of the data in order to generate the checksum. Unlike strings in C, the checksum process cannot end at the first null byte, since this byte could contain valid data.

This checksum is considerably more effective than the parity checking discussed previously. It is capable of discovering corruption of far more than a single bit. Again, two bits will have to be in error before this checksum can be fooled into reporting that invalid data is correct. A single bit, if in error by itself, should show up in the final checksum. However, if two complementary bits are in error such that the error of the second bit offsets the error of the first bit, then the checksum method will not detect this occurrence. Note that the odds of this combination of bits occurring are only 1 in 256. This checksum is therefore far more accurate than the parity check.

Also note the comparative space efficiency of this checksum: it can give some data validation for large blocks of data by using only a single byte. However, as the amount of data verified by this checksum increases past 256 bytes, the error rate of the checksum becomes more troublesome. Let's examine this point by using an 8-byte string consisting of the following binary values (shown in decimal form):

$$128, 128, 128, 128, 128, 128, 128, 14$$

We obtain a checksum of 142—the checksum for the last two bytes. This is because the first six bytes are in pairs that each sum to 256, resulting in a zero checksum through the first six bytes. Any change in the last two bytes (128, 14) will be reflected accurately in the final checksum, with the proviso mentioned previously, that no change in the last byte is commensurately offset in the preceding byte (a 1-in-256 chance). In the preceding example, any 6-byte string that generates a checksum of zero can replace the six bytes of 128 without being detected by the checksum. Pursuing this approach, we soon find that there is a 1-in-256 chance that any 2-byte combination is in error and will be undetected by the checksum. The upshot of this is that the longer the data being checksummed, the greater the chance of error. The generally accepted maximum length where a one-byte checksum can be used without excess risk is 256 bytes.

To increase the reliability of the checksum approach, we could use a two-byte checksum that performs the same calculation. To do so, we would change the code in Listing 10-1 so that the function returns an `int` and so that `sum` is defined as an `int`.

An interesting historical note is the use of the one-byte checksum in Intel records. Not long after the Intel object standard was first published, compiler vendors recognized that they were capable of generating correct Intel object records without needing to verify them with a checksum. And because disk drives average only about 1 error in every 10^{12} bits written, the checksum field, while still being generated, was never used. At some point, compiler writers chose to ignore the field altogether and to simply insert a 0 in the checksum byte. When Intel reissued the standard in 1993 [Intel 1993], the description of the checksum field was updated correspondingly: "Some compilers write a 0 byte rather than computing the checksum, so either form should be accepted by programs that process object modules."

The choice of checksum is determined by the nature of the information being verified. For example, in the early 1980s the United States Postal Service designed a bar code scheme that allowed scanners to read ZIP codes from envelopes and then encode and print the zip codes along the bottom edge of the envelopes. Subsequent mail scanners could then identify these bar codes and use them to route the letter automatically. The bar code system [USPS 1984] uses a parity scheme to encode each digit of the ZIP code and a checksum to verify the entire sequence of digits. The bar code is composed of short lines and long lines, with the long lines representing a 1 and the short lines representing a 0. An example of the postal bar code is shown in Figure 10-1.

Start Bar   End Bar

Figure 10-1.   A U.S. Postal Service bar code showing a 9-digit ZIP code (12345-6789) followed by a checksum digit (5).

The postal bar code scheme works in this way: the checksum is the digit that must be added to the total of the previous nine digits to reach a multiple of 10. In Figure 10-1, the first nine digits total 45, so the checksum is 5. The digits themselves each consist of five bars, with each bar representing a bit that has a value of 0 or 1. The first four bars contain the bits that indicate the digit, while the last bar is used for obtaining even parity. The values of the bars (going from left to right) are 7-4-2-1. The choice of 7 rather than 8 for the left most bar is explained in the next paragraph. We see 1 is represented as 00011 or better—0001 and a parity bit of 1. Likewise, 6 is represented as 01100, or 0110 followed by a parity bit of 0, and 8 is 1001 followed by a parity bit of 0.

By the use of 7, not 8, as the leftmost bar, the Postal Service added a refinement to its scheme: every digit has at least two 1's in it. (This is different from even parity. Recall that with even parity, a number could have *no* bits set to 1.) This refinement means that a digit of 0 must be given a special value: 1100 with a parity bit of 0.

Finally, the bar code has an initial and trailing 1, which indicate the beginning and end of the bar code. Using this scheme, the Postal Service can verify that every digit has been encoded correctly (by the use of parity bits) and that the whole code is correct (by the use of the checksum). A final check consists of counting the 1's: since each digit must have at least two 1's and there is a 1 at the beginning and end of the code, each bar code should have at least twenty-two 1's.

The checksums presented so far are effective for verifying that existing data is encoded correctly. Given a *correct* ZIP code, for example, the postal bar code system can verify quickly that the bar code has been read and printed correctly. Specifically, these checksums can tell you only that the data is represented in a valid form. What they cannot tell you is whether the original data is correct to begin with. In the previous example, the checksum cannot say whether the original ZIP code is correct, but only that a valid sequence of digits has been encoded in a bar code. These checksums address form, not content. This limitation means that these checksums cannot be used to validate data entered by a keypunch operator. With data that is entered manually, you need to check both that the data has a valid form and that it matches the original data being keyed. To do this, you need to use weighted checksums.

Weighted Checksums

Weighted checksums attempt to overcome a critical weakness of simple checksums: detecting transpositions. Suppose that a keypunch operator is entering nine-digit ZIP codes, and we calculate the checksum according to the U.S. Postal Service's method. We compute a tenth digit that, when added to the nine ZIP digits, will generate a total that is a multiple of 10. This checksum digit will tell us whether the ZIP code has a valid form, but it will not tell us whether digits have been transposed. In Figure 10-1, a ZIP code of 12345-6789 generated a checksum of 5. Had the data-entry operator transposed the first two digits (21345-6789), we would obtain the same checksum, and the error would go unnoticed.

To address the problem of transpositions (a major problem in data entry), we have to accord a separate value to the *position* of each digit we are verifying. We do this by giving each position a separate weight. The weight is then multiplied by the digit itself, and the sum of these weighted digits is used as the basis of the checksum. A simple scheme is to give each position in the number a successively higher multiple of 7, as shown in Table 10-1.

Table 10-1. Positional weighting based on powers of 7

Position	Weight
1	1
2	7
3	49
4	343
5	2401
6	16807
7	117649
8	823543
9	5764801
10	40353607

Based on this table, a five-digit number such as 12345 would be encoded as 1∗2401, 2∗343, 3∗49, 4∗7, 5∗1. The sum would be 3267. Then we would take this number modulo 11 (assigning the value 0 to a remainder of 10). When modulo 11 is applied to 3267, the result is 0. This is the checksum digit. Another scheme often used in data processing is powers of 9 modulo 11. We will examine comparative accuracy of these methods shortly.

The use of modulo 11, rather than the last digit of the sum (which would be the equivalent of modulo 10), is based on the dispersal caused by dividing a number by a prime number (11). This topic was first presented in Chapter 3, "Hashing." Divide any number by 11 and it will generate a new remainder (unless the number is an exact multiple of 11). This is not true for 10, since the modulo function for 10 will never change the final remainder digit. The choice of 11 rather than a higher prime—13, for example—allows the minimum mapping of values. In modulo 11, a remainder of 10 is mapped to 0; in the case of 13, three remainders (10, 11, 12) would have to be mapped to single digits for no significant gain in distribution of remainders. Listing 10-3 (*cksmtest.c*, presented later in the chapter), shows how significantly the choice of modulo 10 instead of modulo 11 negatively affects the distribution of checksum digits.

The code for generating the foregoing weighted checksum, along with a small driver that allows you to specify the number to be checked at the command line, appears in Listing 10-2. This code places the values from Table 10-1 in a lookup table and calculates the checksum in a straightforward fashion.

Listing 10-2.   How to generate a 7 mod 11 checksum.

```c
/*--- ck7mod11.c ------------------------ Listing 10-2 ------
 * Demonstrates weighted checksum using powers of 7 and
 * modulo 11
 *---------------------------------------------------------*/

#include <stdio.h>
#include <stdlib.h>
#include <string.h>
#include <ctype.h>

#define DRIVER   1 /* generate a main line when #defined */
#define VERBOSE  1 /* print information about computation */

int Get7Mod11Chksum ( const char *data, int length )
{
    int  i, j;
    int  position;
    unsigned long int sum;

    static long int powers [10] = { 1, 7, 49, 343, 2401,
            16807, 117649, 823543, 5764801, 40353607 };

    /* make sure all digits can be looked up */

    if ( length > 10 )
        return ( -1 );

    sum = 0L;
    position = 0; /* what digit in the data are we at? */

    for ( i = length; i > 0; i--, position++ )
    {
        /* do we have a digit ? */

        if ( ! isdigit ( data[i-1] ))
            return ( -2 );

        /* convert digit character to a number */

        j = data[i-1] - '0';

        /* look up power, multiply by j, add to sum */

        sum += powers [position] * j;
    }
```

```
    /* get the sum modulus 11 */

    i = (int) ( sum % 11L );


    if ( i == 10 )
        i = 0;

#ifdef VERBOSE
    printf ( "Sum is %ld, checksum is %d\n", sum, i );
#endif

    return ( i );
}


#ifdef DRIVER
main ( int argc, char *argv[] )
{
    int i;

    if ( argc < 2 )
    {
        fprintf ( stderr, "Generates checksum using 7 mod 11.\n"
                  "Requires a command line # to validate.\n" );
        return ( EXIT_FAILURE );
    }

#ifdef VERBOSE
    printf ( "Computing 7 mod 11 checksum for: %s\n", argv[1] );
#endif

    i = Get7Mod11Chksum ( argv[1], strlen ( argv[1] ));

    if ( i == -1 )
        fprintf ( stderr,
                  "Number must be ten digits or less\n" );

    if ( i == -2 )
        fprintf ( stderr, "Number is invalid.\n" );

    return ( EXIT_SUCCESS );
}
#endif
```

As you can see in Table 10-2, there are four possible transpositions of 12345. Note that none of these transpositions generates the same weighted checksum as the original number.

Table 10-2. Possible transpositions of 12345 with the corresponding checksums

Transposition	Sum	Checksum
21345	5325	1
13245	3561	8
12435	3309	9
12354	3273	6

Catching two transpositions is a considerably more difficult task, and errors of this kind can slip through. However, in the real world, this situation should not occur frequently. If a keypunch operator regularly makes two transposition errors, there is a qualitative issue that needs to be addressed. Invariably, such quality will be detected quickly, because the checksum will report too many errors for the work to continue unless the operator becomes more accurate.

Before settling on a checksum method, you will find it useful to test the method to see how well it avoids generating checksums for transpositions that are the same as the checksum of the original number. Listing 10-3 (*cksmtest.c*) performs this test. It creates a table, `table`, that holds 100 random ten-digit numbers. It then loops through the table and computes the checksum for each of the 100 numbers and all possible transpositions of that number. It keeps track (in `collisions`) of the number of times that a transposed number generates the same checksum as the original number. It then generates a new table of 100 ten-digit numbers, but uses only the first nine digits of each number to test the transpositions on nine-digit numbers. It continues in this manner until it has tested 100 random numbers for all sizes from ten digits to two digits.

Listing 10-3. A program that tests multiple weighted checksum methods on 100 random numbers, using all possible transpositions.

```
/*--- cksmtest.c ------------------------ Listing 10-3 ------
 *  Test checksum methods to see the distribution of checksums
 *  when transpositions occur. Performs the testing on 100
 *  random 10-digit numbers all the way to 100 2-digit
 *  numbers. Benign transpositions (see text) are not included.
 *------------------------------------------------------------*/

#include <stdio.h>
```

```c
#include <stdlib.h>
#include <string.h>
#include <ctype.h>

char table [100] [10]; /* the table of random digits */
                       /* max: 100 numbers of 10 digits each */

void DisplayUsage ( void );
void LoadTableRandom ( char * );
int  GetChecksum ( char *, int, int );

int main( int argc, char *argv[] )
{
    int  i, j, size, method;
    char *p, *pmax;
    char buffer[10];

    p = (char *) table;       /* start of table */
    pmax = p + 1000;          /* end of table */

    if ( argc != 2 )
    {
        DisplayUsage();
        return ( EXIT_FAILURE );
    }
    else
        method = atoi ( argv[1] );

    switch ( method )
    {
        case 1: printf ( "Using 7 mod 11\n\n" );     break;
        case 2: printf ( "Using 9 mod 11\n\n" );     break;
        case 3: printf ( "Using 7 mod 26\n\n" );     break;
        case 4: printf ( "Using 7 mod 10\n\n" );     break;
        case 5: printf ( "Using 9 mod 10\n\n" );     break;
        default:
                DisplayUsage();
                return ( EXIT_FAILURE );
    }

    /* we loop through for every size from 10 to 2.
     * We don't handle 1-digit numbers since they
     * offer no possibility of transpositions.
     */

    for ( size = 10; size > 1; size-- )
    {
        int collisions = 0;
```

```
/* Load the table with random digits */

LoadTableRandom ( pmax );

/* main test loop: we process 100 numbers
 * of length size. For each number, we do every
 * possible transposition and get its checksum.
 */

for ( i = 0, p = (char *)table; i < 100;
                                    i++, p += size )
{
    int k, l, orig_cksum;

    /* get the original number's checksum */

    orig_cksum = GetChecksum ( p, size, method );

    /* now copy the number to buffer, where we'll
     * do the transpositions.
     */

    memcpy ( buffer, p, size );

    /* do the transpositions and checksums */

    for ( k = 0; k < size - 1; k++ )
    {
        /* is there a transposition possible?
         * if both digits are the same, they cannot
         * be transposed; so skip these, otherwise
         * they will generate bogus collisions.
         */

        if ( buffer[k] == buffer[k + 1] )
            continue;

        /* otherwise, do the transposition */

        l = buffer[k + 1];
        buffer[k + 1] = buffer[k];
        buffer[k] = (char) l;

        /* get the checksum */

        j = GetChecksum ( buffer, size, method );
```

```
                    if ( j == orig_cksum )
                        collisions += 1;

                    /* now undo this transposition */

                    l = buffer[k + 1];
                    buffer[k + 1] = buffer[k];
                    buffer[k] = (char) l;
                }

            }   /* end of loop processing numbers of one size */

            printf ( "%2d digits avg. %1.2f collisions\n",
                        size, (float) ( collisions / 100.0 ));

            collisions = 0;
        }

    return ( EXIT_SUCCESS );
}

void LoadTableRandom ( char *table_end )
{
    int i;
    unsigned short int j;
    char *p, *p2;

    /* 200 random ints will get us close to 1000 digits
     * we presume it gets us at least 500 digits, which is
     * a safe bet, but will not always be the case.
     */

    p = (char *) table;

    for ( i = 0; i < 200; i++ )
    {
        j = (short int) rand();
        sprintf ( p, "%u", j );
        p += strlen ( p );
    }

    /* how many digits left to fill out? */

    i = table_end - p;

    p2 = p - 1;

    /* go backwards from p and copy digits into the
```

```
  * remaining table space. This will copy i digits
  * prior to p and place them in reverse order after p.
  */
 while ( i )
 {
     *p++ = *p2--;
     i--;
 }
}

int GetChecksum ( char *data, int length, int which_test )
{
    int  i, j;
    int  position;
    unsigned long int sum;
    long int *powers;

    static long int powers_of_7 [10] = { 1, 7, 49, 343, 2401,
            16807, 117649, 823543, 5764801, 40353607 };

    static long int powers_of_9 [10] = { 1, 9, 81, 729, 6561,
            59049, 531441, 4782969, 43046721, 387420489 };

    if ( which_test == 2 || which_test == 5 )
        powers = powers_of_9;
    else
        powers = powers_of_7;

    /* make sure all digits can be looked up */

    if ( length > 10 )
        return ( -1 );

    sum = 0L;
    position = 0; /* what digit in the data are we at? */

    for ( i = length; i > 0; i--, position++ )
    {
        /* do we have a digit ? */

        if ( ! isdigit ( data[i-1] ))
            return ( -2 );

        /* convert digit character to a number */

        j = data[i-1] - '0';

        /* look up power, multiply by j, add to sum */
```

```
            sum += powers [position] * j;
        }

        /* get the sum modulus depending on method */

        switch ( which_test )
        {
            case 1:
            case 2:
                i = (int) ( sum % 11L );
                if ( i == 10 )
                    i = 0;
                break;
            case 3:
                i = (int) ( sum % 26L );        break;
            case 4:
            case 5:
                i = (int) ( sum % 10L );        break;
            default:
                DisplayUsage();
                exit ( EXIT_FAILURE );
        }

        return ( i );
}

void DisplayUsage()
{
    fprintf ( stderr,
        "Error: need to specify checksum method to test\n"
        "1. Powers of 7 Mod 11\n"
        "2. Powers of 9 Mod 11\n"
        "3. Powers of 7 Mod 26\n"
        "4. Powers of 7 Mod 10\n"
        "5. Powers of 9 Mod 10\n" );
}
```

The program exercises the two methods mentioned previously—powers of 7 modulo 11 (7 mod 11) and 9 mod 11—and one additional method: 7 mod 26. The results of this program for 7 mod 11 and 9 mod 11 are shown in Table 10-3. It also tests 7 mod 10, as mentioned previously, and 9 mod 10.

Table 10-3. **The results of two separate checksum methods, showing the number of transpositions that have the same checksum as the original number (for 100 random numbers)**

Digits	7 mod 11	9 mod 11
10	9	15
9	11	13
8	12	12
7	10	7
6	5	6
5	4	7
4	6	7
3	4	3
2	3	2

If you run the program in Listing 10-3, you will likely obtain results that differ somewhat from those in Table 10-3. This is because of variations in the number sequences generated by your compiler library's `rand()` function. Even though the table is based on 100 random instances for each number size, the results depend intensely on the generated test numbers. Table 10-3 shows the average results from running the program on compilers from Borland, Microsoft, and Novell's UnixWare. As an illustration of the variance, the run of tests for ten-digit numbers using the 9 mod 11 method generated 16 collisions with Borland's compiler and only 10 with the UNIX product.

From the table, we can see that the 7 mod 11 method is the better one for avoiding checksum collisions when transpositions occur. The numbers in the table show that weighted checksums will generally catch just under 90 percent of numbers that are seven digits or longer where any transposition occurs, and well over 90 percent when the number is shorter than seven digits.

These results, however, are deceptively bad. In Table 10-3 we see that in 100 ten-digit random numbers, there will be 9 unnoticed transpositions when we use the 7 mod 11 method. In actual fact, the percentage is much closer to 100 percent accuracy, because every ten-digit number has 9 possible transpositions. Hence, of the 900 possible transpositions, only 9 go by undetected. Moreover, of the 900 possible transpositions 10 percent will be benign because they are transpositions of the same digit. For example, in the number 1234567890, the possible transpositions (going from left to right) are as follows:

2-1, 3-2, 4-3, 5-4, 6-5, 7-6, 8-7, 9-8, 0-9 (nine transpositions and nine possible errors)

However, in 1223445678, there are these nine possible transpositions:

2-1, 2-2, 3-2, 4-3, 4-4, 5-4, 6-5, 7-6, 8-7 (nine transpositions and *seven* possible errors)

Because transpositions of identical digits (2-2 and 4-4 in the preceding example) do not constitute errors, we deduct these from the pool of possible errors that the checksum needs to catch. Since there is a 10 percent chance that any digit is followed by another matching digit, of the 900 possible transpositions, only 810 are errors. Of these 810 errors, the 7 mod 11 checksum caught all but 9. Hence, it has an error-catching rate of 99 percent, even though only 91 percent of the ten-digit numbers can be guaranteed correct on average.

If these results are insufficient, there are several possible improvements. Not the least of these is to make some part of the number meaningful so that other data can verify its correctness. If you must use long nonmeaningful numbers, however, make the checksum a letter rather than a digit. This offers 26 possible checksums rather than the 10 permitted by a single digit. For example, look at checksum method 3 in Listing 10-3. It uses powers of 7 modulo 26. The results of this change are dramatic: collisions drop off to zero in all but the largest numbers. In numbers up to ten digits in length, this method catches virtually 100 percent of data-entry errors consisting of single transpositions.

Interestingly, this last approach is not widely used. The reason is primarily an issue of speed. Professional data-entry clerks can use a ten-key numeric keypad much more quickly if they do not have to move their hands off their keypads to type a single letter. Typing a single letter during a run of numbers often requires that both hands be brought to the keyboard to position the fingers for the single keypress, or that the operator look down at the keyboard to locate the letter. This invariably slows down the entry process. The trade-off, as ever, is speed versus accuracy. Note that if you choose to use a letter checksum, you should avoid using letters such as O and I, because they are likely to be confused with the numbers 0 and 1. In the code presented in Listing 10-3, checksums of O and I should be explicitly tested for and mapped to other letters.

Another solution for increasing checksum accuracy is to use two-digit checksum (with modulo 101). This approach ensures virtual 100 percent accuracy while making it unnecessary for the operator's hand to leave the numeric keypad. However, this approach has been eschewed by most data-processing methods because of the time required for typing two extra digits, rather than one, and because of the additional disk space occupied by the extra byte.

In real-world situations where long numbers are involved, the general trend is to use bar codes to ensure both speed and accuracy. Bar codes are now standard where long numbers must be entered quickly. Consider an airbill from

Federal Express or other carriers, or parts lists from large suppliers. These firms use bar codes as the primary means of data entry, while still retaining a check digit in the number being bar-coded. In this way, whether the number is scanned in or keyed in, accuracy remains high.

Cyclic Redundancy Check

In the previous discussion of checksums, we found that simple checksums are moderately good at flagging data errors and that weighted checksums are very effective at spotting errors in data entry. Both forms of checksums, however, are limited by the size of the data they can verify. Simple checksums, as discussed previously, are inaccurate for data that is longer than 256 bytes. Weighted checksums are impractical for numbers longer than 12 to 15 digits, because the powers of 7 or 9 become too large to handle within C's integral data types. As a result of this limitation, there arises the need to generate checksums that can validate large blocks of data very accurately. Furthermore, since large amounts of data are involved, the algorithm must work quickly. Telecommunications is a field in which this kind of validation is frequently necessary. In telecommunications, large blocks of data are sent from one site to another. It is imperative that the receiving site be able to determine whether it has received the exact data it was sent. To accomplish this, modern telecommunications protocols use a checksum called a **cyclic redundancy check (CRC)**. The name of this checksum should not be considered as daunting as it sounds. The way the words themselves describe the algorithm is buried deep in the origins of the algorithm and have no special significance—not unlike "hashing" in hashing algorithms (see Chapter 3) and the taxonomy of red-black trees (see Chapter 6).

The origins of CRC are not in telecommunications but in computer hardware. Originally, CRC was used for validating data transfers within a computer. This legacy lives on today as CRC is still used by disk drives to validate reads and writes of data blocks.

CRC computes a number that reflects the value and the position of individual bits in a block of data. It does this by making the individual bits exponents in a polynomial of the form:

$$bit_{n-1} * x^{n-1} + bit_{n-2} * x^{n-2} + ... + bit_0 * x^0$$

(The value of x is special and will be discussed in a moment.) In the implementations of CRC that we examine, this polynomial is established 16 bits at a time. That is, $n = 16$. This polynomial is then divided by one of two polynomials, depending on which form of CRC we decide to use. If we use CRC-16 (the CRC algorithm used in disk-drive controllers), the divisor polynomial is as follows:

$$x^{16} + x^{15} + x^2 + 1$$

If we use CRC-CCITT (CCITT is the worldwide communications-standards organization), the divisor polynomial is this:

$$x^{16} + x^{12} + x^5 + 1$$

CRC-CCITT is used in the Xmodem-CRC protocol (regular Xmodem uses a 1-byte checksum) and in early versions of IBM's SDLC/HDLC telecommunications protocols. Why these two particular divisors are used is the result of considerable mathematical material, much of which is explained without requiring excessive mathematics by Joseph Campbell and David Schwaderer [Campbell 1987; Schwaderer 1988]. Suffice it to say that divisions by these polynomials gives a wide distribution of CRC values and can be done quickly with the use of bit shifts.

CRC-CCITT

The actual CRC value is the remainder from the foregoing division. For example, if we were to obtain the CRC-CCITT value for the ASCII letter g, we would perform the following calculations. The letter g is hex 67. Hence, its binary representation is 01100111. Making this into a polynomial of the form described previously, we obtain the following:

$$0x^7 + 1x^6 + 1x^5 + 0x^4 + 0x^3 + 1x^2 + 1x^1 + 1x^0$$

Removing the terms with coefficients of 0 and simplifying the rest, we get the following equation when we divide by the CRC-CCITT polynomial:

$$\text{CRC-CCITT (g)} = \text{remainder of } \frac{x^6 + x^5 + x^2 + x + 1}{x^{16} + x^{12} + x^5 + 1}$$

At first glance this looks like a virtually impossible equation and certainly one that involves far too many difficult calculations (exponentiations and division) to render a value quickly. However, as stated previously, the CRC polynomials and the magical value of x were chosen carefully to make this division possible using only bit operations. Listing 10-4 (*ccittotf.c,* for *CCITT on-the-fly*) shows how to compute CRC-CCITT on a file by computing the CRC one byte at a time. The first function, GetCCITT(), performs the actual calculation and returns the CRC for a byte. The returned value is then passed back to the function with the next byte to validate. When all bytes in the file have been examined, the final CRC value is displayed. That value is the CRC for the whole file.

Listing 10-4.   CRC-CCITT computed on the fly one byte at a time for an entire file.

```c
/*--- CCITTOTF.C  ----------------------- Listing 10-4 -----
 * Compute CCITT-CRC on-the-fly.
 * Usage:   ccittotf filename
 *
 * Based on a similar program by Nigel Cort in C Gazette 5.1
 * (Autumn 1990).
 *-----------------------------------------------------------*/

#include <stdio.h>
#include <stdlib.h>

#define DRIVER 1 /* DRIVER includes the file processing */


/*  Compute single-byte CRC-CCITT on-the-fly */

unsigned short GetCCITT ( unsigned short crc, unsigned short ch )
{
    static unsigned int i;
    ch <<= 8;                               /* Move to MSB       */
    for ( i = 8; i > 0; i-- )        /* Go through 8 bits */
    {
        if ( (ch ^ crc) & 0X8000 )      /* Perform CRC calc. */
            crc = ( crc << 1 ) ^ 0x1021;
        else
            crc <<= 1;
        ch <<= 1;
    }
    return ( crc );
}

#ifdef DRIVER
int main ( int argc, char * argv[] )
{
    FILE *fin;          /* file we're reading into buffer */
    char *buffer;       /* buffer we're working on        */
    size_t i, j;        /* counters of bytes in buff      */
    unsigned short crc; /* the CRC value being computed   */

    if ( argc < 2 )
    {
        fprintf ( stderr, "Error! Must specify filename.\n" );
        return ( EXIT_FAILURE );
    }

    if (( fin = fopen ( argv[1], "rb" )) == NULL )
    {
```

```
      fprintf ( stderr, "Cannot open %s", argv[1] );
      return ( EXIT_FAILURE );
   }

   /*--------------------------------------------------
    * Set up a very large input buffer of 32K bytes.
    * This program does no good if it doesn't fly!
    *-------------------------------------------------*/

   if (( buffer = (char *) malloc ( 32766 )) == NULL )
   {
      fprintf ( stderr, "Out of memory\n" );
      return ( EXIT_FAILURE );
   }

   crc = 0;

   for (;;)
   {
      i = fread ( buffer, 1, 32766, fin );
      if ( i == 0 )
      {
         if ( feof ( fin ))   /* we're done, so show results */
         {
            printf ( "CCITT CRC for %s is %04X\n",
                                          argv[1], crc );
            return ( EXIT_SUCCESS );
         }
         else          /* read another 32K of file */
            continue;
      }

      for ( j = 0 ; j < i; j ++ )   /* loop through the buffer */
         crc = GetCCITT ( crc, buffer [j] );
   }
}
#endif
```

The value 0x1021 appears prominently in the computation of the CRC value in the CCITT implementation shown in Listing 10-4. This is a magic value used in the bit shifting that mirrors the magic value of x mentioned previously. If you want to know how and why this magic value is necessary for transposing the computation into a series of bit shifts, you will need to delve deep into the mathematics of CRC. The books by Schwaderer and Campbell, mentioned earlier, are good places to start.

It should be clear that the polynomial used in the CCITT polynomial has a constant value for its denominator. Moreover, since there are a maximum of

256 possible bit combinations in a byte, there are only 256 possible numerators in the division of polynomials. Given this, we can create a table of CRC-CCITT values that can be used for looking up the individual CRC for a byte, rather than computing the CRC on the fly. By using a lookup table of the CRCs, the program in Listing 10-4 can be made to run more efficiently, albeit at the cost of 1,024 additional bytes of memory. The table of values appears in Figure 10-2 as it would look in a C program.

Figure 10-2.   A source-code table of the CRC-CCITT values for every possible byte.

```
/* CCITT Lookup Table */
unsigned short ccitt_table[256] =
{

/*    0 -- */   0x0000, 0x1021, 0x2042, 0x3063, 0x4084, 0x50A5, 0x60C6, 0x70E7,
/*    8 -- */   0x8108, 0x9129, 0xA14A, 0xB16B, 0xC18C, 0xD1AD, 0xE1CE, 0xF1EF,
/*   16 -- */   0x1231, 0x0210, 0x3273, 0x2252, 0x52B5, 0x4294, 0x72F7, 0x62D6,
/*   24 -- */   0x9339, 0x8318, 0xB37B, 0xA35A, 0xD3BD, 0xC39C, 0xF3FF, 0xE3DE,
/*   32 -- */   0x2462, 0x3443, 0x0420, 0x1401, 0x64E6, 0x74C7, 0x44A4, 0x5485,
/*   40 -- */   0xA56A, 0xB54B, 0x8528, 0x9509, 0xE5EE, 0xF5CF, 0xC5AC, 0xD58D,
/*   48 -- */   0x3653, 0x2672, 0x1611, 0x0630, 0x76D7, 0x66F6, 0x5695, 0x46B4,
/*   56 -- */   0xB75B, 0xA77A, 0x9719, 0x8738, 0xF7DF, 0xE7FE, 0xD79D, 0xC7BC,
/*   64 -- */   0x48C4, 0x58E5, 0x6886, 0x78A7, 0x0840, 0x1861, 0x2802, 0x3823,
/*   72 -- */   0xC9CC, 0xD9ED, 0xE98E, 0xF9AF, 0x8948, 0x9969, 0xA90A, 0xB92B,
/*   80 -- */   0x5AF5, 0x4AD4, 0x7AB7, 0x6A96, 0x1A71, 0x0A50, 0x3A33, 0x2A12,
/*   88 -- */   0xDBFD, 0xCBDC, 0xFBBF, 0xEB9E, 0x9B79, 0x8B58, 0xBB3B, 0xAB1A,
/*   96 -- */   0x6CA6, 0x7C87, 0x4CE4, 0x5CC5, 0x2C22, 0x3C03, 0x0C60, 0x1C41,
/*  104 -- */   0xEDAE, 0xFD8F, 0xCDEC, 0xDDCD, 0xAD2A, 0xBD0B, 0x8D68, 0x9D49,
/*  112 -- */   0x7E97, 0x6EB6, 0x5ED5, 0x4EF4, 0x3E13, 0x2E32, 0x1E51, 0x0E70,
/*  120 -- */   0xFF9F, 0xEFBE, 0xDFDD, 0xCFFC, 0xBF1B, 0xAF3A, 0x9F59, 0x8F78,
/*  128 -- */   0x9188, 0x81A9, 0xB1CA, 0xA1EB, 0xD10C, 0xC12D, 0xF14E, 0xE16F,
/*  136 -- */   0x1080, 0x00A1, 0x30C2, 0x20E3, 0x5004, 0x4025, 0x7046, 0x6067,
/*  144 -- */   0x83B9, 0x9398, 0xA3FB, 0xB3DA, 0xC33D, 0xD31C, 0xE37F, 0xF35E,
/*  152 -- */   0x02B1, 0x1290, 0x22F3, 0x32D2, 0x4235, 0x5214, 0x6277, 0x7256,
/*  160 -- */   0xB5EA, 0xA5CB, 0x95A8, 0x8589, 0xF56E, 0xE54F, 0xD52C, 0xC50D,
/*  168 -- */   0x34E2, 0x24C3, 0x14A0, 0x0481, 0x7466, 0x6447, 0x5424, 0x4405,
/*  176 -- */   0xA7DB, 0xB7FA, 0x8799, 0x97B8, 0xE75F, 0xF77E, 0xC71D, 0xD73C,
/*  184 -- */   0x26D3, 0x36F2, 0x0691, 0x16B0, 0x6657, 0x7676, 0x4615, 0x5634,
/*  192 -- */   0xD94C, 0xC96D, 0xF90E, 0xE92F, 0x99C8, 0x89E9, 0xB98A, 0xA9AB,
/*  200 -- */   0x5844, 0x4865, 0x7806, 0x6827, 0x18C0, 0x08E1, 0x3882, 0x28A3,
/*  208 -- */   0xCB7D, 0xDB5C, 0xEB3F, 0xFB1E, 0x8BF9, 0x9BD8, 0xABBB, 0xBB9A,
/*  216 -- */   0x4A75, 0x5A54, 0x6A37, 0x7A16, 0x0AF1, 0x1AD0, 0x2AB3, 0x3A92,
/*  224 -- */   0xFD2E, 0xED0F, 0xDD6C, 0xCD4D, 0xBDAA, 0xAD8B, 0x9DE8, 0x8DC9,
/*  232 -- */   0x7C26, 0x6C07, 0x5C64, 0x4C45, 0x3CA2, 0x2C83, 0x1CE0, 0x0CC1,
/*  240 -- */   0xEF1F, 0xFF3E, 0xCF5D, 0xDF7C, 0xAF9B, 0xBFBA, 0x8FD9, 0x9FF8,
/*  248 -- */   0x6E17, 0x7E36, 0x4E55, 0x5E74, 0x2E93, 0x3EB2, 0x0ED1, 0x1EF0
};
```

It would be foolish to try to enter this table manually into a program. One error and the final CRC value for a file will be incorrect. A simpler method is to have the computer generate the table. Listing 10-5 is a short program that generates the table exactly as it appears in Figure 10-2.

Listing 10-5.   A program that creates a CRC-CCITT lookup table.

```
/*---mkccitt.c ------------------------- Listing 10-5 -------
 *  Makes a CRC-CCITT table for lookups in C-usable
 *  format. Outputs to screen; Redirect to disk as needed.
 *  For example:
 *                  mkccitt > ccitt.tbl
 *
 *  Based on code from Nigel Cort in C Gazette 5.1 (Autumn 1990)
 ------------------------------------------------------------*/

#include <stdio.h>

unsigned short CalculateCCITT ( unsigned int );

unsigned short table [256];

void main ( void )
{
   unsigned int i;

   /* first calculate the CRC values */

   for ( i = 0; i < 256; i++ )
      table [i] = CalculateCCITT ( i );

   /* then print out the table */

   printf ( "/* CCITT Lookup Table */ \n" );
   printf ( "unsigned short ccitt_table[256] =\n{" );

   for ( i = 0; i < 256; i++ )
   {
      /* start a new row every eight CRCs */

      if (( i % 8 ) == 0 )
         printf ( "\n   /* %3u -- */   ", i );

      /* print the CRC */

      printf ( "0x%04X", table [i] );
      if ( i != 255 )
```

```
        printf ( ", " );
    }

    /* print closing brace for table */

    printf ( "\n};\n" );
}

unsigned short CalculateCCITT ( unsigned int index )
{
    unsigned short a, i;
    a = 0;            /* serves as an accumulator */

    index <<= 8;

    /* The heart of the CRC-CCITT */

    for ( i = 8; i > 0; i-- )
    {
        if (( index ^ a ) & 0x8000 )
            a = ( a << 1 ) ^ 0x1021;
        else
            a <<= 1;
        index <<= 1;
    }

    return ( a );
}
```

To use the table in Figure 10-2, the CRC-CCITT program presented in Listing 10-4 has to be modified slightly. The function that generates the CRC is removed, of course; then the table lookup is inserted into the main processing loop. The complete program for using the table is presented in Listing 10-6 (*crcccitt.c*). Note that the listing is virtually identical to the main() function in Listing 10-4. Only the last two lines, which do the lookup, are changed. Also note the #include of the table in Figure 10-2.

Listing 10-6.   A program that computes a CRC-CCITT with the lookup table from Figure 10-2.

```
/*--- CRCCCITT.C  ----------------------- Listing 10-6 --------
 * Compute CCITT-CRC using a lookup table
 * Usage:   crcccitt filename
 *
 * Based on a similar program by Nigel Cort in C Gazette 5.1
 * (Autumn 1990).
 *------------------------------------------------------------*/
```

```c
#include <stdio.h>
#include <stdlib.h>

#include "ccitt.tbl"  /* generated by mkccitt.c (Listing 10-5) */

int main ( int argc, char * argv[] )
{
   FILE *fin;           /* file we're reading into buffer */
   char *buffer;        /* buffer we're working on       */
   size_t i, j;         /* counters of bytes in buff     */
   unsigned short crc;  /* the CRC value being computed   */

   if ( argc < 2 )
   {
      fprintf ( stderr, "Error! Must specify filename.\n" );
      return ( EXIT_FAILURE );
   }

   if (( fin = fopen ( argv[1], "rb" )) == NULL )
   {
      fprintf ( stderr, "Cannot open %s\n", argv[1] );
      return ( EXIT_FAILURE );
   }

   /*--------------------------------------------------
    * Set up a very large input buffer of 32K bytes.
    * This program does no good if it doesn't fly!
    *--------------------------------------------------*/

   if (( buffer = (char *) malloc ( 32766 )) == NULL )
   {
      fprintf ( stderr, "Out of memory\n" );
      return ( EXIT_FAILURE );
   }

   crc = 0;

   for (;;)
   {
      i = fread ( buffer, 1, 32766, fin );
      if ( i == 0 )
      {
         if ( feof ( fin ))  /* we're done, so show results */
         {
            printf ( "CRC-CCITT for %s is %04X\n",
                                          argv[1], crc );
            return ( EXIT_SUCCESS );
         }
         else          /* read another 32K of file */
```

```
        continue;
   }

   for ( j = 0 ; j < i; j ++ )   /* loop through the buffer */
     crc =
        (crc << 8) ^ ccitt_table [ (crc >> 8) ^ buffer [j] ];
 }
}
```

CRC-16

Another version of the CRC algorithm is CRC-16, mentioned previously. It uses a different polynomial, which was presented previously. The implementation of CRC-16 presented in Listing 10-7 (*crc16.c*) shows a slightly different approach to the use of lookup tables for CRC. This listing, based on work by William James Hunt, uses a very small table of only sixteen entries and looks up each nibble (half a byte, or four bits). This approach offers greater speed than does calculation on the fly, but it conserves some of the space consumed by the table in the preceding listing. Because it blends speed and size, this approach is ideal for embedded applications where memory is at a premium but speed is still of the essence.

Listing 10-7. A program that generates a CRC-16 value for a file.

```
/*--- crc16.c --------------------------- Listing 10-7 ------
 *    Performs CRC-16 check on a file.
 *    Usage: crc16 finename
 *
 *    Modeled on William Hunt's work and Nigel Cort's port.
 *-----------------------------------------------------------*/

#include <stdio.h>
#include <stdlib.h>

#define DRIVER 1     /* brings in the main line */


/* Compute a CRC-16 value */

unsigned short int GetCRC16 (
            int start,       /* starting value */
            const char *p,   /* points to chars to process */
            int n )          /* how many chars to process */
  {

      static unsigned int crc16_table[16] =   /* CRC-16s */
```

```
            {
                0x0000, 0xCC01, 0xD801, 0x1400,
                0xF001, 0x3C00, 0x2800, 0xE401,
                0xA001, 0x6C00, 0x7800, 0xB401,
                0x5000, 0x9C01, 0x8801, 0x4400
            } ;

            unsigned short int total;  /* the CRC-16 value we compute */
            int r1;

            total = start;

            /* process each byte */

            while ( n-- > 0 )
            {
                /* do the lower four bits */

                r1 = crc16_table[ total & 0xF ];
                total = ( total >> 4 ) & 0x0FFF;
                total = total ^ r1 ^ crc16_table[ *p & 0xF ];

                /* do the upper four bits */

                r1 = crc16_table[ total & 0xF ];
                total = ( total >> 4 ) & 0x0FFF;
                total = total ^ r1 ^ crc16_table[ ( *p >> 4 ) & 0xF ];

                /* advance to next byte */
                p++;
            }
            return ( total ) ;
        }


#ifdef DRIVER
#define BUFSIZE 8192

main ( int argc, char *argv[] )
{
    FILE *fin;
    int  n;         /* number of bytes actually read */
    unsigned short int  crc;      /* CRC value */
    char *buffer;  /* buffer into which we read file */

    if ( argc < 2 )
    {
        fprintf ( stderr, "Error: must provide filename\n" );
```

```
            return ( EXIT_FAILURE );
    }

    if (( fin = fopen ( argv[1], "rb" )) == NULL )
    {
        fprintf ( stderr, "Cannot open %s \n", argv[1] );
        return ( EXIT_FAILURE );
    }

    buffer = (char *) malloc ( BUFSIZE );
    if ( buffer == NULL )
    {
        fprintf ( stderr, "Error allocating memory\n" );
        return ( EXIT_FAILURE );
    }

    crc = 0;

    /* principal processing loop */

    do
    {
        /* read file in 8KB blocks */

        n = fread ( buffer, 1, BUFSIZE, fin );

        /* Fold in this block's CRC-16 */

        crc = GetCRC16 ( crc, buffer, n );
    }
    while ( n == BUFSIZE );    /* Stop when done */

    fclose ( fin ) ;

    /* check for read error */

    if ( ferror ( fin ))
        fprintf ( stderr, "Error in Processing %s\n", argv[1] );

    /* No error, so report CRC-16 */

    else
        printf ( "CRC-16 for  %s = %04X\n", argv[1], crc );

    return ( EXIT_SUCCESS );
}
#endif
```

With a singular exception (discussed in the next section), CRC-16 and CRC-CCITT are extraordinarily effective at catching errors on small blocks of data. Joseph Campbell cites the following statistics showing the size of the data blocks and the ratio of errors caught [Campbell 1987]:

≤16 bits	100%
17 bits	99.9969%
>17 bits	99.984%

The last two figures are averages. It is clear that the more bits that are involved, the greater the likelihood that an error will pass unnoticed. The two CRC methods presented so far are both 16-bit methods; that is, they generate 16-bit CRCs. If the data block being verified exceeds 4K, the error ratio for 16-bit CRCs begins to deteriorate sufficiently that virtually flawless data integrity can no longer be assured. For larger blocks of data, a 32-bit CRC is needed: CRC-32.

CRC-32

The 16-bit CRCs presented earlier in this chapter are the classic implementations of the algorithms for 16-bit checksums. The CRC-CCITT, for example, is the same CRC found in Xmodem-CRC. However, 16-bit CRCs suffer from one serious drawback: they will not catch situations in which leading 0 bits of a data block are dropped. The explanation is logical. The initial value of the CRC is set to 0. You will note that in the tables used by the 16-bit CRCs (see Figure 10-2) the value for a zero byte is also 0. Therefore, a data block consisting of two zero bytes will have the same CRC as a block consisting of five zero bytes. So, if the five-byte block is sent and only two bytes arrive, the CRC will not detect this error.

Xmodem-CRC gets around this problem because it uses 128-byte blocks. Before checking the CRC value at the end of the block, Xmodem-CRC checks to see that it has received a full 128 bytes. In this way, any dropped 0 bytes will be detected prior to the CRC calculation. Likewise, if you use the 16-bit CRCs presented in this chapter to compare two files, the size of the two files must first be checked for equality before the CRC values can be examined for a match.

CRC-32 solves this problem by initializing the value of CRC not to 0 but to 0×FFFFFFFF. The use of a nonzero initial value is known as **preconditioning**. CRC-32 also implements **postconditioning** by altering the final CRC value. It flips the bits of the final CRC value. The postconditioning does not appear to address a specific integrity concern. It is simply part of

CCITT's specification for CRC-32. Other variants of CRC use different pre-conditioning and postconditioning approaches.

The divisor polynomial for CRC-32 is as follows:

$$x^{32} + x^{26} + x^{23} + x^{22} + x^{16} + x^{12} + x^{11} + x^{10} + x^8 + x^7 + x^5 + x^4 + x^2 + x^1 + 1$$

As with CRC-CCITT, the approach used here is to create a table and to look up the CRCs for individual bytes in this table. The table appears in Figure 10-3.

Figure 10-3. A lookup table for CRC-32.

```
/* CRC-32 Lookup Table */
unsigned long crc32_table[256] =
{
  /*   0 -- */  0x00000000, 0x77073096, 0xEE0E612C, 0x990951BA,
  /*   4 -- */  0x076DC419, 0x706AF48F, 0xE963A535, 0x9E6495A3,
  /*   8 -- */  0x0EDB8832, 0x79DCB8A4, 0xE0D5E91E, 0x97D2D988,
  /*  12 -- */  0x09B64C2B, 0x7EB17CBD, 0xE7B82D07, 0x90BF1D91,
  /*  16 -- */  0x1DB71064, 0x6AB020F2, 0xF3B97148, 0x84BE41DE,
  /*  20 -- */  0x1ADAD47D, 0x6DDDE4EB, 0xF4D4B551, 0x83D385C7,
  /*  24 -- */  0x136C9856, 0x646BA8C0, 0xFD62F97A, 0x8A65C9EC,
  /*  28 -- */  0x14015C4F, 0x63066CD9, 0xFA0F3D63, 0x8D080DF5,
  /*  32 -- */  0x3B6E20C8, 0x4C69105E, 0xD56041E4, 0xA2677172,
  /*  36 -- */  0x3C03E4D1, 0x4B04D447, 0xD20D85FD, 0xA50AB56B,
  /*  40 -- */  0x35B5A8FA, 0x42B2986C, 0xDBBBC9D6, 0xACBCF940,
  /*  44 -- */  0x32D86CE3, 0x45DF5C75, 0xDCD60DCF, 0xABD13D59,
  /*  48 -- */  0x26D930AC, 0x51DE003A, 0xC8D75180, 0xBFD06116,
  /*  52 -- */  0x21B4F4B5, 0x56B3C423, 0xCFBA9599, 0xB8BDA50F,
  /*  56 -- */  0x2802B89E, 0x5F058808, 0xC60CD9B2, 0xB10BE924,
  /*  60 -- */  0x2F6F7C87, 0x58684C11, 0xC1611DAB, 0xB6662D3D,
  /*  64 -- */  0x76DC4190, 0x01DB7106, 0x98D220BC, 0xEFD5102A,
  /*  68 -- */  0x71B18589, 0x06B6B51F, 0x9FBFE4A5, 0xE8B8D433,
  /*  72 -- */  0x7807C9A2, 0x0F00F934, 0x9609A88E, 0xE10E9818,
  /*  76 -- */  0x7F6A0DBB, 0x086D3D2D, 0x91646C97, 0xE6635C01,
  /*  80 -- */  0x6B6B51F4, 0x1C6C6162, 0x856530D8, 0xF262004E,
  /*  84 -- */  0x6C0695ED, 0x1B01A57B, 0x8208F4C1, 0xF50FC457,
  /*  88 -- */  0x65B0D9C6, 0x12B7E950, 0x8BBEB8EA, 0xFCB9887C,
  /*  92 -- */  0x62DD1DDF, 0x15DA2D49, 0x8CD37CF3, 0xFBD44C65,
  /*  96 -- */  0x4DB26158, 0x3AB551CE, 0xA3BC0074, 0xD4BB30E2,
  /* 100 -- */  0x4ADFA541, 0x3DD895D7, 0xA4D1C46D, 0xD3D6F4FB,
  /* 104 -- */  0x4369E96A, 0x346ED9FC, 0xAD678846, 0xDA60B8D0,
  /* 108 -- */  0x44042D73, 0x33031DE5, 0xAA0A4C5F, 0xDD0D7CC9,
  /* 112 -- */  0x5005713C, 0x270241AA, 0xBE0B1010, 0xC90C2086,
  /* 116 -- */  0x5768B525, 0x206F85B3, 0xB966D409, 0xCE61E49F,
  /* 120 -- */  0x5EDEF90E, 0x29D9C998, 0xB0D09822, 0xC7D7A8B4,
  /* 124 -- */  0x59B33D17, 0x2EB40D81, 0xB7BD5C3B, 0xC0BA6CAD,
  /* 128 -- */  0xEDB88320, 0x9ABFB3B6, 0x03B6E20C, 0x74B1D29A,
  /* 132 -- */  0xEAD54739, 0x9DD277AF, 0x04DB2615, 0x73DC1683,
```

```
/* 136 -- */   0xE3630B12, 0x94643B84, 0x0D6D6A3E, 0x7A6A5AA8,
/* 140 -- */   0xE40ECF0B, 0x9309FF9D, 0x0A00AE27, 0x7D079EB1,
/* 144 -- */   0xF00F9344, 0x8708A3D2, 0x1E01F268, 0x6906C2FE,
/* 148 -- */   0xF762575D, 0x806567CB, 0x196C3671, 0x6E6B06E7,
/* 152 -- */   0xFED41B76, 0x89D32BE0, 0x10DA7A5A, 0x67DD4ACC,
/* 156 -- */   0xF9B9DF6F, 0x8EBEEFF9, 0x17B7BE43, 0x60B08ED5,
/* 160 -- */   0xD6D6A3E8, 0xA1D1937E, 0x38D8C2C4, 0x4FDFF252,
/* 164 -- */   0xD1BB67F1, 0xA6BC5767, 0x3FB506DD, 0x48B2364B,
/* 168 -- */   0xD80D2BDA, 0xAF0A1B4C, 0x36034AF6, 0x41047A60,
/* 172 -- */   0xDF60EFC3, 0xA867DF55, 0x316E8EEF, 0x4669BE79,
/* 176 -- */   0xCB61B38C, 0xBC66831A, 0x256FD2A0, 0x5268E236,
/* 180 -- */   0xCC0C7795, 0xBB0B4703, 0x220216B9, 0x5505262F,
/* 184 -- */   0xC5BA3BBE, 0xB2BD0B28, 0x2BB45A92, 0x5CB36A04,
/* 188 -- */   0xC2D7FFA7, 0xB5D0CF31, 0x2CD99E8B, 0x5BDEAE1D,
/* 192 -- */   0x9B64C2B0, 0xEC63F226, 0x756AA39C, 0x026D930A,
/* 196 -- */   0x9C0906A9, 0xEB0E363F, 0x72076785, 0x05005713,
/* 200 -- */   0x95BF4A82, 0xE2B87A14, 0x7BB12BAE, 0x0CB61B38,
/* 204 -- */   0x92D28E9B, 0xE5D5BE0D, 0x7CDCEFB7, 0x0BDBDF21,
/* 208 -- */   0x86D3D2D4, 0xF1D4E242, 0x68DDB3F8, 0x1FDA836E,
/* 212 -- */   0x81BE16CD, 0xF6B9265B, 0x6FB077E1, 0x18B74777,
/* 216 -- */   0x88085AE6, 0xFF0F6A70, 0x66063BCA, 0x11010B5C,
/* 220 -- */   0x8F659EFF, 0xF862AE69, 0x616BFFD3, 0x166CCF45,
/* 224 -- */   0xA00AE278, 0xD70DD2EE, 0x4E048354, 0x3903B3C2,
/* 228 -- */   0xA7672661, 0xD06016F7, 0x4969474D, 0x3E6E77DB,
/* 232 -- */   0xAED16A4A, 0xD9D65ADC, 0x40DF0B66, 0x37D83BF0,
/* 236 -- */   0xA9BCAE53, 0xDEBB9EC5, 0x47B2CF7F, 0x30B5FFE9,
/* 240 -- */   0xBDBDF21C, 0xCABAC28A, 0x53B39330, 0x24B4A3A6,
/* 244 -- */   0xBAD03605, 0xCDD70693, 0x54DE5729, 0x23D967BF,
/* 248 -- */   0xB3667A2E, 0xC4614AB8, 0x5D681B02, 0x2A6F2B94,
/* 252 -- */   0xB40BBE37, 0xC30C8EA1, 0x5A05DF1B, 0x2D02EF8D
};
```

The program that will generate this table is presented in Listing 10-8 (*mkcrc32.c*). Except for the calculations and the slight changes in display, this program looks very much like the one shown in Listing 10-5 (*mkccitt.c*). The approach used in Listing 10-8 is based on an article by Mark R. Nelson [Nelson 1992]. A very different approach to constructing this table can be found in Schwaderer [Schwaderer 1988].

Listing 10-8.   A program that creates a CRC-32 lookup table.

```
/*--- mkcrc32.c ----------------------- Listing 10-8 ------
 *  Makes a CRC-32 table for 32-bit lookups in C-usable
 *  format. Outputs to screen; Redirect to disk as needed.
 *  For example:
 *                  mkcrc32 > crc32.tbl
```

```
 *
 *  Adapted from code by Mark Nelson (DDJ, May 1992)
 ---------------------------------------------------------------*/

#include <stdio.h>

unsigned long table[ 256 ];

unsigned long CalculateCRC32 ( int );

void main ( void )
{
   unsigned int i;

   /* first calculate the CRC-32 values */

   for ( i = 0; i < 256; i++ )
      table [i] = CalculateCRC32 ( i );

   /* then print out the table */

   printf ( "/* CRC-32 Lookup Table */ \n" );
   printf ( "unsigned long crc32_table[256] =\n{" );

   for ( i = 0; i < 256; i++ )
   {
      /* start a new row every four CRCs */

      if (( i % 4 ) == 0 )
         printf ( "\n  /* %3u -- */   ", i );

      /* print the CRC */

      printf ( "0x%08lX", (unsigned long) table [i] );
      if ( i != 255 )
         printf ( ", " );
   }

   /* print closing brace for table */

   printf ( "\n};\n" );
}

unsigned long CalculateCRC32 ( int i )
{
    int j;
    unsigned long crc;
```

```
            crc = i;

            for ( j = 8 ; j > 0; j-- )
            {
                if ( crc & 1 )
                    crc = ( crc >> 1 ) ^ 0xEDB88320L;
                else
                    crc >>= 1;
            }
            return ( crc );
    }
```

The actual CRC processing of the file occurs in Listing 10-9 (*crc32.c*). This program looks very much like the one in Listing 10-6, because the mechanics are very similar: a file is read, and the CRC-32 is computed byte-by-byte, using the lookup table in Figure 10-3, which is #included. Note the preconditioning of the variable crc and its postconditioning before the value is returned.

Listing 10-9.   A program that calculates CRC-32 by using a lookup table.

```
/*--- crc32.c --------------------------- Listing 10-9 -------
 * Compute CRC-32 using a lookup table
 * Usage:  crc32 filename
 *-----------------------------------------------------------*/

#include <stdio.h>
#include <stdlib.h>

#include "crc32.tbl"  /* generated by mkcrc32.c (Listing 10-8) */

int main ( int argc, char * argv[] )
{
    FILE *fin;              /* file we're reading into buffer */
    unsigned char *buffer;  /* buffer we're working on        */
    size_t i, j;            /* counters of bytes in buff      */
    int k;                  /* generic integer                */
    unsigned long crc;      /* the CRC value being computed    */

    if ( argc < 2 )
    {
        fprintf ( stderr, "Error! Must specify filename.\n" );
        return ( EXIT_FAILURE );
    }

    if (( fin = fopen ( argv[1], "rb" )) == NULL )
    {
```

```
        fprintf ( stderr, "Cannot open %s\n", argv[1] );
        return ( EXIT_FAILURE );
    }

    /*-------------------------------------------------------
     * Set up a very large input buffer of 32K bytes.
     * This program does no good if it doesn't fly!
     *------------------------------------------------------*/

    if (( buffer = (unsigned char *) malloc ( 32766 )) == NULL )
    {
        fprintf ( stderr, "Out of memory\n" );
        return ( EXIT_FAILURE );
    }

    /* preconditioning sets crc to an initial nonzero value */

    crc = 0xFFFFFFFF;

    for (;;)
    {
        i = fread ( buffer, 1, 32766, fin );
        if ( i == 0 )
        {
            if ( feof ( fin ))   /* we're done, so show results */
            {
                /* postconditioning inverts the bits in CRC */

                crc = ~crc;

                /* now print the result */

                printf ( "CRC-32 for %s is %08lX\n",
                                            argv[1], crc );
                return ( EXIT_SUCCESS );
            }
            else          /* read another 32K of file */
                continue;
        }

        for ( j = 0; j < i; j ++ )  /* loop through the buffer */
        {
            k = ( crc ^ buffer[j] ) & 0x000000FFL;
            crc = (( crc >> 8 ) & 0x00FFFFFFL ) ^ crc32_table[k];
        }
    }
}
```

Which CRC should you use? If you are sending data packets in a telecommunications setting, the chances are that your protocols will select the appropriate CRC. If your packets are greater than 4K, however, make sure you are using CRC-32 and not a 16-bit implementation. If you are using the CRC to verify that two binary files have the same contents (such as in testing data compression/decompression methods), the CRC-32 method is preferable. It is suited to large files and, because it uses preconditioning, it does away with the need of verifying file sizes first. For this reason, data compression utilities such as the current versions of PKZIP use CRC-32 for file verification. (Use the -v option of PKZIP to see the CRC-32 results for each compressed file.) The relationship between data compression algorithms and CRCs is discussed in greater detail in Chapter 9, "Data Compression."

Resources and References

Campbell, Joseph. *C Programmer's Guide to Serial Communications*, Indianapolis, IN: Howard Sams & Co., 1987. This is the definitive book on telecommunications for PC programmers. Although somewhat dated because hardware has improved considerably since this book first appeared, the exposition of the principles of programming for modems and the details of bit operations in CRC are especially lucid.

Intel Corporation. *8086 Relocatable Object Module Formats,* order #121748-001. Santa Clara, CA: Intel Corporation, 1981. Although this document was already somewhat out of date when the PC made its debut, it was the only definitive documentation used by writers of operating systems, compilers, assemblers, and linkers for many years. It has since been supplanted by [Intel 93] (q.v.).

Intel Corporation. *Tool Interface Standards: Portable Formats Specification*, order #241597-002. Santa Clara, CA: Intel Corporation, 1993. This document, available free from Intel, specifies the object file formats for MS-DOS, UNIX, and MS Windows. It also contains information on the format of debugging records.

Nelson, Mark R. "File Verification Using CRC: 32-bit Cyclic Redundancy Check." *Dr. Dobb's Journal*, May 1992, p.64.

Schwaderer, David. *C Programmer's Guide to NetBIOS*. Indianapolis, IN: Howard Sams & Co., 1988. This book contains a good technical overview of CRCs with some unusual implementations for coding them.

U.S. Postal Service. *Preparing Business and Courtesy Reply Mail*. Publication 12, September 1984. Available at most U.S. post offices.

Index

Source Code Disk Order Form

Please send me _____ copies of the source code disk for *Practical Algorithms for Programmers.* Diskettes are 3½-inch, 1.44 MB MS-DOS format.

In the United States: $25 plus sales tax for orders shipped to California or Texas. Payment can be by check, money order, cash, or credit card.

In Canada and Mexico: $28 in US currency payable by check drawn on an American bank, money order denominated in US dollars, cash, or credit card.

All other countries: $32 by cash or credit card only. No checks, bank drafts, or money orders.

Make check payable to Pacific Data Works.

Name _____

Address _____

_____

City _____ State _____

Zip/Postal Code _____ Country _____

Send to: Pacific Data Works
               P.O. Box 272062
               Houston, TX 77277-2062
               USA

If using a credit card:

Credit Card Type: ❐ Visa   ❐ MasterCard   ❐ American Express

Card # _____

Cardholder Name _____

Signature_____Exp. Date _____

Comments to authors: